D1259623

STATE OF WAR

The Violent Order of Fourteenth-Century Japan

The John Whitney Hall Book Imprint
commemorates a pioneer in
the field of Japanese Studies
and one of the most respected
scholars of his generation.
This endowed book fund
enables the Center for
Japanese Studies to publish
works on Japan that
preserve the vision and
meticulous scholarship of a
distinguished and beloved historian.

STATE OF WAR

The Violent Order of Fourteenth-Century Japan

Thomas Donald Conlan

This book was financed in part
through generous grants from the
Suntory Foundation and the
John Whitney Hall
Book Imprint.

Center for Japanese Studies
The University of Michigan
Ann Arbor, 2003

Published by
Center for Japanese Studies, The University of Michigan
202 S. Thayer St., Ann Arbor, MI 48104-1608

Michigan Monograph Series in Japanese Studies
Number 46
Center for Japanese Studies
The University of Michigan

Library of Congress Cataloging-in-Publication Data

Conlan, Thomas.
    State of war : the violent order of fourteenth-century Japan / Thomas Donald Conlan.
       p. cm. — (Michigan monograph series in Japanese studies ; no. 46)
    Includes bibliographical references and index.
    ISBN 1-929280-16-5 (cloth : alk. paper) — ISBN 1-929280-23-8 (pbk. : alk. paper)
    1. Japan—History—Period of northern and southern courts, 1336–1392. 2. Japan—
History—Kamakura period, 1185–1333. I. Title. II. Series.

DS865.5.C67 2003
952'.021—dc21

                                 2003053107

Book design by City Desktop Productions

This book was set in Times.

This publication meets the ANSI/NISO Standards for Permanence of Paper
for Publications and Documents in Libraries and Archives (Z39.48–1992).

Printed in the United States of America

To Mom and Dad
With Love and Gratitude

Contents

Illustrations

Chapter 4

Chapter 6

Tables

Plates

1. The tedium of guard duty. Source: *Heiji monogatari emaki*. Individual Collection. Photograph provided by Chūōkōronshinsha.

2. The tedium of guard duty. Source: *Go-sannen kassen ekotoba*. Permission and photo granted by the Tokyo National Museum.

3. Warrior returning with head. Source: *Shōtoku taishi eden*, "Mononobe Moriya to no kassen" permission of Jōgūji. Photo courtesy Ibaragi Kenritsu Rekishikan.

4. Decapitated heads. Source: *Go-sannen kassen ekotoba*. Permission and photo granted by the Tokyo National Museum.

5. Aiding the wounded. Source: *Heiji monogatari emaki*. Individual Collection. Photograph provided by Chūōkōronshinsha.

6. Extracting an arrow. Source: *Go-sannen kassen ekotoba*. Permission and photo granted by the Tokyo National Museum.

7. The use of shields in battle. Source: *Shōtoku taishi eden*, "Mononobe Moriya to no kassen" permission of Jōgūji. Photo courtesy Ibaragi Kenritsu Rekishikan.

8. Different coloring styles of armor. Note also the tiger skin saddle blanket. *Mōko shūrai ekotoba*, scroll 1, page 9, "The Encampment of Shōni Kagesuke." Possession of Kunaichō Sannōmaru Shōzōkan. Permission for reproduction granted by the Imperial Household Ministry.

9. Unhorsing an opponent. Source: *Kasuga gongen kenki e*, scroll 2, section 2 (partial). Possession of Kunaichō Sannōmaru Shōzōkan. Permission for reproduction granted by the Imperial Household Ministry.

10. Warriors setting off in boats. Source: *Aki no yo no nagamonogatari*. Possession of the Idemitsu Museum of Arts.

11. The inspection process. *Mōko shūrai ekotoba*, scroll 2, page 40, "Suenaga presenting enemy heads." Possession of Kunaicho Sannōmaru Shōzōkan. Permission for reproduction granted by the Imperial Household Ministry.

12. a. Warrior with an *ōdachi*. Illustration courtesy Futaarasan shrine. b. National Treasure Ōdachi mei Bizenshū Osafune Tomomitsu. Illustration courtesy Futaarasan shrine.

13. Warrior with a battle axe. Source: *Go sannen kassen ekotoba*. Permission and photo granted by the Tokyo National Museum.

14. Warriors fighting with swords, pikes and *naginata*. Source: *Aki no yo no nagamonogatari*. Possession of the Idemitsu Museum of Arts.

15. Leg armor of the late fourteenth century. Photograph and permission courtesy the Kyoto National Museum.

16. Three warriors wearing *hōate*. Source: *Aki no yo no nagamonogatari*. Possession of the Idemitsu Museum of Arts.

17. Infantry fighting in poor terrain. Source: *Kasuga gongen kenki e*, scroll 19, section 1 (partial). Possession of Kunaichō Sannōmaru Shōzōkan. Permission for reproduction granted by the Imperial Household Ministry.

18. The market of Fukuoka. Source: *Ippen hijiri e den*, scroll 4, page 7. Jishū Sōhonzan Yūkōji. Photo courtesy Tokyo National Museum.

19. Fourteenth-century castle under attack. Source: *Rokudō-e*, "Jindō no kuso." Permission granted by Shōjuraikōji. Photo courtesy Nara National Museum.

20. Non-combatants fleeing the battlefield. Source: *Aki no yo no nagamonogatari*. Possession of the Idemitsu Museum of Arts.

21. Armed *hyakushō*? Source: *Konda sōbyō engi emaki*, scroll 1, "Ōjin tennō no misasagi o chikuzō suru dan." Possession of the Konda Hachiman shrine. Photo courtesy Habikino city, Bunka rekishi shiryōshitsu.

22. Warring priests. Source: *Aki no yo no nagamonogatari*. Possession of the Idemitsu Museum of Arts.

Acknowledgments

I owe a profound debt to Jeffrey Mass, who has been selfless with his time and support, advice and encouragement. His meticulous care has forever imparted upon me the need to be clear and concise in thought and articulation. Jeff will always remain to me a mentor, friend, and inspiration. I could never have embarked upon this project without him.

Many have helped me during this decade-long journey. I am indebted to Peter Duus and Philippe Buc for the stimulating advice and insights that they have provided. Thanks too to Jim Ketelaar for his advice in the early stages of this work. Also, I am grateful to Hitomi Tonomura, my first teacher of Japanese history, who sparked my interest in the field, and who has encouraged me over the years. I also would like to thank Emiko Moffitt and Naomi Findley, in charge of the East Asian Collection of the Hoover Library for their help in securing much-needed Japanese sources.

Ōyama Kyōhei sponsored during my three years in Kyoto under the auspices of a Japanese Education Ministry scholarship from 1994–1997. During that time, I was fortunate to have Uejima Susumu and Yokouchi Hisatō as tutors of Japanese documents and diaries. I appreciate the efforts on my behalf of Fujii Jōji, Katsuyama Seiji, Yoshikawa Shinji and all of the faculty and staff of the history department at Kyōto University. Profound thanks, too, to Seno Sei'ichirō, for his tireless generosity and wisdom and to Asakuma Sueyoshi for his comradeship, and the long hours spent honing my Japanese prose so as to make it fit for publication.

I am grateful to Kondō Shigekazu for his kind assistance and support, and Noda Taizō for introducing me to the intricacies of medieval castles. The generosity of Hirase Naoki, Kobayashi Motonobu, Kumagai Masao, the representatives of Hiromine shrine, Tanaka Junichirō of the Yamashiro shiryōkan, and Hara Hidesaburō allowed me to view numerous original fourteenth century documents, for which I am thankful.

I cannot adequately thank everyone who has helped me. I would like to offer special thanks to Morita Masaru, Katō Jun'ichi, Jim Conlan, Tom Nelson, Kawabata Shin, Satō Yasuhiro, Michael Como, John Ott, Marjan Boogert, Jeff Irish, Jason Webb, Rob Eskildsen, Mickey Adolphson, Joe Chou, Christopher Bolton, Robert Hellyer, Bruce Batten and Vincent Gerusz for the insights and friendship that they have provided. I also am indebted to Andrew Goble, who helped revealed to me the world of medieval medical manuals and wounds, and who taught me the value of trusting one's *senpai*. Thanks too to Karl Friday, for his insight into the Heian military, and Joan Piggott, for her great help and support over the years. John Rogers deserves thanks for introducing me to medieval Japanese military manuals. Finally, I am grateful to Kidder Smith for reading a draft of the introduction, and providing valuable comments, insights and advice.

Stanford University offered me a graduate fellowship, thereby making this project possible, and I am grateful to the administrators of the FLAS and to the Japanese Ministry of Education for their financial support. Special thanks to Nancy Okimoto and Luccia Hammar at the Institute for International Studies, and Terry MacDougall, Imai Ken'ichi, and everyone at the Stanford Japan Center for providing me with a wonderful office in Japan. My colleagues at the Stanford Humanities Center helped me have a stimulating and productive year in 1997–1998. Conversations with Martin Jay and Charlie Segal in particular, helped me hone chapters six and seven.

The Fletcher Family Faculty Research Fund at Bowdoin College provided funds for securing the photos for this manuscript. I would like to thank Gomi Hikaru of the Sannōmaru Shōzōkan, the Kunaichō, Okuno Toshiaki of Chūōkōronshinsha, Ueno Akira, Ota Satoko of the Equine Museum of Japan, Andō Chieko of the Idemitsu Museum of Arts, Mimi Yiengpruksawan of Yale University, Sumihiro Akiko of the Tōkyō National Museum, Washitsuka Yasumitsu of the Nara National Museum, Nakagawa Hisasada of the Kyōto National Museum, Saitō Yoshirō of the Ibaragi Kenritsu Rekishikan, the Kamakura Kokuhōkan, Tanaka Masanori, Matsumuro Kōji and the Cultural and Historical Sources Department of Habikino City, Shōjuraikōji, Kiburuji, Yūkōji, Jōmyōji, Jōgūji, the Ōyama zumi shrine, Futaarasan shrine, and Konda Hachiman shrine for granting permission and providing photos for this book's illustrations.

Bruce Willoughby has done wonderful work with the editing and production of this book, for which I am grateful. Thanks to him and everyone at the Center for all of their hard work. I am also grateful to the helpful suggestions of the anonymous reader who reviewed my manuscript. Of course, responsibility for any errors or oversights is solely my own.

An earlier version of chapter one appeared as "The Nature of Warfare in Fourteenth-Century Japan: The Record of Nomoto Tomoyuki." *The Journal of Japanese Studies 25.2.* (Summer 1999), and an earlier version of chapter five appeared in Jeffrey Mass, ed., *The Origins of Japan's Medieval World*, ©1997 by the Board of Trustees of the Leland Stanford Junior University. Material from that version appears with the permission of the publishers, Stanford University Press.

Generous support from the Suntory Foundation helped defray a significant portion of the production costs of this book. Mr. Bunno proved particularly helpful, and I am grateful to him, and everyone at the foundation. I would also like to thank G. Cameron Hurst and Paul Varley for offering insightful comments on my manuscript, and providing recommendations on short notice. Both men are models of scholarly integrity, who have greatly helped me over the years. I feel fortunate to know them both. Nagano Masayoshi, Noda Taizō and Asakuma Sueyoshi also generously assisted me in applying for this grant. I am grateful to all.

I am always thankful for the love and support of my wife Yūko. She has helped me with correspondence to Japan, and has made my life brighter and happier. I feel fortunate to be able to celebrate the publication of this book with our son George. And finally to my parents, who encouraged me to choose my own path in life. I dedicate this to them, in memory of those who fought and died so very long ago.

Abbreviations

NBIK   *Nanbukuchō ibun, Kyūshū hen*. Compiled by Seno Sei'ichirō. 7 vols. Tōkyōdo Shuppan, 1980–92.

NBIC   *Nanbokuchō ibun, Chūgoku, Shikoku hen*. Compiled by Matsuoka Hisato. 6 vols. Tōkyōdo Shuppan, 1987–95.

KI   *Kamakura ibun*. Compiled Takeuchi Rizō. 51 vols. Tōkyōdo Shuppan, 1971–97.

DNSR   *Dai Nihon shiryō 6.1–43*. Tokyo: Tōkyō Teikoku Daigaku Shuppan, 1901–.

HI   *Heian ibun*. Compiled by Takeuchi Rizō. 15 vols. Tōkyōdo Shuppan, 1963–80.

CHSS   *Chūsei hōsei shiryō shū*. Edited by Satō Shin'ichi and Ikeuchi Yoshisuko. 5 vols. Iwanami Shoten, 1955–65.

Introduction

A violent order is disorder; and
A great disorder is an order. These
two things are one.

Wallace Stevens, "Connoisseur of Chaos"

THE VIOLENT ORDER

Warfare is instrumental to change rather than being merely expressive of it, and its waging necessitates profound innovations in state and society. The absolute imperative of military victory focuses all components of state and society on this single objective. All other considerations become subsumed to achieving this end, which in turn necessitates a reweaving of the social and political fabric. Legal rights, social privileges, and, for that matter, political authority, can only be maintained through military force. Hence, even the most conservative polities are forced to innovate in order to survive the advent of war. Nevertheless, in comprehending the nature of the transformations engendered by war, one cannot conceive of warfare as an outside force that somehow alters state and society. Instead, war represents a process that encompasses all. Rather than merely hastening change on a static state and society, war creates its own particular and peculiar order.

This view of warfare as a transcendental process has been common currency since the first chroniclers began chanting their epics or writing their tales. War, a plastic term, represents an activity innately human and infinitely variable, bounded only by the common denominator of organized violence, and yet so liminal that nearly every history and epic created prior to the twentieth century was devoted to expounding its constituent triumphs and tragedies. That warfare delineates the boundaries of nearly every historical era, in every land, persuasively attests to its transformative power. Nevertheless, the notion that warfare is the catalyst for change has often been only implicitly understood at best, which explains both the abundance of accounts of war and the relative paucity of explicit testimonies of its power to instigate change.

After the trauma of the great world wars, attitudes regarding war underwent an epochal shift. Instead of singing the praises of the brave and recording their names for posterity, the ultimate glorification was reserved for the Unknown Soldier. Scholarship reflects the spirit of the times. With the rise of "personless" social history (i.e., Marxism and the Annales school), the focus of historical inquiry has become directed either to abstractions—such as shifts in the composition of class and the corresponding transformations in society engendered by the dialectic of these vertical conflicts—or to long-term processes, such as demographic fluctuations or technological innovations. Viewed from such paradigms, war has been dismissed as merely constituting "crests of foam that the tides of history carry on their strong backs."[1] Some historians still slight warfare as representing "only a surface phenomenon."[2] Perhaps unsurprisingly, military history has become confined to analysis of the particularities of battle, such as weapons and tactics, and generally ignores the fundamental social processes of war.

Recently, some scholars have begun to rehabilitate warfare as a focal point of historical inquiry.[3] Some attempt to reconstruct the nature of battle, while others pessimistically assert the impossibility of such an endeavor.[4] Nevertheless, accounts that focus on the experience of battle suffer from a profound limitation, because the systemic demands of supply and organization inherent in the waging of war cannot be comprehended by merely recounting the experience of battle. By contrast, those authors who focus on the impact of

---

1. Fernand Braudel, *The Mediterranean and the Mediterranean World in the Age of Philip II* (Berkeley: University of California Press, 1995), vol. 1, p. 21.
2. Mary Elizabeth Berry, *The Culture of Civil War in Kyoto* (Berkeley: University of California Press, 1994), p. 27.
3. George Duby, in *The Legend of Bouvines*, has examined the lasting repercussions of battle, although he has also emphasized the intractable epistemological difficulties in reconstructing the experience of war. John Keegan has attempted to reconstruct the nature of battle in *The Face of Battle*, while Charles Tilly has argued that the requisites of maintaining and supplying armies proved to be the catalyst for state formation. See Georges Duby, *The Legend of Bouvines* (Berkeley: University of California Press, 1990); John Keegan, *The Face of Battle* (New York: The Viking Press, 1976); and Charles Tilly, *Coercion, Capital and European States, AD 990–1990* (London: Basil Blackwell, 1990).
4. Keegan attempts the former, while Duby argues for the latter.

war upon state creation[5] ignore the precise nature of battle, and instead explore how the process of war proved instrumental to political and institutional change. Such studies are misleading, however, because they fail to recognize that the need to secure victory, rather than the desire to strengthen institutions of the state per se, transcended all other considerations. Furthermore, they misunderstand the nature of warfare by treating it as an exterior force, much like a giant wrecking ball, that somehow shattered the static structures of state and society. In fact, warfare should be conceived as an encompassing process that subsumes and transforms disparate aspects of the social and political order by focusing them on the overriding goal of military victory.

A state of war represents a subversion of the most fundamental tenet of the social order, whereby murder is no longer a crime but a source of merit. When the laws and injunctions promulgated by authorities to limit the endemic violence that plagues mankind are now directed toward the destruction of those designated as "enemy," and the human genius for muddle gives way to the clarity of "friend" and "enemy," man's instinct for violence is focused and magnified exponentially by the legitimating weight of authority.

Once political allegiances are fractured and the legitimating power of authority is redirected, then the need to wage war successfully transcends all other considerations. The significance of war stems from the totality of its demands, rather than how it was waged. Hence, studies of technological change or military organization are unable to reveal fully the transformative power of war, because such changes pale in comparison to the systemic burdens that its waging entails. One must explore how a particular war unfolds in order to fully understand its power, for it profoundly influences spheres seemingly remote from the battlefield, such as the basis for social determination, the state's extraction of revenue, and the very worldview of all contemporaries. These unseen processes belong as much to the violent order of war as do individual battles. Furthermore, the study of war can reveal how state and society actually function as opposed to how they are portrayed in ideal. One can reconstruct aspects of the past that might otherwise have disappeared from the historical record.

This study attempts to reconstruct the complex process of war through a layered approach, whereby each chapter provides distinct historical and temporal perspectives. At the most fundamental level, war is waged by individuals, and each experiences the fear and excitement of battle alone. Accordingly we first recount the nature of war through the experiences of one fourteenth-century Japanese warrior, Nomoto Tomoyuki, over a period of three years. As no one fights alone, the collective experience of warfare in fourteenth century Japan shall then be explored through statistical analysis

---

5. Such as Tilly, *Coercion, Capital and European States*.

of the normative trends of six decades of war and a reconstruction of how armies were organized. Our focus then shifts to the economic, institutional, and social constraints of military organization in Japan over a span of decades, revealing that the need to supply forces led to a profound decentralization of state powers. The outbreak of war also affected the Japanese social matrix by blurring the social structure and transforming social statuses so that they became based solely upon the ability to offer military service and to extract economic resources. In this era of eroding central control, those aspiring to achieve hegemony were forced to rely upon intangible factors of other-worldly authority, trust, and largesse in order to cobble together a modicum of political authority. This authority nevertheless became increasingly constrained by the establishment of a transcendent notion of judicial right, based upon, and legitimated by, the unilateral recourse to violence.

Although the "rise" of warriors has generated considerable scholarly attention in Japan, the wars that propelled these men to prominence have languished in relative obscurity. Such a lacuna in historical studies is puzzling, for the periods in which the "rise" of warriors is thought to have occurred invariably coincide with the outbreak of war. Historians have long thought that Japan's so-called "ancient" or "classical" age gave way to the "medieval" in the 1180s. Many monographs have accordingly devoted considerable attention to warriors in the eleventh and twelfth centuries.[6] However, some scholars have argued recently that the court was not overwhelmed in 1185 and that regional warriors were more closely tied to the capital than had been previously realized. The new political entity that was created in the aftermath of the 1180s—the Kamakura regime—supplemented the court instead of supplanting it. Kamakura's judicial decrees and edicts initially stabilized the realm, and functioned as an insulating cushion to contain violence. A new social and political order was ushered in not by the founding of the Kamakura *bakufu*, but by its violent destruction in 1333.[7]

---

6. See, for example, Karl Friday, *Hired Swords: The Rise of Private Warrior Power in Early Japan* (Stanford: Stanford University Press, 1992); William Wayne Farris, *Heavenly Warriors: The Evolution of Japan's Military, 500 to 1300* (Cambridge: Harvard University Press, 1992); Eiko Ikegami, *The Taming of the Samurai: Honorific Individualism and the Making of Modern Japan* (Cambridge: Harvard University Press, 1995); and Jeffrey P. Mass, "The Emergence of the Kamakura Bakufu," in John W. Hall and Jeffrey P. Mass, eds., *Medieval Japan: Essays in Institutional History* (Stanford: Stanford University Press, 1974), pp. 127–56, and "The Missing Minamoto in the Twelfth-Century Kantō," in *Journal of Japanese Studies* 19.2 (Winter 1993): 121–46.

7. See Jeffrey P. Mass, "Of Hierarchy and Authority at the End of Kamakura," in Jeffrey P. Mass, ed., *The Origins of Japan's Medieval World: Courtiers, Clerics, Warriors, and Peasants in the Fourteenth Century* (Stanford: Stanford University Press, 1997), pp. 17–38, and *Yoritomo and the Founding of the First Bakufu* (Stanford: Stanford University Press, 1999). This view is shared by Amino Yoshihiko, who sees in the fourteenth century a groundswell of change in which the very structure of society was transformed. For his initial exposition of this thesis, see Amino Yoshihiko, *Mōko shūrai*, vol. 10 of *Nihon no rekishi* (Shōgakkan, 1974).

While focusing on the process of change, these scholars have largely ignored the relationship between these innovations and the act of war. Nevertheless, the profound transformations of the fourteenth century, and, for that matter, the important changes of the late twelfth century and nearly every other era as well, coincide with the onset of war. This monograph is intended to illustrate how the process of waging war necessitated a fundamental restructuring of state and society, and to reveal that the wars of the fourteenth century delineate a watershed in Japanese history.

The very fact that the war continued for approximately sixty years during the fourteenth century necessitated a reordering of state and society, much as did the five years of war during the 1180s. But although the older, shorter conflict has received exhaustive attention, the latter wars proved more significant because they ensured that state power would devolve to the provinces and that violence would become a legitimate means of asserting judicial claims. A further innovation, less immediately obvious, was a new basis for determining social status. Instead of being prescribed by those in authority, status came to be based on performance and control over physical resources. In a related process, regional lords increasingly were able to ensure compliance with their orders by their consolidation of regional political and military authority. These lords continued, however, to be commanded by the Ashikaga shoguns, who relied upon notions of sacred kingship, and magnificent largesse, to assert their hegemony, and who were constrained only by a newly transcendent notion of judicial rights.

These disparate metamorphoses can be only fully comprehended as particular responses to the pressing needs of successfully waging war. Few, if any, could remain aloof from the fray, because the need to reward those who provided military service outweighed considerations of ownership and justice, thereby undermining the land rights of all. In order to preserve one's prerogatives, one needed to be associated with a successful political entity that could confirm these rights. Accordingly, reports of the war's outbreak galvanized men from all stations of life, in all regions of Japan, and forced them to profess allegiance with one armed camp or another.

Political authority generated the conflict of the fourteenth century and nurtured its rapid expansion through all of Japan. In order to secure victory, battle must be taken to the provinces, asserted Kitabatake Akiie, a Southern Court general who thrice led armies to the capital.[8] Peace could only return

---

8. Akiie literally stated, "If you attempt to determine the affairs of the realm from one location, all will become disordered. What then could save us from [our] troubles." Kitabatake Akiie *chinjō*. This document is most conveniently found in *Chūsei seiji shakai shiso ge* ed. Kasamatsu Hiroshi, Satō Shin'ichi and Momose Kesao, *Nihon shisō taikei*, 22 (Iwanami Shoten, 1981), vol. 2, pp. 155–62. Go-Daigo apparently heeded Akiie's advice, and coordinated simultaneous offensives from both the north and south. See NBIK, 1254, 9.18 (1338) Go-Daigo tennō *rinji utsushi*.

with the subjugation of one of the two courts. According to Tōin Kinkata, the ranking courtier of the Northern Court, "conquering the South[ern Court] . . . is the basis for peace and stability in the realm (*tenka*)."[9] In other words, the reconstitution of social and political order hinged upon military victory. Warfare was a vital matter the exigencies of which superseded all contemporary political, jurisdictional, and social boundaries.

The onset of war during the 1330s represented an extraordinary mobilization of all landed members of society, or warriors. Most fought in order to preserve or expand land holdings that they believed to be theirs by right. Warriors had little vested interest in the survival of a particular regime so long as they could preserve their rights to the land. The astute warriors ensured that they were confirmed by all competing polities. The destabilization of rights forced nearly all to rely upon autogenic force to assert or defend their claims to the land.

These rights were destabilized with the onset of war because the need to reward those who provided military service outweighed considerations of ownership and justice. Some warriors attempted to ensure the unity of their clan by creating a council in which every major member could voice his opinion on appropriate action for all.[10] Others, upon hearing that the realm was in disorder, used war as a pretext to attack longstanding rivals.[11] A few adopted the dubious strategy of fighting for several political entities. Although family members killing each other in an attempt to preserve their house seems to fly in the face of reason, the Amano apparently penned the following oath:

> To cause the name of a hereditary warrior house (*yumiya no ie*) to suffer extinction violates the wishes of our ancestors. In this time of turmoil, we resolve to preserve, for all time, the Amano lineage. Akiuji, Masayoshi, Akiyuki, Akimitsu, Yukikage, Akikuni, Tsunemasa and Akimori shall ally with the [Ashikaga] shogun's forces. Masasada, Masakuni, Akimune, Hiroaki, and Akishige shall support imperial (*kangun*) forces. If perchance we should meet on the battlefield, let us by no means display any lingering affection. This oath is such.[12]

---

9. *Entairyaku* (Tōin Kinkata), ed. Iwahashi Koyata and Saiki Kazuma (Zoku Gunsho Ruijū Kanseikai, 1970–86), vol. 6, p. 308, of 11.12.1359.

10. NBIK, 383. For an intriguing monograph on the nature of the family council, see Shigekazu Kondō, "Leadership and the Medieval Japanese Warrior Family," in Ian Nearly, ed., *Leaders and Leadership in Japan* (London: Curzon Press, Japan Library, 1996), pp. 14–25.

11. NBIK 408.

12. NBIC, 700. Masaoka Hisatō, the compiler of NBIC, designates this document as a possible forgery, for the time of choosing allies was some two years earlier. As the document is a later copy (*utsushi*) it is impossible to test its veracity; either the document is a forgery, or the copyist misread the date.

Irrespective of the veracity of the Amano oath, this document illustrates that a family could conceivably divide its political loyalties to ensure its preservation.[13] Men of the provinces had to forcibly assert their rights in order to sustain them. Although warriors prized personal glory, their behavior cannot be reduced to a simple desire for attention, nor can it be characterized as fighting for a "higher" national cause, although notions of undying service to the imperial court were not utterly absent. Nevertheless, all rights and prerogatives hinged upon the ability to defend them. Ultimately, the successful prosecution of the war constituted the higher cause obeyed by all.

The autonomy of warriors, bolstered by their refusal to obey blindly the dictates of political authority, thrived in the environment of a civil war during which two courts competed for support. Violence likewise became incorporated into the fabric of daily life, as rights and statuses were defended, or asserted, by hard steel instead of by notarized pieces of paper. Each war they waged unfolded according to its own particular logic. Nevertheless, the tides of warfare altered what they created, for the excessive cost of waging war eroded this very autonomy and allowed regional magnates, or *shugo*, to achieve military and political dominance in the provinces.

War's great constant is its transformative power, for it leads to new associations and new attitudes. Little was external to this war, and little was untouched by its powerful forces. Fourteenth-century warfare transcended all contemporary boundaries and subverted political, intellectual, and social norms. Furthermore, the process of its unfolding ensured that violence would remain woven into the fabric of daily life for centuries to come. In sum, rather than being an eddy of the sea of change, warfare was perhaps the tide—or the very ocean itself. It is doubtful that Emperor Go-Daigo (r. 1318–31, 1333–36) foresaw these consequences when he embarked upon his fateful uprising in the autumn of 1331.

UNLEASHING THE VIOLENT ORDER

The armies that the Kamakura *bakufu* dispatched during the years 1331–33 were perhaps the most formidable forces of the entire fourteenth century, and yet they ultimately suffered a defeat so overwhelming that the *bakufu*, and all hopes for political stability, were destroyed.

Warfare erupted in 1331 as a result of a conflict over the parameters of authority that was focused by a dispute over imperial succession. Late in

---

13. In another example, Migita Sukeie claimed to be ill and dispatched a son in his stead to fight for Go-Daigo. Meanwhile, Sukeie continued to fight for Kamakura. Compare the 5.1333 Migita Sukeie *moshijō*, and the 4.20.1333 *kassen chūmon* found in the Migita *monjo*.

the thirteenth century, the Kamakura *bakufu* had decreed that both contending candidates to the throne were to reign alternately. The emperor of one lineage would pass the throne to the crown prince of the other lineage. This arrangement led to an increased polarization in state and society over the next fifty years. Gradually, nobles and warriors associated with one or the other of the two lineages of imperial contenders until all of society was aligned into two massive factions, much as a cluster of iron filings lined up around two magnetic poles. The two poles of legitimacy, the rival imperial lines, ultimately coalesced into two separate courts—the Northern (of the Jimyōin lineage) and Southern (Daikakuji)—which vied for hegemony from 1331 until 1392.

The regime that brokered this compromise—the Kamakura *bakufu*—quite naturally became the focus of animosity from both imperial factions. Ultimately, Go-Daigo, who desired to rule and pass the throne to one of his own many progeny in the Daikakuji line, came to reject this compromise and rebelled against Kamakura in 1331.

When the first report of Go-Daigo's rebellion arrived in Kamakura, the *bakufu* responded by dispatching forces to the capital.[14] Its men were mobilized following "the Jōkyū precedent," which constituted an extraordinary call to arms for warriors from throughout Japan.[15] Once Go-Daigo's rebellion was summarily crushed, Kōgon of the rival Jimyōin imperial lineage was installed as emperor; Go-Daigo was exiled to Oki Island; and most of his supporters were jailed, banished, or executed. Thereupon, Kamakura disbanded its army.

Prince Moriyoshi and Kusunoki Masashige, Go-Daigo partisans, continued their anti-Kamakura agitation and established forts in Yoshino, Akasaka, and Chihaya.[16] In response, the *bakufu* knitted together an army drawn from provinces close to the capital, instead of undertaking a full-scale mobilization

---

14. Kamakura's army was composed of warriors drawn from Tōtōmi, Owari, Ise, Sanuki, Awaji, Iga, Mikawa, Iyo, Shinano, and Kai Provinces. See KI, 32135–36. For a detailed analysis of this, see "Kōmyōji zanhen shokō" in *Zōtei Kamakura bakufu shugo seido no kenkyū*, comp. Satō Shin'ichi (Tōkyō Daigaku Shuppankai, 1971), pp. 255–74. Nevertheless, Mori Shigeaki asserts that the "Kōmyōji zanhen" merely represents Kamakura's plan for attack. See his *Taiheiki no gunzō* (Kadokawa Sensho, 1991), p. 112.

15. See KI 31950 and KI 32828, for fighting at "Kusunoki castle" lasting from 9.14.1331 until 10.20.1331. For other references to the 1331 conflict, see KI 32044, 31915, and, for the case of Kyushu, KI 31591. For references to the "Jōkyū precedent," Kamakura's victorious war against the court in 1221, see *Kamakura nendaiki*, found in *Kamakura nendaiki uragaki, Buke nendaiki uragaki, Kamakura dai nikki*, in *Zōho zoku shiryō taisei*, vol. 51 (Kyoto: Rinsen Shoten, 1979), p. 64.

16. Although Kusunoki Masashige is more famous, Prince Moriyoshi was instrumental in bringing down Kamakura by issuing numerous calls to arms. See Mori Shigeaki, "Ōtōnomiya Moriyoshi shinnō ryōji ni tsuite," in *Chūsei komonjo no sekai*, ed. Ogawa Makoto (Yoshikawa Kōbunkan, 1991), particularly pp. 210–13.

as it had successfully done in 1331.[17] Kamakura mobilized troops during 1332–33 using methods akin to calling warriors to the capital for guard duty.[18]

In 1332 three of the Kamakura *bakufu*'s armies advanced simultaneously along roads in Kawachi, Yamato, and Kii Provinces.[19] Extant documents reveal that the *bakufu*'s mobilization was on a lesser scale than some sources suggest, with each army constituting no more than several thousand warriors.[20] These Kamakura forces, whose overall commander was Aso (Hōjō) Harutoki, proved capable of a multipronged offensive in spite of their regional base, quickly overwhelming forts at Yoshino's Kinpusenji and nearby Akasaka before converging on Kusunoki Masashige's mountain stronghold of Chihaya. Although Masashige inflicted casualties on Kamakura's forces, he had no hope of breaking Harutoki's siege.

Because of its partial mobilization against Kusunoki Masashige and Prince Moriyoshi in the fall of 1332, Kamakura's resources were stretched thin. When provinces to the west of the capital disintegrated into turmoil, Kamakura's deputies in the west, the Rokuhara *tandai*, dispatched a force to counter the new threat, but they suffered a crushing defeat.[21] So desperate

17. The regional nature of this army was recognized by Aida Nirō, *Mōkō shūrai no kenkyū*, 3rd ed. (Yoshikawa Kōbunkan, 1982), pp. 401–2. Only generals and not troops were dispatched to the west. See KI 31911 and KI 32220; the document dated 11.8.1332 to the Kawano of Iyo is included in the Tenshō version of the *Taiheiki*. See *Taiheiki (Tenshō hon)*, ed. Hasegawa Tadashi (Shōgakkan, 1994), maki 6, "Hyōbu no kyō Yoshino shutsugyo no koto," p. 309.

18. Beginning in the late-twelfth century, "housemen" (*gokenin*) recognized as such by the Kamakura *bakufu* would customarily serve guard duty (*ōban'yaku*) in the capital. When his prescribed period of service had expired, the *gokenin* would submit a document stating he had performed his duties—sometimes on behalf of all the warriors of a province. For translations of such documents during the attempted Mongol invasions of Japan, see Thomas D. Conlan, *In Little Need of Divine Intervention* (Ithaca, NY: Cornell East Asia Series, 2001), pp. 236–37, 244–45. See also the Migita documents of 10.7.1285 for a record of three months of service guarding the retired emperor and 7.2.1301 for six months of service. Both documents are most conveniently found in the "Migita *keizu*," in *Zoku gunsho ruijū, keizubu* (Zoku Gunsho Ruijū Kanseikai, 1975), pp. 145–46. Compare these with Kamakura's documents, found in KI 31911 (for a document addressed to the Suda), 31915 (the Kumagai), 32003 (Tōdaiji), 31933 (Hineno), and Oyama ke *monjo* document 13 Kantō *migyōsho utsushi*, in Amino Yoshihiko, *Nihon chūsei shiryō no kadai* (Kōbundō, 1996), p. 300. One other mobilization order from the Rokuhara *tandai*, addressed to Katsuoji, appears in KI 32052.

19. "Kusunoki kassen chūmon," *Zoku zoku gunsho ruijū*, vol. 3: *Shidenbu* (Zoku Zoku Gunsho Ruijū Kanseikai, 1969–70), p. 548. *Gokenin* on guard duty in the capital were also expected to serve in the Kii and Yamato armies. See KI 31915.

20. According to a notation (*okugaki*) appended to a Buddhist text (the *Bonmojutsu sekishō* located at Tōshōdaiji), Nikaidō Dōun, commander of the Yoshino army, led "several thousand mounted warriors." This source is most accessible in *Taiheiki*, ed. Okami Masao (Kadokawa Nihon Koten Bunko, 1975), vol. 1, n. 7.7, pp. 448–49. The *Taiheiki* consistently exaggerates the size of Dōun's forces, and describes them as consisting of either 37,500 (*Seigenin* text) or 23,000 (*Jingū chōkōkan* text) troops.

21. KI 32052 of 3.10.1333 demanded that Katsuoji priests aided Rokuhara. For evidence of fighting on 2.15.1333 to the west of the capital, see KI 32148.

was the situation that the Kōgon emperor fled to the Rokuhara compound for security.[22]

Into this delicately balanced situation strode Ashikaga Takauji, who led one of the *bakufu*'s two reinforcing armies. Instead of aiding Rokuhara, Takauji secured the support of Go-Daigo, newly escaped from Oki Island, and launched an attack against the hapless Rokuhara *tandai* late in the fourth month of 1333. Takauji also dispatched a number of mobilization orders (*saisokujō*) to warriors throughout Japan. Many turned against Kamakura, and both the *tandai* and the *bakufu* itself were destroyed within weeks. (See figure 1, the graves of the Rokuhara *tandai*.)

Due to the nature of his rebellion against the established order, Takauji had to rely upon personal requests to warriors throughout Japan to join his (and Go-Daigo's) cause. Political exigency undermined the previous system of regional, province-wide mobilization; instead, warriors were enticed to fight with promises of compensation.

Even though the Kamakura *bakufu* had been obliterated, Aso Harutoki managed to keep his army intact by unilaterally granting estates to his followers as reward for their service.[23] Harutoki's still formidable force abandoned its siege of Chihaya and marched to Nara, where an uneasy standoff ensued in the sixth month of 1333. His army, fifty thousand strong according to the *Taiheiki*, holed up in Hannyaji and prepared for a final battle.

Figure 1. The graves of the Rokuhara *tandai*. Rengeji, located in Shiga prefecture, Maibara village. Photograph by the author.

22. *Entairyaku*, vol. 3, 12.8.1350, pp. 379–80.
23. KI 32220.

The end of Harutoki's army reveals much about how strong the principle of adequate compensation for warriors had become. Harutoki's Utsunomiya allies bolted after they received an imperial edict (*rinji*) from Go-Daigo, promising that their lands would be confirmed. Others followed, save for those too tainted by their ties to Kamakura ever to countenance rewards from Go-Daigo.[24] Those that remained became priests and surrendered.[25]

What is most remarkable is not that Harutoki's army crumbled under the enticement of imperial edicts, but that it survived for as long as it did. In spite of the overwhelming defeat of Kamakura and the annihilation of every other component of the regime, this expeditionary force remained. No other army would weather defeat so well. Harutoki and his rank and file have been wrongly forgotten, for their passing marked the end of a systematically organized army for some time to come.

In organization and staying power (if not success), Harutoki's army was the greatest army of the fourteenth century. And yet organization per se was no longer crucial for military success. Instead, as even Harutoki had realized, generals had to compensate their troops in order to sustain their armies. After 1333, military service had to be requested instead of demanded. Armies became nothing but aggregate assemblages of individuals. The standard of obligation would fall so low that by 1363 warriors would boast of their service, which merely consisted of not deserting even once.[26] With the fall of Kamakura there perished the belief that political entities deserved unquestioning loyalty, for everyone now knew that political regimes were inherently fragile.

The need to mobilize and wield military force became both a means of stabilizing authority and an end unto itself. After the downfall of Harutoki, no one knew who would ultimately prove to be the most successful in amassing and sustaining these powers of coercion. Sometime in the spring of 1333, state and society were unleashed from their old moorings and cast adrift in a sea of uncertainties. Ultimately, only the relentless logic of war remained, the sole unsettling certainty in an age of profound contention.

---

24. *Taiheiki* (*Jingū chōkōkan hon*), ed. Hasegawa Tadashi, Kami Hiroshi, Ōmori Kitayoshi, Nagasaka Shigeyuki (Osaka: Izumi Shoin, 1994), maki 11, "Kongōsan no yosetera chūseraruru koto," pp. 304–5. This passage also appears in Helen Craig McCullough, trans., *The Taiheiki: A Chronicle of Medieval Japan* (New York: Columbia University Press, 1959), p. 334.

25. All 189 of these Kamakura partisans were later defrocked. Harutoki and some fifteen others were executed in the middle of the night some nine months later. See "Ōmi Banba no shuku Rengeji kakochō," in *Gunsho ruijū* vol. 22, *Zatsubu* vol. 4, comp. Hanawa Hokinoichi (Naigai Shoseki Kabushiki Kaisha, 1931), p. 577.

26. *Shizuoka kenshi shiryōhen, Chūsei*, comp. Shizuoka Kenshi Iinkai Hensanshitsu (Shizuoka: Shizuoka Prefecture, 1994), vol. 2, document 676, 2.6.1363 Kamakura Kubō *migyōsho*, for references to a warrior's boast that he had never returned once (*kikoku no gi*). See also NBIC 912, 4065, and 4665 for references to warriors readily abandoning offensives.

1

Portrait of a Warrior: The Life and Death of Nomoto Tomoyuki

The passionate desire to be praised by posterity is just as well known to the courtly knight of the twelfth century and the unrefined . . . mercenaries of the fourteenth. . . . The agreement for the *Combat des Trente* (March 27, 1351) between Robert de Beaumanoir and the English captain Robert Bamborough is concluded by the latter with the words, "and let us so act, that people in times to come will speak of it in halls and palaces, in markets and elsewhere throughout the world."

Johan Huizinga, *The Autumn of the Middle Ages*

One crisp October day in 1995, when the coolness of autumn morning gave way to a warm, clear light under deep blue skies, I visited at his home Mr. Kumagai Masao, scion of the Kumagai family and lineal descendent of the twelfth century warrior Kumagai Naozane. After an elegant lunch complete with an excellent saké served from cups several centuries old, Mr. Kumagai brought out a immense pawlonia (*kiri*) box, well burnished with the hue of antiquity, on which was carved "Documents of the Kumagai house." In this box were many carefully wrapped scrolls. In each scroll, several tens of documents had been pasted together sometime during the late seventeenth or early eighteenth centuries. The oldest document consisted of a testament by Naozane himself dating from the waning days of the twelfth century—an indelible reminder that Kumagai fame and prosperity stemmed from his exploits.

That these documents survived is little short of remarkable. The Kumagai prospered in the thirteenth century and managed to navigate the turbulent ensuing centuries and establish a powerful presence in Aki Province. The late sixteenth-century convulsion of Japan's "reunification" buffeted Kumagai fortunes when their overlord, the Mōri, suffered a crushing defeat in 1600. For their part, the Kumagai managed to preserve their holdings only in truncated form, far to the west of Aki, settling in the newly established castle town of Hagi. Here they remained, down to the generation of Kumagai Masao.

The Kumagai documents include records of both the main family (sōryō-ke) and its branch lineages. The documents of the lineages had initially been stored in a separate repository, but, for unknown reasons, they were later entrusted to the main line. A few other documents of uncertain origin are interspersed among the documents, notably a long and detailed petition for reward, tightly wound at the end of one scroll, which describes the exploits of one Nomoto Tomoyuki. For whatever reason, the Kumagai preserved this document along with their own voluminous records. Tomoyuki's battle experiences remain the only aspect of his life that has not been lost to antiquity.

Among the thousands of petitions that survive, one submitted on behalf of Nomoto Tomoyuki is uniquely suited for reconstructing the experience of fourteenth-century war for several reasons. The first is its length. Although most petitions only chronicle a few military encounters, this document summarizes numerous petitions and reports of arrival written from 1335 through 1337 and is thus ideally suited for illuminating the epochal onset of war.[1] The second is its reliability. This document dates from 1338 and its contents can be independently verified. The third reason stems from its comprehensiveness—this document provides vivid insights into nearly every facet of war. Through Tomoyuki's petition, we can flesh out the inherently human experience of waging war through a "braided narrative," whereby personal experiences are supplemented with sources that establish a broader context.[2] The fourth is Tomoyuki's anonymity. This petition

---

1. This distinction of petitions for reward was first recognized by Urishihara Tōru in "Gunchūjō ni kansuru jakkan no kōsatsu," *Komonjo kenkyū* 21 (June 1983): 33–52. All of Tsurujūmaru's petition is translated as it appears in NBIC 654, except the final passages which describe events after Tomoyuki's death and are therefore summarized.
2. David Hackett Fischer advanced the notion of "braided narrative" in *Albion's Seed* (New York: Oxford University Press, 1989).

represents a plea for rewards that largely went unheeded. By understanding how the Nomoto began their descent into obscurity, one can surmise
how warfare altered the structure of state and society. The experiences of
Nomoto Tomoyuki should not, however, be overemphasized, for they are
indicative of broader trends and processes that can be gleaned from other
petitions as well, which shall constitute the basis for the next chapter. With
that caveat in mind, let us therefore turn to the petition submitted by
Nomoto Tomoyuki's son Tsurujūmaru.

> **Attention**
>   **Tsurujūmaru, the son of Nomoto Noto Shirō Tomoyuki, now dead,
> states [his father's] military service.**
>   **The aforementioned Tomoyuki is a descendant of this [the Kuma-
> gai?] house. Since he started serving the shogun [Ashikaga Takauji],
> he has performed unparalleled military service, abandoning his lands
> and fighting with little concern for personal safety. There is no hiding
> his valor. Nevertheless, Tomoyuki was unable to submit [a complete
> record of] his deeds [while alive]. They are now humbly presented.**

Tsurujūmaru's document begins abruptly. Political narratives were unnec-
essary in the 1330s because all contemporaries understood the initial context—an indeterminate period of complex political maneuvering that had
collapsed into the clarity of war.

The turmoil that accompanied the sudden annihilation of the Kamakura
bakufu in 1333 continued in spite of, or perhaps because of, the emperor Go-
Daigo's determined efforts to forge a centralized regime. Several uprisings
sputtered throughout the archipelago, but it was a group of Hōjō partisans, the
beleaguered survivors of the Kamakura *bakufu*, who experienced shocking success in the summer of 1335. From their hideaway in the mountains of central
Japan, they swept down and occupied the burnt-out shell of Kamakura.[3]
Paralysis gripped Go-Daigo's regime until Ashikaga Takauji departed without authorization "for the sake of the realm" and crushed the Hōjō in a series
of battles, occupying Kamakura in the eighth month of 1335.[4]

---

3. Hōjō Tokiyuki, one of the few ranking survivors of Kamakura, fled to the mountainous province of
   Shinano and raised the flag of rebellion in the third month of 1335. *Shinano shiryō*, comp. Shinano
   Shiryō Kankōkai (Nagano: Nagano Prefecture, 1954), vol. 5, p. 260, and, for increasing military
   activity in the fifth month of 1335, pp. 262–64. The Shinano uprising gained strength and, during
   the seventh month, Tokiyuki and his supporters sacked their old stronghold of Kamakura. Ibid.,
   7.1335 Ichikawa Sukefusa *chakutōjō* and 8.1335 Ichikawa Chikamune *gunchūjō*, pp. 264–66.
4. Takauji's justification appears in a pro-Ashikaga work: *Baishōron*, ed. Yashiro Kazuo and Kami Hiroshi
   in *Shinsen Nihon koten-bunko* (Gendai Shichōsha, 1975), p. 70. For documentary references to

After Takauji had ousted the Hōjō, he waited in Kamakura for news from the capital. Tense negotiations continued between Kyoto and Kamakura as Go-Daigo and his ministers vacillated over whether to reward Takauji for his achievements or punish him for his insubordination. During these four months, an uneasy calm settled on the town. Warriors preoccupied themselves in a variety of ways. Some preferred gambling, while others wrote stanzas of linked verse or whiled away the time playing games (*igo*) during the day and judging teas and the merits of poems at night.[5] Others lost themselves in the arms of prostitutes.[6] Their less boisterous companions listened to the yarns of famed poets and skilled minstrels.[7] Lute (*biwa*) players who recited the epic *Tale of the Heike*, with its idealized portraits of men such as Kumagai Naozane and its underlying theme of evanescent glory, proved to be particularly popular.[8] (See figures 2 = pl. 1 and 3 = pl. 2.)

Figure 2. The tedium of guard duty. Source: *Heiji monogatari emaki*. Individual Collection. Photograph provided by Chūōkōronshinsha.

Takauji's expedition, including his 8.2.1335 departure without permission, see *Shizuoka kenshi shiryōhen*, *Chūsei* vol. 2, document 120, and NBIK 544.

5. *Taiheiki*, maki 7, "Chihayajō ikusa no koto," p. 167, and McCullough, *The Taiheiki*, pp. 184–85, contain references to gambling, prostitution, and poetry competitions. For artifacts related to gambling uncovered in Kamakura, see Amino Yoshihiko, ed., *Bushi no miyako Kamakura*, vol. 3 of *Yomigaeru chūsei* (Heibonsha, 1989), pp. 224–25.

6. *Taiheiki*, maki 38, "Tsukushi tandai gekō no koto," p. 1134–35.

7. "Ōtōnomiya monogatari," *Shinano shiryō*, vol. 7, p. 367.

8. *Gen'ishū*, ed. Kaji Hiroe (Heibonsha, 1996), p. 271. For reference to Kō no Moronao also listening to *The Tale of the Heike* while ill, see *Taiheiki*, maki 21, "Enya Hangan zanshi no koto," p. 664.

Figure 3. The tedium of guard duty. Source: *Go-sannen kassen ekotoba*. Permission and photo granted by the Tokyo National Museum.

The waning months of 1335 melted into a flurry of frantic action. Go-Daigo, alarmed by Takauji's flouting of authority, ultimately dispatched an army to chastise him. Both Go-Daigo and Takauji attempted to garner as much support as they could, and each issued numerous mobilization orders to warriors across the land. At some point that fall, Tomoyuki threw in his lot with Takauji. How long it took him to mobilize is unknown, although some warriors reported to camp a mere eleven days after they received their first invitation to fight.[9]

The advancing imperial army mauled Takauji's vanguard, commanded by his brother Tadayoshi. Takauji strove to avert disaster and save his brother when he set out from Kamakura with a small band of men.

> **On the eighth day of the twelfth month of 1335, when the shogun [Ashikaga Takauji] set forth from Kamakura, Tomoyuki was with him. On the eleventh of the same month, at the Battle of Aizawahara in Izu, [Tomoyuki] galloped to the fore and performed the service of fighting in the vanguard. The particulars were witnessed by Uesugi Hyōgo Nyūdō and the [*samurai dokoro*], Miura Inaba no kami.**

9. NBIK 810.

This passage, and each subsequent one, represents Tsurujumaru's summary of a no longer extant petition that had been originally submitted by his father. Tomoyuki's laconic account of the battle at Aizawahara was drawn from a document written during the twelfth month of 1335. Both of Tomoyuki's witnesses, Takauji's uncle Uesugi Hyōgo Nyūdō and Miura Inaba no kami, perished a month later in the capital when things began to go badly for the Ashikaga.[10]

Although Tomoyuki does not mention how he felt the night before his first battle, some of his compatriots turned their thoughts to posterity. A few wrote wills, either shortly after "being called up by the military (*buke*)" or on the night before battle, when fears that "something might happen" were strongest.[11] Sōma Mitsutane, for example, remained preoccupied with family concerns right to the end, passing his documents to an adopted son four days before dying when his castle was stormed.[12] Motegi Kenan, on the other hand, was more concerned with the repose of his soul. He demanded that the eighteenth of each month be treated as the day of his death and requested that the sutra he had been copying be completed as soon as possible.[13]

The night immediately before battle was one of anticipation and trepidation. Few warriors mustered much élan. Yamanouchi Tsuneyuki wrote to his wife and told her that "battle is imminent and I feel so alone."[14] Anxious young warriors asked for combat advice from veterans.[15] Some attempted to purify themselves prior to battle, abstaining from sex or

---

10. Uesugi Norifusa, the older brother of Takauji's mother, Uesugi Seishi, died at the "battle on the river-side." For a description of his death, see "Nantaiheiki" (Imagawa Ryōshun) in *Gunsho ruijū* 17 *kassen bu* 2 *buke bu* 1 (Naigai Shoseki Kabushiki Kaisha, 1930), p. 309. The Miura were disgruntled because they believed that they had been snubbed by Go-Daigo's regime. See Yamada Kuniaki, "Miura shi to Kamakura fu," in *Chūsei no hō to seiji*, ed. Ishii Susumu (Yoshikawa Kōbunkan, 1992), pp. 22–51. Both Uesugi Norifusa and Miura Inaba no kami perished on 1.27.1336, near the Kamo River in Kyoto. See *Baishōron*, p. 89.

11. For the former, see *Hiraoka shishi, shiryōhen* 1, comp. Hiraoka Shishi Iinkai (Hiraoka: Hiraoka, 1966), 2.4.1332 Fujiwara Yasumasa *yuzurijō utsushi*, pp. 408–10. For the latter, compare KI 32042, KI 32056, and the "Hakata nikki," which reveals that these wills were written the same day that the Kikuchi attacked Hakata. For the Kikuchi attack, see "Hakata nikki," in *Zoku zoku gunsho ruijū* 3, *Shidenbu*, p. 551.

12. For Mitsutane's testament, see *Sōma monjo*, eds. Toyoda Takeshi and Tashiro Osamu (Zoku Gunsho Ruijū Kanseikai, 1979), document 34, 5.20.1336 Sōma Mitsunate *yuzurijō*, pp. 29–30; for reference to his death, see ibid., the Sōma Okada genealogy (*keifu*), p. 205.

13. *Tochigi kenshi shiryōhen chūsei*, comp. Tochigi Kenshiryō Hensan Iinkai (Tochigi: Tochigi Prefecture, 1975), vol. 2, Motegi *monjo* document 2, Motegi ke *shōmon utsushi*, pp. 72–73.

14. *Hino shishi shiryōshū Takahata Fudō tainai monjo hen*, Hino Shishi Hensan Iinkai, comp. (Tōkyō Inshokan, 1993), document 36, Yamanouchi Tsuneyuki *shōjo*.

15. *Aro monogatari*, Sawai Taizō, ed. in *Muromachi monogatari shū* 1, *Shin nihon koten bungaku taikei*, ed. Ichiko Teiji et al. (Iwanami Shoten, 1989), pp. 128–33. See also *Genpei jōsuiki*, ed. Furutani Tomochika et al. (Kokumin Bunko Kankōkai, 1911), maki 37, p. 909. Although this text is more commonly known as *Genpei seisuiki*, the consensus of Japanese literary scholars is that *Genpei jōsuiki* is the correct pronunciation.

avoiding deer meat. Few resisted fortifying their resolve with generous amounts of saké.[16]

The only thing that Tomoyuki accomplished in this first encounter was to have been seen. Those who fought desired this above all, for from it stemmed rewards and the possibility of advancing in the world. One said, "If I were to advance, alone, in midst of the enemy, and die in a place where none could witness my deeds, then my death would be as pointless as a dog's death."[17] Another particularly flamboyant man, determined to stand out from his comrades, dyed his horses deep purple, crimson, chartreuse, and sky blue, or embellished them with zebra stripes and leopard spots.[18] Needless to say, when battle was imminent, people from all stations of life crowded onto bridges and climbed the hills, eager to view the spectacle of war.[19]

Tomoyuki was particularly fortunate that men such as the Miura and Uesugi could speak of his valor, for the higher the social rank of the witness, the greater the likelihood of gaining rewards.[20] For example, Yamanouchi Tsuneyuki comforted his son in a letter from the front, writing, "Do not worry . . . for even if I die, the general (*taishō*) and members of the unit (*ikki*)" will ensure that rewards will be granted.[21] All in all, this first day was a good one for Tomoyuki; he received recognition and credit for the military service of his retainers, who fought at nearby Nakayama.

> **On the same day, the battle of Nakayama [erupted]. The enemy was strong to the fore so [Tomoyuki's men] retreated a bit. Tomoyuki's retainers [*wakatō*] Iwase Hikotarō Nobutsune, Matagorō Mitsuie, Matatarō Tanetsune, and Magogorō Ietsuna, some ten horsemen in all, charged into the forces of Officer [*hangan*] Yūki and dropped one enemy rider. [Nobutsune and the others] were about to take the head,**

16. *Zoku gunsho ruijū bukebu* (Zoku Gunsho Ruijū Kanseikai, 1975), vol. 25, part 1, p. 79. The *Taiheiki* roundly criticizes a general for having prostitutes in his camp, and claims that their (defiling?) presence contributed to his defeat. *Taiheiki*, maki 38, "Tsukushi tandai gekō no koto," pp. 1134–35. For the defiling nature of deer meat, see *Genpei jōsuiki*, maki 36, p. 899. For saké, see *Aro monogatari*, p. 131. For drinking saké in order to ensure an enemy's defeat, see *Heihō reizuisho*, ed. Ishioka Hisao in *Shoryūheihō* 1 *Nihon heihō zenshjū* 6 (Jinbutsu Ōraisha, 1967), p. 59.

17. *Genpei jōsuiki*, maki 37, p. 909.

18. *Taiheiki*, maki 34, "Hatakeyama Nyūdō Dōsei jōraku no koto," p. 1011.

19. For examples of crowds watching battle, see *Gen'ishū*, p. 271; "Ōtōnomiya monogatari," *Shinano shiryō*, vol. 7, p. 369; and *Taiheiki*, maki 7, "Chihayajō kassen no koto," p. 163 and maki 29, "Shōgun oyako onjōraku no koto," p. 859.

20. As one warrior stated, "My uncle Yasaburō Kunihiro died in battle right under the eyes of the general (*taishō*); there was no need for any other witnesses." DNSR vol. 14, 12.1350 Ōhara Kosaji *gunchūjō*, pp. 58–59.

21. *Hino shishi shiryōshū Takahata Fudō tainai monjo hen*, document 45, Yamanouchi Tsuneyuki *shojo*.

> **but the general of the day, Yamana Izu no kami [Tokiuji], witnessed his deeds and penned a document of praise [*kanjō*]. Following this order [not to take the head, Nobutsune, Mitsuie, Tanetsune, and Ietsuna] pursued the fleeing enemy to the Hire River. The particulars appear on the document of arrival [*chakutōjō*] dated the following day.**

The battles of Aizawahara and Nakagawa were fought on this same day and in close proximity. Although some battles ended in a few hours, thereby making it possible to fight twice on a given day, Tomoyuki does not mention fighting at Nakagawa.[22] Either he rested, or he fought separately from his retainers. Nevertheless, Tomoyuki received credit for the deeds of the Iwase. Although the latter might have fought separately, they would not have submitted their own petitions for reward. In this sense, the right to submit documents, and not the ability to ride into battle on horseback, proved to be the ultimate sign of status.

The encounter just described was not necessarily typical. Desultory battles could last for days, while sieges could last for months.[23] Commanders often relied upon blockades to strangle their enemies, but the fluid political situation and the ill-defined parameters of political and military allegiance in 1335 contributed to the rapid and decisive outcome in this instance.

When standing armies were about to clash, they exchanged "war cries" (*toki*) which demarcated the advent of battle, as did the eerie, unnerving, husky whistle of specially designed "humming arrows" (*kaburaya*).[24] The war cry constituted an invitation to fight.[25] According to Ise Sadatake, a general would twice call out "Ei, Ei." His troops would reply "Oh."[26] Prior to battle, or so the manuals say, warriors were to start with a pianissimo and

---

22. In another case, we see that Hiromine Seishun fought two battles on the same day—first in Toba, in the southern part of the capital, and later on the Amida peak of Mt. Hiei. *Hyōgo kenshi, shiryōhen chūsei*, comp. Hyōgo Kenshi Henshū Senmon Iinkai (Hyōgo: Hyōgo Prefecture, 1983–97), vol. 2 Hiromine *monjo* document 28, 9.26.1336 Hiromine Seishun *gunchūjō an*, p. 616. For a battle that lasted approximately five hours, see NBIK 1154.

23. "Hakata nikki," p. 556. "A battle [raged] every day for five days which consisted of nothing but an arrow battle. Sword blows were not exchanged [but] a number of enemy were shot (*ya ikusa bakari nite tachi uchi nashi*)." For battles lasting six consecutive days, see NBIK 2536. Some warriors fought a series of battles during little over one month, NBIK 657–63. Others guarded areas and fought indeterminate battles for seven months while besieging a castle, NBIK 794–95, 810.

24. Numerous examples appear in the *Taiheiki*. See, for example, maki 26, "Shijō nawate kassen no koto," p. 779; maki 31, "Musashino kassen no koto," p. 921 for a "battle cry of victory"; maki 33, "Kikuchi Shōni kassen no koto," p. 994; maki 38, "Settsu no kuni kassen no koto," p. 1146; maki 39, "Motouji, Haga kassen no koto," p. 1162 for "three battle cries." For a reference to both armies emitting three battle cries, see *Entairyaku* (Taiyōsha, 1940), vol. 4, 6.9.1353, p. 307.

25. *Teijō zakki*, ed. Shimada Isao (Heibonsha, 1985), vol. 3, p. 319.

26. Ibid.

then crescendo; after victory had been achieved, the war cries were to start
off with a forte and decrescendo. It was commonly believed that a well-
executed battle cry would invariably lead to victory.[27] Once the defeated fled,
triumphant warriors yelled "battle cries of victory," which concluded the
encounter.[28]

Only a small number of men fought at Nakagawa. Even ten horsemen
might slice through the dispersed armies of the fourteenth century, in which
scattered groups of foot soldiers intermingled with small clusters of enemy
horsemen. Although one might imagine that Tomoyuki and his men galloped
on speedy horses, the reality was far more prosaic. Japanese horses of the
Kamakura period were quite small, equivalent in size to the modern pony.
The average horse stood only slightly over four feet at the shoulder (130 cm),
while the smallest horses were only three and a half feet tall (109 cm) and
the largest four feet seven inches (140 cm)![29] (See figure 4.) These short-
legged but sturdy beasts were capable of enduring much punishment over
rough terrain, but they were not particularly fast. Japanese horses wore straw

Figure 4. Native Japanese Horse. Photograph and permission by the Equine Museum of
Japan.

27. For reference to such calls "lead[ing] to a hundred victories in a hundred battles," see *Aro mono-
    gatari*, p. 132. For more on these military manuals, see *Zoku gunsho ruijū bukebu*, vol. 25, part 1,
    p. 79.
28. *Taiheiki*, maki 33, "Kikuchi kassen no koto," p. 995.
29. This is known from horse skeletons excavated from Zaimokuza in Kamakura. See Hayashida Shigeyuki,
    Nihon zairaba no keitō ni kansuru kenkyū (Nihon Chūō Keibakai, 1978), pp. 109–20, and Suzuki
    Hisashi, *Kamakura zaimokuza hakken no chūsei iseki to sono jinkotsu* (Iwanami Shoten, 1956).

sandals instead of iron shoes.[30] When burdened with armor and an armored rider, these horses could only muster a gallop after considerable effort and could not sustain such a pace for long before dropping into a trot.[31] The smallness and slowness of Japanese horses need to be taken into consideration when attempting to reconstruct battle scenes.

In the above account from Tsurujūmaru's petition, the Iwase cut down an enemy horseman, although it is not clear how they accomplished this feat. The act of taking a head was infused with a significant amount of cultural meaning and generated praise from authorities.[32] The overriding purpose of taking a head was to "prove" one's battle service, and thus the act was the apogee of good fortune: "Those who took an enemy's head . . . sallied forth from the castle; those who lost their lords retreated, crying, into the castle."[33] Heads were rigorously inspected because they constituted the most tangible proof of battle service.[34] The heads of those killed would be carefully cleaned and dressed, and names attached to those who could be identified, while those determined to be from low-ranking men would be discarded.[35] Recognition was a crucial concern: taking an unidentified head was "no different from taking the head of a dog or bird."[36] (See figure 5 = pl. 3. See also figure 6 = pl. 4.)

Generals normally discouraged the custom of head-hunting because warriors so engaged might become vulnerable. A man preoccupied with taking a head placed himself in grave danger. According to one petition, one such man was shot and killed by returning opponents.[37] Another warned his

---

30. For more on horse footwear, see Kuroda Hideo, "Uma no sandaru," *Sugata to shigusa no chūseishi, Ezu to emaki no fukei kara* (Heibonsha, 1986), pp. 22–28. For a reference to "horse shoes" (*uma no kutsu*), see *Taiheiki*, maki 29, "Moronao kyōdai yoriki shōgai no koto," p. 883. See also maki 13 of the *Kasuga gongen kenki e*.

31. Suzuki Kenji, *Rekishi e no shōtai* (Nihon Hōsō Shuppankai, 1980), vol. 6, pp. 32–34, and Kawai Yasushi, *Genpei kassen no kyozō o hagu, Jishō Jūei nairanshi kenkyū* (Kōdansha, 1996), p. 53. For horses wearing armor, see *Taiheiki*, maki 23, "Hata Rokurō Saemon ga koto," p. 685.

32. The oldest surviving document of praise lauds the capture of a head. "During skirmishing in the mountains north of Chihaya castle, you took a head, which is most splendid." 4.21.1333 Harutoki *kanjō*, unpublished document, which has been transcribed in Uemura Seiji, *Kusunoki Masashige* (Shibundō, 1962), p. 97. From 1333 onward, many petitions record the decapitation of enemy warriors.

33. *Genpei jōsuiki* (Kokumin Bunko Kankōkai, 1911), maki 37, p. 917. The taking of heads was proudly mentioned in petitions for reward. See NBIC 400 and 1212.

34. *Taiheiki*, maki 24, "Setajō ochiru no koto," p. 715. For one list of those killed in battle, see NBIK 6940. For a visual representation of a warrior presenting heads, and his deeds being recorded by a scribe, see figure 17, pl. 11, *Mōko shūrai ekotoba*, ed. Komatsu Shigemi, vol. 13 of *Nihon no emaki* (Chūōkōronsha, 1988), pp. 114–15 and Conlan, *In Little Need of Divine Intervention*, pp. 182–83.

35. See for example *Genpei jōsuiki* (Kokumin Bunko Kakōkai, 1911), maki 20, p. 489. For examples of heads being pickled in saké, see *Teijō zakki*, vol. 4, pp. 229–30. For a representation of heads on display, with name tags attached, see figure 6, pl. 4, and *Go-sannen kassen ekotoba*, ed. Komatsu Shigemi, vol. 15 of *Nihon emaki taisei* (Chūōkōronsha, 1977), pp. 102–3.

36. *Genpei jōsuiki* (Kokumin Bunko Kakōkai, 1911), maki 37, p. 926.

37. *Tochigi kenshi shiryōhen chūsei*, vol. 3, pp. 346–47, Sano Awa Ichiōmaru *gunchūjō*. See also *Genpei jōsuiki* (Kokumin Bunko Kakōkai, 1911), maki 42, p. 1059 for an instance of a man being shot while trying to take a head.

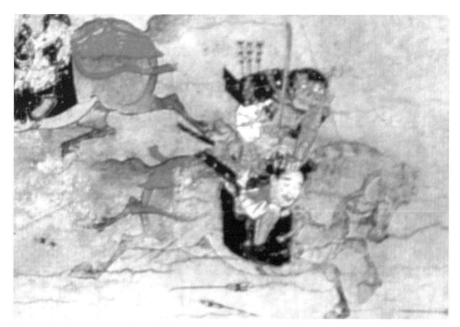

Figure 5. Warrior returning with head. Source: *Shōtoku taishi eden*, "Mononobe Moriya to no kassen" permission of Jōgūji. Photo courtesy Ibaragi Kenritsu Rekishikan.

comrades that "when you try to take a head, you will invariably encounter five or ten enemy."[38] Those who were successful tended to abandon the battlefield, already in possession of the ultimate proof of valor.[39] Some commanders issued standing orders to "cut and toss" these heads.[40] In these circumstances, warriors discarded heads once their valor had been witnessed.[41] A few even contented themselves with a fragment of armor instead of a head. One warrior "cut and tossed" an enemy head and settled instead

38. *Aro Monogatari*, p. 129.
39. A triumphant warrior grasping a head constitutes a standard motif of the successful warrior. See figure 5, pl. 3, figure 9, pl. 7, and *Ibaragi no emaki*, Ibaragi Hakubutsukan, comp. (Mito: Ibaragi Kenritsu Rekishikan, 1989), color plate 2, "Shōtoku taishi eden," and *Go-sannen kassen ekotoba*, p. 50. For forged references to taking seven heads, see NBIC 1685.
40. NBIC 773. This has also been mentioned in Satō Shin'ichi, *Nanbokuchō no dōran*, (Chūōkōronsha, 1974), p. 197. Urushihara Tōru has argued that these "cut and toss" orders represent a modification of the inspection process for rewards. In cases where detailed inspections proved impossible, eyewitness accounts became increasingly relied upon. See his *Chūsei gunchūjō to sono sekai* (Yoshikawa Kōbunkan, 1998), particularly pp. 138–44.
41. For examples of "cut and tossed" heads, see NBIK 674, 1211–12; *Taiheiki*, maki 31, "Yawata ikusa no koto," p. 935; and *Ino Hachimangū monjo*, ed. Tamayama Narimoto (Zoku Gunsho Ruijū Kanseikai, 1983), document 148, Iga Morimitsu *gunchūjō*, of 5.1337. For other examples of heads being taken, see NBIK 732 and 1238.

for a piece of enemy armor because he was in the midst of the enemy and lacked sufficient space to hack off the head.[42] Nevertheless, the custom of head-hunting proved tenacious. Although the Iwase abandoned their quarry at Nakagawa, another of Tomoyuki's retainers managed to take one on 1.30.1336. Likewise, the same general who issued "cut and toss" orders later chose to reward two warriors equally: the first killed an enemy general while the second took his head![43]

Those thirsty for some token of achievement decapitated any wounded enemy they could find. For a wounded man to spend a night unscathed on the battlefield was described as being nothing short of "miraculous" (*fushigi nare*).[44] Prior to the fourteenth century, warriors were praised for securing as many heads as possible. For example, during the Mongol invasion of 1281, Kikuchi Jirō advanced among the Mongol dead, collected a large number of heads, and brought them into the castle, thereby "making a name for himself [to last for] generations."[45] Although some warriors continued to matter-of-factly pick up discarded heads, a stigma eventually accrued to such scavenging.[46] According to the *Taiheiki*, some particularly overzealous warriors

scoured the capital for those dead and wounded who had fallen in moats and ditches and collected heads of the dead, and lined them up—eight hundred and seventy three in all—at the Rokujō riverbed (*kawara*). Of those, most had not been killed in battle. Many were fakes, taken from residents (*zaikenin*), townsmen, and travelers on the roadside. A welter of names were haphazardly attached to the heads. Five placards stated that the designated head was of Akamatsu Enshin. As there was no one who knew how he looked, all five were hung in the same way. . . . The wags of the capital gazed at the heads and murmured, "Those who borrowed these heads returned them with interest."[47] (See figure 6 = pl. 4.)

42. NBIC 457.
43. *Taiheiki (Tenshō hon)*, ed. Hasegawa Tadashi, in *Shinhen Nihon koten bungaku zenshū* (Shōgakkan, 1996), vol. 2, maki 19, "Kokushi Ise no kuni o hete Yoshino dono e mairu koto," p. 528. Nevertheless, Tashiro Akitsune followed his injunctions and "cut and tossed" an enemy, which was witnessed by Kuge Saburō and Miyake Gorō. See *Takaishi shishi*, comp. Takaishi Hensan Iinkai (Takaishi: Takaishi, 1986), document 123, 3.26.1338 Tashiro Akitsune *gunchūjō*.
44. *Taiheiki*, maki 32, "Kōnan ikusa no koto," p. 971.
45. "Hachiman gudō kun," in *Gunsho ruijū*, comp. Hanawa Hokinoichi (Keizai Zasshisha, 1894), vol. 1, p. 468.
46. For an example of nonchalant head-hunting in the fourteenth century, see *Taiheiki*, maki 31, "Usui toge kassen no koto," p. 929.
47. *Taiheiki*, maki 8, "Sangatsu jūninichi Miyako ikusa no koto," p. 195. For a different English translations, see McCullough *The Taiheiki*, p. 214.

Figure 6. Decapitated heads. Source: *Go-sannen kassen ekotoba*. Permission and photo granted by the Tokyo National Museum.

Such ridicule coincides with the origin of rules of etiquette regarding the taking of heads.[48] Transgressors of the norms of head-hunting became the objects of laughter in the 1330s and the focus of scorn in the 1390s.[49] The practice of picking up an abandoned head gradually became a shameful act, and so later military manuals devoted considerable detail to distinguishing whether a head was removed from a living man or a corpse.[50]

> **On the twelfth day of the same month, during the battle of the Sano riverbed . . . [Tomoyuki and the others] joined the main body of troops [*nakate*], crossed the river, and performed military service.**
>
> **On the thirteenth, during the battle at the Izu kokufu, [Tomoyuki's] follower [*chūgen*] Heigorō otoko was killed.**

Heigorō was a member of the base orders (*genin*) who followed Nomoto Tomoyuki into battle. He lacked a surname and was referred to as *otoko* (*onoko*), a disrespectful epithet reserved for those of lower orders or those deserving scorn.[51] Although one can assert with some confidence that Heigorō did not ride a horse, it is not clear whether he was a foot soldier or a laborer accidentally killed in the fray. Speed was of the essence for the

48. For a pioneering study of such a "civilizing process," see Norbert Elias, *The History of Manners* (New York: Pantheon, 1978).

49. For the first criticisms of a man who "picked up heads thrown away by his colleagues," see *Meitokuki*, ed. Tomikura Tokujirō (Iwanami Shoten, 1941), maki 2, "Toki Michisada no koto," p. 106.

50. *Teijō zakki*, vol. 3, p. 318.

51. Women used this epithet to address a rapist. See *Genpei jōsuiki (Kokumin Bunko Kakōkai*, 1911), maki 35, p. 882. For references to "commoners" (*genin*) being addressed in a similar manner, see NBIC 744.

Ashikaga armies in their pursuit of the shattered imperial army, and so little time was spared to minister to the wounded or to bury the dead.

Nomoto Tomoyuki could have demanded compensation for the death of Heigorō, but Heigorō's bereaved could not. Heigorō was in all probability administered last rites and buried in a mass grave by *ji* priests,[52] who collected the corpses, buried them, performed funeral ceremonies, and set up a memorial.[53] If the dead man was a ranking warrior, *ji* priests might erect a commemorative stele, as did Ku and Hen Amidabutsu for three Akima warriors who died defending Kamakura.[54] Heigorō was probably buried in a makeshift grave too shallow to prevent dogs from digging him up and gnawing on his bones.[55] Wandering priests might write sutras or Sanskrit letters on these wretched remains in order to aid the dead on their path to salvation.[56]

> On the third day of the first month of 1336, Tomoyuki's retainer [*wakatō*] Iwase Hikotarō Nobutsune led the vanguard's attack of Ikisumiya [castle] in Ōmi [province]. As he cut his way through the castle walls of the southeast corner, Nobutsune had an arrow pass through his left and right cheeks. This was seen by the general Hyōbu taiyū [Niki Yoriaki] and Yamana Izu no kami. Nobutsune even received a commendation [*kanjō*] [from these men]. In addition, the retainers Maruyama Hikojirō Tametoki and Katakiri Gorō Nariyoshi were wounded. The following day all arrived at Noji station.

Takauji's army hardly paused on its advance to the capital and arrived near the outskirts after two and a half weeks. Speed was essential in such circumstances, for the longer an army remained on the road, the greater the burden on its warriors and, ultimately, the less likely its success in battle.

52. Ippen (1239–89) founded a movement whose followers (*jishū*, congregation of itinerant priests) attempted to continually chant the *nenbutsu*, "Hail the Amida Bodhisattva." *Ji* priests danced while performing *nenbutsu* and traveled throughout Japan. They administered to the dying (see *Meitokuki*, maki 2, "Ieyoshi kurō no koto," p. 89) and were also responsible for medical treatment as well. For a pioneering study of this, see Hattori Toshirō, "Tōdai ni okeru senshō byōsha no kyūgo to shūkyō katsudō," *Muromachi Azuchi Momoyama jidai igakushi no kenkyū* (Yoshikawa Kōbunkan, 1971), pp. 443–52.

53. "Ōtōnomiya monogatari" in *Shinano shiryō*, vol. 7, p. 393. For a reference to twenty or thirty priests collecting corpses after a battle in 1336, see also *Taiheiki*, maki 15, "Shōgun miyako o ochiru koto," p. 444.

54. KI 32175. The purpose of these markers was to ensure that the souls of those killed violently would be reborn in the Pure Land.

55. See Suzuki, *Kamakura zaimokuza hakken no chūsei iseki to sono jinkotsu*, particularly pp. 22–24.

56. See ibid., p. 28–29. The act of writing on the skulls of the dead is also mentioned in the twelfth-century literary masterpiece, *Hōjōki*.

Ashikaga Takauji mastered the quick march, covering the distance between Kyoto and Kamakura in a mere seventeen days.[57] Other warriors, covering a similar distance, might require as long as twenty-five days,[58] while a beleaguered army required over two months.[59]

The fleeing imperial forces regrouped just to the west of the capital at Ikusu "castle," but only managed to hold up Takauji's army for a day. The battle was in all probability waged near the castle's outlying structures, which were reduced through either frontal assault or arson.[60] One of the few surviving pictorial representations of a mountain castle reveals little more than a series of temporary barricades.[61] (See figure 28 = pl. 19.) Ikusu must have been such a humble structure. By contrast, some of the more formidable castles, such as Kusu castle in northern Kyushu, could withstand a siege for almost seven months.[62]

After an arrow pierced the face of Iwase Hikotarō Nobutsune, he was undoubtedly escorted off the battlefield by his companions in a manner similar to that in the *Heiji monogatari emaki*, where one man leads a wobbly warrior away from the melee. (See figure 7 = pl. 5.) In spite of the apparent severity of his wound, Nobutsune nevertheless fought again five days later. Nobutsune's facial wound was in fact relatively minor because the arrowhead was easily extracted. One can reconstruct what Nobutsune must have endured from an illustration in the *Go-sannen kassen ekotoba*, where we see one man restraining and steadying his wounded companion while another is using what look like pliers to extract an arrow from his face (see figure 8 = pl. 6). Nobutsune was fortunate, for those who could not have an arrowhead extracted died agonizing deaths or were crippled.[63]

Many of the seriously wounded died shortly after battle because medical technology was primitive. One rescued warrior, for example, succumbed to seven sword and arrow wounds that evening.[64] Another, wounded in the

---

57. *Shizuoka kenshi shiryōhen* 6, *Chūsei* 2, document 81, Ashikaga Takauji *Kantō gekō shukunami kassen chūmon*, pp. 33–35.

58. *Shinpen Saitama kenshi shiryōhen* 5, *Chūsei* 1, comp. Saitama-ken Shiryō Hensan Iinkai (Saitama: Saitama Prefecture, 1982), document 316, 2.11.1338 Beppu Yukisane *chakutōjō*, p. 246.

59. Ibid., document 318, 3.1338 Kudama Yukiyasu *gunchūjō*, pp. 246–47.

60. For attacks, see NBIC 498, NBIK 657–58, 662–63, 794–96 and 925–26. For burning barricades, see NBIK 658.

61. See the large fold-out plates in Gotō Shigeki, ed., *Nihon koji bijutsu zenshū* (Shūeisha, 1980) vol. 10 depicting one panel from the *Rokudō-e*.

62. See NBIK 810 for mobilization orders being dispatched on 3.13.1336. Kusu castle did not fall until 10.12.1336.

63. One man, shot just below the shoulder by an arrow, was unable to extract it, and "after three days of utter agony, died a screaming death." *Taiheiki*, maki 23, "Hata Rokurō Saemon ga koto," p. 686. Beppu Michizane quit fighting for years because of an arrowhead lodged in his foot. See the 2.1344 Beppu Michizane *gunchūjō utsushi, Shinpen Saitama kenshi shiryōhen* 5, *Chūsei* 1, pp. 264–65. Michizane ultimately perished in battle somewhere in Kii Province during the spring of 1360. See ibid., urū 4.9.1360 Ashikaga Yoshiakira *gohan migyōsho*, p. 310. I am indebted to Andrew Goble for bringing this to my attention.

64. *Taiheiki*, maki 23, "Hata Rokurō Saemon ga koto," p. 686.

Figure 7. Aiding the wounded. Source: *Heiji monogatari emaki*. Individual Collection. Photograph provided by Chūōkōronshinsha.

shoulder, lingered until he reached home a week later to die.[65] One of the few surviving medical manuals from the fourteenth century, the *Fukuden hō*, is remarkably less sophisticated in dealing with wounds than later manuals. It is, however, replete with astute observations. The reader of this text would, in all probability, be able to judge whether a wound was mortal, although treatment was not greatly aided by the text. Nevertheless, some herbs that are mentioned, such as mugwort (*yomogi*), have medicinal value as effective coagulants.[66] Much of this knowledge seems to have been concentrated in Buddhist temples. Yūrin, the author of the *Fukuden hō*, was

65. NBIK 1301.
66. *Yomogi* is actually quite effective in stopping bleeding, as I discovered after treating a wound caused by dropping a refrigerator on my foot! For more on the efficacy of *yomogi*, see the *Yūrin Fukuden hō* maki 11, part of the Fujigawa collection located at Kyoto University. Most medications were mixed with warm saké, which enhanced their effect. See *Yūrin Fukuden hō*, pp. 6–7.

Figure 8. Extracting an arrow. Source: *Go-sannen kassen ekotoba*. Permission and photo granted by the Tokyo National Museum.

a noted Buddhist priest.[67] To use such a manual at all required a good deal of knowledge, as well as the ability to collect and permanently store materials. We can therefore assume that medical specialists existed and that their medicines and techniques were reserved for the most powerful warriors.[68]

The state of surgical techniques for the fourteenth century is evident in the *Fukuden hō*. For abdominal wounds, one was to "cover the intestines with dried feces; then close the wound with mulberry root sutures and spread cattail pollen over the area. Activities to be avoided were anger, laughter, thought, sex, activity, work, sour foods, and saké."[69] Needless to say, the odds of surviving serious wounds were slim.

67. According to the *Kokushi daijiten* (Yoshikawa Kōbunkan, 1979–97) in its explanation of the *Fukuden hō*, Yūrin resided at Nanzenji and founded Tōfukuji, located in Hitachi's Kashima gun.
68. For example, the ailing Niki Yoriaki was treated by the medical priest (*sō'i*) Tsūsen with acupuncture, but to no avail, for he died the next day. *Entairyaku*, vol. 6, 10.12.1359, p. 300.
69. *Yūrin Fukuden hō*, maki 11, p. 4.

Ultimately, Nomoto Tomoyuki arrived at Noji station, which in fact resembled a small town. Hostels lined these stations, providing shelter for troops as well as functioning as staging points, thereby allowing armies to pause and regroup.[70] These areas had other appeals to the soldiers as well, for women known as "station wives" comforted travelers in various ways.[71] Furthermore, bathhouses appear to have been constructed at stations as well, although these baths were occasionally dismantled for shields and barricades if the need arose.[72] (See figures 9 = pl. 7 and 10.)

Some took advantage of the confusion prevalent at these locales in order to abscond with horses and other goods.[73] Likewise, hostels proved to be ideal locations for warriors to defect. For example, the Rusu had served under the Southern Court generals, but they joined enemy Ashikaga forces at Mikawa Province's Yahagi station.[74] In addition to providing lodging to soldiers, deserters, and other travelers, these stations were networks for the dissemination of news and rumors.[75] Unsurprisingly, messages were dispatched from them by a kind of pony express, and at these stations generals attempted to coordinate attacks.[76]

70. When Ashikaga Takauji launched his offensive in the summer of 1335, his army quartered at these lodgings. "Ashikaga Takauji *Kantō gekō shukunami kassen chūmon,*" *Shizuoka kenshi shiryōhen* 6, *Chūsei* 2, document 81, pp. 33–35. For the arrival of warriors at the Yahagi station on 8.2.1335, see Sanekane *gunchūjō,* ibid., document 120, p. 65, and Kenmu 2[3] Takahashi Shigemune *gunchūjō,* Tadaiin *monjo,* document 150, pp. 76–77. For the case of Noji, Hayami Tomotsuna arrived at this station two days before Tomoyuki arrived. See *Waseda daigaku shozō Ogino kenkyūshitsu monjo gekan,* comp. Waseda daigaku toshokan (Yoshikawa Kōbunkan, 1980), document 705, p. 38. More information regarding the names and locations of stations appears in both the DNSR, series 6, vol. 2, 7.22.1335, pp. 501–2 and Yashiro and Kami, eds., *Baishōron,* p. 219, and (in chart form) in Shinjō Tsunezō, *Kamakura jidai no kōtsū* (1967, Nihon Rekishi Soshō Shinsōban, Yoshikawa Kōbunkan, 1995), pp. 373–76. Finally, see *Entairyaku,* vol. 6, 11.4.1359, p. 301, for armies regrouping at Taruii station.
71. For reference to a "station wife," see *Taiheiki,* maki 24, "Masashige onryō kikken no koto," p. 702.
72. For more on baths being dismantled, see NBIC 306 and 394. Inexplicably, Amino refers to these regions as being "immune" from the authority of the state. See his *Muen kugai raku: Nihon chūsei no jiyū to heiwa* 2nd ed. (Heibonsha, 1987), pp. 311–12. Amino supports his assertion on this subject by quoting the *Gen'ishū:* "On days where there were no battles, both friends and enemies met in the bathhouses of the capital and passed the time swapping stories. There were no disturbances." He omits, however, the rest of the passage: "This behavior stems from there being [a battle in] the capital, for in the provinces, men would not stop fighting at such places." See *Gen'ishū,* p. 271.
73. In 1333, Ashikaga Takauji criticized men for "claiming to need fast horses . . . and absconding with the horses and cattle of travelers and locals, and burdening the stations (*yado*) in a variety of ways." KI 32457.
74. *Chūsei Rusu ke monjo,* ed. Misawa Shiritsu Toshokan (Iwate: Misawa Kyōiku Iinkai, 1979), pp. 50–51, 7.6.1350 Kira Sadaie *suikyojō,* which states that the Rusu joined Ashikaga forces in the second month of 1336 at Yahagi. Prior to this time, the Rusu had served under Kitabatake Akiie of the Southern Court. See ibid., p. 46, 10.1.1335 Mutsu *kokusen.*
75. Iwahashi Kotaya ed., *Entairyaku,* Vol. 3 (Taiyōsha, 1938), 8.18.1350, p. 299 for the case of Taruii station.
76. *Taiheiki* maki 21, "Enya Hangan zanshi no koto," pp. 675–77. For an additional example of Ashikaga Takauji dispatching messages in order to coordinate an attack from the Kakegawa station, see 11.26 (1351) Ashikaga Takauji *gonaisho,* in *Shizuoka kenshi shiryōhen* 6, *Chūsei* 2, document 453, p. 218.

Figure 9. The use of shields in battle. Source: *Shōtoku taishi eden*, "Mononobe Moriya to no kassen" permission of Jōgūji. Photo courtesy Ibaragi Kenritsu Rekishikan. Also note the prevalence of arrows, and how mounted warriors managed to decapitate their enemies.

These stations were freewheeling areas, to be sure, but they possessed strategic importance.[77] Occupying a station enabled one to control routes of supply and communication, and to curtail enemy troop movements. For example, the Ashikaga thwarted Kitabatake Akiie's drive to the capital by dispatching an army to Taruii station.[78] Akiie had no choice but to veer to Ise, and then to Izumi, where he was killed and his army annihilated. Because stations might be torched, they were likewise guarded with a sizeable contingent of warriors.[79]

> **On the eighth, Tomoyuki's retainers Iwase Hikotarō Nobutsune, Matagorō, Matatarō, and Magogorō all joined Yūki [family] forces and pursued the enemy to Hachiman. On the edge of the Ōwatari bridge,**

77. For cases where these stations became the focus of military campaigns, see *Niigata kenshi chūsei shiryōhen*, comp. Niigata Kenshi Hensanshitsu (Niigata: Niigata Prefecture, 1981), vol. 4, document 1051(7), p. 16, and KI 32810.
78. *Taiheiki*, maki 19, "Aonogahara ikusa no koto," p. 611–17. For another example, where Ashikaga Takauji dispatched his collaterals to Yahagi station in order to block the retreat of a Kamakura (Rokuhara *tandai*) army, see KI 32810.
79. For stations being burned, see *Taiheiki*, maki 36, "Hatakeyama Nyūdō Dōsei botsuraku no koto," p. 1098. For troops being posted at stations, see *Fukushima kenshi 7, Shiryōhen kodai chūsei*, comp. Fukushima Prefecture (Fukushima: Fukushima Prefecture, 1966), p. 459, Endō Ishikawa *monjo* document 15, 5.1353 Ishikawa Kanemitsu *gunchūjō*.

> these four charged and destroyed a tower [*yagura*] on the bridge and
> slashed their way onto the structure. After kicking [*fumiotoshi*] the mid-
> dle bridge's girders into the river, Iwase Matataro Tanetsune was
> wounded. The particulars were reported to the encampment [*jin*] of Kō
> Musashi no kami [Moronao] because it was located on the bridge.

On the eighth, Nomoto Tomoyuki and his retainers attacked imperial
encampments at Iwashimizu, south of the capital. Several bridges crossing
the Yodo River were the focal point of the battle. Archers stationed in towers on each bridge provided covering fire for Go-Daigo's defenders against
the Ashikaga onslaught. While Nomoto's men were destroying both the
enemy tower and the girders of the middle bridge, other warriors allied to
the Ashikaga, such as Yamanouchi Michitsugu, built their own towers and
"shot long-range arrows down on six enemy horsemen below, knocking some
off their horses and forcing others to flee."[80]

Warriors did not invariably serve under a single commander; instead they
submitted their petitions to the nearest available commander. Although
Nomoto Tomoyuki had his documents previously monogrammed by Yamana
Izu no kami, he submitted his documents of the day to Kō no Moronao
because of the latter's proximity.

> On the battle of the sixteenth, Tomoyuki's retainers Nobutsune and
> Mitsuie galloped to the fore and drove the enemy away from Hōsshōji.
> [Nobutsune?] cut down one horseman wearing dyed and patterned
> [*kōketsu*] armor [*hitatare*].[81] The particulars were seen by Toki Hōki
> Zenmon [Yorisada] and Sasaki Saemon Shichirō.

At this juncture, Takauji's forces managed to occupy the capital, forcing
Go-Daigo to flee to Mt. Hiei northeast of the capital. As Ashikaga reinforcements poured in from the west, the fortunes of their cause dramatically
improved.

Nobutsune cut down a horseman who was identified only by his armor.
The purpose of armor was for both bodily defense and recognition. Not only
could its quality express the general wealth of its owner, but its color scheme

---

80. NBIC 222. Michitsugu was killed at Sanjō kawara on 1.30.1336.

81. For an illustration of *kōketsu*, see *Yusoku kojitsu daijiten*, comp. Suzuki Keizō (Yoshikawa Kōbunkan,
    1995), pp. 208, 222 (an illustration), and 434.

Figure 10. Fourteenth-century temple doors, similar to those used for shields. Jōdoji temple, Onomichi. Photo by the author. (The first photo is of Jōdoji's doors, the other of its Tahōdō.)

identified him as belonging to the Minamoto, Taira, Fujiwara, or Tachibana lineage.[82] Owing to individualistic styles of braiding—over eighteen color com-
binations and methods of braiding are identifiable—even men who wore armor
of a similar style could be identified from afar (see figure 11 = pl. 8).[83] This
armor proved durable and was subject to incremental improvements in design.[84]

The man killed by Nobutsune could be distinguished as an enemy
because warriors attached special badges or emblems to their armor in order
to signal both their allegiances and their intention to fight. These emblems,
of simple cloth, were often emblazoned with patterns and the names of
deities.[85] Those who agreed on a common badge created a fighting unit (*tō*)
of the moment.[86] Conversely, those who sought to change their allegiance

Figure 11. Different coloring styles of armor. Note also the tiger skin saddle blanket. *Mōko
shūrai ekotoba*, scroll 1, page 9, "The Encampment of Shōni Kagesuke." Possession of
Kunaichō Sannōmaru Shōzōkan. Permission for reproduction granted by the Imperial Household Ministry.

82. Of course, this color scheme was not rigorously enforced, but it still provided a general guideline for
    identifying the family background of its wearer. The Genji wore black, the Heishi purple, the Fuji-
    wara light green, and the Tachibana yellow. See "Heishō jinjun yōryaku shō," in *Zoku gunsho ruijū,
    Bukebu*, vol. 25, no. 1, p. 94.
83. *Kassen emaki—Bushi no sekai*, ed. Torugashi Yuzuru (Mainichi Shinbunsha, 1990), pp. 21–23.
84. For example, Kikuchi Takemitsu tested the strength of each plate (*sane*), and constructed a particu-
    larly effective suit of armor which "stopped the arrows of even the strongest archers." *Taiheiki*, maki
    33, "Kikuchi kassen no koto," p. 996.
85. The sole surviving emblem is located in the Ōyamazumi shrine's museum (*hōmotsukan*) on Ōmishima
    in the Inland Sea.
86. *Taiheiki*, maki 14, "Hakone kassen no koto," p. 394.

or sneak into an enemy camp simply exchanged badges,[87] while those who resolved to remain aloof wore no flags or emblems.[88]

Distinguishing friend from foe was no simple matter in an age without uniforms.[89] Family crests constituted the sole marker of identification for many—these crests might be emblazoned on armor, weapons, shields, battle flags, or the sails of ships. By the late Kamakura period, most warriors had taken to using family crests,[90] which were identifiable to nearly all.[91] Others strove to differentiate themselves by festooning their helmets with crimson fans and artificial plum branches, or, season permitting, real plum branches.[92]

At times, family members wearing identical badges but living in different regions allied with opposing forces. They fought against each other with disastrous consequences.[93] According to the chronicles, hundreds might die when such divided families met in battle, until one group, in one instance, improvised by tearing off the right shoulder panel (*sode*) of their armor and attaching it to their helmets.[94] Others devised hybrid crests that combined the motifs of the Ashikaga and Nitta seals with their own.[95] The great increase in family crests during the fourteenth century stems from the tendency of families to divide (and subdivide) their allegiances.[96]

Although some warriors created new crests in order to create distinctions, others used the ambiguity of similar crests to blur their allegiances. For example, the crests of the Ashikaga consisted of a black ring on a white field intersected by two narrow black lines with the center white; the Nitta—who commanded Go-Daigo's imperial armies—had a black circle on a white background intersected by a thick black line. When Ashikaga partisans were defeated, they painted over the white inner circle of the Ashikaga emblem,

87. Ibid., maki 31, "Usui toge kassen no koto," p. 929, for warriors attaching the Ashikaga emblem; see ibid., "Nantei Hachiman ontaishitsu no koto," p. 939, for warriors attaching the Nitta emblem. See also maki 14, "Hakone kassen no koto," p. 396, and maki 8, "Mayajō kassen no koto," pp. 185–86.

88. Ibid., maki 31, "Musashino kassen no koto," p. 920.

89. For an example of a warrior questioning whether arriving warriors were enemy or ally, see *Taiheiki*, maki 14, "Hakone yosete intai no koto," p. 398. For another example of where enemy are mistakenly assumed to be allies, see maki 15, "Miidera kassen no koto," p. 428.

90. Nuta Raiyū, *Nihon monshōgaku* (Shinjinbutsu Ōraisha, 1968), p. 32.

91. For example, Ashikaga Takauji was able to determine who fought for the enemy by inspecting abandoned battle flags. *Baishōron*, pp. 117–18. See also *Taiheiki*, maki 14, "Hakone kassen no koto," pp. 394–95.

92. For the former, *Taiheiki* maki 14, "Hakone Takeshita kassen no koto," p. 394; for the latter, maki 31, "Musashino kassen no koto," p. 920. Those unable to secure adequate flowers settled for crimson fans. *Taiheiki*, maki 29, "Shōgun oyako onjōraku no koto," p. 858.

93. Nuta, *Nihon monshōgaku*, p. 36.

94. *Baishōron*, p. 88–89.

95. Nuta, *Nihon monshōgaku*, pp. 1164–65. Six families are known to have combined their crest with the Nitta crest, while at least twelve utilized the Ashikaga crest. The relative paucity of Nitta crests stems from their ultimate defeat.

96. Ibid., and Satō, *Nanbokuchō no dōran*, p. 189.

thereby causing wags in the capital to joke about how these new seals resembled (*nitta*) the Nitta's seal.[97] (See figure 12.)

Each military unit was identified by a bannerman selected for his bravery.[98] These men proved to be fine targets, and there are many examples of their death or disfigurement in battle.[99] Their banners served to foster a sense of group identity and became invested with considerable emotional value. Indeed, because these warriors fought for honor as much as anything else, they sometimes attacked rashly in order to retrieve a lost flag.[100]

> **During the battle on the twenty–seventh, Tomoyuki's retainers [*wakatō*] Nobutsune, Mitsuie, Tanetsune, Ietsuna, and Takada Yasaburō Mitsuyuki again galloped to the fore. To the west of the middle reaches of the Kamo River, they captured three Kurama priests alive. Their deeds were witnessed on the battlefield by the administrator [*samurai dokoro*] Sasaki Bitchū no kami.**

Reinforcements for Go-Daigo trickled in to the capital as the days passed. Ashikaga Takauji, in his pursuit of Nitta Yoshisada from the east, had neglected to station adequate reserves to his rear. Kitabatake Akiie pursued Takauji's army from the north and his arrival in Kyoto therefore tipped the balance against the Ashikaga. Priests from Mt. Hiei and Kurama now poured into the capital but were initially checked by Takauji and his men. The fortunes of battle hung precariously in the balance, as the imperatives of war slowly sucked in increasing numbers of men and women from throughout the archipelago.

The Kurama priests were apparently bound and thrown into tiny squalid jails, a common fate for prisoners.[101] Those who were imprisoned were among the fortunate because prisoners captured in the heat of battle were often killed

97. *Taiheiki*, maki 15, Shujō kankō no koto," p. 450.
98. Imagawa Ryōshun, "Ōzōshi," quoted in Nuta, *Nihon monshōgaku*, p. 36. According to Ryōshun, three types of flags existed: a familial flag, a white flag, and an imperial brocade flag.
99. References to bannermen being killed appear in the following documents: 9.1335 Kamada *meyasujō* (found under the date 8.18.35 in DNSR); NBIK 552 and 553; NBIC 1097; *Kutsuki monjo*, ed. Okuno Takahiro (Zoku Gunsho Ruijū Kanseikai, 1978), vol. 1, document 232; and *Niigata kenshi shiryōhen*, vol. 4, document 1051(7). For wounded bannermen, see KI 32044, 32050, 32080; NBIC 101, 212, 349, 354, 390, 1173; *Kanagawa kenshi, shiryōhen, kodai-chūsei* 2, 3.1–2, comp. Kanagawa Kenshi Hensanshitsu (Yokohama: Kanagawa Kenshi Hensanshitsu, 1975), vol. 3, part 1, document 3266; *Gunma kenshi shiryōhen* 6, *Chūsei* 2, comp. Gunma Kenshi Hensan Iinkai (Gunma: Gunma Prefecture, 1984), document 744; and *Shinano shiryō*, vol. 5, pp. 333–34. For one whose head was crushed with a rock and was "half dead," see *Hyōgo kenshi*, vol. 8, Nanzenji *monjo*, document 12, p. 26.
100. *Taiheiki*, maki 7, "Chihayajō kassen no koto," pp. 165–66, and NBIC 375.
101. *Taiheiki*, maki 25, "Miyake, Ogino muhon no koto," pp. 745–46 and *Meitokuki*, maki 2, pp. 99–100. The Chancellor Tōin Kinkata briefly describes the process of arrest in his diary. See *Entairyaku*, vol. 3, 11.29.1350, p. 374.

Figure 12. The Ashikaga (left) and Nitta (right) seals.

outright. During Takauji's initial advance to the east in 1335, prisoners and heads taken in battle were synonymous![102] Some prisoners were immediately executed, while others were killed after a lengthy process of appeal.[103]

More men were killed outright than captured. Only thirty men out of some hundreds were captured alive after the battle of Minatogawa.[104] The *Taiheiki* records instances in which more men were killed than captured alive. In one case, two hundred men were killed and a hundred captured alive, and in another example, seventy-three men were killed and sixty-seven captured alive.[105] Those that were captured might be asked to identify the heads of their less fortunate compatriots.[106] The base orders (*genin*) were also frequently captured alive due to an apparent reluctance to take the heads of men of lower statuses.[107] Nevertheless, for those of higher status, capture could entail a humiliating and degrading death, which explains why suicide was, by contrast, a relatively attractive option.

> **On the same day, when the Yamakawa Officer [*hangan*] attacked the middle reaches of the Kamo River from the north, [Nobutsune, Mitsuie et al.] again attacked the edge of the enemy's shields. The horse Nobutsune was riding was shot with an arrow. The Yamakawa Officer and his followers saw this.**

102. *Shizuoka kenshi shiryōhen* 6, *Chūsei* 2, document 81, "Ashikaga Takauji *Kantō gekō shukunami kassen chūmon*," "Jū-shichi nichi Hakone kassen," pp. 33–34.
103. Compare NBIC 1031 with NBIC 331, NBIK 550, and *Taiheiki*, maki 13, "Hyōbu no kyō shinnō kōji," pp. 365–66.
104. NBIK 617.
105. For the former, see *Taiheiki*, maki 38, "Miyakata hōki no koto," pp. 1133–34; for the latter, see maki 34, "Kishū ryūmonsan ikusa no koto," p. 1018.
106. NBIC 1203, *Taiheiki*, maki 32, "Miyako ikusa no koto," p. 976, and maki 38, "Miyakata hōki no koto," p. 1134.
107. Again, see NBIK 810 and "Hakata nikki," p. 555 for references to a "commoner" (*genin*) and a nun (*bikuni*) being captured alive. Apparently all warriors were killed, for thirty-two heads and two *genin* were brought to Hakata. It is not known if the *genin* were later executed or not. For more on the culture of taking heads, and of some being of too low a status to be identified, see Ikushima Terumi, "Chūsei kōki ni okeru 'kirareta kubi' no toriatsukai," *Bunka shigaku* 50 (November 1994): 131–50. The wealthy merchant who bankrolled Kusu castle was also captured alive, but his ultimate fate is unknown. NBIK 810.

From this passage, one can see that warriors might mass behind a barricade of shields. Safely ensconced in favorable terrain, they frightened enemy horses who refused to charge directly. Skilled horsemen compensated by harrying the fringes of such a force, although this was a risky endeavor, as Nobutsune discovered to his chagrin. Nevertheless, Nobutsune was relatively lucky. Although he had undoubtedly been unhorsed, he was apparently unscathed. His mount also survived, for deaths of horses involved considerable financial loss and were therefore invariably recorded in petitions.

> On the battle of the thirtieth, in front of the west gate of Hōjūji, Tomoyuki's man [*rōtō*] Sugimoto Yōichi Yoshihiro grappled with Seki Magogorō, a houseman [*kenin*] of Ota Hangan, and took his head. This was seen [and inspected] by Sasaki Bitchū no kami, the battle administrator [*samurai dokoro*].

The Ashikaga's position in the capital was becoming untenable. During the waning days of the first month of 1336, they were overwhelmed by the Kitabatake's reinforcements, suffered severe casualties, and fled. Two of those mentioned in this narrative—Uesugi Norifusa and Miura Inaba no kami—died on the twenty-seventh at the edge of the Kamo River, while another, Yamanouchi Michitsugu, who had unleashed his arrows so accurately at the bridge near Iwashimizu, died on the thirtieth.

What was it like to grapple with an enemy? One might use a "bear claw" (which resembles a giant rake) to unhorse a fleeing opponent, who would presumably be cut up by foot soldiers following close behind. (See figure 13 = pl. 9.) Otherwise, one might circle behind an opponent, overtake him, and stab him in the throat from behind.[108] (See figure 9 = pl. 7.) These deeds were rarely recorded, although blows from behind were common enough to lead to an improvement in the rear portion of Japanese helmets, and the development of leather helmet liners.[109]

The act of grappling required considerable horsemanship, for Japanese war ponies were ponderous beasts that could gallop for only a short distance. First the warrior had to trot within striking distance, then spur on his mount, overtake, and unhorse his fleeing opponent with either a long sword or a "bear

---

108. Depictions of stabbing from the rear commonly appear in fourteenth-century picture scrolls. See "Shōtoku taishi eden," in *Ibaragi no emaki*, p. 2, and *Go-sannen kassen ekotoba*.

109. Helmet liners increased in sophistication as well in order to prevent the wearer from being knocked senseless after being pummeled. Takahashi Masaaki, *Bushi no seiritsu bushizō no sōshutsu* (Tōkyō Daigaku Shuppan, 1999), pp. 242–43. Furthermore, the addition of leather liners coincided with an increase in helmet size. For a good English survey, see Hatirō Yamaguchi, ed., *Japan's Ancient Armor* (Japan Tourist Library, 1940), p. 34.

Figure 13. Unhorsing an opponent. Source: *Kasuga gongen kenki e*, scroll 2, section 2 (partial). Possession of Kunaichō Sannōmaru Shōzōkan. Permission for reproduction granted by the Imperial Household Ministry.

claw"—a rather perilous act, for horses, skittish creatures, were easily startled by an enemy's sword or the shadow of its rider's blade.[110] Those warriors who preferred projectiles would slow their horses to a trot in order to unleash a volley of arrows.[111]

> **On the first day of the second month, Tomoyuki traveled together with the shogun from Shinomura in Tanba to Hyōgo Island in Harima. During that battle of Nishinomiya in Settsu [Province], [Tomoyuki] served under the command of Sama no kami [Ashikaga Tadayoshi]. When [Tadayoshi] ascended the mountain, [Tomoyuki] performed military service. The particulars were witnessed by Ōtaka Iyo no kami.**
>
> **On the eleventh, at the battle of Tejima riverbed in Settsu, just as [Tomoyuki] encamped at the river's edge, [Ashikaga Takauji] suddenly returned to Hyōgo. That night [Tomoyuki and his men were] summoned and followed.**

110. See *Taiheiki*, maki 15, "Tadarahama ikusa no koto," p. 458, and maki 29, "Moronao shatei yoriki shōgai no koto," p. 883.
111. Kondō Yoshikazu, *Chūseiteki bugu no seiritsu to bushi* (Yoshikawa Kōbunkan, 2000) pp. 219–21.

Ashikaga Takauji, in defeat, fled the capital and sought refuge at Shinomura, to the west. It was here, where his mother held extensive lands, that he had first raised his flag of rebellion against Kamakura two and a half years before, and it was here that he reflected upon the precipitous reversal of his fortunes.[112] With the battle for the capital now lost, the indomitable Takauji regrouped and set off for the south, where his troops were once again hammered at Nishinomiya. They fled to the bustling port at Hyōgo Island in order to avert annihilation. (See figure 14 = pl. 10.)

> **On the twelfth, Sama no kami [Tadayoshi] departed from Mana castle at Hyōgo. Tomoyuki was about to follow with him, but then saw a notice claiming that all had been killed. [Tomoyuki] believed this; and then suddenly under the cover of darkness, the [Ashikaga] boats departed; Tomoyuki did not know of this. Not being able to follow [the Ashikaga in battle, Tomoyuki] lost his will [_hon'i_]. Although it might seem to resemble the epitome of disservice, particularly when considering that relatives resided in the west, Tomoyuki nevertheless did not know the lay of the land. The enemy was in full pursuit. Having no other recourse, Tomoyuki crept into the capital and fled eastward on the thirtieth. At Mikawa [Province], a number of skirmishers [_nobushi_] repeatedly tried to take Tomoyuki's life. Any particular queries can be answered by Kō Gorō Hyōe no jō and Kō Mimasaka Tarō, etc. Tomoyuki eventually arrived at Ihara castle in Tōtōmi [Province] and, after the enemy fled, took his leave and departed for the east [the Kantō].**

Poor Tomoyuki was left behind in the chaos of the Ashikaga defeat. He decided to return to his homelands, a recourse adopted as well by other Ashikaga partisans, such as Kutsuki Yoshiuji.[113] Others, old and feeble, remained hidden in the capital.[114] Remarkably few warriors surrendered to Nitta Yoshisada or Go-Daigo.[115] Most fled to where their power was strongest in order to observe what punishments might be meted out to Ashikaga supporters. The fact that these men did not readily join Go-Daigo's resurgent

---

112. *Nanbokuchō jidai no Tanba Kameoka*, Kameoka Shi Bunka Shiryōkan, comp. (Kameoka, 1993), pp. 1–2.
113. *Kutsuki monjo*, vol. 2, document 428, 1.28.1336 Kutsuki Yoshiuji *gunchūjō*. No Kutsuki exploits are mentioned after Yoshiuji arrived at Hyōgo Island, so one can only assume that he returned to his homelands after the Ashikaga fled to Kyushu.
114. NBIK 905–6.
115. *Baishōron*, pp. 96, 117–18.

Figure 14. Warriors setting off in boats. Source: *Aki no yo no nagamonogatari*. Possession of the Idemitsu Museum of Arts.

allies reveals the depth of mistrust and dissatisfaction that many felt for his regime. A few doughty warriors continued open hostilities in spite of the fact that their cause appeared hopeless. The indefatigable Hatano Kageuji would later boast that "when the shogun [Ashikaga Takauji] departed for Hyōgo Island, the victorious enemy surrounded my castle. I wanted to join the shogun's forces, but could not. I thought I would die where I stood. I had all but resolved to kill myself in the garden any number of times, but somehow I managed to preserve my unworthy life. If one were to carefully consider the extent of my service (*chūkin*), then it would be the equivalent of dying in battle. After all, most merely ran away."[116]

Takauji likewise continued to struggle. He commandeered some three hundred boats and set off for Kyushu. There was a good deal of confusion as his large forces attempted to board a small number of boats, but Takauji was still able to issue mobilization orders on the thirteenth, the day he actually departed from the port of Hyōgo Island.[117] Two days later, Takauji received an imperial edict from the retired Jimyōin emperor Kōgon, and thus secured the legitimation necessary to rebound from his defeat. He immediately issued a flurry of confirmations to dissatisfied warriors, ordered warriors to guard the sea lanes of the Inland Sea, and granted lands to important temples.[118] By the seventeenth, he had decided before arriving there to stay

---

116. NBIC 259. The greatest service one could perform was to die in battle. As death merited the most compensation—understandably—Hatano Kageuji is stating that his merit was of the first order.
117. For the details of Takauji's arrival at Hyōgo Island, see *Baishōron*, pp. 94–98.
118. NBIC 247–51, documents dating from 2.15.1336 until 2.18.1336, and NBIK 417.

at Akamaseki, which was the port near the straits that separated Honshu from
Kyushu.[119] A day later (and only five days after Takauji had actually fled the
capital), a number of Kyushu warriors now began to align themselves with
his movement.[120] While marching westward, he protected his back by dispatching collaterals to mobilize forces in areas he had passed through.[121] On
the twentieth, he arrived at Akamaseki.[122]

Rapid communication more than compensated for the institutional instability of the Ashikaga forces. One by one, groups of warriors arrived at Akamaseki.[123] Save for a core of Ashikaga generals and a few Kyushu warriors,
most of those who joined with the Ashikaga had not previously fought in the
capital.[124] These warriors mobilized with stunning speed. Takauji's first calls
to arms to western warriors are dated on the thirteenth, and yet, six days later,
the first Kyushu warriors were joining his forces before he even reached Akamaseki![125] Within a week, warriors from Awa Province arrived, and within
a further three days, warriors from as far afield as Hizen, Aki, and Satsuma
reported as well.[126]

A well-developed relay system ensured the rapid dissemination of messages. We find numerous references to "express ponies" and indeed even to
"fast boats" transmitting information.[127] During the second month, however,
various lines of communication were effectively cut in the east and west.
Ashikaga partisans in the east, such as Sōma Mitsutane, were left in the dark
and were vulnerable to "the enemy spreading many lies."[128] Conversely, Go-
Daigo's partisans knew nothing of Takauji's whereabouts or the political situation in the west.[129] Go-Daigo even dispatched words of praise to the head

---

119. For a mobilization order to a local warrior, see NBIK 418, of 2.17.1336.
120. NBIK 419.
121. NBIC 254, in this case, the Imagawa to Izumo. *Baishōron* provides a detailed account of the
     provinces to which a number of supporters were dispatched on pp. 97–98.
122. *Baishōron*, p. 98.
123. For documents concerning the arrival of these warriors to Akamaseki, see NBIK 420, 422, 439, 445,
     and 1111.
124. See NBIK 756 and 905 for the exploits of Sebama Masanao and Shiga Yorifusa, two Kyushu war-
     riors who traveled with Takauji from the east to Kyoto and then to Kyushu.
125. NBIK 419.
126. Indeed, the Miike of Aki (who also had holdings in Chikugo Province) were first requested on the
     seventeenth day of the second month to go to Akamaseki, and they arrived exactly ten days later.
     See NBIK 418, 445.
127. See "Hakata nikki," pp. 552-54 for the former, and Amino, *Nihon chūsei shiryō no kadai* Oyama
     ke *monjo*, document 8, 7.17 Taishōgun bō *migyōsho*, p. 295, for the latter.
128. *Sōma monjo*, document 27, 2.18.1336 Sōma Shigetane *sadamegaki*, pp. 22–23. Sōma Mitsutane
     lamented that "I have heard that Shigetane has killed himself in Kamakura. Furthermore, since his
     elder brother Chikatane went to the capital, I have heard nothing concerning his whereabouts." Ibid.,
     document 34, 5.20.1336 Sōma Mitsutane *yuzurijō*, pp. 29–30.
129. Nitta Yoshisada only began searching for the fleeing Ashikaga on the nineteenth of the second
     month—the day before Takauji and his army had arrived at Akamaseki. NBIC 253.

(*daigūji*) of Aso shrine some twenty-two days after his death at the battle of Tadarahama![130]

Nomoto Tomoyuki knew little about the whereabouts or ultimate fate of Takauji. Although there were some orders written on tiny pieces of paper[131] or penned on silk so that they might be hidden in the top-knot of a messenger,[132] Nomoto Tomoyuki was not important enough to have received such a secret message. Instead, he made his way east to the best of his abilities.

The battle of Oyama castle. After the shogun departed for the west, an uprising by the forces of Kitabatake Akiie caused the people to be unsettled. All those allied [to the shogun] arrived at the encampment near this castle. Those of this family who were of such a mind, headed toward [Oyama's] castle, where they performed continuous military service for many days. On the third day of the eleventh month of 1336, during the battle of Yokotamohara, [Tomoyuki?] took [*buntori*] one head, which was seen by the commanding general. In addition, his man [*rōtō*] Obuchi Hikokurō Nyūdō was wounded, which was recorded in Tomoyuki's report of arrival. This sequence of events was witnessed by the members of this family. Both the commanding general and the grandmother of Oyama Tsune-inumaru monogrammed this document. [Tomoyuki] also received a document of arrival from Momonoi Suruga no kami [Naotsune].

On the tenth day of the third month of this year (1337), Oda Kunai gon no taiyū and Masado Tora Hosshimaru led powerful rebel forces toward the Hitachi provincial headquarters. Tomoyuki's representative [*daikan*] Iwase Hikotarō Nobutsune cut down one enemy horseman. Masado Hitachi no suke Hiromasa rode forth and received notice for his deeds. The approved petition for reward, signed by Satake Gyōbu no taiyū, makes this clear.

---

130. For the order, see NBIK 497, 514; for his death, see NBIK 1182.

131. The smallest document I have seen personally is a *ryōji* by the Hitachi Prince (of the Southern court) two and one–half inches square. This document, and another by Emperor Go-Murakami, are reproduced between pp. 218 and 219 of Tōkyō Teikoku *Dai Nihon komonjo iewake* 14, *Kumagai ke monjo*, comp. Daigaku Shiryōhensanjo (Tōkyō Teikoku Daigaku Shuppankai, 1937).

132. One such document, of 4.29.1333 and dispatched to Aso Koretoki is reproduced between pp. 142 and 143 of *Dai Nihon komonjo iewake* 13, *Aso ke monjo*, comp. Tōkyō Teikoku Daigaku Shiryōhensanjo (Tōkyō Teikoku Daigaku Shuppankai, 1932–34), vol. 1. See also the Shimazu document of 4.29 (1333), a photo which appears on p. 37 of Satō Kazuhiko, *Zusetsu Taiheiki no jidai* (Kawadeshobō Shinsha, 1990). A reference to such a method of transmission appears in *Taiheiki*, maki 18, "Urifu Hangan hata o ageru koto," p. 558. For more on such documents, see Matsui Teruaki, "Origami no chakutōjō ni tsuite," *Komonjo kenkyū*, 34 (May 1991): 2–38.

The confusion and uncertainty that pervades the tumultuous year of 1336 permeates Tomoyuki's petition. Kitabatake Akiie, after dislodging Takauji from the capital with his northern army, returned to pacify the east. This proved to be a strategic blunder, for Takauji was able to regroup in Kyushu to the west and to retake the capital during the fifth month of 1336. Tomoyuki's actions during these decisive few months are unknown—perhaps he hid himself and waited for a more favorable time to counterattack. By the eleventh month, Tomoyuki was again active, although his movement was confined to Shimōsa Province in the east, where both Oyama castle and his homelands were located.[133] Ashikaga supporters in eastern Japan were on the defensive and remained holed up in the fortified dwellings of the Oyama. Since the head of the Oyama family was an infant, the boy's grandmother took an active role in leading the house, even to the extent of placing her monogram on warriors' petitions for reward.

Southern Court forces dominated the east early in 1337. In the battle for Seki castle, in Hitachi Province, Shintsuma Matajirō Taneshige, Nomoto Gorō Takanobu, and four of his retainers (wakatō) were killed on 7.8.1337. The battle then spread to Shimōsa's Taga district (gō) in Kanzaki no shō, where the representatives (daikan) of Tomoyuki burned the Nomoto residences while Nomoto wives and children hid in the forests in order to avoid the forces of Kitabatake Akiie and the Oda. These daikan probably included Iwase Nobutsune, who performed valorous acts on 3.10.1337. Their fate is unclear. As for Nomoto Tomoyuki himself, he died on 3.27.1337. It is not known whether he died in battle or peacefully, although the wording "he departed for the other world," as opposed to his being killed (uchishi), suggests that he might not have died violently. Still, the days of peace that Tomoyuki had waited for prior to submitting his petition did not arrive in his lifetime. It seems unlikely that Tomoyuki ever knew that the regime that he had fought and died for would ultimately triumph and come to dominate Japan's political landscape for two and a half centuries.

Nomoto's son, Tsurujūmaru, succeeded him but was unable to travel to the capital to submit his petition for reward until later. In the meantime, he and his retainers (wakatō) were busy seeking just to survive the Kitabatake onslaught.

Not that death was a matter for great fear, because to die gloriously in battle meant that one's descendants would receive great rewards. Thus Hitomi On'a offered sentiments such as "I think I shall die ahead of others and leave a name for the men of a later day."[134] Yamanouchi Tsuneyuki also wrote

---

133. Nomoto Tomoyuki's homelands, Kanzaki no shō, were located in Shimōsa Province's Taga district, where the Chiba and Southern Court supporters fought a battle. NBIC 654.

134. *Taiheiki*, maki 6, "Akasakajō kassen no koto," pp. 148–49 and McCullough, *The Taiheiki*, p. 166. The Hitomi episode is not a *Taiheiki* fabrication. See the "Kusunoki kassen chūmon" of 2.22.1333, in *Zoku zoku gunsho ruijū*.

to his son and told of how his actions had been praised: "Don't worry if I die in battle, for the general and members of the unit (*ikki*) [will take care of you]."[135] One oath penned by the members of the Kadochigai *ikki* expressly states "if any member of this group (*shūchū*) is killed or dies of illness, the upbringing of his orphans will be provided for. If someone attempts to seize [an orphan's] holdings on the pretext that he is a minor, the members of this unit will come to his aid."[136] And indeed, Yamanouchi Tsuneyuki's final thoughts seem to be for his family's welfare: "I do not believe I shall return from this battle alive. My only regret is that there is not one [retainer] left [to take care of things back home]."[137] Nomoto Tomoyuki's worries must have been the same but, unlike Tsuneyuki, he still had loyal retainers fighting for the welfare of his son.

Here the petition ends its narrative of Tomoyuki's exploits. The Nomoto must have felt the strain of prolonged warfare which was exacerbated with Tomoyuki's untimely death. Nomoto Tsurujūmaru ended his account by boasting of his undivided service (*muni chūsetsu*) for the Ashikaga, thereby suggesting his belief, widely shared at the time, that death in battle deserved compensation in the form of land rights, such as *jitō shiki*.[138] Confirmations of existing lands, or rewards of new holdings, were cherished above all else because land rights had been destabilized with the outbreak of civil war.

Tomoyuki's brief abandonment of the Ashikaga cause early in 1336 did not preclude his son from requesting compensation in a manner acceptable to a commander of unknown origins, in 1338. Others received substantial rewards for transferring their allegiances at this time. In 1343, for example, the Southern Court stalwart Yūki Chikatomo joined the Ashikaga after receiving a confirmation of all his holdings (*chigyō*) awarded before 1335."[139] Yūki Chikatomo was assured of adequate compensation because he had been the linchpin of the Southern Court's defenses in eastern Japan. In contrast to Chikatomo, whose defection crippled the Southern Court's resistance in the east, Tomoyuki accomplished nothing of strategic consequence. Accordingly, Tsurujūmaru only managed to be recognized by a lesser commander who affixed his pedestrian monogram to this petition.[140]

135. *Hino shishi shiryōshu, Takahata Fudō tainai monjo hen*, document 45, Yamanouchi Tsuneyuki *shojō*.
136. NBIK 6848.
137. *Hino shishi shiryōshū, Takahata Fudō tainai monjo hen*, document 50, Yamanouchi Tsuneyuki *shojō*.
138. Descendants of warriors who had been killed would write of their father's "loyal service" in being cut down in battle (*uchishi chūkin*). NBIK 6294–95. Some fathers who lost their sons could receive praise and *jitō shiki* for their son's service (*chūsetsu*). NBIK 5776–77.
139. DNSR, series 6, vol. 7, of 2.25.1343, p. 573.
140. Photos of Motegi house petitions suggest that Momonoi Rokurō, an Ashikaga collateral commander, signed both Nomoto and Motegi documents. See *Motegi chōshi*, vol. 2, *Shiryōhen* 1, comp. Motegi Chōshi Hensan Iinkai (Motegi, 1997), photos 16, 19, pp. 469, 477.

   As no other documents survive, it is impossible to ascertain whether Tsurujūmaru received rewards for Tomoyuki's battle service. Whether
Tsurujūmaru was able to maintain his holdings with the help of Iwase Nobutsune is also unclear, though the paucity of later records pertaining to the
Nomoto suggests that he may have been ultimately unsuccessful. Only this
single trace survives of these men and the drama of their lives, rolled in a
scroll containing Kumagai house documents. And yet if Nomoto Tomoyuki,
Iwase Nobutsune, and the others could but know that their exploits are
remembered in some small way after six hundred and sixty years, I suspect
they would not be displeased. (See figure 15.)

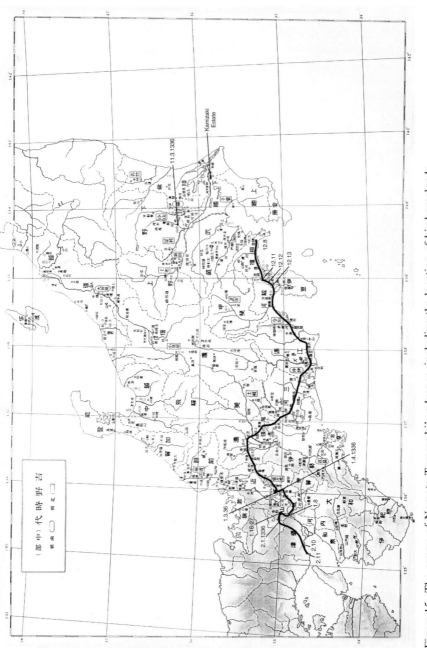

Figure 15. The course of Nomoto Tomoyuki's advance, including the location of his homelands.

CHAPTER
2

Tactics, Innovation, and Organization: A Statistical Narrative of War

---

And there he told how Arthur and the two kings had sped at the great battle, and how it was ended, and told the names of every king and knight of worship that was there. And so Bleise wrote the battle word by word, as Merlin told him how it began, and by whom, and in likewise how it was ended, and who had the worse. All the battles that were done in Arthur's days, Merlin did his master Bleise do write; also he did do write all the battles that every worthy knight did of Arthur's court.

Sir Thomas Malory, *Le Mort D'Arthur*

Battle is by nature a chaotic experience; a myriad of individual decisions and deeds intertwine in the course of a single organic process. Each man witnesses the events of his locality. Although horribly aware of his own situation, he is not necessarily aware of events a hundred yards away, let alone the general contours of the battle. The intensely personal experience of war belies its quintessentially social nature. Victory is decided regardless of any one man's valor. Nevertheless, individual acts are hardly irrelevant, for the overlapping actions, fates, and decisions of the multitude balance into a simple result of victory, defeat, or stalemate, with profound ramifications for all. Inasmuch as battle consists of an amalgamation of individual deeds, the general contours of battle can only be discerned when the voices of the many are assembled in a single narrative.

Reconstructing an action as confusing and fleeting as a battle poses epistemological difficulties, for all that remains after the dust has cleared and the dead have been buried are the recollections of survivors. The experiences of fourteenth-century warriors were preserved in documents. These written traces functioned as a means of assuring that a man be compensated for the expenses incurred and the damages suffered as a result of battle. Because warriors in Japan needed proof of their valor in order to secure rewards, they provided verifiable accounts of the date, location, and nature of their military service. The authorities rigorously inspected these documents, sometimes adding annotations rendering them more accurate.

An unparalleled body of source materials survives pertaining to fourteenth-century warfare, which is indicative of its contemporary importance. Nearly 1,500 records survive in two documentary forms, the report of arrival (*chakutōjō*) and the petition for military rewards (*gunchūjō*).

A report of arrival attests that a warrior had arrived at a particular encampment; such reports thereby reveal how troops assembled. These documents do not conform to a single pattern. Some were composed immediately after arriving at a staging point or fighting in a battle, while others were written weeks or months after the events that they described.[1] Warriors, or their scribes, recorded who had arrived at a particular location. The commanding general or a member of his board of retainers would, after confirming that the said person was in fact present, scrawl "received" as well as his monogram on the document. Some generals refused to monogram the documents of warriors who arrived late in camp, but such strictness could cause unintended consequences. One warrior so "wronged" vented his frustration by attacking his nominal superiors and burning the city of Hakata.[2] Likewise, to report and to fight were different matters entirely. Some warriors, after receiving such a monogrammed document, thereby "proving" their arrival in camp, returned home.[3]

A report of arrival is useful in mapping the geographic and temporal movement of its subject. A typical example is as follows:

1. For an illuminating article, see Urushihara Tōru, "Chakutōjō no kisoteki kōsatsu," *Shigaku* 54.2–3 (March 1985): 65–82, particularly p. 72.
2. "Hakata Nikki," pp. 548–56.
3. NBIK 787.

Arrived: The Province of Sagami
Yamanouchi Sudō Saburō Tokimichi has come to this location.
Hence his arrival is thus.
The third year of Kenmu (1336), eighth month, nineteenth day
Received (Monogram of Shiba Iekane)[4]

This report merely verifies that Yamanouchi Tokimichi arrived in Sagami.
What he did before or after 8.19.1336 can only be reconstructed through other
reports of arrival, or battle reports and petitions for reward, which record how
one fought and what damages were incurred as a result of battle.

Battle reports (*kassen chūmon*) were submitted to battle administrators
(*kassen bugyō*), who sometimes rigorously inspected these documents,
thereby rendering them more accurate. For example, Migita Sukeie submitted a document on behalf of a follower (*wakatō*), Hachirō Ietsuna, who had
been wounded in battle on the fourteenth day of the fourth month of 1333.
Sadahisa and Sukekiyo, a pair of battle administrators, verified Ietsuna's
wounds. Sadahisa added the comments "armor pierced" and "shot through
the jaw by and arrow; lodged in chest," while Sukekiyo added in his char-
acteristic light colored ink the notation "shallow."[5] All documents pertaining to Ietsuna's wounds were submitted by his lord, Sukeie, who alone would
receive compensation for his retainer's injuries.

Once a warrior completed his battle report, he used it as evidence to
"prove" his military service (*chūsetsu*) and thereupon submitted a petition
for rewards, or *gunchūjō*. Most petitions summarize the information found
in battle reports, which explain why, because of their preliminary nature, relatively few survive. After each petition was verified, it was signed and then
returned to the petitioner. Several men in camp would record the exploits of
a number of their comrades, each of whom later submitted a petition to his
commander of the moment.[6] After each document was verified, it was signed
and then returned to the petitioner.

These petitions almost invariably record the date and location of battle.
Some describe wounds, deaths, damages inflicted upon oneself, and, on
occasion, verifiable "valor" such as arson, while others, the majority perhaps,
are singularly lacking in noteworthy accomplishments. For example, Kutsuki

---

4. NBIC 451.
5. I would like to thank Tanaka Junichirō of the Yamashiro shiryōkan for allowing me to view the original Migita documents. For a printed version, see the Migita genealogy in *Zoku gunsho ruijū,
   Keizubu*, vol. 7, 129–65.
6. At times the same men wrote petitions for several warriors. Petitions submitted in 1333 by Harima
   warriors, the Azumi and Hiromine, were written by the same man. For a printed version of these
   documents, see KI 32157 and 32150. In other cases, a scribe could be one warrior's retainer. In the
   case of the Migita, for example, reports of arrival written in 1314 and petitions submitted in 1333
   are in the same hand. Urushihara, "Gunchūjō ni kansuru jakkan no kōsatsu,"describes how petitions
   constitute summaries of several previously submitted documents.

Yoshiuji stated that he performed "military service" at three distinct locations, but the nature of his service remains shrouded in this vague turn of phrase.[7] Kutsuki Yoshinobu, fighting half a year later, only records the names of the two men who witnessed the death of his retainer, Nomura Kosaburō.[8] As the following translation of his petition reveals, however, Kutsuki Yoriuji fought with considerably more élan:

> The military valor (*gunchū*) of Sasaki Dewa Shiro Hyōe no jō Yoriuji:
>
>   After joining [the Ashikaga cause], I traveled to Kurochi [in Mino Province] on the twenty-eighth day of the first month, where I performed the service (*chū*) of constructing fortifications. Next, on the fifth day of the fourth month, I fought a battle at Aiga castle [in Ōmi Province], where I defeated the enemy. Next, on the final day of the fourth month, I broke through the mountain barrier at Arachi [in Echizen Province] and on the same day attacked Hikita, where I defeated Tajima Bō and his rebels, and burned their castle. On the same day, the fourth, I fought a battle at Kanegasaki, and shot a horseman. Next on the eighteenth day of the seventh month, because of an attack by the Okinoshima rebels, I was on my way to Ehama harbor, in Takashima district [in Ōmi Province]. The Okinoshima rebels launched a night attack, and I fought them off with abandon, fearing not for my life. My retainers (*wakatō*), Sasamoto Uemon Saburō and Tsuji Hyōe Tarō, were killed. Additional wounded followers included Ogasawara Jūrōgorō, Tako Hyōe Jirō, Matsui Jibu, Hioki Hikoshichirō, and two lowly followers (*chūgen*). Even I, Yoriuji, sustained a head wound. Nevertheless we managed to capture an enemy boat. Next, my representative for the Kurihara Ippaku estates, in [the northernmost province of] Ōshū, Itazaki Jirō Saemon no jō Tameshige, performed noteworthy military service and received documents of praise from the shogun [Ashikaga Takauji] and the governor of Mutsu, Iyo Shikibu Daibu [Shiba Iekane]. Tameshige received a copy of a report, submitted [by Iekane], recommending that he should receive rewards. Because the following exceptional service (*chūsetsu*) has been performed, I desire to immediately receive a signature in order to prove my exploits for later days. Respectfully, thus.
>
>   The Fifth Year of Kenmu [1338], Seventh intercalary month
>   Received [the monogram of Kyōgoku Dōyo][9] (See figure 16.)

---

7. *Kutsuki monjo*, vol. 2, document 428, 1.28.1336 Kutsuki Yoshiuji *gunchūjō*.
8. *Kutsuki monjo*, vol. 2, document 429, 9.17.1336 Kutsuki Yoshinobu *gunchūjō*.
9. *Kutsuki monjo*, vol. 2, document 431, 7.1338 Kutsuki Yoriuji *gunchūjō. Kanjō* were only granted for particularly noteworthy deeds, and were valued since they helped a warrior to prove that his valor was exceptional and deserving of reward.

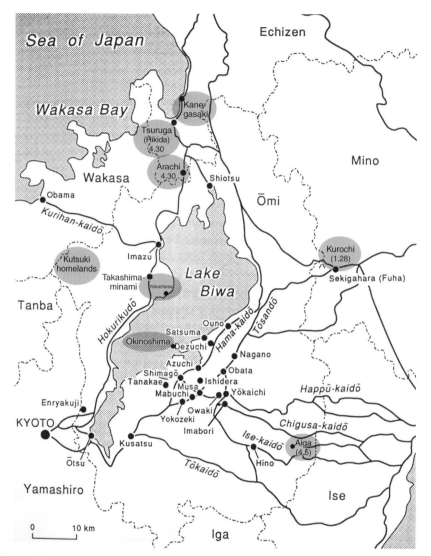

Figure 16. An illustration of the locations mentioned in Kutsuki Yoriuji's petition. Map is adapted from Hitomi Tonomura, *Community and Commerce in Late Medieval Japan* (Stanford: Stanford University Press, 1992), p. 118.

In this document, Yoriuji records the exploits of himself and ten followers. He fought in three contiguous provinces over a period of seven months, and likewise recorded the deeds of his representative, who fought in the distant northern province of Ōshū (Mutsu). Yoriuji fought against at least two different forces, while he and his representative served under two different generals. This document also records two fatalities and seven injuries, although it remains unusually reticent about the nature of the wounds sustained, for Yoriuji refers only to his own head wound.

Yoriuji and his followers performed the following acts of military service: he constructed a castle; destroyed an enemy's toll barrier and burned one of their castles; shot an enemy horseman; suffered wounds and fatalities among himself and his followers; engaged in several attacks and skirmishes; and stole an enemy boat. The specific and verifiable nature of his service made him more likely to be compensated that his compatriots. Finally, his representative received a document from Ashikaga Takauji and a document of praise from Shiba Iekane.

Yoriuji's narrative, much like that of Nomoto Tomoyuki's in the previous chapter, provides a fascinating glimpse into the actions of one individual and his followers. Nevertheless, it remains difficult to distinguish typical behavior from the unusual in such a limited sample of documents. One cannot discern whether Yoriuji fought with unusual valor or suffered typical casualties unless his document is compared with the thousands of others that survive. By engaging in statistical analysis, however, one can record the numbers of those appearing in these documents, as well as how many were killed and wounded. For that matter, one can, wherever possible, record how these individuals were wounded. These data allow highly accurate, quantifiable reconstructions of the fleeting order of battle.

One profitable way of reconstructing the experience of battle is to provide a holistic, statistical analysis of the data found in a much larger sample. The information provided in the thirteen hundred surviving petitions of reward can be woven into a single composite narrative. These numbers have their own tale to tell about the collective endeavor of war. (See figure 17 = pl. 11.)

A STATISTICAL NARRATIVE OF BATTLE

Although military petitions have recently generated historical interest, studies have tended to concentrate on their creation and transmission, while their content remains relatively unexplored.[10] To date, only Shakadō Mitsuhiro has analyzed the nature of wounds recorded in battle reports (*kassen chūmon*), but his work is problematic for several reasons. He only relies upon battle reports and ignores the more common petitions for reward. Further, he divides warriors into categories such as "warriors" and "*wakatō* . . . and retainers" and assumes that these men invariably fought differently, when, in fact, both

---

10. Urushihara Tōru's "Gunchūjō ni kansuru jakkan no kōsatsu," *Komonjo kenkyū*, 21(June 1983): 33–52, remains the definitive study of petitions for reward. For Urushihara's fullest elaboration of this topic, see his *Chūsei gunchūjō to sono sekai* (Yoshikawa Kōbunkan, 1998).

Figure 17. The inspection process. *Mōko shūrai ekotoba*, scroll 2, page 40, "Suenaga presenting enemy heads." Possession of Kunaichō Sannōmaru Shōzōkan. Permission for reproduction granted by the Imperial Household Ministry.

warriors (*tozama*) and retainers (*wakatō* or *miuchi*) fought on foot and on horseback.[11] Finally, Shakadō presents his data synchronically and seems oblivious to the possibility of change through time.

A comprehensive survey of extant petitions for reward and reports of arrival during the years of 1331–92 reveals how the intensity and magnitude of warfare varied during the era of the Northern and Southern Courts. This data was collated from extant petitions for reward and all other documents that describe military encounters, including the occasional judicial edict. For example, the events recorded in Kutsuki Yoriuji's document would be distilled as follows: Total number of warriors—fifteen; fatalities—two; wounds—seven; documents—one.

---

11. Shakadō Mitsuhiro, "Nanbokuchōki ni okeru senshō,"*Nairanshi kenkyū* 13 (August 1992): 27–39. For horse-riding retainers (*wakatō*), see NBIC 654, translated in chapter one. For a *tozama* fighting on foot, see *Fukushima kenshi* 7, Okamoto Mototomo *kazō monjo*, document 38, 11.2.1342 Okamoto Shigechika *dai* Yamada Shigenori *gunchūjō*, p. 225.

I arrived at this figure by counting all individuals, including all commanders mentioned as well as those who signed the documents. Such a policy overrepresents the numbers of commanders, but this bias is mitigated by the fact that only three "enemies" are recorded: the single horseman shot by Yoriuji, Tanba no Bō, and the Ikijima rebels. Casualties were only counted when the names of the wounded and the dead were recorded. Instances where the enemy was reported as being killed, such as the horseman shot by Yoriuji, were not recorded because their veracity could not be independently verified. Likewise, I only recorded documents that survive as originals, or as reliable copies, and omitted petitions or documents of praise alluded to in the text of these sources.

These numbers provide a rough barometer of the intensity of battle. Nevertheless, these data should not be considered definitive for several reasons. The first is that many records have been destroyed or lost during the intervening six centuries. The second is that some warriors, particularly commanders, were undoubtedly counted several times. Another problem is that a survey based on records of wounds might overestimate the casualty rate. In order to mitigate against this, the data found in reports for arrival and other documents that describe battle were counted as well. With these caveats in mind, the total number of petitions, men, and casualties recorded is as follows:

TABLE 1

Troop numbers, casualties, and petitions of reward

Period	Warriors	Fatalities	Wounds	Documents
Period One (1333–38)	3678 (**43**)	704 (**60**)	537 (**43**)	517 (**40**)
Period Two (1339–49)	1237 (**14**)	169 (**14**)	155 (**12**)	219 (**17**)
Period Three (1350–55)	1777 (**21**)	108 (**09**)	303 (**25**)	278 (**21**)
Period Four (1356–94)	1460 (**17**)	167 (**14**)	255 (**21**)	277 (**21**)
Unclear	482 (**06**)	25	0	11
Total	8634	1173	1250	1302

Note: Numbers indicate named individuals while the bold figures in parentheses show the relative percentage of warriors, fatalities, wounds, and documents in each of the time blocs. Percentages do not invariably add to one hundred because of rounding.

From this table and figure 18 one can discern that political developments influenced the intensity of battle. By comparing this data with a narrative of political events, it is possible to divide the warfare of these sixty years into four discrete periods, with periods one and three representing two distinct peaks of military activity.

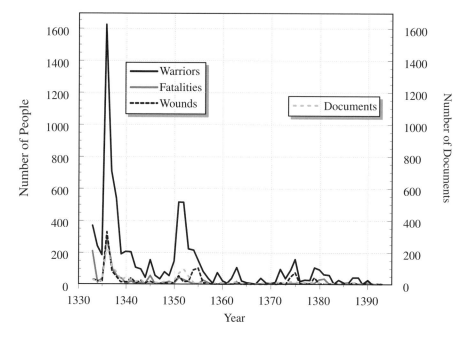

Figure 18. Trends in fourteenth-century warfare.

Most petitions for reward survive from period one (1333–38), when fierce battles raged. This period encompasses the destruction of the Kamakura *bakufu*, and all of the events that have been recounted in our narrative about Nomoto Tomoyuki in the first chapter. Nevertheless, the Southern Court suffered several crushing defeats in 1338, and the ensuing ten years (period two) remained mostly quiescent. Military campaigns were thereupon confined to eastern and northern Japan during the early 1340s. After Southern Court resistance was quelled in 1343, the conflict thereupon spread to central Japan and the southern island of Kyushu. Just as the situation was stabilizing in favor of the Ashikaga, a dispute erupted within the *bakufu* in 1350 and led to the dissolution of the Ashikaga regime into two warring factions, both of which fought against the resurgent forces of the Southern Court (period three: the Kannō disturbance). Finally, from 1356 (period four) onward the military situation stabilized as the members of the defeated Ashikaga faction gradually returned to the fold and reduced the Southern Court's strongholds.

The number of extant petitions for reward functions as a barometer of military activity, because no significant variations regarding the average number of warriors mentioned in each petition exist. In fact, the documents of each time period have rates of 7.1, 5.6, 6.4, and 5.3 warriors mentioned in each, respectively. For example, the number of petitions for reward in 1339 drops to a mere one third of the previous year, which indicates a profound decrease in military activity. Thus, one can divide the fourteenth century into two six-year peaks of war (period one, 1333–38, and period three, 1350–55).

The initial years of warfare (1333–38) and the later Kannō disturbance of 1350 vary in character. Sixty percent of all recorded deaths occurred during the first period. These six years witnessed the annihilation of several armies. For example, four hundred and thirty died with the Rokuhara *tandai*, seven hundred perished with Kusunoki Masashige at Minatogawa, and again, in 1338, seven hundred members of Kitabatake Akiie's army were killed at Otokoyama.[12] On the other hand, the mortality rate for period three (the Kannō disturbance) is low in spite of an increase in military activity throughout Japan. Even the relatively peaceful periods two and four witnessed a higher percentage of fatalities. In other words, although battles sputtered throughout the archipelago during the 1350s, they appear to have been fought in a more desultory manner.

Warriors apparently became more adept at preserving their lives as the fourteenth century progressed. When dividing the number of deaths and wounds by the number of recorded warriors for each period, one comes up with mortality rates of nineteen, fourteen, six, and eleven percent, which confirms the intensity of period one. One surprising development, however, is that the lowest rate of fatalities for the whole century appears in period three, in spite of otherwise increased amount of military activity. Perhaps as the Ashikaga *bakufu* fractured, former comrades-in-arms fought against each other with less intensity. Battles waged solely against the Southern Court invariably resulted in higher mortality rates, even during the final decades of the fourteenth century, than were witnessed during period three.

These four periods witness relatively constant wound rates of fifteen, thirteen, seventeen, and seventeen percent. A comparison of mortality rates reveals, however, that the mortality rate exceeds that of wounds in period one, while in period two these rates become virtually identical. Thereafter, the mortality rate remains consistently lower. This comparison again confirms the relatively high fatality rate for period one and the low rate for period three.

More insight regarding the nature of war can be determined from another survey of the nearly thirteen hundred documents pertaining to warfare in

---

12. For the destruction of the Rokuhara *tandai*, see KI 32137. Information pertaining to Minatogawa appears in *Baishōron*, p. 124. For the seven hundred killed in 1338, see NBIK 1201–3, 1215–7, 6996–8. As 189 of the Rokuhara forces were recorded by name, they were included in the database; the remaining 241 were not specifically mentioned and so were excluded from calculations. Likewise, a chronicle mentions the seven hundred dead at Minatogawa and so this figure is excluded. Finally, although reports of seven hundred dead in 1338 appear in documentary form, the figure remains suspiciously vague, and so it was excluded. Even if the Rokuhara dead are excluded from statistical analysis, the mortality rate of period one remains at fifty-three percent, significantly higher than that of any other period.

fourteenth-century Japan. In approximately half of the instances (721 out of 1250), the nature of wounds, and how they were caused, is precisely recorded. When arranged according to the four periods already defined, one comes up with the following table:

TABLE 2
Wounds by weapon

Period	Arrow	Sword	Pike	Rock	Total
One (1333–38)	229 (**64**)	117 (**33**)	6 (2)	4 (1)	356 (**49**)
Two (1339–49)	90 (**76**)	23 (**20**)	4 (4)	1 (1)	118 (**16**)
Three (1350–55)	160 (**85**)	23 (**12**)	5 (3)	0 (**0**)	188 (**26**)
Four (1356–94)	44 (**75**)	15 (**25**)	0 (**0**)	0 (**0**)	59 (**8**)
Total	523 (**73**)	178 (**25**)	15 (2)	5 (1)	721

Note: Numbers in parentheses indicate percentage in each time bloc, save for those in the total column, which designate the relative percentage of these records in comparison with other time blocs. Figures below one percent were rounded up.

From this data, one can ascertain that the bow remained the dominant weapon throughout the fourteenth century. By contrast, pikes and rocks were rarely used. Sword wounds were most common during period one, when battle was most intense, and rarest during the Kannō disturbance. Arrows caused anywhere from two–thirds to three–quarters of all wounds, while swords caused one–third of all wounds initially, but were later used increasingly infrequently. Pikes and rocks, however, were used rarely at all.

Although this chart illuminates general trends in how weapons were used, not all weapons can be directly compared. Handheld weapons functioned differently from those that unleashed projectiles; hence one type was incapable of supplanting the other because they were used in different circumstances. One can only recount how the prevalence of swords and pikes shifted through time, or for that matter, how arrows were eventually supplanted by bullets. As should be obvious from this chart, no major shifts favoring one type of weapon are evident. Rather, the different percentages of sword and arrow wounds indicate varying intensities of battle. Projectile weapons were useful in skirmishes or cases when masses of men did not come in direct contact, but they did not influence how battles were waged in close quarters until the development of precision artillery and high-powered rifles. Hence, one can ascertain that warriors engaged in hand to hand combat most often in period one, which is supported by the fact that period one witnessed the highest mortality rates of the fourteenth century.

Anecdotal evidence regarding these weapons also reveals much about the nature of battle.

The bow remained the dominant weapon throughout the fourteenth century, causing an average of seventy–three percent of all wounds. Although widely used, arrows were not particularly lethal. Twenty arrows were required, it was said, to do in Imagawa Yorikuni.[13] Horses perished only after enduring multiple hits as well.[14] On the other hand, a warrior's armor could stop "tens" of arrows, keeping him unscathed.[15]

The lack of stopping power by arrows is reflected in fourteenth-century vocabulary. Warriors were rarely described as being "shot to death" (*igoroshi*). For example, a skilled archer pierced Nagoe Owari no kami right between the eyes. Thereupon he boasted that he had shot to death (*igoroshitaru zo*) the enemy general with a single arrow, undoubtedly a notable feat.[16] By contrast, those who died lingering deaths as a result of arrow wounds were described as being "killed" (*uchishi*), which explains why *igoroshi* appears so rarely in contemporary sources.[17]

When warriors were shot in the extremities, they were barely incapacitated. For example, an arrow passed through the middle finger of Beppu Michizane on 4.24.1343, and yet two days later the same Michizane was again in the thick of battle.[18] Being hit by an arrow was not necessarily a trifling event, however. On 8.23.1343 the indefatigable Beppu Michizane was shot in the foot, and the arrowhead remained lodged. Thereupon, Michizane was confined to guarding boats and encampments.[19] In most cases, however, warriors wounded in the extremities required little treatment

---

13. See p. 312 of the "Nantaiheiki."
14. See NBIC 233, *Taiheiki*, maki 29, "Kokiyomizu kassen no koto," p. 871 and maki 16, "Minatogawa kassen no koto," p. 490.
15. *Kanoshiryō, Nanbokuchō* I, comp. Kano Shiryō Hensan Iinkai (Ishikawa Prefecture, 1992), 9.1346 Tokuda Akina *gunchūjō*, p. 334.
16. *Taiheiki*, maki 9, "Koga nawa kassen no koto," p. 221.
17. Compare *Iwate ken chūsei monjo* 1, comp. Iwate Ken Kyōiku Iinkai (Morioka, 1960), document 171 with document 226. The terminological distinction is most evident in the 9.1335 Kamada *meyasujō*, DNSR6.2 of 8.18.1335, where the standard bearer (*hatasashi*) Yajirō otoko was shot to death (*igoroshi*), and yet the following day(8.19), a retainer (*kenin*) was described as being killed (*uchishi*). For another example of *igoroshi*, see the 3.1336 Migita Sukeyasu *gunchūjō*. For the *igoroshi* of horses, see NBIK 1190 and *Sōma monjo*, p. 114, Sōma Okada *monjo* document 22, 3.1336 Sōma Nagatane *gunchūjō* (2 horses).
18. *Shinpen Saitama kenshi shiryō hen* 5, *Chūsei* 1, 2.1344 Beppu Michizane *gunchūjō utsushi*, pp. 264–65. For another warrior wounded a second time within a span of three weeks, see *Fukushima kenshi* 7, Okamoto *monjo*, document 32, p. 223. Nejime Kiyotane was also wounded in the arm on 12.18.1336 and later on the hand on 1.10.1337. See NBIK 823.
19. *Shinpen Saitama kenshi shiryōhen* 5, *Chūsei* 1, pp. 264–65, 2.1344 Beppu Michizane *gunchūjō utsushi*. Michizane nevertheless managed to recover somewhat from this debilitating injury, for he perished in battle in 1360. See document 433, p. 310.

and soon returned to the battlefield. Shots to the head, face, and neck were, however, almost invariably serious wounds. One man had an arrow pierce his head above the right eye, and was thereupon described in a petition as "half-dead."[20] In another case, an arrow penetrated the right side of Soga Mitsutoshi's neck, ultimately causing his death.[21]

By contrast, rocks were rarely used, except when defending forts. Nearly every instance of a warrior being wounded by a rock occurred when a castle was being stormed. For example, the Date Yoshitsuna's hapless bannerman Ōjirō was described as being "half-dead" after having his head crushed by a rock while an enemy castle was being stormed, while Tashiro Mototsuna's bannerman Hikoshirō had his neck broken by rocks in a similar attack. Nevertheless, save for those instances where boulders were dropped on warriors, they were not particularly lethal weapons.[22]

The prevalence of sword wounds in the fourteenth century does not indicate that warriors fought in tightly massed groups. Rather, swords were better suited for conflicts among widely scattered clusters of men. Some swords reached seven feet in length and were useful in breaking the legs of charging horses.[23] A few long swords (ōdachi) were only partially sharpened, with half of the blade near the hilt blunt and rounded like a "clamshell," which indicates that they were used to bludgeon opponents instead of slashing them.[24] (See figure 19 = pl. 12.)

Mounted warriors wisely refrained from wielding swords because skittish mounts might dump them after seeing the shadow of the blade, or, for that matter, an enemy's sword.[25] If a mounted warrior were to use a sword, he would in all probability wield it as a lance, although some scholars have asserted that wielding a sword was virtually impossible on horseback. More typically, a warrior would dismount and hammer an opponent's helmet with his sword.[26] Unsurprisingly, references to broken weapons are

20. KI 32830. The expression used in this document literally, is "half-dead half-alive."
21. *Iwate ken chūsei monjo* 1, document 171, p. 62, and document 226, p. 78.
22. For the former example, see *Hyōgo kenshi shiryōhen chūsei*, vol. 8, Nanzenji *monjo* document 12, p. 26; for the latter, see *Takaishishishi 2, Shiryōhen* 1, document 145, 10.11.1341 Tashiro Ryōken *gunchūjō*, pp. 591–93. See also KI 32043–4, and NBIK 657, 926.
23. One fourteenth-century long sword can be seen at Futaarasan shrine, near Nikkō. For the use of such weapons against horses, see *Taiheiki*, maki 8, "Santo Kyōto ni yosuru koto," p. 200.
24. *Taiheiki*, maki 32, "Kōnan kassen no koto," p. 969. For more on "clamshell blades" (*hamaguriha*) see *Buke myōmokushō*, comp. Hanawa Hokinoichi (Meiji Tosho Shuppan, 1954), 8 vols. sword section 17 (*hamaguri*).
25. For a flustered swordsman being dumped from his own horse, see *Taiheiki*, maki 29, "Moronao shatei yoriki shōgai no koto," p. 883; for an enemy's blade frightening a horse, see *Taiheiki*, maki 15, "Tadarahama ikusa no koto," p. 458. See also NBIC 2533.
26. For analysis of the difficulty of using swords on horseback, see Kondō Yoshikazu, "Buki kara mita nairanki no sentō," *Nihonshi kenkyū* 373 (September 1993): 60–74. See also his *Chūseiteki bugu no seiritsu to bushi* (Yoshikawa Kōbunkan, 2000), particularly pp. 257–65, where he postulates that

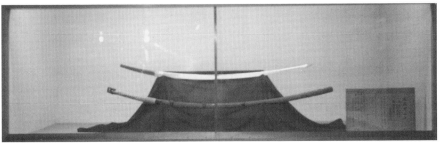

Figue 19. a. Warrior with an *ōdachi*. Illustration courtesy Futaarasan shrine. b. National Treasure Ōdachi mei Bizenshū Osafune Tomomitsu. Illustration courtesy Futaarasan shrine.

---

the great length of *ōdachi* stems from their use by mounted warriors. Conversely, for an example of horsemen dismounting to use their swords, see *Taiheiki*, maki 31, "Nantei hachiman ontaishitsu no koto," p. 938.

common.[27] Not only could blades be damaged from ferocious blows, but a warrior could lodge his weapon in his opponent's body, which led to some special prayers designed to free a weapon from the corpse.[28] Conversely, the long swords so favored at this time could not be effectively used with an enemy who was too close.[29]

A fleeing enemy is easier to kill than one actively resisting. When the city of Kamakura was sacked in 1333, over a hundred men, women and children were slaughtered. Slash wounds appear on the skulls and limbs of sixty percent of the men, thirty percent of the women, and ten percent of the children.[30] Most sword wounds were either to the forehead or the top of the head. Blows to the top of the head were sometimes of such force that the sword would bounce off the skull, leaving several parallel strokes. Other skulls were fractured or crushed by the force of the blade's impact.

Armed opponents were far more difficult to kill: they understandably remained as distant from each other as possible. Some warriors survived multiple blows, which indicates that they were repeatedly nicked by the tip of an enemy's sword. One man survived thirteen cuts, while one horse endured seven slashes.[31]

Some preferred battle-axes and halberds (naginata), but these were not particularly durable weapons for their wooden handles could be broken.[32] Akamatsu Ujinori, for example, crushed the helmets of several adversaries with his battle-ax until one opposing warrior slashed the wooden handle of Ujinori's ax and rendered it useless.[33] Due to the weakness of their handles, naginata and battle-axes were shorter than long swords.[34] Thus, long swords were the most effective and durable weapon of the fourteenth century. (See figure 20 = pl. 13.)

Recorded pike wounds are rare. One might assume that this stems from their efficacy, as Muromachi-era medical manuals state that "those impaled by short sword or pike cannot be easily saved."[35] According to chronicles such as the Taiheiki, pike wounds were virtually synonymous with instant death. Hosokawa Yoriharu is described as expiring immediately after being

27. Taiheiki, maki 29, "Shōgun oyako onjōraku no koto," p. 860; maki 31, "Musashino kassen no koto," p. 921; and maki 32, "Kōnan kassen no koto," p. 972.
28. See Heihō reizuisho, p. 70.
29. Taiheiki, maki 32, "Miyako ikusa no koto," p. 977.
30. Suzuki, Kamakura zaimokuza hakken no chūsei iseki to sono jinkotsu, particularly p. 70.
31. For the man, see NBIK 1497; for the horse, see Iriei monjo, ed. Ueda Jun'ichi (Zoku Gunsho Ruijū Kansekai, 1986), maki 7, p. 304.
32. For a broken naginata, see Taiheiki, maki 31, "Musashino kassen no koto," p. 924.
33. Taiheiki, maki 32, "Yamana Uemon no suke teki to naru koto," pp. 949–50.
34. The longest naginata were five feet long, two feet shorter than long swords. See Taiheiki, maki 14, "Ōwatari kassen no koto," p. 410.
35. Hosokawa Katsumoto, Reiranshū, Kinsō (unpublished manuscript, possession of the author), p. 2.

Figure 20. Warrior with a battle axe. Source: *Go sannen kassen ekotoba*. Permission and photo granted by the Tokyo National Museum.

struck in the throat, while an impaled horse is depicted as collapsing instantly as a result of the blow.[36] One warrior stabbed by a pike is likewise described in the petitions as "half-dead."[37] Another survivor, grievously wounded after being stabbed with a pike on the right side of his face and the elbow of his left arm, was forced to dispatch a representative (*daikan*) to fight in his stead while he recovered from these wounds.[38]

Pikes were nevertheless ill-suited for use in scattered melees. Because of their small blade, pikes were effective at stabbing but not slashing. Pikes could be easily broken in encounters with opponents wielding seven-foot long swords. Not until massed formations of infantry were developed did the fragility and unwieldiness of pikes cease to be problematic. In a tight formation, one only needed to stab at enemies in front. Accordingly, pikes lengthened considerably in the fifteenth and sixteenth centuries. Indeed, some sixteenth-century examples attained a length of fifteen feet, three times as long as those of the fourteenth century.

Pikes were not the only weapons used to stab. In the *Aki no yo no nagamonogatari*, one encounters a scene of hand-to-hand combat. (See figure 21 = pl. 14.) One warrior is holding a pike, two have *naginata*, and one has a long sword.[39] Both swords and *naginata* are being used to stab adversaries. Thus swords and *naginata* proved most versatile for one could use them to

36. For references to Hosokawa Yoriharu, see *Taiheiki* maki 30, "Shichijō Ōmiya kassen no koto," p. 907. For a speared mount collapsing instantly after such a blow, see *Taiheiki* maki 38, "Sagami no kami Kiyouji uchishi no koto," p. 1143.

37. KI 32830.

38. *Fukushima kenshi* 7, Koaraii monjo, document 1, pp. 782–83.

39. Also found in Miya Tsugio, *Kassen no emaki* (Kadokawa Shoten, 1977), monochrome illustration number 11.

Figure 21. Warriors fighting with swords, pikes, and *naginata*. Source: *Aki no yo no naga-monogatari*. Possession of the Idemitsu Museum of Arts.

beat, stab, *and* slash opponents, while one could use a pike only to impale opponents in front of oneself or smash adversaries to one's side.

As swords were unwieldy on horseback, mounted soldiers instead generally relied upon arrows. Hence, the prevalence of sword wounds attests to the fact that foot soldiers engaged in hand-to-hand combat most frequently during the first years of war in the fourteenth century. One can also surmise that period one witnessed sieges and battles in constricted terrain, where horsemen had to dismount. Likewise, battle during period one was fought intensely, with warriors closing in on their enemy instead of merely harrying them with arrows. The decrease in sword wounds and increase in arrow wounds suggests that warriors came to prefer fighting at a distance. Most battles after 1338 consisted of skirmishers, or squads of cavalry, firing salvos of arrows.

Further insight into the nature of warfare comes from the 627 wounds that are precisely recorded in battle reports and petitions for reward. When arranged chronologically, they illuminate the changing pattern of woundings and, by extension, the efficacy of armor.

The first noteworthy trend is that in period four, the number of recorded wounds dramatically decreases. One sees a sudden decline in leg wounds (minus eleven percentage points) and an increase in body wounds (plus seven percentage points), although it is not clear whether this indicates an improvement in armor or merely a statistical aberration. In contrast to visual sources created prior to the fourteenth century, those dating from later in the fourteenth century prominently display leg armor. (See figure 22 = pl. 15.)

Neck and face wounds declined precipitously throughout the fourteenth century.[40] The prevalence of such wounds can be partially attributed to the

---

40. They appear most commonly in 1333. See KI, 32043–4, 32050 and *Migita keizu* in *Zoku gunsho ruijū, Keizubu* (Zoku Gunsho Ruijū Kanseikai, 1975), p. 148. Perhaps unsurprisingly, veterans

TABLE 3
The location of wounds

Location	Period One (1333–38)	Period Two (1339–49)	Period Three (1350–55)	Period Four (1356–94)	Total
Face	26 (**10**)	10 (**8**)	6 (**3**)	1 (**2**)	43 (**7**)
Neck	8 (**3**)	4 (**3**)	2 (**1**)	2 (**4**)	16 (**3**)
Head	7 (**3**)	4 (**3**)	7 (**4**)	3 (**5**)	21 (**3**)
Body	52 (**21**)	26 (**20**)	42 (**22**)	16 (**29**)	136 (**22**)
Arm	68 (**27**)	38 (**29**)	60 (**32**)	18 (**33**)	184 (**29**)
Leg	91 (**36**)	49 (**37**)	73 (**38**)	15 (**27**)	227 (**36**)
Total	251 (**40**)	131 (**21**)	190 (**30**)	55 (**9**)	627

Note: Numbers in parentheses indicate percentage in each time bloc, save for those in the total row, which designate the relative percentage of these records in comparison with other time blocs.

inexperience of those warriors fighting during 1333, because sixty-three percent of all wounds pertaining to the 1333 siege of Chihaya castle were to the face and neck. Nevertheless, a reduction from ten percent to a mere two percent over sixty years suggests a more systematic explanation: warriors had become more adept at protecting their faces and necks because of improvements in armor.

The marked decrease in face wounds stems from the dissemination of protective gear such as face guards (*hōate*).[41] Although armor specialists believe that *hōate* were not widely used in the fourteenth century, four references appear in the *Taiheiki*.[42] Furthermore, *hōate* are depicted in fourteenth-century illustrated scrolls such as the *Go-sannen kassen ekotoba* and the *Aki no yo no nagamonogatari*.[43] (See figure 23 = pl. 16.) As the bow was the preferred weapon in the fourteenth century, and because the face and neck remained vulnerable to arrows, protecting these regions became a

---

advised novices to "protect your face [from] incoming arrows with your armor's shoulder boards (*sode*)." *Genpei jōsuiki* (Kokumin Bunko Kankōkai, 1911), maki 37, p. 909.

41. Face guards (*hōate*) consist of a piece of metal rounded to fit the neck, chin, and cheekbones.

42. *Taiheiki*, maki 38, "Sagami no kami Kiyouji uchishi no koto," p. 1142; maki 14, "Ōwatari kassen no koto," p. 410 (the Izumi version is in error, for it mentions "shin guards" when in fact the correct term appears in the Seigen in *Taiheiki* text); maki 23, "Hata Rokurō Saemon no jō Tokiyoshi no koto," p. 685; and maki 17, "Yama seme no koto," p. 507. For the skepticism of specialists, see Yamagishi Sumio, *Nihon kachū no kisoteki chishiki* (Yūzankaku, 1990), pp. 118–20.

43. *Go-sannen kassen ekotoba*, chūkan dai ichidan, fourth page. Three examples appear in *Aki no yo no nagamonogatari emaki*, chūkan dai go dan (figure 23, pl. 16), found in Miya, *Kassen no emaki*, monochrome illustration 10. Three more examples appear in ibid., *chūkan dai nana dan*, number 12.

Figure 22. Leg armor of the late fourteenth century. Photograph and permission courtesy the Kyoto National Museum. This famous portrait of a mounted warrior has commonly been though to portray Ashikaga Takauji. Recent scholarship has revealed, however, that the illustration depicts a warrior from the mid-fourteenth century (probably the 1360s). The armor contains the Kō family crest, revealing that this warrior is a member of the Kō family. Kuroda Hideo has postulated that this warrior is Kō no Moroakira, a warrior who died defending the second shogun, Ashikaga Yoshiakira, whose monogram appears above the portrait.

pressing concern. Armor was improved in order to prevent the most danger-ous wounds caused by the most common weapon.

Further insights regarding the nature of battle and the efficacy of weapons emerge from a survey of horse casualties. When a warrior was killed, the cause of his death was not mentioned, but it was for horses. Although the number of recorded horses is statistically insignificant, these thirty-one cases can nevertheless prove illuminating.

TABLE 4

Horse casualties[44]

Period	Sword (k)	Sword (w)	Arrow (k)	Arrow (w)	Pike (k)	Pike (w)
One (1333–38)	4	4	3	11	1	0
Two (1339–49)	2	1	0	1	0	0
Three (1350–55)	1	1	0	0	0	0
Four (1356–94)	1	1	0	0	0	0
Total	8	7	3	12	1	0

(k)=killed; (w)=wounded

Of the thirty-one horses recorded, twelve (thirty-nine percent) were killed and nineteen (sixty-one percent) wounded. Seventy-four percent of all horse casualties (eight [twenty-six percent] killed and fifteen [forty-eight percent] wounded) occurred in period one, which again underscores the intensity of the 1333–38 conflict.

The continued appearance of sword wounds throughout the fourteenth century suggests that horsemen continued attacking infantry or other horse-men, although such encounters were most common in period one. In period one, sixty-one percent of the recorded horses were struck with an arrow, thirty-five percent were slashed, and four percent were impaled. In period two, twenty-five percent of wounds stemmed from arrows while seventy-five

44. For the relevant documents, see NBIK 459, 544, 651, 868, 1190, 1220, 1375, 1497, 2536 (4 horses), 3936; NBIC 233, 238, 291, 654, 773, 2533, 3644; *Niigata kenshi shiryōhen* 4, *Chūsei* 2, document 1422; *Sōma monjo*, p. 114, Sōma Okada *monjo* document 22, 3.36 Sōma Nagatane *gunchūjō* (2 horses), and ibid., Daihisa *monjo* document 7, 8.1337 Sōma Tomotane *gunchūjō*; *Tochigi ken-shi* 5, pp. 84–85, 4.1338 Motegi Tomomasa *gunchūjō* (3 horses) (also *Kanagawa kenshi shiryōhen, Kodai-chūsei* 3, no. 1, document 3359); *Shinano shiryō* 5 (1954), p. 364, 4.1337 Ichikawa *gunchūjō*, and *Shinano shiryō* 7 (1956), pp. 192–93, 9.1387 Ichikawa Kai no kami Yorifusa *gunchūjō*; *Gunma kenshi shiryōhen* 6, *Chūsei* 2, document 700, 5.1336 Sano Yoshitsuna *gunchūjō*; and *Kanagawa kenshi* 3.1, document 3269.

Figure 23. Three warriors wearing *hōate*. Source: *Aki no yo no nagamonogatari*. Possession of the Idemitsu Museum of Arts.

percent were caused by swords. The reason for the disappearance of arrow wounds is not, however, clear. Most horsemen studiously avoided perilous situations, choosing, for example, to do nothing for a fallen comrade save watch the unfolding drama.[45] As warriors were ill-disposed to risking their horses, which were, after all, valued assets, they perhaps became more adept at protecting their mounts. One might also attribute this decline to the dissemination of horse armor.[46]

Since the cause of horse fatalities is recorded, one can estimate the effectiveness of weapons. Of the thirty-one horses, fifteen (forty-eight percent) were slashed by swords, fifteen (forty-eight percent) were pierced with arrows, and one (three percent) was impaled by a pike. The only impaled horse died instantly (one hundred percent), while over half of those slashed (eight animals, fifty-three percent) expired. By contrast, only twenty percent of those shot with arrows (three out of fifteen) perished. Thirty-nine percent of recorded horses were killed while sixty-one percent were wounded. The ratio of killed to wounded for swords is 53/47; for arrows 20/80, and for spears 100/0 (only one example). This ratio provides a general index of how lethal respective wounds were: those slashed perished roughly half the time,

45. *Heike monogatari*, ed. Takagi Ichinosuke et al. in *Nihon koten bungaku taikei*, vols. 32–33 (Iwanami Shoten, 1964), maki 11, "Yumi nagashi. "
46. For a reference to horse armor, see *Taiheiki*, maki 23, "Hata Rokurō Saemon ga koto," p. 685. According to the *Keichō hon* version of the *Taiheiki*, *Nihon koten bungaku taikei*, maki 22, this was chain armor.

one out of five of those shot with an arrow died, while those impaled generally expired.

In conclusion, bows and arrows were the most commonly used weapon in the fourteenth century, while long swords were best suited for hand-to-hand combat. The relative paucity of pike wounds, coupled with the shortness of pikes, indicates that fourteenth century battles were fought by scattered warriors. Although the intensity of battle waned in the fourteenth century, no new patterns of weapons usage or tactical shifts are evident.

FOURTEENTH-CENTURY TACTICS

The insight provided by the preceding statistical narrative contrasts sharply with the descriptions of fourteenth-century battle by most historians, who have characterized warriors of the eleventh through the fourteenth centuries as bow-wielding men who fought in single mounted combat. This "class" of warriors was undermined with the advent of "commoners" fighting on foot and using pikes. The fourteenth century has thus been posited as a turning point, when pike-wielding soldiers bloodied horsemen and broke the hitherto unquestioned dominance of cavalry.[47] This advent of infantry supremacy—the shift from "individuals" on horseback to "massed" tactics involving foot soldiers,[48] —has been perceived as the catalyst for epochal changes in state and society.[49] According to this paradigm, changes in technology—here narrowly defined as the adoption of new weapons—influenced the structure of social and political organization. Weapons such as pikes enabled "commoners" to achieve political prominence as a result of their newfound military power. The wielders of pikes, in other words, caused the military and political decline of the old warrior order by defeating them in battle.

This thesis is, however, problematic for several reasons. The first is that no apparent tactical changes are evident. The second is that the adoption of the pike proved to be the catalyst in profound military and societal changes. Nevertheless, as the preceding statistical narrative has revealed, no major tactical innovations arose at this time. And, the third reason is that no class or social order monopolized the use of a particular weapon or style of fighting. Men of diverse backgrounds were capable of riding horses and wielding bows, swords, pikes, clubs, rocks, and battle axes. Hence, one cannot claim that changes in tactics reflect either transformations in social organization or the relative strength of different orders.

47. For such a characterization, see Seki Yukihiko, "Busō," in *Chūsei o kangaeru ikusa*, ed. Fukuda Toyohiko (Yoshikawa Kōbunkan, 1993), pp. 13–14.
48. Satō, *Nanbokuchō no dōran*, pp. 194–95.
49. Amino Yoshihiko emphasizes this in his *Nihon no rekishi* 10 *Mōko shūrai* pp. 372–73.

How then can this image of battle be reconciled with the standard inter-pretation that the fourteenth century witnessed a shift from "individual" to "massed" tactics? Much of the misunderstanding stems from a misunder-standing of the term *nobushi*.

Many historians have believed that *nobushi* refers to "commoner infantry." Seki Yukihiko, for example, states that "Victory in the fourteenth century hinged upon the [decisive impact] . . . of large numbers of commoner infantry (*ashigaru* and *nobushi*). [Accordingly,] massed tactics undermined the previous [pattern] . . . of individual horsemen fighting each other."[50] From this account, one might assume that *nobushi* designates a phalanxlike infantry formation dominated by "commoners." Implicit in this summary is that social orders can be broadly associated with modes of combat and types of weapons. Pikes are ipso facto a "commoner" weapon that must be used by men in tightly packed groups, all of which are described by the term *nobushi*. In fact, this represents a fundamental misunderstanding, for the term *nobushi* desig-nates scattered skirmishers regardless of their social origins.

The term *nobushi* was used to describe men who ranged in status from the unfree to autonomous warriors.[51] All those who "did" *nobushi* were called *nobushi*.[52] Such men did not belong to a single social order. This is manifest in the following report: "feigning retreat we lured enemy *nobushi* into [open] fields and our horsemen surrounded them. Fourteen *nobushi* were captured or killed. Of the fourteen, five were samurai; three with surnames were [also] captured alive."[53] *Nobushi* were neither massed troops nor com-moners, but simply skirmishers.

The original meaning of the word *nobushi* was "those who hide in fields."[54] Engagements in which warriors crouched in fields and peppered opponents with arrows were known as "*nobushi* battles." In the actual lan-guage of surviving petitions, some warriors claimed to have "performed the outstanding military service of [engaging in a] *nobushi* battle," while others boasted that they "fought *nobushi* battles continuously for many days."[55] "*Nobushi* battle" describes a conflict fought by dispersed warriors "who hid

50. Seki, "Busō," pp. 13–14.
51. For a warrior "doing *nobushi*," e. g. launching a night raid, see *Fukushima kenshi*, p. 225, Okamoto monjo, document 37, 10.17.1342 Okamoto Shigechika *dai* Yamada Shigenori *gunchū chakutōjō*.
52. *Taiheiki*, maki 38, "Settsu kassen no koto," p. 1148, and NBIK 6636.
53. NBIK 5667.
54. *Kokinchōbunshū*, in *Nihon koten bungaku taikei* 84 (Iwanami Shoten, 1967), maki 9, Buyū 12, pas-sage 337, "Minamoto Yoshiie Ōe Masafusa ni heihō o narabu koto," which mentions "times of lying in fields" (*no ni fusuru toki*). For a brief summary of *nobushi* in English, see Paul Varley, *Warriors of Japan as Portrayed in the War Tales* (Honolulu: University of Hawaii Press, 1994), pp. 173–74. "*Nobushi*" may also have been pronounced "*nobuseri.*"
55. For the former, NBIK 2597; for the latter, NBIK 5171. For a reference which equates "*nobushi* bat-tles" with "arrow battles"(*ya ikusa*), see *Kano shiryō, Nanbokuchō* I, pp. 526–27, 9.1352 Tokuda Dōso *dai* Saitō Akifusa *gunchūjō*.

in fields." Thus, rather than proving the existence of infantry formations, the term *nobushi* indicates that battles were fought by scattered skirmishers of diverse statuses.

Cavalry and Infantry

The armies of the fourteenth century consisted of foot soldiers and horsemen mixed together. This haphazard amalgamation is most tellingly depicted in the *Kasuga gongen kenki-e*. In one scene, a few horsemen direct foot soldiers in battle; in another, infantry cowers among rocks and trees while groups of horsemen thunder by.[56] (See figure 24 = pl. 17.) In diaries one sees references to armies composed of fifty on foot and sixty on horse.[57]

Cavalry easily mopped up infantry caught in the open. As one horseman proclaimed, "even the strongest soldiers cannot withstand the bite of arrows, nor can the fastest of men outrun a horse." Hence, one sees examples in the *Taiheiki* where even the most skilled swordsmen were easily dispatched by mounted archers.[58] The supremacy of cavalry hinged upon mobility. Mounted

Figure 24. Infantry fighting in poor terrain. Source: *Kasuga gongen kenki e*, scroll 19, section 1 (partial). Possession of Kunaichō Sannōmaru Shōzōkan. Permission for reproduction granted by the Imperial Household Ministry.

56. *Kasuga gongen kenki-e*, maki 2, page 5, in Komatsu Shigemi, comp. *Zoku Nihon no emaki* 13 *Kasuga gongen kenki-e* (Chūōkōronsha, 1991).
57. "Kannō ninen hinamiki," in *Zoku gunsho ruijū* 29.2 (Zoku Gunsho Ruijū Kanseikai, 1975), for the actions of 9.7.1351.
58. *Taiheiki*, maki 8, "Shigatsu mikka miyako ikusa no koto," pp. 204–25, and McCullough, *The Taiheiki*, pp. 224–27.

soldiers preferred open spaces and would resort to arson to burn down all the dwellings for some four hundred to five hundred yards in order to create an open space for horses to charge.[59] Otherwise, skirmishers (*nobushi*) might climb to the roofs of houses and shoot at the enemy passing below.[60]

Cavalry suffered when trapped in narrow areas. The Hosokawa, for example, were harried mercilessly because they:

> could not pass to the north for they had not finished burning the dwellings (*zaike*) of Ōtsu. A deep lake to the east was [likewise] impassable, forcing [the Hosokawa army] to advance in single file along a narrow . . . road. The enemy . . . rowed [parallel to the Hosokawa] . . . and shot them from the side . . . killing five hundred in all.[61]

Every instance of cavalry being defeated by infantry occurred when its mobility was hampered by impassable terrain, such as by narrow mountain roads or swampy paddies. In situations where the terrain was poor prudent horsemen dismounted and went on foot.[62] The supremacy of mounted warriors remained unchallenged in open spaces. Infantry could achieve supremacy—and withstand a cavalry charge—only when massed formations such as the phalanx were developed. This was still in the future in the fourteenth century, for units of pikemen and foot soldiers would not be able to defeat cavalry until the outbreak of the Ōnin war in 1467.

No significant tactical innovations arose in the fourteenth century in spite of sixty years of endemic warfare. The absence of innovation cannot be equated with an absence of change, for armor was improved and military organization was rationalized. The transformations engendered by fourteenth-century war did not, however, arise as a result of changes in tactics per se.

MILITARY ORGANIZATION

Save for an improvement in neck armor, no major innovations characterize the process of waging war in the fourteenth century. No changes appear in how weapons were used, or how the enemy was engaged. Nevertheless, military organization was rationalized after 1350 as provincial constables (*shugo*) came to direct regionally mobilized armies. A comparison between the armies of 1336 and those of a generation later illuminates this increasing sophistication in regional military organization.

---

59. *Taiheiki*, maki 35, "Shodaimyō kasanete Tennōji ni mukau koto," p. 1040.
60. *Taiheiki*, maki 30, "Shichijō Ōmiya ikusa no koto," p. 907. See also maki 8, "Shigatsu mikka miyako ikusa no koto," p. 202, and McCullough, *The Taiheiki*, p. 223 for archers blocking the streets.
61. *Taiheiki*, maki 15, "Miidera kassen no koto," p. 429.
62. NBIK 704. Those who attacked Mt. Hiei also dismounted and advanced on foot. *Baishōron*, p. 126.

In the battles of 1336, warriors fought heedless of their regional origins. A veteran group of Kyushu and eastern warriors had, after two months of running battles, seized the capital under the command of Ashikaga Takauji. They were reinforced at Hōsshōji by a contingent from Aki and other provinces of western Japan. When battle erupted on 1.16.1336, Takauji's battle-hardened troops fought at the western and southern gates of the temple complex, interspersed with Aki warriors. Although the Aki warriors were mobilized by the *shugo* of the province (Takeda Nobutake), they did not fight under his command. Rather, warriors rushed to whichever gate they preferred.

TABLE 5
The battle of Hōsshōji, 1.16.1336[63]

Name	Origin	Location
Tomikuru Tadashige	Bungo	Hōsshōji
Tonami Raison	Bungo	Southern Gate, Hōsshōji
Yoshimatsu Kintō	Buzen	Sanjō kawara/Hōsshōji
Asakura Butsu'a	Aki	Southern Gate
Sūo Chikaie	Aki	Western Gate
Mito Yoriaki	Aki	Southern Gate/Sanjō kawara
Kutsuki Yoshiuji	Ōmi	Hōsshōji
Henmi Aritomo	Aki	Western Gate
Sebama Masanao	Bungo	Western Gate
Nomoto Tomoyuki	Musashi	Hōsshōji
Nokami Sukeuji	Bungo	Hōsshōji
Hatano Kageuji	Aki	In front of Hōsshōji
Sudō Kaganari (Kikkawa *dai*)	Aki	Hōsshōji
Mōri Motoharu	Aki	Hōsshōji
Tashiro Ichiwakamaru	Izumi	Sanjō kawara
Tsuchiya Munetada	Kawachi	Sanjō kawara
Mizaki Masataka	Izumo	Sanjō kawara
Kondō Mitsukage	?	killed at the Hōsshōji battle
Katayama Takachika	Tanba	? kawara

(See figure 25.)

63. NBIK 543–544, 546, 757; *Kutsuki monjo*, vol. 2, document 428; NBIC 225, 233, 259, 304, 348, 350–51, 383, 654, and 4250; and *Hirakata shishi 6, Shiryōhen 1*, Tsuchiyashi *monjo*, document 4, 1.24.1336 Tsuchiya Tadamune *gunchūjō*, p. 223. For Kondō Mitsukage's death, see DNSR, series 6, vol. 2, p. 1015. Katayama Hiko Saburō mentions fighting in Kyoto battles near the Kamo river from 1.16 through 1.27.1336. See *Wachi chōshi shiryō shū 1, Chūsei kinsei* no. 1, comp. Wachi chō (Wachi chō, 1987), Katayama ke *monjo*, doc. 33, 10.13.1337 Katayama Hiko Saburō Tadachika *gunchūjō*, p. 39.

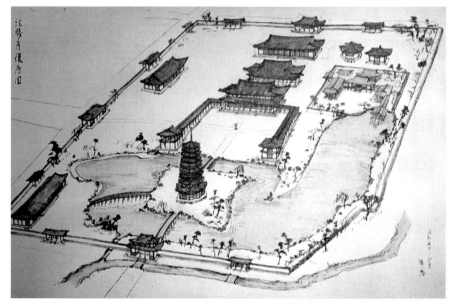

Figure 25. A recreation of Hōsshōji in 1077. Drawing by Fujishima Gaijirō.

Petitions dating from 1337 likewise reveal that men from different provinces fought in cross proximity, for a Tanba warrior, Katayama Mago Saburō, witnessed the deeds of Suwabe Shin'e, from Izumo Province.[64] These armies were ephemeral entities. When the Ashikaga fought in the capital seven months later, only two veterans of Hōsshōji—Sebama Masanao and Tashiro Ichiwakamaru—returned.[65]

The battles of the latter half of 1336 were considerably greater in magnitude than those at Hōsshōji. For example, at least seven distinct groupings fought on 8.25.1336. (See figure 26.) The first, the Ogasawara, defeated the priests of Mt. Hiei on its eastern slopes, captured two generals, and then advanced to the Seta bridge. This encircling action effectively cut Go-Daigo's

64. *Gunma kenshi*, p. 546, document 758 for a Suwabe petition that describes the actions on the evening of 3.5.1337. Katayama Mago Saburō was the witness from Tanba. Suwabe Shin'e was from Izumo although he possessed Inaba lands as well. See NBIC 379, 715, and 736. For proof of Katayama Mago Saburō's Tanba origins, see *Wachi chōshi shiryō shū* 1, *chūsei kinsei* no. 1, Katayama ke *monjo* docs. 38–39, 10.1355 Katayama Toramatsu *mōshijō an*, pp. 41–42. His grandson, Katayama Hiko Saburō Takachika, can be documented as fighting at the same location (Echizen Province's Kanegasaki castle) as Suwabe Shin'e on the evening of 3.5.1337. See ibid., Katayama ke *monjo* doc. 27, 3.15.1337, Katayama Hiko Saburō Takachika *gunchūjō*, p. 38. For the relationship between Takachika and his grandfather Mago Saburō, see the Katayama genealogy in ibid., pp. 81–82.

65. Compare the preceding table with appendix 2a. Katayama Takachika fought in Kyoto during the first and sixth months of 1336, and guarded a castle in Yamashiro from 8.12-29.1336 but he abandoned the Ashikaga when they fled to Kyushu. See *Wachi chōshi shiryō shū* 1, *Chūsei kinsei* no. 1, Katayama ke *monjo* docs. 23-25, pp. 36–37.

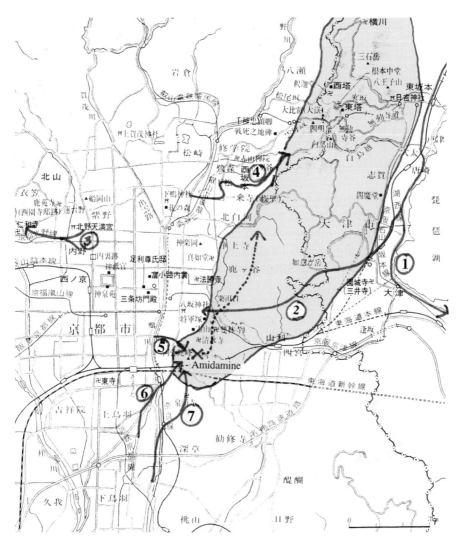

Figure 26. The battles of 8.25.1336. Source: *Taiheiki*, vol. 2 (Shōgakkan, 1996). Note: The shaded area designates the Southern Court's original lines of defense. Solid arrow lines indicate the initial course of the Ashikaga attacks. Dotted arrow line indicates Ashikaga pursuit after Southern Court forces fled from Amidamine.

supply lines and ensured his defeat. A second auxiliary force crossed the mountains and cut Southern Court defenses in half north of Amidamine. Shōni Yorihisa led the third force, composed of Buzen warriors, in the northwest quadrant of the capital. Shōni forces blocked enemy reinforcements from the west.

The fourth identifiable force, composed of Nagato and Aki warriors (the Tairanogo and Kamishiro), was led by Yamana Tokiuji. These men staged a probing attack on Imahiei Nakao, a strategic road leading to Ōmi, cutting enemy lines of communication in the process. An auxiliary force composed of Aki and Hizen warriors (the Kikkawa and Yasutomi) attacked Shin Hiei and advanced to Amidamine.[66]

The main thrust was from the south. The sixth identifiable force, composed of warriors from Kyushu and central Japan, fought under the command of Hosokawa Akiuji and advanced from Takeda to Inariyama and Amidamine. Kō no Moroyasu commanded a closely supporting group composed of Harima and Izumo warriors that proceeded from Toba to Amidamine.

The armies of the 1330s were not regionally organized. Aki and Settsu warriors participated in two separate units while Kyushu warriors fought in three. Nevertheless, after twenty years of war, great strides were made in military organization as the first regionally organized regiments were formed.

In contrast to the battles of the previous generation, when warriors were drawn from provinces throughout Japan, most of those who fought in 1354 resided close to the capital (Izumi, Ōmi), or resided in provinces to the immediate north or east (Etchū, Shinano, Mino) or the west (Harima, Bingo, Tajima, Hōki, Bitchū, Aki). Those few who came from afar, for example, Kantō or Kyushu, fought solely under the command of the Ashikaga shogun. Thus, one can detect a two-tiered pattern of mobilization. Warriors of middling means fought under a *shugo*'s command, while their more powerful brethren—those capable of traveling long distances—preferred serving under hegemonic figures such as the Ashikaga shogun. Powerful warriors resisted serving under regional magnates.[67]

Some military units were regionally organized. For example, all Izumi warriors who supported the Northern Court fought together under the command of Hosokawa Kiyouji. Thus, cohesive, regionally based units were forged after twenty years of hostilities. The number of warriors who maintained their autonomy and resisted serving in a *shugo*'s army steadily dwindled as the fourteenth century progressed.

CONCLUSION

Fourteenth-century battle was fought by widely scattered troops. Most warring consisted of skirmishing. An average of seventy-three percent of all

---

66. These men received the monogram of the *samurai dokoro*, Komata Tarō Nyūdō. For more on the Komata see NBIK 740.

67. For more on some warriors' reluctance to serve under regional commanders (e.g. the Oyama's resistance to Shiba Ienaga), see Matsumoto Kazuo, "Nanbokuchō shoki Kamakura fu gunji taisei ni kansuru ichi kōsatsu," *Komonjo kenkyū* 41, 42 (December 1995): 63–80.

wounds stemmed from arrows. Even in the fiercest of battles, only a few mustered the courage to fight hand-to-hand.[68] As bows were the dominant weapon, the most pressing concern was to prevent serious arrow wounds. Hence, face guards (*hōate*) were developed and disseminated.

The onset of indeterminate warfare did not lead to any changes in tactics. Squads of cavalry dominated the battlefield and were defeated only when their mobility was hampered by poor terrain. Otherwise, horsemen could easily slice through scattered skirmishers. Accordingly, an army primarily composed of infantry preferred fighting in inaccessible terrain, while horsemen opted for (or created) open spaces. Finally, the prevalence of long swords and the paucity of pike wounds indicates that no "massed" infantry formations existed in the fourteenth century.

Armies were impermanent, unstable entities. Powerful warriors resisted serving regional magnates. Nevertheless, after the Kannō disturbance (1350–52), *shugo* began to direct cohesive, regionally based—albeit small-scale—military units. The transformation was not caused by the act of war per se. Rather, as we shall see, the delegation of fiscal powers of taxation enabled magnates to sustain semistanding armies. In short, although battle was determined by the social and political matrix of the time, it proved to be an essential ingredient of that matrix's very reconstitution.

---

68. Cases where warriors exchanged blows with an enemy were rare enough to merit special praise. NBIK 6308.

Appendix 1
Troop Numbers, Casualties and Petitions for Reward

Year	Warriors	Fatalities	Wounds	Documents
1333	370	210	34	32
1334	242	14	23	17
1335	179	36	14	25
1336	1633	300	336	253
1337	714	90	85	115
1338	540	54	45	75
1339	191	39	15	25
1340	208	6	16	48
1341	204	19	43	29
1342	106	2	7	20
1343	97	5	17	28
1344	41	1	9	6
1345	161	60	21	10
1346	58	1	6	12
1347	36	3	9	12
1348	81	14	11	21
1349	54	19	1	8
1350	150	2	15	25
1351	518	46	54	72
1352	516	31	16	99
1353	223	16	20	51
1354	216	7	94	17
1355	154	6	104	14
1356	84	31	9	10
1357	42	5	8	7
1358	8	1	2	3
1359	75	3	5	12
1360	25	1	4	11
1361	8	0	0	4
1362	43	4	3	14
1363	108	5	17	17
1364	21	1	3	5
1365	13	3	0	2
1366	10	0	3	4
1367	6	1	1	3
1368	41	1	2	12
1369	11	0	0	2
1370	7	1	0	2
1371	16	1	0	8
1372	96	1	9	20

APPENDIX 1—CONTINUED

Year	Warriors	Fatalities	Wounds	Documents
1373	34	1	0	4
1374	86	4	45	18
1375	159	5	77	17
1376	15	2	0	8
1377	28	1	4	12
1378	26	0	1	12
1379	106	8	44	9
1380	92	31	4	12
1381	62	36	0	7
1382	60	2	1	13
1383	0	0	0	0
1384	28	0	0	3
1385	14	0	0	2
1386	13	1	0	5
1387	45	3	13	8
1388	44	3	0	4
1389	2	1	0	1
1390	27	10	0	3
1391	0	0	0	0
1392	4	0	0	2
1393	0	0	0	0
1394	1	0	0	1
Unknown	482	25	0	11
Total	8634	1173	1250	1302

APPENDIX 2A
THE BATTLES OF 8.25.1336[1]

Name	Origin	Location	Commander
Ogasawara Sadamune	Shinano	Higashi Sakamoto, the Seta bridge	?
Takahashi Shigemune	Settsu	From Hiei shrine to Yamashina; in front of Gion	auxiliary (*karamete*) forces
Sebama Masanao	Bungo	Takedagawa, Amidamine	? [Hosokawa Akiuji]

continued on next page

1. *Shinano shiryō*, vol. 5, p. 343; *Habikino shishi*, vol. 2, document 87, 3.1337 Kishiwada Haruuji *gunchūjō*, pp. 286–89; *Shizuoka kenshi* 6, *Chūsei shiryōhen* no. 2, document 150, 1335[6] Takahashi Shigemune *gunchūjō*, pp. 76–77; *Hyōgo kenshi shiryōhen chūsei*, vol. 2, Hiromine *monjo* document 28, 9.26.1336 Hiromine Seishun *gunchūjō an*, p. 616; NBIK 740, 755–56, 763; NBIC 457, 465, 467, 499, 503; and for the Tashiro and others, DNSR, series 6, vol. 3, pp. 689–91, 694, 698.

APPENDIX 2A—CONTINUED

Name	Origin	Location	Commander
Suwabe Shin'e	Izumo	Toba, Amidamine	Kō no Moroyasu
#Ninomiya Hyōgo no kami	Izumo?	Toba, Amidamine	Kō no Moroyasu
#Tako Yatarō	Izumo	Toba, Amidamine	Kō no Moroyasu
Hiromine Masatoshi	Harima	Toba, Ima Hiei, Amidamine	Kō no Moroyasu auxiliary forces on Amidamine
Tairanogo Shigetsugu	Nagato	Ima Hiei Nakao	Yamana Tokiuji
Kamishiro Kaneharu	Aki	Ima Hiei Nakao	Yamana Tokiuji
Kawachi Dōkaku (Kikkawa Tatsukumamarudai)	Aki	Shin Hiei	Komata monogram
Yasutomi Yasushige	Hizen	Amidamine	Komata monogram
Kikkawa Tsunehisa	Aki	Shin Hiei, Amidamine	Komata monogram
Tashiro Ichiwakamaru	Izumi	Takeda, Inariyama, Kowata, Amidamine	Hosokawa Akiuji monogram
Itano Raiin	Settsu	Takeda, advance to Kowata, Inariyama, Amidamine	Hosokawa Akiuji
Sugita Rokurō	?	?	Akiuji's battle administrator (*kassen bugyo*)
Ishino Matajirō	?	?	Akiuji's *kassen bugyo*
Narita Shigechika	?	?	?
Taguchi Shigetsura	Buzen	Uchinoto Ninnaji	Shōni monogram
Nagano Suketomi	Buzen	Kitanoto Ninnaji	Shōni monogram
Hatano Ietaka	Tanba	?	?
Seki Kurōdo Nyūdō	?	?	?
Yada Zen Shichirō	?	?	?
Daigen Noritsuna	Mino?	killed at Higashiyama Amidamine	?
#Kangen Sōzu*	Enryakuji (?)	"Hachiman road" general	[Southern Court commander, captured]
#Echigo Matsujūmaru*	?	"Hachiman road" general	[Southern Court commander, captured]
Kishiwada Haruuji*	Izumi	Kowata yama Amidamine	?
Aso Koresada*	Higo	Amidamine	Shijō dono

Note: Those italicized fought with the Ashikaga at Hōsshōji. Asterisks designate Southern Court supporters. Those with a # are either witnesses or retainers mentioned in petitions for reward.

APPENDIX 2B
THE BATTLES 1354[2]

Date	Location	Warrior	Province (Origin)	Commander [Monogram]
12.24.1353	guard Ōmi	Hineno Tokimori	Izumi	Hosokawa, Kiyouji
12.24.53	Ōmi	Tashiro Akitsuna	Izumi	Kiyouji
12.24.53	Ōmi	Ninomiya En'a	Etchū?	Shibata?
1.20.54	Mushaji	Hineno Tokimori	Izumi	Kiyouji
1.20.54	Mushaji	Tashiro Akitsuna	Izumi	Kiyouji
1.21.54	Higashi/Nishi Sakamoto	Hineno Tokimori	Izumi	Kiyouji
1.21.54	Tōji, Ima Hiei	Hineno Tokimori	Izumi	Kiyouji
1.21.54	Higashi/Nishi Sakamoto	Tashiro Akitsuna	Izumi	Kiyouji
1.21.54	Ima Hiei	Tashiro Akitsuna	Izumi	Kiyouji
1.21.54	Guard Seta bridge	Ninomiya En'a	Etchū?	Shibata?
1.22.54	Sakamoto	Ninomiya En'a	Etchū?	Shibata?
1.24.54	Riverside of Settsu station	Azumi Morikane	Harima	Akamatsu
1.29.54	Climb Mt. Hiei	Ninomiya En'a	Etchū?	Shibata?
2.3.54	Nishi Sakamoto	Ninomiya En'a	Etchū?	Shibata?
2.6–7.54	Kawachi? Kamiyama	Azumi Morikane	Harima	Akamatsu
2.6.54	Kawachi Yama Minamio	Kageyama Tokitomo	Bingo	Iwamatsu
2.6.54	Mt. Kaminashi (Settsu)	Nuta Tanemitsu	Higo	?
2.6.54	Battle (Harima/capital)	Kobayakawa Shigekage	Aki	?
2.6.54	Mt. Kamiminami and Kyoto	*Kanamochi Sakon Shōgen	Hōki	?
2.7.54	Yamazaki encampment	Kageyama Tokitomo	Bingo	Iwamatsu
2.7.54	Yamazaki encampment	Azumi Morikane	Harima	Akamatsu
2.8.54	Battles [Ima Hiei?]	Hineno Tokimori	Izumi	Kiyouji
2.8.54	Battles [Ima Hiei?]	Tashiro Akitsuna	Izumi	Kiyouji
2.9.54	Washio Kiyomizusaka	Ninomiya En'a	Etchū?	Shibata?

continued on next page

2. *Sano Izumi shishi shiryōhen*, comp. Sano Izumi Shi (Osaka, 1958), Hineno *monjo*, document 36, 3.1355
   Hineno Tokimori *gunchūjō*; *Hyōgo kenshi shiryōhen chūsei*, vol. 3, Azumi *monjo*, document 10,
   p. 6; NBIC 2707, 3.1355 Kamada Tokimiki *meyasujō*; NBIK 3795–96; NBIC 2723, 2726–27, 2729,
   2731; *Kutsuki monjo*, vol. 1, document 18 of 5.20.1355. For the Tashiro, Ninomiya, and the mention of deaths in various genealogies, see DNSR, series 6, vol. 19, pp. 441–42, 748.

APPENDIX 2B—CONTINUED

Date	Location	Warrior	Province (Origin)	Commander [Monogram]
2.13.54	Nishiyama Minedo encampment	Kageyama Tokitomo	Bingo	Iwamatsu
2.15.54	Battle (?)	Hineno Tokimori	Izumi	Hosokawa Kiyouji
2.15.54	Battle(?)	Tashiro Akitsuna	Izumi	Hosokawa Kiyouji
2.15.54	Kyoto Battle	Kageyama Tokitomo	Bingo	Iwamatsu[†]
3.8.54	Kyoto Battle (Nishi Shichijō)	Kageyama Tokitomo	Bingo	Iwamatsu[†]
3.8.54	Kyoto, Shichijō, Higashi	Kamada Tokimiki	Hitachi	?
3.8.54	Ima Hiei	Ninomiya En'a	Etchū?	Shibata?
3.12.54	Shichijō (Kyoto)	Ninomiya En'a	Etchū?	Shibata?
3.12.54	Tōji	Nasu Suketō	Bitchū	(perish)?
3.12.54	Tōji	Satake Kaneyoshi	Hitachi?	(perish)?
3.12.54	Tōji	Toki Yoriyasu, Mino	Harima	Akamatsu
3.13.54	from Tōji to Yodo	Azumi Morikane	Harima	Akamatsu
3.13.54	Shichijō-Nishi Ōmiya	Kageyama Tokitomo	Bingo	Iwamatsu

Note: (*) indicates supporters of Ashikaga Tadafuyu (Southern Court); (†) fought under Niki command.

CHAPTER
3

The Sinews of War: Military Supply and the Consolidation of Regional Authority

War begun without good provision of money beforehand for going through with it is but as a breathing of strength and blast that will quickly pass away. Coin is the sinews of war.

Francois Rabelais, *Gargantua and Pantagruel*

Paradoxical as it may seem, endemic civil wars were waged on the crest of rising prosperity. Once the energies of people were no longer concentrated upon subsistence, their surplus wealth could be channeled into sustaining military bands. Political power flowed from this ability to manifest one's interests by force. Since military power depended upon the ability to extract surplus wealth, prosperity had the unintended consequence of increasing the number of those capable of asserting their rights. Political power ultimately accrued to those able to wield the most formidable fighting forces, which in turn depended upon their ability to link economic surpluses to the waging of war.

Japan prospered from the mid–thirteenth century onward as paddy lands were reclaimed and trade flourished. Elite demand in the cities of Kyoto and Kamakura fueled this growth, which, in turn, was spurred by Chinese specie flooding into the archipelago. Luxury industries clustered in the vicinity of the capital, although regional smithies were also established. With rising prosperity came increasing violence, as some came to possess the means to defend their rights. By 1333, perhaps several thousand warriors controlled enough resources to maintain bands of fighting men. These men had the means and the presence of mind to fight for whomever they pleased.

Most historians have assumed that political and military power in "premodern" societies was based on control over arable land. Ever since the seminal work of John Hall, ranking warriors (*jitō*) have been characterized as "land stewards" who collected rents and taxes in kind and not in cash.[1] Likewise towns and markets were thought to have remained underdeveloped and a cash economy was perceived as being next to nonexistent.[2]

Such an outlook is understandable, for a paucity of sources relating to trade has caused scholars to overlook the flourishing market economy of thirteenth- and fourteenth-century Japan. Nevertheless, as we shall see, this economy was based on a sophisticated network of trade, which in turn depended upon the exchange of cash. This trade flowed along contours established by political authority. Although these markets were driven by elite consumption, all regions witnessed increasing prosperity as goods and coin filtered into the countryside.

"Control" over the land was manifested by extracting revenue from it. Produce might be levied, of course, but increasingly it came to be translated into cash. Profit from trade also underpinned authority. Unlike the warriors of the early modern period who possessed a visceral, ideologically inspired disdain for wealth, their fourteenth century forebears were deeply involved in commerce and trade. Warriors amassed revenue through levies, moneylending, and trade in order to purchase those supplies—such as foodstuffs, horses, weapons, and armor—that were required for war.

War's most significant repercussions were systemic, for the existing socio-economic fabric was suddenly burdened with unprecedented demands, thereby forcing innovation upon those who desired to maintain the status quo. Battle typically entailed ruinous expenses. Local authority became increasingly precarious as fighting continued, because warriors steadily consumed their surpluses of political and economic capital. Although trade underpinned military power, the prosecution of war undermined trade, thereby causing some warriors to extract provisions from their lands instead of paying for them. Ultimately, most warriors either unilaterally assumed local powers or relied upon magnates for supplies and funds.

---

1. John Whitney Hall, *Government and Local Power in Japan* (Princeton: Princeton University Press, 1966), pp. 157–77. One finds on p. 177 reference to a levy in cash, but otherwise revenue is almost solely expressed in bales of rice (*koku*).
2. For a recent expression of this assumption, see Ikegami, *The Taming of the Samurai*, pp. 101–12.

The relentless need for provisions complicated the task at hand for both authorities and men of the provinces. The armies of the 1330s were plagued with shortages, for no institutionalized mechanisms existed for procuring provisions. Warriors were instead responsible for providing themselves and their followers with weapons and victuals. Hence, even the briefest of campaigns entailed a great economic burden. An army defending its homelands might rely upon harvested provisions, but one engaged in an offensive campaign could best secure supplies by paying for them.

Insufficient funds and not insufficient foods caused shortages in supply. Although a warrior's fighting prowess ultimately hinged upon his fiscal resources, even the wealthiest warriors were ill-prepared to supply themselves and their followers for an extended campaign. Some hard-pressed warriors stole grains, but most preferred to seize gold and valuables that could be exchanged as cash.

Military commanders struggled to keep their armies supplied. At times they might loan warriors extra suits of armor, or horses from their herd, but such haphazard attempts to alleviate their plight could not solve this endemic crisis. Generals and constables (*shugo*) seasoned by several years of war began to earmark revenue from parcels of land for supplies. Nevertheless, this provisional assignment of lands suffered from a fundamental flaw, for lands were finite but the demand for military service was less so. A further inadequacy was that revenue assigned to a particular warrior was not shared with others. A grant of land did not even ensure that its recipient would report to battle.

Military exigency necessitated innovations in state and society. Due to the limited scale and regional nature of battles fought after 1338, commanders were able to muddle through the logistical crisis that plagued their armies. With the renewed outbreak of full-scale war in 1350, however, these ad hoc measures proved hopelessly inadequate. The *bakufu*, controlled by Ashikaga Takauji, passed a far-reaching law in 1352 that authorized *shugo* to earmark half of a province's revenue for military provisions (*hanzei*), thereby linking the machinery of tax collection to the procurement of provisions. This law allowed commanders to control enough cash to bankroll their forces, thereby solving the endemic deficiencies of supply, and contributing, in the process, to the sudden appeal of the *shugo* office among the ambitious. The prohibitive expense of war forced most warriors to abandon their cherished autonomy and serve under *shugo*. Thus, *shugo* were able to translate fiscal powers into regional lordships and assume prerogatives that had hitherto been monopolized by the center.

The demands for provisions, the dictates of strategy, and the concurrent strengthening of regional political authority ensured that all areas became subsumed into the political sphere. As we shall see, areas that had hitherto enjoyed a degree of immunity, or "unattachedness" (*muen*), could no longer exist after

1333.[3] Armies torched and occupied these "immune" areas, thereby destroying the notion that they were somehow divorced from the political realm.

When war erupted in the 1330s, the fate of each competing regime was ultimately tied to its ability to generate support and to harness funds and supplies systematically. As the goal of authority became focused on the annihilation of opponents, the energies of public order became directed toward procuring troops, money, weapons, and supplies. Any authority that could not generate adequate support, revenue, or supplies suffered defeat and, ultimately, extinction. Because each regime's survival depended upon its successful prosecution of war, all other considerations were secondary. As long as two competing political entities remained, the relentless logic of war continued to be paramount. The goal of authority lay not in the accumulation of wealth and power as an end to itself, but rather in being able to exercise it in order to achieve military victory.

MATERIAL CONSTRAINTS

Production

Inadequate production proved to be the most unyielding constraint on sustainable military power. Weapons manufacture in fourteenth-century Japan is best characterized as a luxury industry. Demand was driven by elite consumption; hence, craftsmen tended to gravitate toward major political centers.[4] For example, an analysis of noted smiths reveals that there was a wave of migration to Kamakura after the *bakufu* was established. Smiths from western and central Japan (e.g., Bizen and Yamashiro) set up shop in Kamakura during the thirteenth century, but their numbers dropped off precipitously after the *bakufu* fell in 1333.[5]

Throughout the thirteenth and fourteenth centuries, Kyoto was the hub of arms production.[6] The most valuable products, such as armor, were crafted in the environs of the capital. Constructing armor was a laborious, time-consuming task, for approximately two to three thousand small lacquered

---

3. Amino Yoshihiko has published an enormously influential series of monographs in which he outlines the theory of "unattachedness" (*muen*). Amino postulates that certain geographic locations were detached from the jurisdiction of the state. Some of these areas include bridges, inns, temples, and graves. See Amino, *Muen kugai raku*, pp. 168–69.

4. For more on archeological traces of Kamakura smiths, see Kawano Shinchirō, *Chūsei toshi Kamakura* (Kodansha, 1995), pp. 235–36.

5. Honma Junji, *Nihontō* (Iwanami Shoten, 1939), pp. 11–16. Noted smiths in Sagami declined from eight to two after 1333. Of the eight famous smiths who had previously resided in Kamakura, one was from Yamashiro and two were from Bizen.

6. For an early reference to armor craftsmen residing in the Shichijō ward of Kyoto, see *Azuma kagami*, ed. Kuroita Katsumi in *Shintei zōho kokushi taikei* (Yoshikawa Kōbunkan, 1975–77), vol. 1, maki 6, 2.25.1186, p. 201.

plates had to be woven together. It generally required two years to create one set of armor, although in an emergency, a suit could be constructed in as little as ten months.[7] One can gain a relative sense of armor's worth from a Heian-era document—one suit of armor (ōyoroi) is worth four times as much as a more simplified type of armor (haramaki) and eight times as much as a sword.[8] Although archeological excavations have revealed that armor repairers resided in Kamakura,[9] the best armor seems to have been manufactured in Kyoto, as noted by the Kamakura official Kanazawa Sadaaki.[10]

Temple multiplexes, whose foundries produced Buddhist statuary, also functioned as sites of weapons manufacture. One long sword (ōdachi) produced in 1366 bears the name "Senjuin Nagayoshi." Here the smith adopted the name of the Senjuin valley, site of the workshops of smiths affiliated with Tōdaiji temple.[11] By the fourteenth century, even religious institutions of the far north, such as Dewa's Gassan, supported sword smiths.[12] Some temples even maintained "smith's fields" (tanji hatake) for their craftsmen.[13]

Religious institutions thus spurred the development of regional manufacturing. By the fourteenth century, the production of swords, for example, had been disseminated throughout much of Japan. One list of the most skilled smiths is as follows:[14]

> *Eastern Japan*: Sagami (2), Mino (5)
> *Central Japan*: Yamashiro (4), Yamato (2), Settsu (1), Ōmi (1)
> *Hokuriku*: Echizen (1), Kaga (2)
> *Chūgoku/Western Japan*: Inaba (1), Iwami (1), Bizen (9), Bitchū
>   (3), Bingo (3), Suō (1), Nagato (2)
> *Shikoku*: Tosa (1)
> *Kyushu*: Chikuzen (3), Bungo (1)

7. Takahashi, *Bushi no seiritsu bushizō no sōshutsu*, pp. 274–77. The number of plates in armor had steadily increased—in the eighth century, only about eight hundred were required.

8. HI 1679.

9. Kamakura craftsmen also produced armor, saddles, and other horse accoutrements. For a useful summary of archeological excavations in Kamakura, see Kawano, *Chusei toshi Kamakura*, pp. 235–36.

10. He stated, "Armor and simplified armor (*yoroi* and *dōmaru*) [produced in] the capital are of incomparably better quality than [armor produced in] other regions." KI 29258, Kanazawa Sadaaki *shojō*.

11. Unfortunately for the historian, in most cases smiths affiliated with temples did not sign their blades, thereby making it difficult estimate their overall productivity. For more on this weapon, located in Ehime's Ōyamazumi shrine, see *Nihon no kokuhō* 25, *Ehime* (Shūkan Asahi Hyakka, 8.10.97): (2–)141.

12. A sword inscribed with the name "Gassan" dating from the mid–fourteenth century can be found in the Dewa Sanzan Hakubutsukan. This sword was on display at the Nara Art Museum's "Gassan Sadaichi kaikoten" exhibit of 1.6–1.28.1996.

13. For the Kamakura-era reference to "smith's fields" in land registers, see *Fukui kenshi shiryōhen* 9, *Chū-kinsei* 7, Fukui Prefecture, comp. (Fukui, 1982–92), Myōtsūji *monjo*, document 17, Myōtsuji Inzu Raizen *okibumi utsushi*, p. 568. This document is a copy dating from 1365.

14. Honma, *Nihontō*, pp. 13–16. The number of smiths was, however, even more widespread than this list would suggest. According to pp. 11–13, noted smiths in the Kamakura era were found also in Mutsu, and in the Chikuzen, Chikugo, Higo, and Satsuma provinces of Kyushu. Smiths were active in Dewa as well. See note 12.

Most swords were either manufactured in the capital region, or in Bizen in western Japan. Anecdotal evidence also suggests that Bizen was a dominant manufacturing center of steel weapons.[15]

Production became increasingly regionalized as the fourteenth century progressed. Simplified armor and weapons came to be produced in the Kumano region of Kii Province. Not only were faceguards (*hōate*) produced, but both full armor (*yoroi*) and simplified armor (*haramaki*) were constructed in Kii Province and nearby Izumi.[16] One can also find references to Kii warriors wearing identical armor, though most died subsequently from arrow wounds, a telling indictment of its quality.[17]

Unlike smiths, who migrated to entrepots of trade, bow makers and other less sophisticated craftsmen resided in the provinces. For example, leather was used to bind lacquer plates of armor. Leather makers and dyers resided in Nuta no shō in Aki province.[18] Likewise, bow craftsmen congregated from central Japan westward, where bamboo—the raw material for first-rate bows—flourished. These men were specialists who produced bows throughout the year.[19] Finally, the finest horses were bred in the rugged pastures of the north (Mutsu), the east, or the uplands of Shinano.[20]

The capital was the locus of arms production, which contributed to the strategic necessity of controlling its environs. Although the Southern Court failed in this endeavor, and its sway over much of Japan was limited, provincial centers of weapons production remained under their control, which helps

---

15. *Taiheiki*, maki 14, "Shōgun onshinpatsu Ōwatari Yamazaki nado kassen no koto," p. 367, and maki 15, "Shōgatsu nijū shichinichi kassen no koto," p. 422, mention "Bizen *naginata*" and arrowheads (*yajirushi*) made at Bizen's Nagafune. One fourteenth-century arrow, now located in the Ōyamazumi shrine, was crafted by Kunimasa of nearby Iyo Province.

16. See *Taiheiki*, maki 23, "Hata Rokurō Saemon no jō Tokiyoshi no koto," p. 685 for reference to a faceguard (*hōate*) produced in Kumano. For the armor produced in Izumi and Kii provinces, see the *Shakuso ōrai*, in *Buki kōshō maki 6, Kaitei zōhō kojitsu shosō* 19, comp. Kojitsu Sōsho Henshūbu (1993), p. 246.

17. *Taiheiki*, maki 17, "Yamaseme no koto," pp. 507–10.

18. KI 6157, 2.1243 Kobayakawa ke *shōmon*. See p. 411 for the holdings of a leather dyer (*kawa some*), and vol. 10, document 7497, p. 339 for another reference to a leather dyer and a leather maker (*shirakawa tsukri*).

19. Bowmaking was a year-round profession. For example, the best time to cut bamboo was in the eighth lunar month, for wood, the fourth month. Composite bows could only be glued in spring and autumn. Most of this information stems from a conversation with Shibata Kanjurō, a Kyoto bow maker, on 12.9.1995. In addition, some of this craftsmen's lore can be gleaned from the *Taiheiki*, for we see references to the best arrows being produced from three-year-old bamboo. See maki 15, "Miidera kassen no koto," p. 432. Some arrows were treated in fire, or lacquered as well. See *Teijō zakki*, vol. 3, "Yumiya no bu," pp. 87–90.

20. A warrior bought one prized mount from Mutsu. *Genpei jōsuiki* (Kokumin Bunko Kankōkai, 1911), maki 36, pp. 906–7. For a reference to horses from Shinano not being dispatched for the *koma hiki*, which involved the presentation of horses to the emperor from throughout Japan, see *Entairyaku*, vol. 5, 8.17.1355, p. 37. Although compiled centuries prior to the fourteenth, the *Engi shiki*, Koten

to explain the long duration of the conflict.[21] Religious institutions maintained their position as regional centers of manufacture, although, as we shall see, *shugo* acquired the ability to produce weapons late in the fourteenth century. In short, diverse regions possessed comparative advantages in production.

The Market

Autarky was impossible in fourteenth-century Japan. No warrior could procure the arms and armor he needed without resorting to trade. High quality armor and weapons could only be purchased in the capital. Warriors from Mutsu and Shinano relied on sales of their horses to purchase needed goods, while those from the west levied a tax on bow makers, thereby providing themselves with ready access to a supply of bows. A bow maker from Nuta no shō, for example, was taxed ninety bows a year, with the largest share being reserved for the *jitō* and the estate manager (*azukari dokoro*) (thirty-two bows each).[22]

Trade flourished in thirteenth and fourteenth-century Japan. Markets were common. Something of their atmosphere can be gleaned from picture scrolls such as the *Ippen hijiri e*, where one can see a number of stalls engaged in the sale and exchange of pottery and other goods.[23] (See figure 27 = pl. 18.) Local authorities attempted to channel trade and control markets. For example, once Andō Taira Uemon Nyūdō Rensei created a port, "wealthy merchants built dwellings nearby, and boats plying their way to and from the capital invariably anchored there."[24] Archeological excavations in the city of Kamakura illuminate the developing economy of the thirteenth century. No coins exist prior to the advent of Kamakura rule in 1185, but gradually their numbers expanded, becoming a flood by 1300.[25] Kamakura served

---

kōkyūkai, comp. (Zenkoku Shinshokukai, 1992), reveals that more pastures were located in the four provinces of Shinano, Musashi, Kai, and Kōzuke (32) than the rest of Japan combined (27). The *Engi shiki* omits, however, the northern provinces of Mutsu and Dewa. Some horses were, however, raised in areas of western Japan such as Izumo. See *Taiheiki*, maki 13, "Ryūme shinsō no koto," p. 347.

21. At Ōmishima's Ōyamazumi shrine, one can still view a fourteenth-century long sword (*ōdachi*) created by a Yamato smith and inscribed with a Southern Court–era name.

22. KI 6157, 2.1243 Kobayakawa ke *shōmon*, p. 411. According to the same document, another maker was taxed thirty-six bows—seventeen to the *jitō*, two to the *azukari dokoro*, and seventeen to the state (*kōmotsu*). See p. 417. The rate assessed was apparently tolerable. According to Shibata Kanjurō, despite seasonal variation, a single bow maker can average approximately twenty to twenty-four bows a month.

23. Some analysis of this scene appears in Kuroda Hideo, "Ichi no kōkei," *Sugata to shigusa no chūseishi, Ezu to emaki no fukei kara* (Heibonsha, 1986), pp. 104–11.

24. "Mineaki," in *Hyōgo kenshi shiryōhen chūsei*, vol. 4, pp. 62–63.

25. Kawano, *Chūsei toshi Kamakura*, pp. 217–19.

Figure 27. The market of Fukuoka. Source: *Ippen hijiri e den*, scroll 4, page 7. Jishū Sōhon-zan Yūkōji. Photo courtesy Tokyo National Museum.

as a magnet for trade that attracted products and raw materials from through-out the archipelago.[26]

The outbreak of war led to a flurry of arms sales. Warriors from eastern Japan, for example, unable to produce bows of the highest quality on their own, instead had to purchase them from the west.[27] Well-to-do warriors, regardless of their origins, regularly bought new horses before going into bat-

---

26. Ibid., pp. 225–32. An immense amount of pottery from the Inland Sea and Ise areas was uncovered in Kamakura. For more on the nature of fourteenth-century trade, see Matsushita Shōji, ed. *Yomi-gaeru chūsei 8 Umoreta wanchō Kusado sengen* (Heibonsha, 1994).

27. *Hino shishi shiryōshu, Takahata Fudō tainai monjo hen*, document 28, Yamanouchi Tsuneyuki *shojō*. Admittedly, the origin of the bows Tsuneyuki ordered is not clear. Theft was also an option for those desperate to procure bows. See *Ino Hachimangū monjo*, ed. Tamayama Narimoto (Zoku Gunsho Ruijū Kanseikai, 1983), maki 2, document 26, Mune Taiyura *sojō*, and *Minoo shishi shiryōhen*, Minoo shishi hensan iinkai, comp. (Minoo, 1973), vol. 2, document 615, 9.18.1338 Gon no Risshi Kōyū *ukebumi an*, p. 19.

tle.[28] Even before battle was joined, warriors' finances were severely strained by the demands of military preparation. Those in dire need of cash could pawn their suits of armor, but this was a recourse of last resort.[29]

Battle constituted a financial risk as well, for the death of a horseman and the subsequent loss of his armor and mount translated into a considerable loss of capital. Some prohibitively expensive assets, such as armor, could not be easily replaced. Owing to its value, armor sometimes became the focal point of inheritance disputes.[30] The loss of even one suit could prove devastating. Conversely, warriors attempted to recoup their losses through the capture of horses—a "glorious" (and lucrative) prize,[31] or their accoutrements.[32] Warriors who received suits of armor as a reward for their military service acquired one of the most cherished gifts possible.[33] The fiscal burden of war forced most warriors to rely to a degree upon the largesse of their commanders.

No institutional mechanism assured armies of a steady flow of provisions from the outbreak of war in 1331 until 1352. In the absence of other support, warriors had to supply their own victuals, which proved burdensome in protracted campaigns. A series of letters uncovered in 1988, written by Yamanouchi Tsuneyuki, reveals the considerable tribulations a warrior had to endure. Tsuneyuki, while in Kamakura, asked his wife and family to sell one house (*zaike*) and use the proceeds to purchase dyed robes (*kosode*), which were essential for battle.[34] Tsuneyuki also requested relatives to ship him tea, dried persimmons, and chestnuts.[35] Accoutrements were Tsuneyuki's responsibility as well, as evidenced by the following complaint: "As I do not

---

28. *Genpei jōsuiki*, maki 36, pp. 906–7. Horses were expensive. For fourteenth-century prices of three or four *kan*, see *Fukui kenshi shiryōhen 9, Chū-kinsei 7*, Myōtsūji *monjo* document 40, 2.24.1365 Myōtsūji Rakandō *narabini* Shokudō *kuyō ryōsoku chūmon*, p. 585.

29. KI 13773, 11.30.1279 Shōgun ke *mandokoro gechijō* for reference to a pawned suit of simplified (*haramaki*) armor.

30. For a dispute in the Sagara family, see KI 5966, 11.25.1241 Kantō *gechijō*. For one in the Edo family, see KI 25139, 5.12.1314 Kantō *gechijō* (translated in Jeffrey P. Mass, *Lordship and Inheritance in Early Medieval Japan: A Study of the Kamakura Soryō System* [Stanford: Stanford University Press, 1989], document 142, pp. 281–83) and KI 28611, 12.12.1323 Kantō *gechijō* (translated in Mass, *Lordship and Inheritance*, document 148, pp. 288–89) concerning a contested inheritance which included armor, swords, and flags.

31. Soga Kōzuke no kami's capture of both a horse and human head earned him "great praise." See *Baishōron*, p. 107.

32. *Shizuoka kenshi shiryōhen 6, Chūsei 2*, document 456, pp. 221–22, and NBIK 2536.

33. NBIC 5389. This document could be a forgery, which ipso facto indicates that armor represented an ideal gift. See also *Taiheiki*, maki 36, "Nangun nyūraku Kyōsei botsuraku no koto," p. 1102, for the gift of a suit of armor and a sword.

34. *Hino shishi shiryōshū, Takahata Fudō tainai monjo hen*, document 27, Yamanouchi Tsuneyuki *shojō*.

35. Ibid., document 37, Yamanouchi Tsuneyuki *shojō*. Residual funds were to pay for bows. See document 28.

have a saddle and other equipment, I am forced to fight on foot."[36] "I needed a horse, and got one thanks to Eitono. I also borrowed a helmet, and have arrived at the front."[37]

Military encampments concurrently functioned as markets. The inflated prices of the camps further contributed to the hardship of warriors. Tsuneyuki, while in Kamakura waiting for a dispute to be adjudicated, complained that he possessed merely one container (*tō*) of saké, an amount insufficient to give to officials, and asked his son to buy more saké and ship it to Kamakura.[38] The financially strapped Tsuneyuki was ultimately forced to borrow two or three *kan* from a certain priest, Daishin bō.[39]

The financial strain of an extended campaign caused warriors to ignore both secular and divine authority. Warriors stole objects in order to pay for provisions,[40] while those in the most dire straits either sold their horses for food or broke down and ate them.[41] Likewise, during one campaign:

> the shogun issued a prohibition, but as time passed the soldiers . . . forced their way into the shrines and temples . . . and stole the sacred treasures. Later . . . [wooden statues of] lions, ponies and dogs were broken up for kindling, and statues of the Buddhas and sutras were sold to buy fish.[42]

Each camp constituted a captive market. Hence a swarm of itinerant merchants and middlemen plied their lucrative trade while hovering around the fringes of each camp. Some industrious souls even sold materials that they had scavenged from the battlefield.[43]

---

36. Ibid., document 38, Yamanouchi Tsuneyuki *shojo*.
37. Ibid., document 42, Yamanouchi Tsuneyuki *shojo*. Eitono (another name for Ebina perhaps?) was apparently a follower of the general of the campaign, Kō no Morofuyu.
38. Ibid., document 1, Yamanouchi Tsuneyuki *shojo*.
39. Ibid., documents 34 and 44, Yamanouchi Tsuneyuki *shojo*.
40. *Taiheiki (Keichō hon)*, ed. Gotō Tanji and Kamada Kisaburō in *Nihon koten bungaku taikei* (Iwanami Shoten, 1961–62), vol. 2, maki 16, "Oyamada Tarō Takaie aomugi o karu koto," p. 163. This section does not appear, however, in the oldest *Taiheiki* texts.
41. *Taiheiki*, maki 36, "Hatakeyama Nyūdō Dōsei botsuraku no koto," p. 1097. For a late thirteenth-century example of a warrior selling his horse and saddle in order to pay for a long journey, see the account of Takezaki Suenaga, in Thomas D. Conlan, *In Little Need of Divine Intervention* (Ithaca, N.Y.: Cornell East Asia Series, 2001), p. 86. For the eating of horses, *Baishōron*, pp. 136–37.
42. *Taiheiki*, maki 34, "Yoshiakira ason Nanpō shinpatsu no koto," p. 1016. The commander of the army, Hatakeyama Dōsei, was criticized as being "a hundred times worse than Kō no Moroyasu," one of the primary villains of the *Taiheiki*. Whether his army was in fact so ill-disciplined deserves further research.
43. *Gen'ishū*, p. 271. This accounts for the paucity of weapons and armor found at battle sites. See also Kawano Shinjirō, "Naze bugu ga shutsudo shinai ka," in Amino, *Yomigaeru chūsei 3 Bushi no miyako Kamakura*, pp. 222–23. Unusual circumstances surround archaeologically excavated weapons. For example, the two swords discovered near Seki castle and photographed in *Sekijō chōshi, Kodai chūsei shiryōhen*, comp. Sekikijō (Sekikijō, Ibaragi Prefecture, 1988) had been dropped in a swamp.

Trade and Blockade

Authorities were cognizant of the strategic value of trade. During times of war, commanders relied upon blockades to strangle their enemies, for an army starved of supplies rapidly disintegrated. Ashikaga Takauji brought Go-Daigo to his knees by throttling his supply lines and blockading the capital.[44] Once the seven roads to the capital were blocked, Go-Daigo's soldiers sustained themselves for a while by selling their horses, but they finally stormed the temples and houses of eastern Kyoto and stole food.[45] Although the Southern Court seized the capital three times after 1336, its partisans could not hold it because Northern Court supporters blockaded the capital's supply routes (one of which was known as "provisions road").[46] Kyoto was more vulnerable to blockade than to attack.

Besieged defenders relied on blockade runners to maintain their supplies. Mōri Motoharu, for example, boasted that he prevented a castle's capture by replenishing its depleted provisions after a series of running battles.[47] Conversely, besiegers attempted to block those who shipped goods into a castle, like a "base" (*genin*) follower of Hida Narabara Hyōe Jirō who was captured while on such a mission.[48]

As trade was the basis for procuring supplies, control over merchants and porters became strategically important. In battle areas, a sophisticated network of passes and tolls hindered desertion and prevented supplies from being delivered to the enemy. A pass was even required to forage for fodder such as beans for a general's horses.[49] Unhindered travel was guaranteed by passes, which were, of course, recognized by only one of the competing polities. Ashikaga Takauji, for example, issued the following order: "To the roadside forces (*roji gunzei chū*): Ōkawabe Saburō Saemon is joining our forces. Do not thwart his passage."[50] Safe passage for noncombatants was guaranteed in principle but not in fact. According to another order:

44. For the Ashikaga blockade, see *Shinano shiryō*, vol. 5, pp. 335–37; *Baishōron*, p. 134; and NBIC 403 for an order to stop all shipping on Lake Biwa. A document in the *Sugaura monjo*, in *Sōson no jiritsu to seikatsu*, comp. Shiga University (Shiga, 1996), pp. 4–5, document 19, recounts how the *hyakushō* of Ōura shimo no shō transported supplies across Lake Biwa when Go-Daigo resided at Sakamomo, at the base of Mt. Hiei.

45. *Taiheiki*, maki 17, "Sanmon no chō Nantō no koto," p. 522.

46. *Taiheiki*, maki 31, "Yawata kassen no koto," p. 933, and maki 32, "Miyako kassen no koto," pp. 974–77, 979–80, illustrate the military significance of a blockade. For the term "provisions road," see Kōsaka Konomu, *Akamatsu Enshin, Michisuke* (Yoshikawa Kōbunkan, 1970), p. 96.

47. NBIC 4065, 4665. See also *Aioi shishi shiryōhen*, comp. Aioi shi, vol. 8, no. 1 (Aioi Shi, 1990–95), document 407, pp. 415–17.

48. NBIK 810.

49. *Taiheiki*, maki 18, "Urifu Hangan hata o ageru koto," pp. 559–60.

50. Hozawa ke *monjo* document 4, 5.30.1333 Ashikaga Takauji *kasho*, in *Sendai shishi shiryōhen kodai chūsei*, comp. Sendai Shi (Sendai, 1995), p. 255.

The rebels of Hitachi's Seki and Taihō castles have fled this past eleventh and twelfth. I hear reports that they may sneak into [Mutsu] province. Set up barriers (*sekisho*) in all districts and guard these areas. Capture all suspicious looking people. If you use this as a pretext to hound merchants or travelers, you shall be punished.[51]

Exhortations not to "hound merchants" reveal how common this practice must have been. According to other documents, shellfish merchants were detained under the suspicion of being spies.[52] In short, the market underpinned the procurement of provisions, but warriors did not possess enough capital to maintain an adequate flow of supplies.

A complaint by the residents of Akanabe no shō aptly illustrates the disruptions caused by war:

> Since the winter [of 1335] the realm has been disordered. As it is impossible to set up markets, or [utilize] harbors, we have been unable to sell (*kokyaku*) our grains, and so money (*yotō*) is in short supply. . . . We have been waiting for peace to return, but in the ensuing days, armies (*gunzei*) of both courts passed through day and night. . . . [They have] forcibly entered the *shōen*, and taken countless oxen, horses, other valuables and even rice and beans. . . . We are nearing the point of starvation. . . . As a result of guarding the estate . . . the most egregious offenses have stopped, although the expenses [involved in guarding the area] defy calculation. Furthermore, as both a *shugo* and provincial governor (*kokushi*) are [stationed] in the province, we believed [the situation] would soon settle down, but orders to provide military forces, provisions (*hyōrōmai*), horses and other accoutrements continue unabated. In spite of [our compliance], we heard rumors that we were going to be branded as "enemy" and have hostages taken and our houses burned.[53]

One recourse adopted by generals lacking adequate funds was to rely upon political authority to secure supplies. Levies in kind proved problematic over the long term. Excessive exactions undermined the ability of *shōen* residents to sell their produce, which in turn led to a shortage of cash and a decrease in productivity.

Purchase proved to be the optimum mechanism for securing supplies.[54] As long as an army had sufficient capital, it could ensure a steady flow of

51. *Sekijō chōshi*, documents 93–94, 11.1343 Sōma Chikatane *ate* Ishidō Yoshimoto *gunzei saisokujō* and Shirakawa Yūki Chikatomo *ate* Ishido Yoshimoto *gunzei saisokujō*, p. 381.
52. DNSR, series 6, vol. 4, p. 244, of 6.11.1337.
53. *Gifu kenshi, kodai-chūsei shiryō*, comp. Gifu Prefecture (Gifu, 1969–72), vol. 3, document 367, p. 899.
54. This was true even prior to the outbreak of war in the 1330s. For a 1313 example, where "evil bands" (*akutō*) borrowed several hundred *kan* of cash from a temple in order to purchase provisions for war, see KI 26211.

goods. Some wealthy merchants (*fukunin*), such as a certain Uokaeshi Saishō no bō, bankrolled armies by paying for their provisions.[55] Nevertheless, such men could only provisionally pay for an army's supplies. Uokaeshi's army held out in a castle for six months, until both the defenders' resolve and his pocketbook were exhausted. An army could only be sustained when the vast resources of public revenue were mobilized for military use. This innovation arose after a decade and a half of experimentation.

POLITICAL AUTHORITY AND SUPPLIES

Armies engaged in extended campaigns seemed to prefer plundering valuables to grains. One army, unable to secure supplies in the vicinity of the capital, went to Kaga, where they stole countless artifacts from shrines and temples over a period of ten days.[56] Temples presented a natural target because of their wealth. During the outbreak of hostilities in 1333, for example, Nikaidō Dōun ransacked Kinpusenji and stole its valuables.[57] Some generals, such as Kō no Moroyasu, plundered gold grave goods from the ancient mounded graves (*kofun*) that dot the Yamato basin.[58]

Some wealthy generals strove to alleviate the situation of hard-pressed warriors by paying for their supplies. Nawa Nagatoshi, who held considerable stores of rice and provisions, paid for the transportation of the bales by giving five hundred *zeni* to each porter; soon, according to the *Taiheiki*, he had five thousand bales (*koku*) of rice.[59] Hard-pressed leaders, such as Kitabatake Chikafusa, had to rely upon gifts, such as seven *ryō* of gold dust, to pay for the provisions of his Taihō castle.[60] Generals were ideally responsible for provisions and provided, whenever possible, horses, saddles, weapons, shields, suits of armor, and cash

---

55. For references to his supplying a castle with provisions, see NBIK 810.

56. *Taiheiki*, maki 20, "Echigo no sei Echizen ni uchikoeyuru koto," p. 622.

57. *Kinpu jinja monjo eshabon* (Manuscript copy. Tōkyō Shiryōhen Sanjo), 2.1334 Yamato Kinpusen Kichisui-in *inzu* Shinhen *funshitsujō*.

58. *Entairyaku*, vol. 2, 2.3.1348, p. 300. Moroyasu authorized this during his 1348 offensive against the Southern Court "pretender" (*gishu*). This characterization is that of the courtier Tōin Kinkata. See DNSR, series 6, vol. 11, p. 376, and *Entairyaku*, vol. 2, p. 292.

59. *Taiheiki*, maki 7, "Sentei funa-ue rinko no koto," pp. 179–80. Texts differ on whether Nawa Nagatoshi paid fifty or five hundred *zeni*. The "Hōki no maki" also claims Nagatoshi paid two hundred *kan*. In any event, Nagatoshi was a wealthy merchant. See Hyōdō Hiromi, *Taiheiki "yomi" no kanōsei* (Kōdansha, 1995), pp. 81–83 and the Nawa genealogy.

60. *Sekijō chōshi*, document 86, 5.1343, Shirakawa Yūki Chikatomo Saemon no jō *gon ate shōshō shojō*, p. 377. For other examples of Chikafusa pleading for cash, see *Sekijō chōshi*, document 74, 11.1342 Shirakawa Yūki Chikatomo *ate* Hōgen Senshū *shojō utsushi* and document 75, Shirakawa Yūki Chikatomo *ate* Hōgen Senshū *shojō tsuijō*.

(*yotō*).[61] Nevertheless, the cost of war soon exceeded the resources of even the wealthiest commanders.

Generals who lacked the funds to pay for supplies chose instead to rely upon their authority to force temples, which were replete with weapons, horses, and fodder,[62] to provide bows and quivers of arrows on demand, along with cash, swords, and "a mountain of supplies, ranging from military provisions (*hyōro*) . . . to 'rice chaff' (*nuka*) for horses."[63] Some religious institutions were levied troops as well, such as Takeo shrine, whose representative was ordered to provide "one horse fully equipped, each with one bow, one [quiver of] arrows, one shield (*koshitate*) and one foot soldier."[64]

Although generals might order religious institutions to supply their armies with weapons and fodder,[65] their demands enabled some temples and shrines to secure a patron in the process. For example, Katsuoji performed the "service" of providing twenty bales of rice as provisions.[66] Katsuoji later relied upon this general (Prince Moriyoshi) to grant them a confirmation of disputed land rights, based upon a forged document. In an age of instability, a "payment" in the form of a land grant or confirmation constituted an enduring form of remuneration.

Generals also encouraged followers to extort supplies. One such order states, "You may borrow supplies from the districts (*gun*) of Kōrai and Sonoki."[67] Although warriors themselves lacked the authority to unilaterally confiscate lands, they could rely upon orders from above to justify any particular seizure.[68]

61. For the loaning of materials, see *Hino shishi shiryōshū, Takahata Fudō tainai monjo hen*, documents 38, 42, Yamanouchi Tsuneyuki *shojō*; for armor, *Taiheiki*, maki 26, "Shijō nawate kassen no koto," p. 782; for horses, NBIC 4071 and *Kitabatake Chikafusa monjo shūko*, comp. Yokoi Akio (Dai Nihon Hyakka Zensho Kankōkai, 1942), p. 289. Examples of monetary loans appear in *Kano shiryō, Nanbokuchō* I, pp. 295–96, Kanazawa bunkō bō *shojō*, while a comprehensive delineation of a general's responsibilities is elucidated in *Baishōron*, p. 114.

62. See, for example, KI 24228. A photograph found in *Shūkan Asahi hyakka, Shiro to kassen Nihon no rekishi bekkan Rekishi o yominaosu* no. 15 shows that even as late as the nineteenth century, temples maintained impressive stockpiles of weapons. Temples could supply, among other things, "horses, saddles, bows and arrows, swords, *naginata*, cloth and provisions." *Taiheiki*, maki 24, "Yoshisuke ason Yoshū gekō no koto," p. 701. This section is missing from some versions of the *Taiheiki* and located in different chapters in other versions. For a reference of Ashikaga Takauji receiving "horses and armor" from Munakata shrine, see *Baishōron*, p. 101.

63. *Taiheiki*, maki 29, "Shōgun oyako ontaishitsu no koto," p. 862; for Katsuoji providing fifty bows and quivers, see *Minoo shishi shiryōhen*, vol. 2, document 614. Katsuoji later complained of the theft of three swords (*tachi*), twelve short swords, and thirty *kanmon* of cash. See Ibid., documents 615 and 624.

64. NBIK 495.

65. See KI 32079 for an order to a temple to provide provisions for five days.

66. KI 32436.

67. NBIK 1066.

68. NBIC 4260. Miyoshi Michihide claimed that Yamanouchi lands were appropriable, and received an edict (*kudashibumi*) legitimating his claims before forcibly entering the lands. See also *Entairyaku*, vol. 2, 2.5.1348, p. 300.

Another method of securing supplies was to tax the lands that one controlled. The earliest attempts, in this case money for a "bow levy" (*kyūji sen*), are coterminous with the first major battles of 1333.[69] Nevertheless, because war disrupted trade, some authorities came to prefer levies in kind to cash. By the mid–fourteenth century, for example, horses and kettles were requisitioned.[70] As one had to adopt the mantle of public authority in order to secure supplies,[71] one's political control over a particular region was soon translated into a mountain of food and material.[72] Levies in produce were not subject to inflation. Likewise, those defending their lands did not need to rely on trade as much as armies on a campaign did. In this regard, those who exercised direct political control over a province possessed an inherent advantage over those fighting far from their homelands.

Conversely, expeditionary forces advancing into enemy territory faced grave difficulties. Some astute generals counteracted the inherent advantage of local defenders by launching a sudden attack, harvesting the provisions of neighboring *shōen*, and conscripting the residents as laborers.[73] In other cases, an army would not advance until it had seized the autumn harvest.[74]

Nevertheless, this reliance on produce contributed to the long-term impoverishment of the provinces. Once an estate was plundered, it could not resupply an army for some time. Commanders quickly realized the counterproductivity of ransacking estates and chose instead to grant lands to their troops, who extracted revenue or produce as they saw fit. The first example of lands being granted for military provisions appears in 1339.[75] This innovation was soon copied by the Southern Court.[76] A few years later, Kō no Moroyasu, in the midst of his campaign against the Southern Court, divided

---

69. *Okayama kenshi, iewake shiryō*, comp. Okayama Prefecture (Okayama, 1986), document 212, 11.1333, Niimi no shō *higashikata jitō kata denpata narabi ni nengutō saimotsu chūmon*, pp. 577–78. A total of one *kan* nine hundred *mon* was levied.

70. *Tōji hyakugo monjo*, 11.1358 *hyakushō moshijō*, and Imatani Akira, "Jū-yon go seiki no nihon," *Iwanami Kōza Nihon tsūshi 7 chūsei 1* (Iwanami Shoten, 1993), pp. 24–25. During the Kannō disturbance, Sasaki Dōyo seized a herd that was destined for the imperial stables as part of the *koma hiki* ceremony of the eighth month. Only six beasts eluded his grasp and reached the capital. *Entairyaku*, vol. 3, 8.16–19.1349, pp. 103–4. For the theft of horses, see *Gifu kenshi*, vol. 3, document 367, p. 899, and *Entairyaku*, vol. 6, 11.9.1359, p. 307.

71. Horses appear to have been a partial exception. Some generals seem to have given warriors mounts from their personal herds. See *Taiheiki*, maki 18, "Urifu Hangan hata o ageru koto," p. 559 and *Hino shishi shiryōshū, Takahata Fudō tainai monjo hen* document 42.

72. The integral relationship between supplies and control is evident in the following passage: "Because the Kusunoki have controlled Kawachi and Izumi for two years, they have collected an immense amount of supplies." *Taiheiki*, maki 6, "Akasakajō kassen no koto," pp. 153–56.

73. *Taiheiki*, maki 37, "Hatakeyama Nyūdō muhon no koto," p. 1115.

74. *Baishōron*, p. 112. For autumn and winter being the best times to launch campaigns, see *Zoku gunsho ruijū bukebu* 25.1, p. 78.

75. *Hirakata shishi 6, shiryōhen 1*, comp. Hirakata Shishi Hensan Iinkai (Hirakata, 1969), Tsuchiyashi *monjo* document 12, 8.16.1339 Hosokawa Akiuji *kakikudashi*, p. 225.

76. *Habikino shishi, shiryōhen*, comp. Habikino Shi (Habikino, 1981–85), vol. 2, document 96, 8.21.1340 Musha dokoro *chō*, and document 102, 1.14.1345 Go-Murakami tennō *rinji*.

lands and granted half of them to his troops for provisions.[77] The tendency to grant lands for provisions originated in those areas of southern Kyushu and central Japan where warfare was endemic.

A grant of land rights was an ongoing source of income that was well-nigh irrevocable. Even if a general attempted to cancel these rights, the warrior adversely affected would resist with the tenacity of the wronged, and switch his allegiance to a rival. Hence all grants of land would generate both allies (the recipients) and enemies (the dispossessed). Thus, although supply was based upon monetary transactions, this method of securing wealth and provisions was based upon political rights. Unfortunately for these generals, potentially appropriable parcels of land were finite, while the demand for military service knew no bounds.

This quandary was resolved in 1352 by the *hanzei* edict, which allowed *shugo* to earmark half of a province's tax revenue for securing provisions. With a stroke of the brush, *shugo* could alleviate the situation of financially strapped warriors, establish a system of patronage, directly appropriate goods, and mobilize labor.[78] Hence, warriors who were appointed *shugo* soon exceeded their non-*shugo* counterparts in wealth, prestige, and power. In a stark contrast to their unappointed brethren, *shugo* constructed castles and shipped supplies at public expense.[79] Laborers were conscripted, and lumber and charcoal were procured at the bequest of public authority. Some *shugo*, such as the Akamatsu, even established foundries.[80] Although powerful warriors were also able to levy "bow taxes,"[81] their authority paled in comparison with that of *shugo*. Accordingly, after the mid–fourteenth century, the acquisition of the *shugo* office became essential for those aspiring to become magnates.[82]

77. *Tannowa monjo* (Original manuscript. Kyoto University Museum.), 10.27.1348.
78. CHSS, vol. 2, amendment (*tsuikahō*) 56, p. 29. This has been translated by Kenneth A. Grossberg and Kanamoto Nobuhisa, in *The Laws of the Muromachi Bakufu: Kemmu Shikimoku (1336) and Muromachi Bakufu Tsuikahō* (Monumenta Nipponica and Sophia University Press, 1981), p. 48. For contemporary references to the *hanzei*, see *Takaishi shishi 2, Shiryōhen* 1, document 196, 12.1359 Ōtori no shō *ryōke shiki shomu ukebumi*, and NBIC 5386.
79. Documents relating to Yano no shō reveal this most clearly. See NBIC 3216–7 for references to a number of porters being used to carry provisions to castles controlled by the Akamatsu (*shirahatajō*), and also being used to harvest lumber for the *shugo*'s new Kinoyama castle. See also NBIC 5266 for reference to laborers being conscripted by the *shugo*, and 5417, 5531 for the *shugo*'s procurement of charcoal and firewood, and for the conscription of several men as messengers. For complaints about the intolerable burden of taxes, see NBIC 5386.
80. Surviving tax records indicate that charcoal was taxed in 1388 and 1410. The first reference to "smith charcoal (*kaji sumi*)" appears in 1410. *Aioi shishi* 8.1, p. 807, document 665, Gakushū kata *nengu tō sanyōjō narabi ni mishin chōfu*, 2.9.1410. References to "*shugo* charcoal" appear in the 1360's. Ibid., p. 260, document 276, Gakushū kata *nengu tō sanyōjō*. See also Imatani, "Jū-yon go seiki no nihon," pp. 30–31.
81. NBIC 4263.
82. Mori Shigeaki has pointed out in his *Taiheiki no gunzō*, p. 249, that after the Kannō disturbance, competition for *shugo shiki* became severe. For perceptive studies on the limitations of the powers of

The Warrior's Burden

Warriors flexed their authority in order to defend their lands, rights, and pre-rogatives. With the outbreak of war, these men had to transform the geography of the provinces from one in which convenience and mobility were paramount to one in which the movement of people and goods could be controlled and defended. Avenues of trade were barricaded while dwellings were abandoned in favor of defensible locales. Hence a flurry of construction commenced with the onset of war. A finite amount of available lumber exacerbated the situation, for a considerable number of shields and barricades were required for this task.

When news of war's outbreak reached Sōma Shigetane early in 1336, for example, he ordered his son Mitsutane to:

1) build a castle within the moats of Kotaka in Namekata district (*gun*), Ōshū Province, and from there to hold off enemy rebels;

2) try to persuade those enemy relatives and *gokenin* of the [neighboring] seven districts to switch sides; and

3) put some two hundred bales (*koku*) of rice from Sue Kurō Saemon no jō into the castle as provisions. In addition, all the villages under the control of the Sōma relatives should order the resident tax collector (*kyūshu*) to ensure [that provisions be dispatched to the castle].[83]

Mitsutane relied upon local authority to construct fortifications and collect provisions. Mitsutane's mandate was enormous. To understand the magnitude of the task that awaited him, let us turn our attention to provisions and fortifications.

PROVISIONS

Since drinkable water was plentiful in Japan, warriors did not need to bring their own supply. The only time water became of critical importance was during the siege, for its absence ensured the defenders' surrender.[84] Saké was, however, indispensable. Warriors often drank saké on the eve of battle and carried it, along with a bag of food, in their quiver (*ebira*).[85] Saké helped

---

pre–1352 *shugo*, see Urushihara Tōru, "Nanbokuchō shoki ni okeru shugo kengen no ichi kōsatsu," *Komonjo kenkyū* 27 (July 1987): 57–72, and "Nanbokuchō shoki ni okeru shugo hakkyū kanjō ni kansuru ichi kōsatsu," *Komonjo kenkyū* 38 (March 1994): 18–31.

83. *Sōma monjo*, document 27, 2.18.36 Sōma Shigetane *sadamegaki*. The *kyūshu*, often a priest, was a resident of the *shōen* who was entrusted with collecting revenue, and who received a portion of this revenue as his salary.

84. *Taiheiki*, maki 6, "Akasakajō kassen no koto," pp. 154–56.

85. For an example of the drinking of saké prior to battle, see *Aro Monogatari*, p. 129; for warriors carrying saké (and fish), see *Taiheiki*, maki 26, "Shijō nawate kassen no koto," p. 780.

fortify their resolve, and indeed, a military manual advised, "when going to battle, you should drink saké."[86]

The phrase "saké and fish" became a metaphor for provisions in general, which indicates their ubiquity.[87] Other foods consisted of beans, which, along with *nuka* (rice chaff), were also used for fodder.[88] Warriors occasionally ate venison.[89] The dietary staple was apparently grains, such as barley, wheat, or rice, along with beans.

Sōma Mitsutane preferred extracting two hundred bales of rice because it fulfilled the immediate military imperative of stocking his fort with supplies. Although this was less profitable than selling these grains, military exigency overruled other considerations. Several hundred bales were necessary if a castle was to have any chance of surviving a siege.[90]

FORTS AND BARRICADES

Prior to the fourteenth century, permanently manned castles did not exist. Warriors lived in fortified dwellings with prominent earthen walls through the 1330s. Although the walls of these dwellings may have deterred random robbery attempts, they were unable to withstand concerted attacks.[91] With the onset of warfare, warriors took to building barricades with alacrity.[92] Many were hurried affairs. For example, according to a complaint by the residents of an estate, the manager (*daikan*) of Tara no shō commandeered the harvest for military provisions, and then forced the residents of the estate to dig moats and "build a castle." The raw materials for this "castle" consisted

86. *Heihō reizuisho*, p. 59. At times, after an unsuccessful attempt to storm a castle, the triumphant defenders sent some saké to fortify the defeated attackers. "It is customary to send saké to [enemy] encampments and it is proper to request saké [from the enemy] on the field of battle." *Genpei jōsuiki*, maki 22, p. 528.

87. See *Taiheiki*, maki 17, "Urifu Hangan kokoro kawari no koto," p. 541, and maki 18, "Echizen no kokufu ikusa no koto," p. 562, and *Genpei jōsuiki*, maki 22, p. 526.

88. *Taiheiki*, maki 18, "Urifu hata o ageru koto," pp. 559–60, mentions laborers scouring the mountains for beans. For *nuka*, see maki 29, "Shōgun oyako ontaishitsu no koto," p. 862. Warriors also plundered rice and beans from *shōen*. See *Gifu kenshi*, vol. 3, document 367, p. 899.

89. *Genpei jōsuiki*, maki 36, p. 899.

90. The *Taiheiki* refers to warriors collecting "several hundred *koku*" of provisions, while the figure of seven thousand *koku* seems to be referring to an immense quantity of supplies. *Taiheiki*, maki 23, "Hata Rokurō Saemon no jō Tokiyoshi no koto," p. 683. For seven thousand *koku*, see maki 18, "Urifu hata o ageru koto," p. 560. "Several tens of thousands" of *koku* were apparently considered sufficient to withstand a siege of several years. See maki 36, "Hayami Shirō kokoro kawari no koto," p. 1094. For more on requisitioning bales of rice, see *Hyōgo kenshi shiryōhen chūsei*, vol. 6, p. 138, 12.23.1363, Ōyama no shō *teishi* Dōshō *kishōmon*, and KI 32436.

91. For example, the Mataga residence, near Kikugawa in Shizuoka Prefecture, is ringed with extensive earthen works. Nevertheless, when warfare erupted, the Mataga constructed fortifications in the nearby hills of Yokochi.

92. Armies constructed bridges as well. For examples of residences being dismantled by armies to make bridges, see *Taiheiki*, maki 31, "Hachiman kassen no koto," p. 935. See also maki 14, "Shōgun onshinpatsu no koto," p. 407.

of the lumber from a certain Ryōgen's fields (*myōpata*) and dwellings (*zaike*), which were obtained after the *daikan* claimed that he had an order to destroy the dwellings of the *hyakushō* in order to build fortifications.[93] Many of these hastily built structures were only fleetingly manned. For example, one erected on 3.6.1346 endured one assault ten days later, but quickly succumbed on 5.4.1346—a life span of slightly under two months.[94]

Fortifications did not conform to a single pattern. Some were only manned in times of crisis, while others were a suitably reinforced dwelling.[95] Still others were located within the precincts of mountain temples.[96] Regional variation was such that dispersed mountain castles predominated in central and western Japan, while a cluster of supporting structures dominated the mountainous countryside of Kyushu. Elaborate ramparts compensated for the relatively disadvantageous terrain of the east. For example, Seki castle, built on the plains of Hitachi, was able to withstand a prolonged siege chiefly because of the care taken in its construction.[97] Some areas, however, witnessed no pronounced pattern. In north central Japan, one can pinpoint nine mountain castles, eight located on hills, four situated at the base of mountains, and seven constructed on level ground.[98]

Fourteenth-century castles were humble affairs, far less imposing that the enormous structures of the early modern period. The most illuminating visual source for these forts is the fourteenth-century *Rokudō-e*, which depicts a besieged mountain castle.[99] (See figure 28 = pl. 19.) Bow-wielding defenders, perched behind rough barricades and moats, are numerous, and yet no permanent walls or towers are evident. The barricades that are depicted appear flimsy.[100]

---

93. *Dai Nihon komonjo iewake* 10, *Tōji hyakuga monjo*, comp. Tōkyō Teikoku Daigaku Shiryōhensanjo (Tōkyō Shiryōhensanjo, 1925), vol. 1, pp. 709–12, *Tōji hyakugō monjo, ha*, 8.1334 Wakasa Tara no shō *hyakushōra moshijō narabi ni kishōmon*.

94. *Toyama kenshi, Shiryōhen chūsei*, comp. Toyama Prefecture (Toyama, 1975), document 279, p. 266.

95. Compare the wording of documents 13 and 14 of the *Motegi monjo*, most conveniently located in *Tochigi kenshi shiryōhen chūsei*, vol. 3, pp. 80–81. See also Saitō Shin'ichi, "Honkyo no tenkai; 14–5 seiki no kyokan to jōkaku yōgai," *Chūsei no shiro to kōkogaku* (Shinjinbutsu Ōraisha, 1991), pp. 247–48.

96. To mention a few examples, Kusunoki Masashige constructed fortifications near Kongōsan; Tsuchiya Munetada describes how temple buildings *inside* his castle were destroyed in an attack. See *Hirakata shishi* 6, Tsuchiyashi *monjo* document 8, 11.1337 Tsuchiya Munetada *gunchūjō*, p. 224.

97. The remains of saps constructed by the besiegers of Seki were discovered early in the twentieth century. See Seya Yoshihiko, *Ibaragi ken no rekishi* (Yamakawa Shuppansha, 1975), pp. 76–77.

98. Satō Kiyoshi, "Tokue Yorikazu chūjō ni mieru Nanbokuchōki Echizen no shiro to kassen ni tsuite," *Fukui kenshi kenkyū*, no. 9 (March 1991): 29–52, particularly pp. 42–44. I am indebted to Usami Masaki for bringing this article to my attention.

99. For a highly informative article, see Fujimoto Masayuki, "Chūsei no eiga ni mieru chusei jōkaku," *Chūsei jōkaku kenkyū*, no. 8 (July 1994): 4-43. See also his "Eishō bunko shozō 'Aki no yo no nagamonogatari' ni mieru jōkaku ni tsuite," *Chūsei jōkaku kenkyū* 10 (1996): 330–33.

100. For the fragility of walls, see *Hyōgo kenshi shiryōhen chūsei*, vol. 3, p. 363, Kuge *monjo* document 3, 3.5.1337 Niki Yoriaki *kanjō*.

Figure 28. Fourteenth-century castle under attack. Source: *Rokudō-e*, "Jindō no kuso." Permission granted by Shōjuraikōji. Photo courtesy Nara National Museum.

In times of desperation, fortifications were erected in inhospitable terrain.[101] Strategically constructed fortifications were built, however, near vital roadways in order to block supply routes.[102] Such structures were easily resupplied. Nevertheless, even the most invincible forts could be starved into submission. Accordingly, the most formidable sites were part of a network of supporting strong points that were impervious to blockade.[103]

These castles were small. In Echizen, Northern and Southern Court partisans were entrenched in fortifications separated by little more than a few kilometers.[104] Only a handful of warriors manned each castle. According to the *Hakata nikki*, fifty were stationed in one,[105] while sixty defended another.[106] One of the largest castles was defended by a hundred men.[107] Even when an attack was successfully repulsed, the defenders were too few to pursue the defeated enemy.[108]

Dwellings were also commandeered to billet troops.[109] According to the *Hakata nikki*, some fifty men manned one particular castle, while five hundred hid in nearby villages.[110] On other occasions, as in the case of Tara no shō, dwellings could be dismantled for their lumber. The homes of the well-to-do could even be converted into forts.[111] As no clear distinction was evident between fortifications and "civilian" residences (*zaike*), both were put to the torch when attacked.[112]

Armies building defensive structures likewise destroyed *zaike* in order to deprive an attacking army of a ready source of lodging and materials for

---

101. Shirahata castle, where Akamatsu Enshin successfully held off Nitta Yoshisada's attack in early 1336, was built in such mountainous terrain. Kōsaka, *Akamatsu Enshin, Michisuke*, p. 52. For another example, see *Genpei jōsuiki*, maki 22, p. 525.

102. *Taiheiki*, maki 19, "Nitta Yoshisada Echizen no fu o otosu koto," p. 599. For another example, see *Taiheiki*, maki 38, "Miyakata hōki no koto," p. 1131 for the Akamatsu, who, expecting an enemy attack, "built a castle in Ōyama and blocked the road to Tajima."

103. *Taiheiki*, maki 19, "Nitta Yoshisada Echizen no fu o otosu koto," p. 599. The situation depicted in the petition for reward of Gotō Motokage is illustrative. Two sections of an enemy's defenses were captured on the twenty-fifth day of the fourth month, but the final structure was not captured until two additional weeks had elapsed. *Hyōgo kenshi, shiryōhen chūsei*, vol. 2, pp. 718–19, Gotō *monjo* document 13, 5.1352 Gotō Motokage *gunchūjō*.

104. Satō, "Tokue Yorikazu chūjō ni mieru Nanbokuchōki Echizen no shiro to kassen ni tsuite," p. 35.

105. "Hakata Nikki," p. 554.

106. NBIC 4646. When the castle fell, "thirty disemboweled themselves and thirty were taken prisoner."

107. *Fukushima kenshi* 7, Yūzōkan Yūki *monjo*, document 69, 2.12 (1351)Yūki Akitomo *shojō*, p. 442.

108. NBIK 1374.

109. NBIK 1109.

110. "Hakata nikki," p. 554.

111. For reference to building fortifications (*jōkaku*) in the residence (*jūtaku*) of a person named Tōkaku, see *Takaishi shishi*, vol. 2, document 93.

112. *Hyōgo kenshi shiryōhen chūsei*, vol. 3, Azumi *monjo* document 10, p. 6. Dwellings might also be burned prior to battle. See *Taiheiki*, maki 38, "Hosokawa Sagami no kami uchishi no koto," and 10.1338 Kawachi no kuni Takaki Hachirō Hyōe no jō Tōmori *gunchūjō* (Migita *monjo keizu uragaki*), for the deeds of 8.18.1337. Up to several hundred dwellings might be incinerated. *Sōma monjo*, document 39, 2.22.1337 Sōma Chikatane *gunchūjō*.

counterfortifications. One army burned all the houses in a five mile (*li*) perimeter.[113] Another army, after dismantling dwellings to use for their castle, consigned all remaining structures to the flames.[114] The construction of fortifications and the defense of those fortifications impacted the lives of all those unfortunate enough to live nearby.

SHIELDS

Many of the "outrages" associated with the outbreak of war stemmed from the chronic demand for shields. Although some made do by using tatami or lacquering screens, most preferred shields of solid wood.[115] Temples were a favorite source of shields.[116] According to a complaint by the Anyōji, a marauding army "tore down the temple's bath house for shields, and destroyed its dormitory for firewood."[117]

Most foot soldiers, seeking protection from projectiles, charged from behind shields.[118] An immense number of shields had to be replaced after each skirmish.[119] Accordingly, the temptation to dismantle temples and shrines and to clear forests in order to replenish them proved irresistible.[120] Shortly after one battle, Hosokawa Kiyouji tore apart the reliquary (*shari*) doors of Tōji in order to secure shields, an act which appalled the courtier Tōin Kinkata.[121] The "outrages" which accompanied the prosecution of war transcended customary boundaries and prohibitions. In response to these unprecedented violations, encompassing regulations were issued. Political authority had to guarantee immunities in order to ensure their preservation.

The Consolidation of Regional Authority

In order to prosecute battle, warriors had to translate their authority into a reallocation of revenue, lands, and supplies for military use. The burdens of an extended campaign were so great that all available resources came to be utilized, even from areas that had previously enjoyed tax exemptions or other

---

113. *Taiheiki*, maki 18, "Urifu Hangan hata o ageru koto," p. 560.
114. See NBIK 2536 for the actions of the 5.1343. See also the upper right hand corner of figure 28, pl.19.
115. Reference to two or three hundred "tatami shields" appears in *Taiheiki*, maki 29, "Shōgun oyako onjōraku no koto," p. 857. For lacquered shields and shields made from bamboo and boxes, see the "Mineaiki," in *Hyōgo kenshi shiryōhen chūsei*, vol. 4, p. 65. Shields depicted in picture scrolls such as the *Kasuga gongen kenki-e* are almost invariably constructed of wood. See figure 24, pl 17. For shields in another scroll, see figure 21, pl. 14.
116. NBIK 495.
117. NBIC 306, 394.
118. For such a battle scene, see *Kasuga gongen kenki-e*, in *Zoku Nihon no emaki*, vol. 13.
119. For a catapult (crossbow?) (*ishiyumi*) destroying many shields, see *Taiheiki*, maki 30, "Sattasan kassen no koto," p. 900. For references to shields being used and destroyed in battle, see KI 32044, 32080.
120. *Taiheiki*, maki 32, "Miyako ikusa no koto," pp. 974–75.
121. *Entairyaku*, vol. 5, 3.24.1355, p. 13, and Ogawa Makoto, *Ashikaga ichimon shugo hattenshi no kenkyū* (Yoshikawa Kōbunkan, 1980), pp. 119–20.

immunities. This breakdown in previously recognized immunities caused local authorities to issue prohibitions. These prohibitions ultimately functioned as an assertion of political responsibility over these spheres, for the revocation of immunities had to be enforced.

Amino Yoshihiko has postulated that medieval society is best characterized as consisting of areas of "unattachedness" or "sanctuary" (*muen*). According to his hypothesis, bridges, way stations, graveyards, and temple compounds were detached from the authority of the state.[122] Nevertheless, these areas of sanctuary offered scant protection from marauding armies. (See figure 29 = pl. 20.) Such immune (*muen*) regions are better conceived as constituting peripheral areas to the administration of the state. Once these regions assumed importance, their immunities ceased to exist. For example, the case of bridges is indicative. Although some historians have characterized bridges and stations as possessing a sacral, otherworldly aura,[123] during times of war, their strategic value became paramount. Some bridges were guarded and fortified with towers while others became the sites of battles or were torched.[124] Conceptions of "otherworldly" aura did little to stop warriors from burning bridges, bathhouses, or stations, or from encamping in *muen* regions. One army even camped in the macabre location of a graveyard![125]

In sum, once the need arose, and the attention of authorities became concentrated on peripheral regions, fragile immunities were simply ignored. Once military power was wielded, it could not be easily curtailed; once immunities were compromised, they could not be successfully reasserted. War transcended all boundaries, negated all immunities, and forever transformed the political and economic terrain.

CONCLUSION

Nothing was exempt from the requisites of war. At times, buildings and bridges were destroyed. Areas spared from physical destruction were nevertheless forced to provide funds, provisions, manpower, and weapons to armies. The

---

122. Furthermore, Amino asserts that "unattached" (*muen*) social orders, such as priests, commoners (*bonge*), merchants, and women were immune from the vagaries of warfare, a topic which I address in chapter four. Mary Elizabeth Berry, in a similar argument, discusses "protocols designed to limit violence." See her *The Culture of Civil War in Kyoto*, pp. 31–32.

123. Amino, *Muen, kugai, raku*, pp. 164–76, particularly p. 169.

124. For the former, see NBIK 543, 756, 905; NBIC 222, 595, and *Shinpen Saitama kenshi*, p. 239, 9.30.1336 Beppu Yukitoki *gunchūjō* for action on Ōwatari bridge. See also NBIC 654, Nomoto Tomoyuki *shisoku* Tsurujūmaru *gunchūjō*. For the guarding of bridges, see NBIC 731, and the 11.4.1350 Onjōji *monjo* document in *Nanzan junjū roku tsuika* 3, in *Shinkō zōho shiseki shūran* 7 (Kyoto, 1967), pp. 83–84; for the latter case of burning bridges, see DNSR, series 6, vol. 14, pp. 58–59, 12.1350 Ōhara Kosaji *gunchūjō*, and NBIC 4269, p. 127.

125. *Yoshida ke hinami ki*, 5.24.1402, partially transcribed in DNSR, series 7, vol. 5. Compare this to Amino, *Muen kugai raku*, p. 153–64.

Figure 29. Non-combatants fleeing the battlefield. Source: *Aki no yo no nagamonogatari*. Possession of the Idemitsu Museum of Arts.

exigencies of warfare placed demands upon institutions and society that hastened the pace of change. And, as we shall see in the following chapter, these transformations altered the very structure of society as well.

Cash purchases played an essential role in keeping armies supplied in the field. Warriors might rely upon their own lands for food and provisions, but they were not self-sufficient. Weapons and victuals had to be purchased or plundered. Although the need for money was great, warriors were not initially remunerated in cash. Instead, they were granted *shiki*, or rights to land revenue. Land rights were, however, finite, and could only be transferred with difficulty. Some suffered severe financial hardship. Others fought to retain rights which had been confiscated by one polity or another. Hegemons labored under difficulties as well, for grants of lands satisfied the grantees, but angered the dispossessed.

The responsibility for supplies remained with public authority. This authority was delegated to regional commanders, be they generals, *shugo*, or provincial governors. The epochal 1352 *hanzei* edicts, which allowed *shugo* to use half of a province's tax revenue to procure military provisions, enabled those fortunate few who were appointed *shugo* to outstrip their counterparts in wealth and military power. Indeed, the powers *shugo* wielded superseded all existing judicial and political immunities. An army's insatiable appetite for supplies ultimately led to the creation of regional magnates, who assumed powers with the Ashikaga *bakufu*'s blessing that had hitherto been the sole prerogative of the state. Powers delegated to provincial figures continued to elude the grasp of the reconstituted state for some time to come.

CHAPTER 4

Status Creation, Social Mobility, and War

The name that can be named is not the eternal name.

Lao-tzu, *The Way of Lao-tzu*

In the intensely hierarchical society of fourteenth-century Japan, the status of each man determined his rights and obligations. Competition for estate and property was condoned among equals, but condemned between men of diverse status. Hence, those men belonging to privileged orders strove to clarify the boundaries of their order and create social distinctions, while those who aspired to raise their lot in the world relied upon ambiguities to muddle their origins, thereby making social mobility possible.

Warfare proved conducive to social mobility—those adept at fighting could rise in the world while the inept might sink in status—but at the same time, the rights and privileges of all were buffeted by the inherent unpredictability of battle. Nevertheless, the most profound legacy of battle transcended individual success and failure, for, as a result of war, the matrix of rights and privileges that pervaded society subtly shifted in unforeseen ways.

Not only might this result in changes in social identity—that is, distinct groupings coalescing into a single order; previously inchoate distinctions hardening into divergent orders; or a gradual shifting in the composition of some orders—but the very basis of status determination might shift. In this last instance, as we shall see, the body of rights and privileges encompassed by social status evolved from being prescriptive, or determined by confirmation, to being performative, or determined by wealth and by the ability to wage war and maintain control of economic resources.

Status terms constitute markers that enable one to reconstruct a fluid social order. Much like radioactive isotopes, these terms serve as traces that reveal the nature of a particular social system. Their gradual decay or shift in meaning, or for that matter, the appearance of new categories, reveal sea changes in social identification that otherwise remain obscure. The meaning of these terms did not shift at a constant rate; rather, periods of barely perceptible ebbing were punctuated by tidal swings corresponding to times of war.

The term *hyakushō* constitutes one such residue of social change. This word initially designated all members of society who had not attained the fifth court rank or above. Save for a coterie of nobles (that is, those appointed to the fifth court rank and above), "*hyakushō*," or quite literally, "[members of] the hundred surnames," identified all members of society who held an obligation to pay taxes (literally *kōmin*, or "the public").[1]

The existence of a general term to describe nearly all members of society reflects the egalitarianism of eighth-century Japan. State administration was geared to ensure that all, save those possessing court rank, would be treated alike. Accordingly, each man, woman, and child was assigned parcels of agricultural land on the basis of sex or age. These lands were redistributed, in theory, upon death. Beginning in the late eight century, however, this system of equitable land redistribution began to misfire sporadically after developers of the land were allowed to transmit their parcels by heredity. These exceptions began to clog the machinery of administration, thereby lengthening the intervals between cycles of redistribution until finally the whole system sputtered to a halt. Once this happened, the principle of egalitarianism was dead, and the separate strata of powerful locals and disenfranchised tenants separated further.[2]

---

1. Proof that *hyakushō* described people ranking as high as the sixth court rank can be found in HI 181. This document mentions the "*hyakushō*'s residence" of Hata Sukune Ariyo, who was of the sixth court rank. Initially, this term appears to have been read as *hyakusei*, but phonetically written passages reveal that is was pronounced as "*hyakushō*" during the fourteenth century. See NBIK 1182, and the *Migita monjo*, 12.12 (1347) Ōtsuka Koremasa *shojō*, in Yokoi, *Kitabatake Chikafusa monjo shūkō*, p. 639. For a brief commentary of the high status of *hyakushō* in the Ritsuryō period (seventh through eighth centuries), see Amino Yoshihiko, *Chūseishi o minaosu* (Yushisha, 1994), p. 55.

2. The most powerful provincials continued to be known as *hyakushō*. For a fine summary, see Kimura Shigemitsu, '*Kokufū no bunka' no jidai* (Aoki shoten, 1997), pp. 51–53. For "*hyakushō*" who possessed enough resources to reclaim land, see HI 50 and 60.

Although the term *hyakushō* lost its comprehensive meaning, no distinct social orders crystallized while society remained at peace. Through default, "*hyakushō*" came to designate provincials who possessed surnames and were entrusted with *shiki* office. Contemporary word associations suggest that "*hyakushō*" was synonymous with holders of local public office, be they *gunji, toneri,* or *zaichō kanjin,* and with *shōen* estate officers (*shōkan*).[3] A "*hyakushō* petition" dating from 1150 was signed by an estate manager (*gesu*) and several other *hyakushō,* all of whom possessed surnames.[4] Nevertheless, with the outbreak of war in the 1180s, a new status of provincial warriors coalesced from the ranks of *hyakushō.*

One legacy of the Genpei war (1180–85) was that a hierarchy of rights and privileges was created. When Minamoto Yoritomo rebelled in 1180, he relied upon his own authority to issue confirmations. Some of Yoritomo's early edicts (*kudashibumi*) were directed to the *hyakushō* of a particular district or estate.[5] Nevertheless, at the same time, Yoritomo created a distinct order of *gokenin* that encompassed those provincials who served him in battle.[6]

Gokenin status became predicated upon the performance of guard duty and the possession of documents (*kudashibumi*) from Kamakura. Although the creation of *gokenin* allowed some provincials to claim membership in a hitherto unknown social entity—that is, that of a "honorable houseman" (*gokenin*)—the advantages of their newly found status were not initially clear to all. Guard duty entailed a considerable burden, while the privileges of *gokenin* status were not explicitly delineated. Likewise, the durability of Yoritomo's regime was not manifest to his contemporaries.[7] Nevertheless, as time passed, privileges, codified by Kamakura law, accrued to *gokenin.* By the mid–thirteenth century, the benefits associated with *gokenin* status

---

3. For references to "*gunji, negi,* and *hyakushōra*" being ordered to enforce an order, see HI 2133; for the "Nabari *gunji narabi ni hyakushōra*" being commanded to stop the despoilments of Ōno no shō residents, see HI 2202; and, finally, for mention of *zaichō kanjin gunji hyakushō,* see HI 2876. For references to *shōkan hyakushō,* see HI 4892, p. 3791; for a variation "*shōkan to ii; hyakushō to ii,*" see HI 3687.

4. See HI 2709 for a petition submitted by the *hyakushō* of Yūge estate, which included the *gesu,* Taira Sukemichi, and ten other *hyakushō* who possessed surnames such as Minamoto, Taira, or Fujii. See also HI 2712 and 3305. Taira Sukemichi's name was written highest on the paper and last, typical for the ranking signer of a document. For another list of *hyakushō* composed of priests and surnamed elites, see HI 4237. Finally, a list of *hyakushō* dating from 1185 lists "Taira Kunimoto, Tanba Takeyasu, and Takeno Munetō," HI 4261. Munetō was, at the very least, highly literate, for he signed his name with an elaborate monogram (*kao*).

5. See HI 3972 and 5073. For similar orders, issued by men other than Yoritomo, see HI 3806 and 4021.

6. For one reference to the *gokenin* of the various provinces, see HI 3974. For the most recent coverage of this, see Jeffrey P. Mass, *Yoritomo and the Founding of the First Bakufu* (Stanford: Stanford University Press, 1999), particularly pp. 93, 141–55.

7. I owe much of this analysis to a conversation with Kondō Shigekazu on 8.22.1997.

outweighed the burdens of guard duty.[8] Thereupon, the most ambitious men of the provinces aspired to become *gokenin*.

There existed no ironclad method of determining who was in fact a *gokenin*. Kamakura initially compiled province-wide registers, but these lists were not made public, and they were not updated. All descendants of *gokenin* who possessed authority over some lands could claim to be of that status, and, as time passed, it became impossible to judge who was descended from these original *gokenin*. In the absence of any other certificate of *gokenin* status, those who were descended from *gokenin*, or for that matter, aspired to become *gokenin*, thirsted for documents from Kamakura, for these pieces of paper concurrently functioned as "proof" of their *gokenin* rank.

Although the *bakufu* lost control over the creation of *gokenin* to heredification, Kamakura's ability to certify *gokenin* remained unquestioned. Every scrap of paper issued by Kamakura allowed its recipient (or his descendants) to claim to be a *gokenin*. Hence all documents issued by Kamakura were jealously guarded. The social significance of Kamakura's documents enhanced the prestige of the regime.

Kamakura lost its monopoly over status certification during the tumultuous years of 1331–33. The outbreak of war led to a proliferation of documents as each competing political entity dispatched mobilization orders to all noted provincials, irrespective of their rank. All men who received these documents became *gokenin*. In other words, civil war ensured that status was no longer expressly linked to the Kamakura *bakufu*, or for that matter, to any single political regime, but rather based upon the ability to wage war. Nevertheless, warrior status was determined by both prescription and performance, for military service remained linked to the possession of documents.

After warfare erupted, a comprehensive social order gained currency: those who were capable of performing autonomous military action, irrespective of their origins, became known as *tozama*, while *miuchi* were their dependent followers. The distinction between *gokenin* and non-*gokenin* vanished as all powerful provincials crystallized into a single *tozama* order. The leveling of *gokenin* and non-*gokenin* into a single performative order was coterminous with the onset of war.[9]

Battle provided some men with an opportunity to change their status. This could be achieved several ways. One was for *miuchi* retainers to usurp the prerogatives of *tozama* after amassing military might. Another was for members of the base orders (*genin*)—men who lacked a name and were ineligible for remuneration although obligated to fight—to receive a name and become

---

8. By the later thirteenth century, *tokusei*, or "virtuous government" edicts, ensured that *gokenin* could repossess pawned lands, which thereby increased the appeal of *gokenin* status.

9. Nevertheless, the term *gokenin* was used throughout the fourteenth century. Conversely, the term *tozama* predates the annihilation of Kamakura and yet continued to be used, with varying meanings, for centuries.

catapulted into the ranks of *miuchi* retainers. Conversely, some *tozama*, weakened after defeat, might chose to become another's retainer. And finally, there were those who could take advantage of the opportunity that war provided and adopt a new social identity. With the outbreak of war, the division between noble scions and provincials dissolved. Those who fought together considered each other equals. *Tozama*, irrespective of their provincial or capital origins, referred to each other as "comrades." Likewise, women who fought in battle were treated as "comrades." Status distinctions, in other words, outweighed differences in gender.

The most profound transformation engendered by war was that status determination became decoupled from prescriptive confirmation. *Tozama* status was characterized by autonomy in war, and warfare was becoming a prohibitively expensive endeavor. As the fourteenth century progressed, few controlled sufficient resources to act with autonomy. The burden of war was so great that the descendants of *tozama*, even if they suffered no devastating setbacks, could no longer afford to maintain enough military might to preserve their autonomy. For those *tozama* who possessed indisputable proof of their status, and yet struggled to maintain their independence, the need to secure sufficient funds overruled all other considerations. *Tozama* in need resorted to selling their cherished documents of investiture, while those who encountered success could buy documents and enhance their status.

Instead of written legitimation, practical control over economic and military resources assumed ultimate importance. The ability to extract revenue and to mobilize manpower from landholdings, and to profit from the markets that flourished within them, proved to be essential for asserting or maintaining *tozama* power. Authority could no longer create a status with a piece of paper; instead, status had to be bolstered by wealth and power. Control of land and wealth became the ultimate determinate of *tozama* status. This shift arose as a result of seventy years of civil war.

The glacial evolution of society was punctuated by periods of rapid change, the catalyst for which was war. In order to comprehend the transformations of the fourteenth century, it is first necessary to analyze how the social matrix coalesced in the aftermath of the battles of the twelfth, and how tensions and ambiguities mounted throughout the intervening 150 years.

THE ORIGINS OF GOKENIN

Hyakushō and Gokenin

Gokenin were apparently created from the ranks of *hyakushō* during the Genpei war (1180–85), but this informal term was not standardized until 1189, when Minamoto Yoritomo called on men "capable of fighting" from throughout the archipelago to "bring their weapons" and join his offensive against the Northern Fujiwara. These men, who displayed the functional ability to fight, began to be systematically enrolled as *gokenin* from 1190 onwards.[10] Nevertheless, it is important to remember that these *gokenin* were selected from the ranks of provincials of the *hyakushō* order.

The *hyakushō* origins of *gokenin* are significant for several reasons. The first is historiographical. Until the groundbreaking work of Amino Yoshihiko, *hyakushō* were generally equated with "peasant" agriculturalists. The thrust of Amino's thesis is that *hyakushō* were not merely agriculturalists; instead they fished, traded, and produced goods.[11] Amino has also pointed out that *hyakushō* initially referred to all men who paid taxes,[12] but he nevertheless fails to mention that all warriors were once *hyakushō* as well. This curious omission is also reflected in the writing of Thomas Keirstead. Keirstead has astutely indicated that the designation *hyakushō* was based upon hereditary right, making the English rendering of "peasant" problematic. He states: "Although enmeshed, like the serf, within an estate-based agrarian regime that extracted land rents and labor services, *hyakushō* did not belong life and limb to the lord. They were juridicially free and could own and alienate land, and their right to leave an estate was established in law."[13] Keirstead correctly emphasizes that "the *hyakushō* is defined here as that which is *not* of servile rank or tainted by criminality,"[14] but he nevertheless ultimately chooses to define *hyakushō* as "the normative peasant subject of the shōen system."[15] This characterization is problematic, for the *hyakushō* of the twelfth and thirteenth centuries included office-holding managerial elites— men who have been, until now, classified as "warriors." The simple fact that an estate manager, a warrior, and a *hyakushō* could be the same person prior to 1180 necessitates a rethinking of eleventh and twelfth-century Japanese history.

Second, the fact that *gokenin* arose from the ranks of *hyakushō* set off a chain reaction in which men attempted to create as many social distinctions as possible. Before 1180, or 1190 for that matter, no clearly defined set of privileges and responsibilities had accrued to any social group. Rather, the

---

10. For the most recent elaboration on this topic, see Mass, *Yoritomo and the Founding of the First Bakufu*, pp. 141–42, 151–55 and 93. For earlier coverage of *gokenin*, see "Yoritomo and Feudalism," in Jeffrey P. Mass, *Antiquity and Anachronism in Japanese History* (Stanford: Stanford University Press, 1992), pp. 78–88.

11. For Amino's recent ruminations on *hyakushō*, see *Nihon chūsei ni nani ga okita ka* (Nihon Editor's School, 1997), particularly pp. 45–68.

12. For a brief commentary of the high status of *hyakushō* in the Ritsuryō period, see Amino, *Chūseishi o minaosu*, p. 55.

13. Thomas Keirstead, *The Geography of Power in Medieval Japan* (Princeton: Princeton University Press, 1992), pp. 25–27.

14. Ibid., p. 28.

15. Ibid., p. 158.

term *hyakushō* retained its residual meaning of "the public." Nevertheless, once a distinct order of *gokenin* crystallized, then those office-holding elites who did not become *gokenin* began to develop an aversion to their *hyakushō* identity, for it implied inferiority to others—such as *gokenin*—who had once been their equals. Powerful *hyakushō* asserted their own rights and privileges by adopting new names and establishing new identities.

The parameters of the *hyakushō* order remained unclear because, unlike newly created categories, such as *gokenin*, this term came to delineate a social category by default. What had once designated "the public" now began to exclude the most powerful men of the provinces. To be a *hyakushō* was to belong to a group of men inferior to the captains of local society.

Hyakushō were obligated through custom to act collectively[16] and to pay their taxes. In other words, *hyakushō* labored under horizontal obligations to their peers and maintained no encompassing bonds to a "lord." *Hyakushō* ties with authority, then, were collective. Those who became *gokenin* were liberated from the need to achieve consensus with their peers.

Those *hyakushō* who entered into a direct relationship with Kamakura during the 1180s and 1190s became known as *gokenin*. The distinction between these *gokenin* and those who remained *hyakushō* is evident in a 1238 regulation (*kotogaki*), which states that "all those confirmed [as *gokenin*] received an investiture edict (*onkudashibumi*) [from the Kamakura *bakufu*] while those [without an edict] are nothing but *hyakushō* (*hyakushō ni ochirareru beki nari*)."[17] thereby establishing the prescriptive nature of *gokenin* status. Although *gokenin* were the superiors of *hyakushō*, the social distance between the two groups was not yet necessarily vast. Initially, only the possession of an investiture edict separated *gokenin* from *hyakushō*.

Nevertheless, this investiture edict proved to be profoundly important, for *gokenin* were no longer obliged to achieve consensus with their peers. Rather, their ties with authority became paramount. In other words, by sacrificing their vertical autonomy, these newly anointed *gokenin* were able to act independently from their (former) equals. Such autonomy contributed to the appeal of *gokenin* status. With privilege came new obligations. *Gokenin* were, for example, forced to perform guard duty on behalf of the *bakufu*.

Kamakura wielded great power in the provinces, for each document of investiture penned by the scribes of the *bakufu* functioned like a magic wand transforming a provincial "maid" (*hyakushō*) into a "Cinderella" (*gokenin*).

---

16. Such as, "the custom of *hyakushō* [consists of acting] in accord (*ichimi*)"; see KI 6254, 11.25.1243 Rokuhara *saikyojō*.
17. KI 5243, 5.14.1238 Kantō *gechijō an*. A more precise designation for this document appears in *Hyōgo kenshi, shiryōhen chūsei*, vol. 1, 5.14.1238 Tadaiin no shō *shōmu no jōjō kotogaki*, Tada Jinja *monjo* document 15, pp. 236–37.

Hence ambitious locals strove to curry favor with the *bakufu*, and cherished all communiqués as "proof" of their *gokenin* status.[18]

The decay of the term *hyakushō* was gradual, for men of exalted rank continued to be designed as *hyakushō* a generation after *gokenin* first appeared. For example, in 1203, the *hyakushō* of Yoshikawa kami no shō signed an agreement in which the "estate officers and temple priests resolve to be in accord."[19] Twenty-two Hōkōji priests and thirty-three *hyakushō* signed this document. Among the latter were the *kumon*, Tachibana; the deputy *jitō*, Fujii; the *azukari dokoro*, Fujiwara; and the "new *kumon*," Yama.[20] All thirty-three of these men were literate, and each signed the document with an elaborate monogram. Thus, as of 1203, the *hyakushō* of Yoshikawa kami no shō constituted a regional elite that dominated this estate's local administrative apparatus. At the very least, the Fujii, Fujiwara, and Yama would have belonged to the "warrior order," for they held name and office and possessed administrative responsibilities. These men, in contrast to *gokenin*, possessed limited individual autonomy. They acted collectively as evidenced by their signing of the agreement of 1203. Nevertheless, because they were appointed to estate offices, they possessed more authority than did their non-office-holding *hyakushō* peers, thereby rendering the designation of the latter problematic. Increasingly, *hyakushō* began to prefer being referred to as *myōshu*.

Myōshu

Once some men established ties to the Kamakura regime and became designated as *gokenin*, the formerly encompassing label of *hyakushō* lost its appeal as a social designation. Those powerful men of the provinces who possessed no ties to the Kamakura *bakufu*, or chose to remain aloof, tended to distinguished themselves from their less powerful brethren by adopting the label *myōshu*, or lord of the *myō*.

18. For assertions that "non-*gokenin* do not individually receive documents," see KI 27089, 7.7.1319 Kantō *gechijō*, p. 165.

19. *Hyōgo kenshi shiryōhen chūsei*, vol. 2, Hōkōji *monjo* 1, 8.5.1203 Yoshikawa kami no shō *hyakushōra renshojō*, pp. 114–15. Hōkōji managed this estate and was invested with *bettō shiki*. See ibid., p. 739. This document has been translated by Jeffrey P. Mass, *The Kamakura Bakufu: A Study in Documents* (Stanford: Stanford University Press, 1976), document 56, p. 77, and appears as KI 1373, although all but four names are inexplicably missing from this published version. Examples of *hyakushō* holding estate offices were not limited to Yoshikawa no shō. For other references to *gesu* and *kumon hyakushōra*, see *Hyōgo kenshi shiryōhen chūsei*, vol. 2, Daisanji *monjo* document 3 of 2.10.1183. p. 69. For a Minamoto Yoritomo *kudashibumi* addressed to *hyakushō* (lit., *hyakushō no tokoro*), see HI 5073.

20. In addition, there were two other Fujii, three Fujiwara, three Yama, two Minamoto, two Hioki, four Takemukai, two Ishino, two Ayando, two Shima, one Tomo, one Waida, one Kamimura, one Hayashi, two Taki, and one Doshi.

Myō constituted an artificial unit of landholding liable to taxation.[21] The person originally assigned to collect taxes on these lands adopted the term "lord of the *myō*" in order to asset his privilege of collecting these taxes. The first such reference to a *myōshu* appears in 1047, but this term was clearly an autogenic designation.[22] References to the "office of *myōshu*" (*myōshu shiki*) do not appear until after the consolidation of the Kamakura *bakufu* in the 1190s.[23] This "office" continued to be coveted by those possessing considerable local authority.

Thirteenth-century *myōshu* were not, as it has commonly been assumed, "peasants." Rather, they were ranking provincials who possessed considerable authority. Something of the status of a *myōshu* can be gleaned in one example which appears shortly after the Genpei war. Tachibana Mitsuie, a *hyakushō* who had been divested of his estate office (*gesu shiki*), petitioned for a unit of taxable land, referred to as a *myō*, in order to be able to assess a corvée on other *hyakushō*.[24] Thus, those men who possessed taxable lands could make levies on *hyakushō*, thereby padding their purses and distinguishing themselves from their "inferiors" in the process.[25] Ultimately, *myōshu* were able to translate their powers of taxation into local lordships. Indeed, by the early fourteenth century, the term *myōshu* was synonymous with *jinushi* (地主); "the lord of the land."[26] *Myōshu* established social distance from other *hyakushō* and achieved a degree of autonomy from them, for *hyakushō* were, as we have seen, customarily bound to act collectively.

The creation of the *myōshu* order generated considerable social tension, for *myōshu* began to consider themselves roughly equal in rank to *gokenin*. Nevertheless, an important distinction remained. Unlike the prescribed status

---

21. For a fine summary of the debate concerning the status of the *myō*, see Keirstead, *The Geography of Power in Medieval Japan*, pp. 46–51, 66–67.

22. The first reference to a *myōshu* appears in HI 646, but was, in the opinion of Dana Morris, purely a fictitious name. See Morris, "Land and Society" in Donald Shively and William McCullough, eds., *The Cambridge History of Japan*, vol. 2 (Cambridge: Cambridge University Press, 1999), pp. 222–23.

23. Although Hara Hidesaburō equates tenth century elites with "*myō*" in his "Denshi to tato to nōmin," *Nihonshi kenkyū* no. 80 (November 1965), Ōyama Kyōhei's assertion that *myōshu shiki* originated coterminous with the founding of the Kamakura *bakufu* seems correct. See his "Nihon chūsei shakai to nomin," *Nihonshi kenkyū* no. 59 (March 1962). One can trace the development of *myōshu shiki* through documents translated by Mass in *The Kamakura Bakufu*, documents 44–46, 78, and in *Lordship and Inheritance*, documents 49, 112; see also *Lordship and Inheritance*, p. 97. Hitomi Tonomura also provides an informative survey of the *myō* and *myōshu* in fourteenth and fifteenth-century Ōmi in her *Community and Commerce in Late Medieval Japan: The Corporate Villages of Tokuchin-hō* (Stanford: Stanford University Press, 1992), pp. 82–88.

24. KI 869. For Mitsuie's dismissal as the estate's *gesu*, see KI 495.

25. For a document attesting to the distinction between *myōshu* and *hyakushō* see KI 24079.

26. KI 24079. This reference clearly distinguishes *myōshu* from *hyakushō*. Some *myōshu* even possessed enough local authority to act as guarantors for bills of sale. *Dai Nihon komonjo iewake 6, Kanshinji monjo* (Tōkyō Teikoku Daigaku Shiryōhensanjo, 1917), document 285, 12.21.1306 Sō Keijun *denchi baiken* pp. 220–21. This document is not found in KI.

of *gokenin*, the rank of *myōshu* was solely based upon de facto control over land instead of investiture edict from Kamakura. Possession of an edict was all that separated the two groups; otherwise *myōshu* and *gokenin* were practically the same. Beginning in the early thirteenth century, for example, some *myōshu* fought in battle,[27] and by 1273 other *myōshu* resisted serving guard duty in the capital under a *jitō*'s command,[28] which indicates that *myōshu* came to consider themselves to be the equals of *gokenin*. On the contrary, *gokenin* originally invested by the *bakufu* naturally considered themselves to be superior to *myōshu*. Inasmuch as *gokenin* status was determined in practice by the possession of communications from the Kamakura regime,[29] non-*gokenin* did what they could to be on the receiving end of such documents. Nevertheless, in 1284 the Kamakura *bakufu* attempted to alleviate the tension between *gokenin* and *myōshu* and, at the same time, assert its control over the latter by confirming (*ando*) the office (*shiki*) of *myōshu*.[30] Although parity between *myōshu* and *gokenin* remained a debated issue, *myōshu* were able to successfully distance themselves from *hyakushō* during the course of the thirteenth century.

Thirteenth-Century Hyakushō

In spite of the disassociation of *gokenin* and *myōshu* from the aegis of "*hyakushō*," those who continued to use the old label out of ignorance, conservatism, or a lack of ambition were nevertheless elites and not "commoners" or "peasants." Although *hyakushō*, the most numerous local elite of the Kamakura period, remained bound to act collectively, they might actually possess their own weapons[31]—such as the case of one who owned "two short swords, two long swords (*tachi*), three bows, and two quivers (*koshi*) of arrows (*ōya*)."[32] Indeed, as Asakawa Kan'ichi observed, the Kamakura-era *hyakushō* were "resident upon land . . . capable in an instant's notice of donning their armor, saddling their horses and riding out to battle as fully

27. *Myōshu* fought in the Jōkyū war. See KI 31881 and Jeffrey P. Mass, *The Development of Kamakura Rule, 1180–1250: A History with Documents* (Stanford: Stanford University Press, 1979), p. 19.
28. KI 11464, 11.14.1273 (Bun'ei 10) Gyōkenra *rensho hōsho utsushi*. For fourteenth-century complaints of *myōshu* intransigence, see NBIK 1255, 1261.
29. During the Kamakura period, one man successfully defended his claim of being a *gokenin* by claiming that he had received a document from a Kamakura official. See KI 28933, 12.21.1324 (Shōchū gannen) Kantō *gechijō an*.
30. KI 15302, 9.10.[1284] Hōjō Naotoki *shojō* and CHSS, vol. 1, amendment 514, p. 252. For more on this, see Mass, *Lordship and Inheritance*, p. 97. For a 1282 petition requesting *bakufu* confirmation of *myōshu shiki*, see KI 14590. This document has been translated by Mass, ibid., p. 244, document 112. This policy of confirming *myōshu*, instigated by Adachi Yasumori in 1284, was abandoned shortly after his assassination in 11.1285. See Murai Shōsuke, *Hōjō Tokimune to Mōko Shūrai: Jidai, sekai, kojin o yomu* (NHK Books, 2001), pp. 210–24.
31. KI 18512.
32. *Ino Hachimangū monjo*, maki 2, document 26, Sixth month (1330?) Sō Taifura *sojō*, pp. 21–22.

equipped soldiers."[33] Some *hyakushō* even possessed unfree servants (*genin*).[34] (See figure 30 = pl 21.)

Nevertheless, the social designation of *hyakushō* possessed enough appeal that "commoners" began a creeping association with higher-ranking *hyakushō* by adopting the term of "cultivator (*sakunin*) *hyakushō*" to describe themselves during the later decades of the thirteenth century.[35] This blurring of distinctions between cultivators and *hyakushō* elites was furthered by the tendency of some thirteenth-century *hyakushō* tended to become beholden to their superiors. The *hyakushō* Tachibana Shigemitsu, for example, was obligated to his lord, a *myōshu* named Terashima.[36]

In the thirteenth century, social ambiguities and contextualized identities were tolerated. Tachibana Shigemitsu was, in the context of an estate, a *hyakushō*, and yet he also was a retainer to his *myōshu* lord. Shigemitsu was

Figure 30. Armed *hyakushō*? Source: *Konda sōbyō engi emaki*, scroll 1, "Ōjin tennō no misasagi o chikuzō suru dan." Possession of the Konda Hachiman shrine. Photo courtesy Habikino city Bunka rekishi shiryōshitsu.

33. Kan'ichi, Asakawa, *The Documents of Iriki* (Japan Society for the Promotion of Science, 1955), p. 207.
34. KI 30628.
35. For a 1272 example of the term "cultivator (*sakunin*) *hyakushō*," see *Minoo shishi shiryōhen*, vol. 1 document 265, undated (circa 1272) Gein no shō *hyakushō* Hase Yoshinobu *moshijō an*. See also *Takaishi shishi 2 shiryōhen* 1, document 175, undated (circa 1343) Tashiro Ryōken *meyasu an*. Although the precise period when *hyakushō* became synonymous with cultivators merits further research, this transition was apparently gradual. Even as late as 1462, eighteen out of one hundred and six *hyakushō* who signed an oath possessed illustrious names such as Mitsuyasu, Sadahisa, and Sadamori, and penned elaborate monograms. These eighteen were elites, while their eighty-eight compatriots, humbly named and only capable of blotting a clumsy circle by their names, were, presumably, cultivators. *Dai Nihon komonjo iewake 10, Tōji hyakugō monjo*, 11.9.1462 Yamashiro no kuni Kamikuze no shō *hyakushōra rensho kishōmon*. A photograph of this document appears in *Kyōto gekidō no chūsei*, Kyōto Bunka Hakubutsukan, comp., 11.1996, p. 75.
36. Ishii Susumu, "Tōgoku no 'myōshu' to 'hyakushō,'" in *Chūsei o yomitoku komonjo nyūmon* (Tōkyō Daigaku Shuppankai, 1990), pp. 76–87.

bound both to his lord Terashima and to his peers. Such competing obligations might be ignored in the ambiguity of civil life, but ties to a lord tended
to supersede other obligations in a time of war. With the outbreak of war, a
man had to determine where his most encompassing obligations lay. Many,
but not all, abandoned ties with their peers and instead became retainers.

FOURTEENTH-CENTURY WAR AND STATUS CREATION

Gokenin, Samurai and Hyakushō

Precisely at the moment when the Kamakura *bakufu* collapsed, new *gokenin*
were created. This seeming paradox stems from the fact that those who
received a mobilization order or who submitted a report upon arriving in camp
used this piece of paper to assert *gokenin* status. *Myōshu* strove to translate
their practical status into the prescriptive status of *gokenin*. For some non-
gokenin, the outbreak of warfare was perceived as a splendid opportunity to
raise their status. For example, the Tannowa of Izumi reported to Ashikaga
Takauji in Kyoto immediately after the Rokuhara *tandai* was destroyed, and
were thereupon recognized as *gokenin*.[37] The Azumi of Harima likewise
became *gokenin* by answering Prince Moriyoshi's call to arms.[38]

Although *gokenin* status had previously depended upon ties with the
Kamakura *bakufu*, it now became based on ties with any regime. A status
once attained could not be easily revoked. Thus the Azumi remained *gokenin*
long after their patron, Prince Moriyoshi, had been jailed and executed.[39]
Once divorced from political patronage, the prescriptive status of *gokenin*
became largely practical, and based on the ability to wage war.

The profusion of fourteenth-century calls-to-arms, which concurrently
functioned as investitures of status, enabled most *myōshu* to achieve parity
with *gokenin*. Some submitted petitions for reward (*gunchūjō*)—the hallmark
of an autonomous warrior—in which they still referred to themselves as

---

37. KI 32154. In the early thirteenth century, the Tannowa held *gesu shiki* and clearly were not *gokenin*.
See KI 3747 and Mass, *The Kamakura Bakufu*, document 69, p. 87. The Tannowa were invested
with *kumon shiki*, a higher ranking post, in 8.1262, but were not listed in *gokenin* registers. See
Takaishi shishi 2, Shiryōhen 1, document 60, 10.6.1272 Izumi *gokenin oban'yaku* (KI 11115). Similarly, Kosaji Motouji began referring to himself as a *gokenin* upon submitting his report of arrival.
Compare the 5.16.1333 Kosaji Motouji *chakutōjō* (which has, to my knowledge, never been published) with the 1.6.1336 Kosaji Motouji *chakutōjō*, the 6.1336 Kosaji Motouji *gunchūjō*, the 4.1336
Kosaji Motouji *gunchūjō*, and the 10.1336 Kosaji Motouji *gunchūjō*. The Kosaji *monjo eshabon* is
located at the Tōkyō Shiryōhen Sanjo.
38. *Hyōgo ken shiryōhen chūsei*, vol. 3, Azumi *monjo* document 1, 5.2.1333 Ōtōnomiya Moriyoshi *ryōji*;
2, 5.10.1333 Azumi Moriuji (?) *chakutōjō*. For mid–eighteenth-century commentary of the significance of Moriyoshi's edict, see Azumi *monjo* document 21,1.15 Azumi Ichi daibu *shojō*, and document 22, 10.15 Azumi Morikatsu *shojō*.
39. Moriyoshi was killed by his jailers when rebels sacked Kamakura in the summer of 1335.

myōshu.[40] As the two ranks coalesced, the "office" of *myōshu* (*myōshu shiki*) became, in the mid–fourteenth century, associated with *gokenin* status.[41]

The central authorities failed to realize the degree to which *gokenin* status had become an autogenic social designation, free of any ironclad association with any political entity. Emperor Go-Daigo, for example, sought to abolish the position of *gokenin* after the destruction of the Kamakura *bakufu*, based on his perception of a link between the two.[42] *Gokenin* resisted less out of a visceral loyalty to the defunct Kamakura regime than out of a realization that Go-Daigo was attempting to establish the court as the sole arbiter of social status.

Gokenin complaints that they were now indistinguishable from commoners (*bonmin*) and little better than "slaves and servants" indicate that many felt threatened by this attempt to crowd out their social space.[43] In addition to being tantamount to a personal insult, attempts to abolish *gokenin* status created a pervasive state of social ambiguity. *Gokenin* resisted and continued to refer to themselves as *gokenin* in documents addressed to the Kenmu regime, a practice they maintained with the new *bakufu* and the Southern Court.[44]

Authority could no longer monopolize all sources of legitimation, for statuses enforced by hereditary privilege and control over lands could no longer be negated by edicts from above. That *gokenin* status had evolved into an autogenic social designation did not bode well for Go-Daigo's absolutism. His attempts to determine social rank not only alienated *gokenin*, but also invited disobedience against his "despotism," which thereby highlighted the weakness of his imperial will.

The outbreak of war eroded the collective, lateral bonds that epitomized *hyakushō* status. Some *hyakushō* preferred becoming the retainers of a magnate capable of offering protection. Those *hyakushō* who became retainers were known as samurai, and were empowered to act individually with the consent of their lord. This is evident in a document dating from the 1330s, which states: "If those *onbyakushō* from among the samurai (*samurai no naka*

---

40. NBIK 2248. For other instances of *myōshu* leading substantial forces, see NBIK 2159.

41. *Aioi shishi shiryōhen*, vol. 8, no. 1, p. 137, document 176, 6.1350 *myōshu* Madono Moritaka *shisoku* Kei Wakamaru *kasane moshijō*.

42. Analysis of Go-Daigo's abolition of *gokenin* status appears in Andrew Edmund Goble, *Kenmu: Go-Daigo's Revolution* (Cambridge: Harvard College, Council on East Asian Studies Monograph, 1996), pp. 155–56. Goble claims that usage of this term was fairly unusual, but in fact the Migita of Izumi, among others, continued using the term. See ibid., p. 256.

43. *Taiheiki*, maki 13, "Ryūme shinsō no koto" (Osaka: Izumi Shoin), p. 351, and maki 14, "Yahagi kassen no koto," p. 386. For more on social space, see Pierre Bourdieu, *Language and Symbolic Power* (Cambridge: Harvard University Press, 1991), pp. 229–51.

44. See for example DNSR, series 6, vol. 1, pp. 265, 298, 10.18.1333 Migita Sukeie *chakutōjō* and 11.1333 Migita Sukeyasu *gonjōjō*; DNSR, series 6, vol. 2, p. 687, 1.4.1336 Ogawa Shigeharu *hirōjō*; KI 32383, 32728; and NBIK 85. Warriors referred to themselves as *gokenin* into the 1350s. See DNSR, series 6, vol. 14, pp. 703, 719, 1.1351 (?) Yokomine Nagatane *moshijō* and 6.1351 Migita Sukeuji *gunchūjō*.

no onbyakushō) interfere with the size of [tax] measuring cups (*masu*) . . .
they will be reported to the proprietor. The *gokenin* will all act upon this
matter . . . and punish perpetrators accordingly."[45] Accordingly, the term
samurai came to indicate a distinct social stratum of warriors who were
bound to their lord and not to their peers.

In spite of the separation out of a new order of samurai, those who
remained *hyakushō* continued to constitute "elites" eligible for military service. Indeed, these men, some of whom rode horses,[46] continued to be called
to arms.[47] Nevertheless, the collective obligations of *hyakushō* ensured that
they would not attain individual recognition. *Hyakushō* were neither eligible
to receive documents nor proprietary rewards. Even though a general might
commend *hyakushō* for their military service, his praise would be publicly
posted and not addressed to individual *hyakushō*.[48] Furthermore, although
hyakushō might be granted a remission in taxes for their battle service,[49] they
were ineligible to be granted parcels of proprietary rights. The collective
responsibility of a *hyakushō* to his peers remained encompassing.

Late in the thirteenth century, those *hyakushō* who held name and office
but who did not become retainers came to be called *satanin hyakushō*, or
hyakushō holding *shōen* administrative offices.[50] In the 1330s, *satanin*

45. *Hyōgo kenshi shiryōhen chūsei*, vol. 1, Tada Jinja *monjo* document 91, 4.8.1337 Tadaiin *no gokenin
    rensho moshijō*, p. 284. This process has been perceptively analyzed in Tanaka Minoru, "Samurai
    bonge kō," *Shirin* 59.4 (July 1976): 1–31.
46. At times, hard-pressed *gokenin* even borrowed horses and saddles from them. *Hino shishi shiryōshū,
    Takahata Fudō tainai monjo hen*, document 38.
47. For references to exempted "military service (*gunchū*) of estate officers (*shōkan*) and *hyakushō*," see
    DNSR, series 6, vol. 4, 6.13.1337, p. 248. This document exempts these men from provisional tax
    levies. For another example, see *Kitabatake Chikafusa monjo shūkō*, p. 639; DNSR, series 6, vol.
    11, 12.12(1347) Ōtsuka Koremasa *shojō*; and Iimori Tomio, "Nobushi to sonraku," *Nairanshi
    kenkyū* 12 (May 1992): 34–41.
48. *Kōyasan monjo*, comp. Kōyasan Shi Hensanjo (Kyoto, 1935–41), vol. 11, *Kyū Kōya ryōnai*, no. 3,
    document 231, 9.5.1348 Sakon Shōgen *kanjō*, p. 226. This document was addressed to a certain
    Ueda Isatō Tarō, who was to post this commendation publicly. The proprietor of an estate was respon-
    sible for recording the names of those *hyakushō* who fought. One general wrote, "I am in the midst
    of battle. Join my forces quick. Have the . . . *hyakushō* of the Gein, Takayama, and Mikawara estates
    (*shō*) . . . fight mixed with skirmishers [*nobushi*]. Submit a list of names (*chōhon o meshisusume*)
    [of those participating] and a petition for reward (*gunchūjō*)." *Minoo shishi shiryōhen*, vol. 2, doc-
    ument 594, Ashikaga Takauji *migyōsho*, pp. 9–10.
49. *Fukui kenshi shiryōhen 6 Chū-kinsei*, p. 529. See also Satō Kiyoshi, "Tokue Yorikazu chūjō ni mieru
    Nanbokuchōki Echizen no shiro to kassen ni tsuite," p. 41. One third of the *hyakushō*'s taxes were
    exempted, with the promise of further reductions contingent upon service.
50. For example, all the "*satanin hyakushō*" of two harbors in Wakasa conferred together, and were
    appointed to be jointly responsible for "public duties." See KI 11373, 8.1.1273 Bō *kudashibumi*.
    Satanin hyakushō also exercised "fair administration" (*kōhei no sata*) over Ichihara village in Tanba.
    Hyōgo kenshi shiryōhen chūsei, vol. 2 Kiyomizudera *monjo* document 40, 11.13.1337 Hikitsuke
    Tōnin hōshoan, and document 41, 11.21.1337 Taira Morishige *shojō*, p. 164. In Ōbe no shō, for
    example, the *satanin hyakushō* were ordered to report the particulars of a battle between the *jitō*
    and their *daikan*. KI 19846, 10.10.1298 Harima Ōbe no shō *hyakushōra moshijō*.

hyakushō fought in battle,[51] and maintained a degree of autonomy. Nevertheless, they could not submit their own petitions. As time passed and the term "*hyakushō*" increasingly began to be associated with cultivators, the term *satanin hyakushō* thereupon gradually fell out of disuse in favor of *satanin myōshu*, which had higher social connotations.[52] By the late–fourteenth century, men capable of autonomy in battle preferred other labels to that of *hyakushō*, but this was because members of the lower orders were using the opportunity of war to raise their status as well.

Warfare and Social Mobility

THE BASE

No social orders were immune from the vicissitudes of war. Commoners, referred to in contemporary terminology as "the base" (*genin*), fought in battle, although they lacked the armor, horses, and accoutrements necessary to perform outstandingly on the field of battle.[53] These men, obligated to their masters, were ineligible for rewards and could not enjoy any communication with military commanders.[54] *Genin* fought under their master's personal command. A *genin*'s master received compensation for his death or disability. For example, Kikkawa Tatsukumamaru recorded the names of two wounded *genin* in his petition for reward, while Yamanouchi Tokimichi mentioned the death of his *genin*, Yajirō.[55] Of course, *genin* did not invariably fight in battle—some performed menial functions such as carrying their lord's helmet.[56]

By belonging to strata below that of the politically responsible orders, *genin* were considered to be expendable. Accordingly they made excellent spies. Two were dispatched in order to grasp the extent of a rebellion.[57]

51. For a 1305 example of *satanin hyakushō* coming to blows with the Sasaki in a border dispute, see KI 22443, intercalary 12.12.1305 Kantō *gechijō*.
52. For a mid–fourteenth-century example, see *Dai Nihon komonjo iewake 13, Aso ke monjo*, vol. 1, document 125, 7.19.(1349?) Era Koreo *shojō* (and for a slightly differently transcribed version, NBIK 2614). Furthermore, in 1380, Ashikaga Yoshimitsu ordered the *gokenin* and "*satanin myōshu*" of Iyo Province to serve under the *shugo*, Kawano Michiyoshi. NBIC 4627. Some discrepancy exists between this version and the one found in the *Iyo shiryōhen chūsei* edition of the *Kawano Kōno ke monjo*, comp. Kageura Tsutomu (Matsuyama, 1967). The NBIC version reads, "*jitō gokenin narabi ni honsho azukaridokoro satanin myōshu*," while Kageura Tsutomo's version states, "*jitō gokenin narabi ni honshoryō satanin myōshu*."
53. For *genin* wielding a *naginata* in battle, see *Genpei jōsuiki* (Kokumin Bunko Kankōkai, 1911), maki 20, p. 486.
54. Generals were advised: "If you rely upon [an army composed of] the base (*bonge*) you will later regret it. Carefully inquire into the surname, name, and office (*kando*) [of troops called to arms]." *Aro monogatari*, p. 120. *Genin* and *bonge* were synonymous.
55. For the former, NBIC 744; for the latter, NBIC 315.
56. *Sakaiki*, comp. Kansai Daigaku Chūsei Bungaku Kenkyūkai (Sonkei Kakubunkozō, Izumi Shoin, 1990), pp. 61–62.
57. "Hakata Nikki," in *Zoku zoku gunsho ruijū 3, Shidenbu*, p. 554.

Another passed through enemy lines in order to report to the chancellor, the courtier Tōin Kinkata.[58] After defeat in battle, members of higher orders might be killed or forced to commit suicide, but *genin* were spared.[59] Although they might be captured and interrogated, their heads were not deemed to be worth taking.[60]

Although those of the higher orders—including samurai—were generally spared from physical punishment and execution for crimes, *genin* were subject to torture.[61] Military regulations likewise ensured that the most severe punishments were meted out to *genin*. According to instructions issued by officials of the Kamakura *bakufu*, "the base (*bonge*) [who violate orders] will be summarily executed, while those [of] samurai [status] will have their names forwarded."[62] *Genin* suffered the most brutal punishments in a time of peace, and were most likely to be dispatched on hazardous missions. Nevertheless, the absence of social privileges for *genin* meant that they were more likely to be captured and tortured than to be killed outright, which had its advantages in times of war.

THE ADVANTAGES OF DEPENDENCE

Although *genin* were social inferiors to *hyakushō*, their obligations were both encompassing and individual. *Genin* had no choice but to do their master's bidding. In cases of exemplary service, *genin* could be catapulted into the ranks of retainers. For example, according to the *Taiheiki*, Kō no Morohisa spurred on his forces by promising that "those who cut down the enemy, destroy their encampment and take prisoners will, if base (*bonge*), be made samurai; and if *gokenin*, be granted a recommendation for rewards."[63] *Genin*

---

58. *Entairyaku*, vol. 3, 11.10.1350, p. 368.
59. "Hakata Nikki," p. 554. After a castle was taken, thirty-two defenders were decapitated while two *genin* were captured.
60. See for example *Genpei jōsuiki*, pp. 487–89, for contrasting treatment of the head of a *genin*, which was thrown to the ground, with that of a ranking warrior, which was carefully washed. Ikushima Terumi provides more information of how *genin* heads did not even merit identification in her "Chūsei kōki ni okeru 'kirareta kubi' no toriatsukai." Such a prejudice also appears when Tōin Kinkata disparaged the inspection of a hundred heads because the names of most were unknown. *Entairyaku*, vol. 5, 3.13.1355, p. 12.
61. According to Kamakura law, *bonge* were branded on the forehead for forgeries, while samurai merely had their lands confiscated. CHSS, vol. 1, article 15 of the *Goseibai shikimoku*, pp. 10–11. Likewise, *bonge* (*genin*) were executed for murder while *gokenin*, again, only had their lands confiscated. CHSS, vol. 1, article 10, p. 8, for *gokenin* and amendment 704, p. 308, for *bonge*. According to *Hyōgo kenshi*, *shiryōhen chūsei*, vol. 8, Konoe *monjo* document 28, Tanba no kuni Miyada no shō *zasshō moshijō an*, p. 633, samurai were, unlike *genin*, immune from torture. In cases of rebellion, or war, however, injunctions against the killing of *gokenin* did not apply.
62. "Kusunoki kassen chūmon," p. 549. For an early–fifteenth-century contrast between samurai with names and nameless "*zatsunin*," see *Shinano shiryō*, vol. 7, p. 392.
63. *Taiheiki*, maki 17, "Yamaseme no koto," p. 504.

were ineligible to receive rewards from anyone other than their master, with the exception of a surname. Those who were granted or adopted a name could, however, become retainers (samurai) of their master. Military service provided these men with an opportunity for social mobility.

The process through which a *genin* raised his status is revealed in a dispute concerning *myōshu shiki* that erupted in Harima's Yano no shō in 1350.[64] Jitsuen claimed to be a *myōshu*. Nevertheless, according to a complaint by the *myōshu* Madono Kei Wakamaru, Jitsuen was the son of a *genin*. "How could such a weak, base (*bonge*) slave (*nuhi*) sully the office (*shiki*) which had been held by *gokenin* for generations?" retorted Kei Wakamaru.[65] From this rhetoric one can deduce that it was deemed inappropriate for a *genin*, or for that matter a retainer, to hold *myōshu shiki*.

In his rebuttal, Jitsuen claimed: "since the time of my grandfather . . . we have been the housemen (*kenin*) of Nagoe Tōtōmi no kami. Our name . . . is without a doubt that of a samurai."[66] Jitsuen declared himself to be a samurai who "received his lands through military service."[67] In other words, Jitsuen sprang from *genin* stock. Nevertheless, Jitsuen's grandfather became a houseman, which enabled Jitsuen to assert that he was a retainer (samurai) of the Nagoe. His claims were strengthened after he received lands from his master. Thereupon, it was a relatively easy matter for Jitsuen to assert that he was a *myōshu*, for he did, after all, possess holdings in *myō*. Jitsuen's creeping association with *myōshu* incensed established *myōshu* who resented his encroachment on their social space.

Genin constituted an unprivileged order of landless commoners. Unlike the more elite *hyakushō*, *genin* were beholden to their master and not their peers. *Genin* subservience paved the way for social mobility, for a grateful master might grant them a name and lands, thereby transforming them into retainers. The move from *genin* to retainer was an easy one because the obligations between the two varied only in degree. With the grant of a name and lands, *genin* were able to assert some important rights, such as immunity from torture. In short, obedience to one's master proved to be the surest route to social advancement. Although the boundary between *genin* and retainers was relatively fluid, the division between retainers and autonomous warriors was not easily surmounted.

---

64. For more on this incident and the relationship between samurai and *bonge*, see Ōyama Kyōhei, "Chūsei mibunsei to kokka," in *Nihon chūsei nōsonshi no kenkyū* (Iwanami Shoten, 1978), pp. 373–90.

65. *Aioi shishi*, vol. 8, no. 1, document 176, 6.1350 *myōshu* Madono Moritaka *shisoku* Kei Wakamaru *kasane moshijō*, p. 137.

66. Ibid., document 177, 6.1350 Jitsuen *kasane chinjō*, p. 140.

67. Ibid., document 177, 6.1350 Jitsuen *kasane chinjō*, p. 140.

Comrades

NOBLE COMRADES

War's influence was not confined to providing some with an avenue for social advancement; instead, it also allowed some nobles to "become" warriors. Fourteenth-century war softened the social matrix and dissolved the distinctions between noble and provincial warrior, for both tended to perform similarly in war.

The term "comrades" (*bōhai*) described all those who willingly joined armies. Although comrades were equated at times with "everyone,"[68] this comradeship excluded both hereditary retainers (*miuchi*) and generals.[69] Nevertheless, a sense of comradeship knitted together men from the capital and the provinces. For example, "the nobles Saemon Tarō Toshiaki and Yajirō Toshiyasu" witnessed the deeds of Kishiwada Kaichi and Haruuji.[70] These nobles are named in warrior style, and references to their court ranks are absent, indicating that Kaichi and Haruuji considered them to be their equals. Such an attitude is understandable, for even in imperial processions, Southern Court nobles wore armor.[71] Battle proved to be a leveling experience for courtiers and landed men of the provinces.

The highest echelons of the nobility were predisposed to military command. Thus, Nijō Yoshitada, grandson of the Chancellor Nijō Yoshizane, led an army in 1333, while Tōin Saemon no kami, nephew to the Chancellor Tōin Kinkata, commanded an army as well.[72] Imperial princes also directed armies. Prince Moriyoshi, a son of Go-Daigo, fomented the dissent that led to the

---

68. NBIC 514, 517. In addition, Tashiro Akitsuna mentioned that his actions had been seen by all his comrades (*bōhai minna miru tokoro ni oyobi sōrō*). *Takaishi shishi, Shiryōhen* 1, document 119, 10.27.1337 Tashiro Akitsuna *gunchūjō*, and NBIK 795.

69. One wrote in his petition for reward, "My participation in battle should be evident. Please question *miuchi* . . . or *bōhai* if you have any doubts." Tannowa *monjo*, 10.21.1337 Tannowa Shigeuji *gunchūjō* of the Kyoto University collection. For the distinction between commanders (*shugo* or generals) and *bōhai*, see the passage for 1.9.36 in NBIK 905, which states that "on top of the bridge . . . an arrow pierced my right thigh. This was seen by everyone there. In addition, the shogun's chief of staff (*shitsuji*) (Kō no Moronao) and Shimazu Shirō Saemon no jō realized (*kenchi*) what happened." When generals witnessed a deed, there was no need for other *bōhai* witnesses. See DNSR, series 6, vol. 14, 12.1350 Ōhara Kosaji *gunchūjō*, pp. 58–59 and NBIK 2536. For a Kamakura era example of *shokan bōhai* as witnesses, see KI 26327, 8.25.1317 Chinzei *gechijō*. Finally, Kasamatsu Hiroshi, *Hō to kotoba no chūseishi* (Heibonsha, 1993), pp. 10–28, provides insightful analysis of *bōhai* as well.

70. 8.1337 and 11.1337 Kishiwada *gunchūjō*, found most readily in the Migita genealogy, in *Zoku gunsho ruijū, keizubu*, vol. 7, pp. 160–64.

71. *Entairyaku*, vol. 4, urū 2.29.1352, p. 130. See also Ichizawa Tetsu, "Nanbokuchō nairanki ni okeru Tennō to shoseiryoku," *Rekishigaku kenkyū* 688 (September 1996): 1–16.

72. NBIC 238. Hino Kunimitsu also directed resistance against the Ashikaga in Nagato: NBIC 994–95.

73. For a fine monograph concerning Moriyoshi, see Mori Shigeaki, "Ōtōnomiya Moriyoshi shinnō ryōji ni tsuite," in Ogawa Makoto, ed., *Chūsei komonjo no sekai* (Yoshikawa Kōbunkan, 1991), pp. 192–218.

destruction of the Kamakura *bakufu*, and briefly held the post of shogun.[73] Two other princes played a role in the struggle against Kamakura in 1333,[74] while Go-Daigo dispatched numerous sons throughout Japan.[75] Rank, in other words, outweighed considerations of social origin.

No great cultural difference existed between courtiers and provincial warriors. Recently, some scholars have assumed that because "death was . . . regarded as the most dangerous pollution" members of the "aristocracy" could not compete with "warriors" in battle, but this dichotomy of cultural differentiation is facile and misleading.[76] Fear of pollution did not influence how war was fought; rather, it merely affected the behavior of both courtiers and warriors in the aftermath of battle.[77] For example, Ashikaga Tadayoshi decided merely to offer a written prayer at the Kibitsu no miya shrine, instead of worshipping in person after he had inspected 1350 heads.[78]

Although no great dichotomy existed between how courtiers and warriors behaved in battle, the former status, based upon appointment to court rank and office, remained invariably prescriptive. Of course, some illustrious families monopolized court positions, but not all of those born into a "noble house" were able to achieve court rank. Belonging to a certain family aided one in securing employment as a courtier, but one's social origins were not decisive. Conversely, such origins did not preclude one from waging war.

Some men from the capital criticized both the fraternization of nobles and warriors and cases where the boundary between noble and warrior remained ill-defined. Evidence of a hardening in social attitudes during the mid–fourteenth century can be gleaned from statements that men who followed "the way of the bow and arrow" (warriors) were distinguished from "the way of the capital" (courtiers).[79] A nascent ethos regarding the "way of the warrior" was initially manifested as ridicule of nobles' military prowess. Fourteenth-century chronicles occasionally reflect this bias, in an attempt to

74. One prince was Moriyoshi (守良) (not to be confused with the Moriyoshi (護良), who was appointed shogun). See Okubō Jinichi, *Mino no kuni Kasugadani no kassenshi* (Yahashi Insatsusho, 1982), pp. 93–101. Another prince's arrival in Kyushu helped hasten the end of the Chinzei *tandai*. "Hakata nikki," 3.17.1333.

75. For the best summary of the princes, see Mori Shigeaki, *Ōjitachi no Nanbokuchō* (Chūkōshinsho, 1988). A "Prince Hanazono" also led Southern Court forces in southern Shikoku. NBIC 928.

76. Ikegami, *The Taming of the Samurai*, pp. 49 and 97.

77. For an informative article about how pollution did not prevent warfare in medieval Europe, see Karl Leyser, "Early Medieval Canon Law and the Beginnings of Knighthood," in Lutz Fenske, Werner Rosener, and Thomas Zotz, eds., *Institutionen, Kultur and Gesellschaft im Mittelalter: Festschrift für Josef Fleckenstein zu seinem 65. Geburtstag* (Sigmaringen: Jan Thorbecke Verlag, 1984), pp. 549–66.

78. *Taiheiki*, maki 16, "Fukuyamajō botsuraku no koto," p. 476. Tadayoshi was a brother to the first Ashikaga shogun, Takauji. Hyperbole pervades the *Taiheiki*, as is evident by the number of heads mentioned here.

79. *Taiheiki*, maki 14, "Hakone kassen no koto," p. 395. NBIK 1232 also refers to the "way of the bow and arrow."

show that performance in war was the sole prerogative of provincial warriors. According to one passage from the *Taiheiki*, "those warriors (*buke no tomogara*) who follow the way of the bow and arrow (*yumiya no michi*) will invariably defeat poetaster courtiers in battle." Nevertheless, on this occasion the poetasters won.[80] Yoshida Kenkō, author of the *Tsurezuregusa*, claimed in the 1330s that even courtiers capable of military success could not be considered as "true" warriors:

> A great number of priests, nobles (*tenjō bito*) and even men of the highest rank[81] enjoy the military arts. Nevertheless, even if such men win a hundred battles they cannot win the name of a warrior. Every man blessed by the fortune of victory is brave. . . . Only one who prefers death to surrender after his forces have been scattered and his arrows exhausted can achieve the name of a warrior. The living have no right boasting of their military prowess. Only those born to a warrior house, remote from humanity and close to beasts, can profit from war.[82]

In short, Kenkō attempted to divorce warrior status from mere performance in battle, and instead link it to hereditary origins. This forging of a "warrior ethos" reflects the gradual hardening of social boundaries, beginning in the center and spreading throughout the peripheries during the late–fourteenth and early fifteenth centuries.[83]

WOMEN, COMRADES, AND "UNATTACHEDNESS" (*MUEN*)

Unlike men, social mobility remained easier for women because their status was invariably practical, rather than prescriptive. Women could traverse social boundaries because their status was based upon their relation to others. One should not, however, assert that women were somehow "unattached" from the

---

80. *Taiheiki*, maki 8, "Chigusa dono miyako semuru koto," p. 208, and McCullough, *The Taiheiki*, pp. 230–31. The Date Nanzenji *monjo* (*Hyōgo kenshi shiryōhen chūsei*, vol. 8) indicates that Chigusa Tadaaki, portrayed as being effete in the *Taiheiki*, directed formidable armies in 1333. See also KI 32149 and 32164.

81. Literally "*kandachime*" or those above the third rank.

82. *Tsurezuregusa*, dai hachijūdan, maki 1, section 80. This has been translated by Donald Keene, *Essays in Idleness: The Tsurezuregusa of Kenkō* (New York: Columbia University Press, 1967), p. 69. Events undermined Kenkō, for a high percentage of noble generals perished in battle and thereby ironically "achieved the name of a warrior." For example, the courtly Nijō family suffered grievously. Nijō Takasuke died in battle at Yawata in 1352, one son was executed in 1333, and another died serving Prince Moriyoshi; *Ōsaka fushi, chūsei* 1, comp. Osaka Fu (Osaka, 1981), p. 713. For more on a Nijō serving in battle with Nitta Yoshisada, and perishing, see *Baishōron*, p. 75. For other nobles in Nitta's army, see *Baishōron*, pp. 80, 123.

83. For an interesting study of how "warriors" were essentialized as provincial landholders, and "nobles" as courtly poetasters, see Takahashi, *Bushi no seiritsu bushizō no sōshutsu*, pp. 291–330.

social matrix, but rather that they assumed the status of their husbands. Women who married, or consorted with warrior men, became known as "comrades" (*bōhai*). One unattached (*muen*) *shirabyōshi* entertainer became, for example, a comrade (*bōhai*) after marrying into a warrior household.[84] Once a women became a "comrade," she could no longer return to her former unattached status. For example, the Rusu family, nearly annihilated during the Kannō disturbance (1350–52), was saved from extinction because a *shirabyōshi*, who had given birth to a son, was able to escape capture.[85] Her equality with the Rusu is evidenced by the fact that she was chased by the Rusu's opponents, and also that her son was ultimately designated as the Rusu heir.[86] Such cases were common, for during the mid–thirteenth century, Ōtomo Yoshinao also fathered two of his twelve sons from such entertainers. One, born from a *shirabyōshi*, was openly recognized, while the other, whose mother was a Kyoto prostitute (*yūjo*), apparently did not become accepted as an heir until he turned eighteen.[87]

Nevertheless, a stigma appears to have been developing regarding "lowly" *shirabyōshi* parentage. A 1267 Kamakura *bakufu* law equated non-*gokenin* women, including *shirabyōshi*, as members of the base orders.[88] One can see the gradual influence of rhetoric on reality, as standing relationships become a source of embarrassment. For example, early in the fourteenth century, one warrior characterized the accusation that his grandmother was a *shirabyōshi* as slander; nevertheless, he was forced to admit the truth of the assertion![89] Entertainers and members of the lower social

---

84. *Kongochōbunshū* (Kokumin Kankōkai, 1910), maki 9, "Buyū," p. 537. Compare this to Amino, *Muen kugai raku*, pp. 200–10.

85. See the "Ōshū yomoku kiroku," in *Sendai shishi shiryōhen*, vol. 1, pp. 230–49, particularly p. 233.

86. In another case, Ashikaga Tadafuyu, the product of a liaison between Ashikaga Takauji with a certain "Echizen no tsubone," became a powerful magnate in spite of his mother's lowly origins. Little is known about Tadafuyu's mother. According to the *Sonpi bunmyaku*, in *Shintei zōho kokushi taikei* (Yoshikawa Kōbunkan, 1964), vol. 3, p. 253, she was merely a woman of the house (*ie no nyobō*). The Ashikaga genealogy, found in *Gunsho ruijū*, states that she was Echizen no tsubone. See *Zoku gunsho ruijū, keizubu*, vol. 2, maki 111, p. 301. For more on Tadafuyu, see *Taiheiki*, maki 27, "Tadafuyu saigoku gekō no koto," and *Moromoriki*, in *Shiryō sanshū* (Zoku Gunsho Ruijū Kanseikai, 1969), vol. 2, 6.17.1344, p. 166.

87. See the Ōtomo (Shiga) genealogy, found in *Bungo no kuni Ōno no shō shiryō*, comp. Watanabe Sumio (Yoshikawa Kōbunkan, 1979), p. 205. For more on the Ōtomo see Conlan, *In Little Need of Divine Intervention*, particularly pp. 210–13.

88. CHSS, vol. 1, amendment 435, pp. 226–27. For the most recent study of *shirabyōshi*, and the issue of prostitution in medieval Japan, see Janet Goodwin, "Shadows of Transgression: Heian and Kamakura Constructions of Prostitution," *Monumenta Nipponica* 55.3 (Autumn 2000): 327–68. Goodwin mentions the 1267 amendment, but she ignores the reference to non-*gokenin*. See p. 348.

89. KI 24376, 7.22.1311 Chinzei *gechijō*. Kokubun Dōhon, a Kyushu *gokenin*, likewise disinherited his son in 1311 for twice running off with a *shirabyōshi*. See the urū 6.24.1311 Shami Dōhon *gizetsujo an*, located most conveniently in Aida Nirō, *Nihon no Komonjo*, vol. 2 (Iwanami Shoten, 1954), p. 572. This document does not however appear in KI.

orders became objects of discrimination as the thirteenth and fourteenth centuries progressed.[90] In short, women's status was becoming more pre-scribed by social origins, while the practical consideration of whom they consorted with became increasingly disregarded. Nevertheless, this process was gradual, for as we have seen, considerable social fluidity remained throughout the fourteenth century.

Throughout the thirteenth and fourteenth centuries, differences in social rank transcended those in gender. Warrior women were treated virtually indistinguishably from their men.[91] When Kamakura was sacked, many were butchered.[92] In the *Go-sannen kassen ekotoba*, one can find graphic illus-trations of men slaughtering enemy women.[93] Accordingly, when enemy forces pillaged the countryside, women and children fled to the mountains.[94]

Warrior women fought in battle just like their men. At times, they even warred against them, for one can find references to one hapless man who bat-tled his ex-wife at Ōishi no shō.[95] Further proof of their performance of battle can be found at the Ōyamazumi shrine, where a suit of armor tailored to female anatomy remains to this day.[96] (See figure 31.) Likewise, the Chancellor Tōin Kinkata mentioned in his diary "a feeble force" of predominately female cav-alry,[97] although it is not clear whether his comments reflect their military inad-equacies, or simply reflected a courtier's bias against women performing in battle. Provincial warriors did not seem to share such qualms, because a woman validated petitions of reward—the prerogative of military leaders—by signing her monogram on them, and this elicited no comment from other warriors.[98]

One cannot ascertain how many women fought in battle. Women warriors were common enough that their presence did not elicit surprise or, for that matter, commentary. Nevertheless, this paucity of references indicates that

---

90. This is also reflected by laws which warn against a *gokenin*'s lands being taken by non-*gokenin* women and *shirabyōshi*. See CHSS 1, p. 226. The Kobayakawa also forbade warriors to marry women who resided in their lodgings; NBIC 2470. This assertion has been made Amino Yoshihiko in his *Muen, kugai, raku*, pp. 139–52. Amino claims that women were invariably "unattached," but this asser-tion is problematic.

91. The decapitation of some women in battle merited documents of praise (*kanjō*). For one example, although dating from the fifteenth century, see *Hyōgo kenshi shiryōhen chūsei*, vol. 9, p. 631, Kakiya *monjo* document 1, 7.20 Yamana Mochitoyo *kanjō*. A picture of this document appears on plate 5. For reference to a "female *jitō*," see NBIK 4559.

92. Suzuki, *Kamakura zaimokuza hakken no chūsei iseki to sono jinkotsu*, p. 70.

93. *Go-sannen ekotoba*, vol. 15, pp. 71–72, chūkan, godan, sheet 23–25. This scroll dates from the mid–fourteenth century.

94. NBIC 654.

95. KI 30790.

96. This armor dates from the early sixteenth century.

97. *Entairyaku*, vol. 4, 6.2.1353, p. 305. At times female *gokenin* dispatched male relatives to fight in their stead. NBIK 494, 667–70.

98. NBIC 654. In addition, chronicles are littered with references to warring women. See for example Tomoe *gozen* in the *Tale of the Heike* and *Koji ruien* (Koji Ruien Kankōkai, 1896–1912), *Heijibu*, no. 1, pp. 312–18.

women constituted a distinct minority of warriors. The "feeble force" mentioned by Tōin Kinkata was exceptional precisely because most of its members were women. This unit originated in western Japan, as do most references to warring women, which suggests that women from the west were most likely to serve in battle, although this assumption merits further research.

Women's status remained performative, for a clear distinction was made between provincial warriors and those women of the capital, who were incapable of fighting in battle. Rape seems to have been particularly reserved for the women of the capital, who could not easily resist. One graphic reference appears in the *Genpei jōsuiki*: "Higuchi Kanemitsu captured [several] ranking women, tore off their clothes . . . and for five or six days exposed them to shame (*haji o misetatematsuritarikeru*)."[99] Accordingly, whenever

Figure 31. *Konito suso sugake odoshi dōmaru* armor tailored to the female anatomy. Attributed to Tsuruhime, of the Hauri family. Possession of Ōyamazumi shrine. Photograph courtesy of Ōyamazumi shrine.

99. *Genpei jōsuiki*, maki 35, p. 882. The women threatened either to become nuns or kill themselves unless Kanemitsu was punished; in spite of an earlier pardon, he was executed. From this passage, one can establish that "exposed to shame" was a euphemism for rape. For reference to a man exposing another's wife and children to shame, see KI, vol. 38, p. 296, document 29940, 8.25.1327 Kantō *gechijō*.

armies entered the capital, ranking women sought shelter in the compounds of relatives.[100] Warrior women, maintaining local ties and autonomy, remained less likely to suffer such indignities.

Thus, "comradeship" was reserved for those capable of fighting as they chose in battle, or those who married into warrior households. Noble scions who fought in the provinces might also be considered "comrades," but their sisters and wives could not. The boundary between "unattached" women and warrior wives remained permeable—although such mobility was becoming increasingly difficult—while the distinction between "noble" and non-noble wives remained firm.[101] Likewise, although nobles could become "comrades," those lacking sufficient resources to behave with autonomy, irrespective of their social origins, could not. Thus, the distinction between warrior and noble was more fluid than the division between autonomous warriors and their retainers.

HEREDITARY WARRIORS

Warrior obligations varied between "insiders," or *miuchi*, who maintained strong ties to a lord, and autonomous "outsiders" or *tozama*. *Tozama* exercised powers of lordship over *miuchi*, who were analogous to "vassals." In other words, *tozama* and *miuchi* labored under different obligations and expectations, which in turn were based upon their varying control over land.

The distinction between *miuchi* and *tozama* appears with deceptive clarity in the *Sata Mirensho*, a law primer of the early fourteenth century. "*Tozama* are *jitō gokenin* who serve the Shogun's house. *Miuchi* are vassals (*miuchi-hōkōnin*) of the Lord of Sagami [the Hōjō]."[102] According to the *Sata Mirensho*, a warrior's relationship with the Kamakura *bakufu* determined his status as either *tozama* or *miuchi*.

One might assume that the categories of *tozama* and *miuchi* would disappear with the Hōjō and the Kamakura *bakufu*, but they did not. In fact, belying the *Sata Mirensho*'s political definition, these terms had gradually become social categories.[103] *Tozama* status, based upon control over land and

---

100. *Entairyaku*, vol. 3, 11.8.1350, p. 366.

101. The daughters of nobles were forbidden to receive lands from *gokenin* by the Kamakura *bakufu*. See CHSS, vol. 1, p. 122. Such prohibitions were enforced because "those who take a noble wife rely on the power of such great houses (*kenmon*) to avoid public service." Kiyowara Nobukata Shikimokushō, quoted in Kasamatsu Hiroshi, *Chūseinin to no taiwa* (Tōkyō Daigaku Shuppankai, 1997), p. 101.

102. Carl Steenstrup, "*Sata Mirensho*: A Fourteenth-Century Law Primer," *Monumenta Nipponica* 35 (1980): 405–35, p. 418. Steenstrup translates *jitō gokenin* as *jitō* and *gokenin*. I believe these two were a compound term. See "Sata Mirensho," in *Zoku gunsho ruijū*, vol. 25, no. 1, pp. 1–14.

103. *Miuchi*, in particular, were not limited to followers of the Hōjō *tokusō*. See Ogawa Makoto, *Ashikaga ichimon shugo hattenshi no kenkyū* (Yoshikawa Kōbunkan, 1980), p. 355; *Genpei jōsuiki*, maki 38, p. 940; and NBIC 406.

enshrined as a hereditary right, was a practical status that would retain significance apart from the existence of any political entity. For example, approximately two decades after the destruction of the Kamakura regime, a *miuchi* of Ashikaga Yoshiakira, Myō no Shimotsuke, indignantly refused an overture from Ashikaga Tadafuyu, whom he denounced for "sending a messenger who makes no distinction between *miuchi* and *tozama*."[104] Believing himself to be a *miuchi* of the Ashikaga shogun, Myō no Shimotsuke could not countenance receiving rewards from another lord.[105] Conversely, no leader could override the pervasive belief that *miuchi* lacked autonomy in determining allegiances and that they were thereby ineligible to receive rewards from anyone other than their lord.

Miuchi

INDIVIDUAL *MIUCHI*

Miuchi were warriors who could not alone determine their allegiances. Those who shifted their loyalties independently of their lord were castigated as traitors. One Ashikaga houseman (*kerai no mono*) who had fought for the Nitta was, upon his capture, summarily executed.[106] In a variation, the treachery of a member of the Shōni house proved to be the catalyst for Shōni Sadatsune's suicide.[107] Or again, it was declared entirely "the punishment of heaven" that a retainer who stripped off and hid the armor of his dead Hōjō lords (*shu*) should be captured and ignominiously executed.[108] A *miuchi* who was willful enough to rebel but too weak to succeed could expect to be severely punished because his behavior transgressed the bounds of social acceptability. *Miuchi* were personally bound to their lord, having taken an oath of fealty (*ryōju no reigi*), which explains why *miuchi* treachery was vigorously punished.[109]

Striking examples of *miuchi* loyalty frequently appear. The powerful *tozama* Utsunomiya Kintsuna joined Ashikaga Takauji's forces upon the defeat of the Southern Court's Nitta Yoshisada. Unaware of this development, two Utsunomiya bands of warriors (*tō*), the Ki and Sei, marched with Kitabatake Akiie of the Southern Court to the capital. However, "when they heard that Utsunomiya [Kintsuna] had joined [Ashikaga Takauji's] forces, they all took their leave [and] . . . went up to the capital."[110] After "galloping toward

104. *Taiheiki*, maki 38, "Miyakata hōki no koto," p. 1129. Ashikaga Tadafuyu was the estranged son of Takauji.
105. *Taiheiki*, maki 38, "Miyakata hōki no koto," pp. 1129–30.
106. *Taiheiki*, maki 17, "Kankō kyōhō kinsatsuseraruru koto," p. 539.
107. *Taiheiki*, maki 15, "Shōni, Kikuchi to kassen no koto," pp. 455–56.
108. *Taiheiki*, maki 10, "Shioda oyako sannin jigai no koto," pp. 270–71 and McCullough, *The Taiheiki*, pp. 297–98.
109. For the relationship of an oath of fealty to retainer status, see KI 24656 and 29236.
110. *Taiheiki*, maki 15, "Ōshū sei sakamoto ni tsuku koto," p. 427.

their lord (*shu no moto*),"[111] these two bands built forts and subsequently bore the brunt of Akiie's offensive.[112] *Miuchi* followed the lead of their lord even when his choice entailed grave personal sacrifice.

Miuchi who abandoned their lord merited strict censure but this did not preclude the possibility of some achieving autonomy. A *miuchi* had to be resourceful in order to switch allegiances successfully independently of his *tozama* lord. For example, one Haga Hyōe Nyūmon Zenka barricaded himself in a castle with an infant son of his Utsunomiya lord (*shu*) and joined an opposing military alliance. Although a contemporary chronicle decried Haga's behavior as "disturbing the oath of lord and retainer (*shujū no reigi o midare*)," Haga Zenka successfully legitimated his de facto autonomy by acting in the name of his lord's son.[113] Zenka's actions generated enough ambiguity of social position to allow for his success, but he could not openly behave like a *tozama*. Perhaps a generation or more had to pass before the autonomy of such *miuchi* became hereditarily enshrined and the descendants of a *miuchi* became widely accepted as *tozama*.

In fact, most *miuchi* remained *miuchi* although their lord, or focus of loyalty, could shift. When Hosokawa Kiyouji was destroyed by the forces of the Ashikaga *bakufu*, for example, many of his *miuchi* transferred their allegiance and became followers of Hosokawa Yoriyuki.[114] A few of Kiyouji's most powerful *miuchi* used the opportunity to achieve independence, among them Hayami Shirō.[115] Formerly a *miuchi* of Kiyouji, he turned over a strategic castle to Ashikaga forces and thereby severed his *miuchi* relationship with the Hosokawa while securing his autonomy. In the process, he ensured Kiyouji's destruction.[116]

The only *miuchi* who achieved independence were those who, in addition to seeking autonomy, controlled substantial lands and followers. Those of little means reaped benefits from their *miuchi* status by participating in distant military campaigns and sharing the rewards that accrued to their lord. Thus, unless internal dissension weakened a *tozama*'s support, the lord could normally crush the rebellion of a *miuchi* who would have to overcome military inferiority and the stigma of treachery. For most *miuchi* the advantages of service and protection outweighed the drawbacks of dependence.

The stability of a *tozama*'s band of *miuchi* depended on the extent of the lands they controlled. *Miuchi* who administered or were entrusted with extensive lands, such as Hayami Shirō or Haga Zenka, could behave, or at least

111. *Taiheiki*, maki 15, "Miidera kassen no koto," p. 428.
112. *Taiheiki*, maki 15, "Shōgatsu nijū shichi nichi Miyako kassen no koto," pp. 440–41.
113. *Taiheiki*, maki 21, "Tenka jisei shō no koto," p. 651.
114. Ogawa, *Ashikaga ichimon shugo hattenshi no kenkyū*, p. 339.
115. Ibid., p. 338.
116. *Taiheiki*, maki 36, "Hayami Shirō kokoro kawari no koto," pp. 1094–96.

attempt to behave, as *tozama*. In other words, *miuchi* loyalty was contingent upon the maintenance of social distance between *miuchi* and *tozama* lords, which was predicated upon a disparity of directly controlled resources. Those with few, if any, lands were most loyal, while those with significant holdings tended to be unreliable. As Imagawa Ryōshun observed, "men should perform service commensurate with their rank. Those whose service exceeds their status (*mi no hodo*) will invariably resent [their lord]."[117] When the distinction between *tozama* and *miuchi* collapsed in all but name, a volatile situation developed which frequently led to the disintegration of ties of dependence.

Corporate *Miuchi*

Not all *miuchi* were capable of becoming individually recognized followers of their lord. Some maintained collective responsibilities and identities. Some *hyakushō* became direct vassals (*miuchi*) to a lord, while others established relations with a lord while concurrently preserving obligations to their peers. The latter formed corporate organizations known as either bands (*tō*) or military units (*ikki*). For example, sixty-seven obscure warriors signed an oath and formed the Kadochigai *ikki* sometime during the 1330s.[118] Their individual landholdings were minuscule; indeed, their collective landholdings were far from substantial. Each member sacrificed some individual freedom in order to belong to a group which maintained tight organization and collective responsibility. For instance, one of the oath's clauses contains provisions that progeny who were orphaned should be raised by other *ikki* members.[119]

Such corporate organizations retained limited autonomy in determining how to fight. Although one clause of the Kadochigai *ikki* oath contains the acknowledgment that regional peace and stability were based on the prowess of their Ōtomo lords, another states as follows: "Concerning military service: the core group (*shūchū*) shall decide what is appropriate . . . but this shall not violate the [wishes] of the majority (*tabun no gi*)."[120] Inasmuch as these warrior bands (*tō*) and *ikki* were unlikely to rebel, their limited autonomy posed no threat to their lord. Moreover, the immense social distance between *ikki* participants and local magnates enabled the former to behave with more latitude than was generally possible for individually bound *miuchi*. At the same time, *ikki* might be collectively granted rewards, for example *jitō shiki*, as in the case of awards by Ashikaga Takauji and Yoshimitsu to the Kadochigai *ikki* in incidents that were nearly thirty years apart.[121]

117. "Nantaiheiki," p. 318.
118. NBIK 6847.
119. NBIK 6847.
120. NBIK 6847.
121. NBIK 2197 and 5233. One of these *jitō shiki* was granted to Aso Koresumi in 1347 by the Southern Court's Prince Kaneyoshi. See NBIK 2391.

As should be evident, corporate *miuchi* were not ephemeral organizations. The Kadochigai *ikki* survived for at least thirty years. Furthermore, the Ki and Sei bands (*tō*) who fought for the Utsunomiya through the 1350s also participated in an attack against the Andō family of Tsugaru in 1323.[122] Thus *miuchi* organizations existed from at least the late-Kamakura period and were capable of surviving a period of political turmoil. By contrast, other less comprehensive allegiances were prone to disintegration. In an age of instability, assemblages of *miuchi* were a bastion of support for *tozama* and an important source of stability for dependent warriors themselves, who were able to enjoy in the process a degree of autonomy.

Tozama

Like most social designations, *tozama* status is more identifiable than definable; some men were clearly *tozama*, while others were not. The *Sata Mirensho*'s equation of *tozama* status with the rank of *gokenin* is singularly unhelpful since both suffered from the same inherent ambiguities. Although the authors of the law primer bravely attempted to distinguish *gokenin* from non-*gokenin*, their claim that the former were men "whose ancestors held since time immemorial ownership of land . . . and received a *bakufu kudashibumi* [investiture edict]" cannot be sustained.[123] In fact, many hereditary landowners, particularly those of western Japan, received no edicts, even though their forebears had appeared on *gokenin* registers.[124] Furthermore, those with no lands but who possessed an investiture edict could also claim to be a *gokenin*.[125] In spite of these ambiguities, one can infer from the *Sata Mirensho* that *tozama* status was determined by genealogical justification (such as "ancestors since time immemorial") and lands.

Status remained integrally linked to lordship over the land. The founder of the Yamana's family fortunes would reminisce in the mid–fourteenth century that "prior to 1333, we were little more than *hyakushō*. Nevertheless, we managed to come into our own and make a name for ourselves in the world after [securing] a place called Yamana, in Kōzuke [Province]."[126] The Yamana based their claims of warrior status on possession of lands, which were legitimated according to the principle of hereditary succession.

---

122. According to the "Suwa Daimyōjin e-kotoba," in *Zoku gunsho ruijū jingi bu* 3, comp. Zoku Gunsho Ruijū Kanseikai (Zoku Gunsho Ruijū Kanseikai, 1975), p. 512, Ki and Sei bands of "Utsunomiya housemen" (*kenin*) suffered heavy casualties while fighting in the far north.

123. Steenstrup, "*Sata Mirensho*" p. 418.

124. Indeed, this was the "custom of western *gokenin*." KI 27089, 7.7.1319 Kantō *gechijō*.

125. See CHSS, vol. 1, Kamakura *bakufu tsukahō*, pp. 280, 289, for rulings that any grandson of a *gokenin* who had his lands confirmed with a *kudashibumi* could be considered a *gokenin*, even if he had no lands.

126. "Nantaiheiki," p. 306.

Although genealogies might be fabricated and embellished, this did not undermine their role as a principal vehicle of social classification. An investigation of the veracity of a warrior's hereditary rights, or genealogical claims, was well-nigh impossible; merely to accuse a warrior of being a non-*gokenin* constituted slander.[127] However, one should not overestimate the autogenesis of *gokenin* or *tozama* status, since men of manifestly inferior social rank, such as hereditary *miuchi*, could be recognized as *gokenin* (*tozama*) only with difficulty. Nevertheless, for those men possessing considerable autonomy and ambiguous rank, such as *myōshu*, a forged genealogy could reap dividends. Thus, *gokenin* status expanded along two avenues. First, those who possessed military power ruthlessly exploited all ambiguities in order to rise in the world. Second, as some *gokenin* prospered, all landholding members descending from such a family could use the *gokenin* designation for themselves. The determining factor of such status was simply a man's plausible, genealogically justifiable claim that he was a *gokenin*.

As the number of *gokenin* expanded in the mid–1330s, those who had been *gokenin* in the Kamakura era sought to "prove" their *gokenin* status by appending a genealogy to their petition for rewards.[128] These men resented being considered equals to former non-*gokenin*, but their attempts to achieve social distinction based on genealogical claims failed to exclude social climbers. Upstarts such as the Tannowa "lost" their genealogy "when the province was in disorder," and thus had their comrades, the local *tozama* of Izumi, sign an affidavit attesting to this fact.[129]

Autonomy in war, or "freedom of movement" (*kyoshū no jiyū*), a cherished desire of nearly all warriors, is more a function of *tozama* status than its defining feature.[130] The autonomy of *tozama* was manifest in their method of military mobilization and rewards. Military commanders requested *tozama* service through orders of mobilization (*saisokujō*). A formal request to fight ipso facto implies conditional obligation; true loyalty is not contingent upon invitation. An oath written in 1336 also expresses the fundamental autonomy of the Nejime *tozama*. All who signed, landholders of *gokenin* status,

---

127. For one example, see *Hizen Matsura tō Ariura monjo*, ed. Fukuda Ikuo and Murai Shosuke (Osaka: Seibundō Shiryō Sōsho, 1982), pp. 42–43, document 17 4.16.1314 Chinzei *gechijō an*, a document missing from KI. Seno Sei'ichirō also addresses this question in *Chinzei gokenin no kenkyū* (Yoshikawa Kōbunkan, 1975), pp. 159–60.

128. These examples date from the early 1340s. See, for example *Minakuchi chōshi* 2, comp. Minakuchi (Minakuchi, 1959), Yamanaka *monjo* document 38, 4.1341 Yamanaka Michitoshi *gonjōan*; *Takaishi shishi* 2, *Shiryōhen* 1, document 181, Tashiro Akitsuna *sojō an*; *Niigata kenshi, shiryōhen* 4, *Chūsei* 2, document 1051, 8.1341 Irobe Takanaga *mōshijo narabi ni gunchūjō an*; and NBIC 4065, 4665.

129. 8.22.1396 Tannowa Inaba no kami Morinaga *funshitsujō*, unpublished document, Kyoto University collection. No members of the Migita, a powerful Izumi *gokenin* family, signed this document.

130. Satō Shin'ichi used the phrase "freedom of movement" to describe *jitō gokenin* in *Nanbokuchō no dōran*, pp. 175–78.

promised "as a lineage (*ichimon*) . . . to act in complete accord (*ichimi dōshin*) concerning everything." Furthermore the signers vowed, "Let there be no differences of opinion (*igi*). Everything shall be discussed in council (*shūgi*). If some disobey this purport, they shall suffer the punishment of all of the middling, small, and great gods of the country of Japan in heaven, earth, and hell."[131] Formal unity among Nejime *tozama* was forged through an oath, indicating the voluntary nature of this agreement and alliance. Nejime *miuchi* labored under informal and unconditional obligations which required no oath; those truly obligated to fight remain largely unrecorded in documentary sources.

Autonomous warriors submitted their own documents. Nejime Kiyonari, the head or *sōryō* of the Nejime, received documents which ordered him to mobilize the Nejime family (*ichizoku*).[132] Kiyonari was responsible for followers and family members who fought under him, and received credit for their actions and compensation for their losses.[133] Nejime Kiyotane, a *gokenin* cousin of Kiyonari, was wounded at the very engagement where Kiyonari fought, but his wounds are not recorded in the latter's petition for reward (*gunchūjō*). Instead, Kiyotane fought independently of Kiyonari and submitted his own petition.[134] Conversely, warriors lacking autonomy could not submit their own documents. Powerful family chieftains (*sōryō*) forbade their relatives to submit documents, for this would imply that they were *gokenin* and thereby autonomous. For example, Migita Moriie, who "followed the orders of the chieftain (*sōryō*) Migita Sukeie, could not submit his own petition even though he had performed battle service (*gunchū*)."[135] Separate petitions and recognition implies autonomy, not disunity. Nejime Kiyotane could fight where and when he pleased, while relatives and hereditary followers, such as the Nejime *miuchi* or Migita Moriie, could not.

Separate residence constituted a rough determinant of *tozama* status—those who lived independently could fight as they wished while house resi-

---

131. NBIK 383. Kiyonari and Kiyotane signed this document, as did the Nejime *gokenin* named Kiyotake, Dōkei, and Kiyoyoshi. One Nejime signer, Yoritomo, remains otherwise obscure. Kiyotake was a *gokenin* summoned to fight in 1333 and 1336. See KI 32383, Kenbu Kiyotake *chakutōjō*. See also NBIK 787–88, for the *chakutōjō* of Kiyotake and Kiyotane. For Kiyoyoshi's *gunchūjō* see NBIK 634. Dōkei controlled some land holdings. See KI 28560, 10.20.1323 Kenbu Takakiyo [Dōkei] *yuzurijō*.

132. NBIK 519, 937, and 1391.

133. NBIK 1391, 1684, 1883, 3166, and 3174–75.

134. For Kiyotane's wounds, see the actions of the battle of 12.18.1336 and 1.10.1337, recorded in NBIK 823, 1394, and 3177. Compare these documents with Kiyonari's (NBIK 1391, 1684, and 3174–75), particularly document 1684 which does not mention Kiyotane's wounds on 1.10.1337, but does refer to those of Kiyonari's retainer (*rojū*) Hyōe Saburō. A close comparison of these documents reveals that the Nejime cousins often fought on different days in slightly different locations, although at times (such as on 8.13.1350) they were attached to the same armies as well.

135. DNSR, series 6, vol. 10, pp. 67–68.

dents could not. This is evident in Makabe Hiromiki's petition which states "although his father might not perform military service . . . the son should not be punished. When a father and son live separately and act independently (*bekko no koi*), it has been customary not to punish [one for the crimes of the other]."[136]

Occasionally the distinction between *tozama* and *miuchi* seems vague. When *miuchi* were entrusted with substantial lands or castles by their *tozama* lord, tension arose because a nominally landless retainer controlled land holdings, which were, after all, a hallmark of *tozama* status. *Miuchi* who viewed their possession of lands as a delegation of *tozama* authority would scorn offers of outside rewards, though there were always those who opted the other way—particularly when a lord was otherwise preoccupied. The ambiguous position of a land-holding *miuchi* made social mobility a possibility, but attempts to change one's status were invariably risky.

Although the categories of *miuchi* and *tozama* maintained a degree of permeability—landed *miuchi* could, with luck and skill, achieve *tozama* status, while a weakened *tozama* could become the *miuchi* of a particularly influential man—expectations regarding warrior behavior remained constant throughout the fourteenth century. *Tozama* status designated all those capable of autonomous military action.

The increasing fiscal burden of war meant that some *tozama*, even those with impeccable documentary and genealogical credentials, were no longer able to behave with autonomy. Some *tozama* preferred to become the *miuchi* of a few powerful men. Others simply sold their prized documents of investiture. For example, although Takeda Jōnin had been appointed a *gokenin* in 1336 by Ashikaga Takauji and invested with the managerial post of *kumon shiki* in 1351, this office continued to be disputed for thirty years. Enervated by this internecine struggle over *kumon shiki* rights, Jōnin's progeny relinquished their claims to the office. Claiming to be "in great need of cash," Jōnin's descendants sold their investiture edicts in 1385 to Tōji temple, whose representative was one of their competitors, and thereupon descended into obscurity.[137] Status and rights to the land were becoming marketable commodities to be sold once they could no longer be asserted effectively.

The purchase of documents and genealogies ensured that wealth ultimately came to determine social status. Status had, in the 1330s, initially

---

136. Makabe *monjo*, 3.1356. *Ibaragi kenshi, Chūseihen*, comp. Ibaragi Prefecture (Mito, 1986), p. 215. See also DNSR, series 6, vol. 6, pp. 234–35.

137. *Mukō shishi shiryōhen* 1, comp. Mukō Shi (Mukō, 1988), 7.25.1385 Takeda Mitsumoto *uriwatashijō*, p. 232. Takeda Jōnin was granted *myōden* as *jitō shiki* and invested with *gokenin* status. Ibid., 12.24.1350 Ashikaga Takauji *gohan migyōsho an*, p. 221. Jōnin was also invested with *kumon shiki* on 2.13.1351. Ibid., Ashikaga Takauji *gohan migyōsho an*, p. 222. For more on the Takeda, see *Mukō shishi, jōhan*, comp. Mukō Shi (Mukō, 1983), vol. 1, pp. 647–49.

become divorced from any political regime, but *tozama* still hungered for certification of their rank. By the waning decades of the fourteenth century, however, the principle of documentary determinism had withered as well. Control over economic resources and not possession of pieces of paper assumed paramount importance. Once warrior status had become completely practical, however, a movement arose to prescribe its members according to the dictates of heredity. With the establishment of wealth as the basis for social rank and privilege and the advent of a modicum of peace, the ranks of society congealed, and a viscous social order continued throughout the mid–fifteenth century.

CONCLUSION

Although the highest echelons of warrior status had remained prescriptive throughout much of the Kamakura era, status became primarily performative once the wars of the fourteenth century erupted. The social distinctions in the fourteenth century were primarily based upon how one fought. The most salient differences were between *tozama*, *miuchi*, and *genin*. *Tozama* were autonomous men, exercising lordly rights over the land. *Miuchi* were their vassals or kin. *Miuchi* in turn could be divided into two groups; those more powerful men who became retainers (samurai), and those of lower status who formed corporate *miuchi* organizations and yet managed to maintain some autonomy in battle. Finally, *genin* had no name and no immediate recourse for autonomy. Instead, they aspired to become retainers. At times, these hereditary bondsmen could receive a name and lands through battle service and, as a result, become a *miuchi*.

The meaning of *hyakushō* evolved in tandem with these shifts. Throughout the thirteenth century, *hyakushō* designated elites. These men were obligated, however, to act in accord with their peers. With the establishment of the *gokenin* order, those powerful *hyakushō* who remained non-*gokenin* adopted the name of *myōshu* to distinguish themselves from other *hyakushō*, and thereby achieved a degree of autonomy. When war erupted in the fourteenth century, the most powerful of those who were still *hyakushō* became the *miuchi* of *tozama*, while their slightly less illustrious compatriots formed corporate *miuchi* organizations.

Ranking men, regardless of their pedigree, were suitable candidates to become regional magnates. On the other hand, those scions of the nobility lacking rank and office were indistinguishable from *tozama*. Accordingly, the term *tozama* does not represent a closed class, but rather an inclusive, egalitarian status encompassing nobles, autonomous warriors, and their wives.

Finally, in the hierarchical society of fourteenth-century Japan, practical considerations of status outweighed differences in gender.

Political turmoil and the fortunes of battle allowed some to embark upon the perilous endeavor of raising their status. The impact of war was more profound, however, than simply providing some with an opportunity to rise in the world. As we have seen, it also contributed to the creation of new social orders. Thus, with the outbreak of war *tozama* status expanded to include both Kamakura-era *gokenin* and *myōshu*. Furthermore, some *hyakushō* tended to establish social distance between themselves and their compatriots by becoming samurai. Yet, as the fourteenth century progressed social distinctions solidified and a sense of camaraderie faded.

Shifts in the mechanisms of social determination had profound ramifications for the nature of the Japanese polity as well. In the Kamakura era, status was created by edicts. With the establishment of *gokenin* status, all locals aspired to receive documents of investiture in order to claim a more exalted status. Heredification ensured that the ranks of *gokenin* would expand through time. Nevertheless, it was not until the destruction of the Kamakura *bakufu* that social determination became divorced from ties to a political regime. This ensured that the polities of 1333 onward had lost an important lever of social and political control. As we shall see, hegemons were forced primarily to rely upon largesse and ritual prerogatives in order to assert their political authority.

By the late fourteenth century, the monetary demands of battle exceeded the purses of some *tozama*. As these men no longer had the means to act independently in battle, their hard-won *gokenin* status ceased to have any real meaning. These warriors accordingly began selling their prized documents of investiture. Thus, although the veneer of documentary certification remained, status came to be ultimately determined by wealth.

The establishment of wealth as the basis of military power inadvertently undermined hereditary privileges, for those who prospered could purchase lands and rights that others had "owned" since "time immemorial." This inexorable process was resisted by others who created genealogies in order to enshrine their privileges. The need to "prove" one's origins through genealogical evidence suggests, to the contrary, a hereditary system under siege. Genealogical compendia mark a conservative reaction to the process by which status came to be determined by wealth.[138] Upstarts recognized this, and either forged or "mislaid" their genealogies. The full ironic potential of genealogies was not reached until the fifteenth century, when they were purchased by the ambitious to bolster their social claims.[139]

---

138. Genealogical encyclopedias, such as the *Sonpi bunmyaku*, were initially compiled late in the fourteenth century.

139. See Katsumata Shizuo, "Jūgo-roku seiki no Nihon," *Iwanami kōza Nihon tsūshi* 10, *chūsei* 4 (Iwanami Shoten, 1994), p. 7, for a diarist's quote on this matter.

The monetary economy represented a new vehicle of social determination independent of hereditary principle. Documents and genealogies, formerly ironclad sources of legitimacy, could be purchased by the newly rich in the fifteenth century, thereby subverting the principle of heredity while at the same time ironically contributing to its longevity. Genealogies merely became another commodity that allowed upstarts to achieve a status suitable for their ambitions and, concurrently, to funnel talent and wealth into established lineages. The establishment of cash as the foundation for both military endeavors and social rank was perhaps the most profound legacy of fourteenth-century war.

CHAPTER 5

Largesse and the Limits of Loyalty: Lordly Obligations in the Age of Two Courts

A largess universal, like the sun,
His liberal eye doth give to everyone.

Shakespeare, *Henry V*, act IV

It would seem to have been a misjudgment. Shortly after storming an enemy castle, Imagawa Ryōshun invited Shōni Fuyusuke to a banquet on the twenty-sixth day of the eighth month of 1375, whereupon he had the hapless Fuyusuke cut down in the midst of festivities. Imagawa Ryōshun justified his guest's slaughter by claiming that Fuyusuke's duplicity and disloyalty demanded drastic punishment. The Shimazu and Ōtomo, powerful Kyushu warriors who had joined Imagawa Ryōshun's expeditionary force, disagreed: the former defected to the opposing Southern Court, while the latter wavered, persuaded to maintain wary allegiance only after being liberally compensated.[1] Even

1. These incentives for the Ōtomo were *jitō shiki* grants. For a summary of the events surrounding Fuyut-suke's death, see *Kaei sandaiki*, in *Gunsho ruijū* 12, comp. Hanawa Hokinoichi (Naigai Kabushiki Kaisha, 1929), p. 203, and *Yamada Shōei jikki* (Yamada Shōei), *Kagoshima kenshiryōshū* 7, ed. Kagoshima Ken Kankō Iinkai (Kagoshima, 1967), pp. 70, 94–95. For the Imagawa offers to the Ōtomo and Shimazu, see NBIK 5229, 5232. For one of the few contemporary documentary references to Fuyusuke's "chastisement," see NBIK 5392.

though Ryōshun had been on the verge of annihilating the Kikuchi and other Kyushu supporters of the Southern Court, his offensive collapsed after Fuyusuke's death.

The dissolution of Ryōshun's army is perplexing, since victory and the prospect of lucrative rewards seemed to be at hand; the enervated forces of the Southern Court faced imminent defeat. Instead, the latter's beleaguered forces were rejuvenated by defectors from the Imagawa. This turn of events suggests that warriors of the fourteenth century were not as unscrupulous and aggrandizing as they have long been imagined. In fact, the disintegration of the Imagawa army may have stemmed from Ryōshun's demand for unconditional loyalty.

The episode remains significant, for it reveals a disjunction between scholarly assumptions regarding warrior loyalty and the actual behavior of fourteenth-century warriors. The underlying assumption in nearly all historical narratives of this epoch is that "loyalty was the highest value . . . [in] an age when disloyalty was commonplace. From Ashikaga Takauji until Tokugawa Ieyasu, *gekokujō*, the overthrow of lords by their vassals, was one of the most salient features of political life."[2] Or as proclaimed by James Murdoch in his well-known indictment of the era, the fourteenth century was "a golden age, not merely of turncoats, but of mediocrities."[3]

Murdoch is hardly alone in portraying fourteenth-century warriors as rebellious, disloyal men. For example, Peter Arnesen describes how Mōri Motoharu, an Aki warrior who had repeatedly fought for Ashikaga Takauji, "rebelled" against Takauji's *shugo* in 1350, but later fought for the Ashikaga in the 1360s.[4] Arnesen admits being baffled both by the ease of Mōri's "treason" and his subsequent reinstatement. How could it be that rebellion and treason, among the most egregious offenses of the modern era, seemed to evoke hardly a shrug in the fourteenth century? The existence of carefully preserved documents addressed to the same man, but emanating from both the Ashikaga *bakufu* and the Southern Court—incontestable proof that he was a "turncoat"—throws doubt on the notion that stigma adhered to those whose loyalty shifted. Moreover, warriors who repeatedly switched sides suffered little ill-consequence and may even have been generously rewarded, revealing

---

2. Albert Craig, *Chōshū in the Meiji Restoration, 1853–1868* (Cambridge: Harvard University Press, 1961), p. 145.

3. James Murdoch, *A History of Japan* (Kobe: "The Chronicle," 1910), vol. 1, p. 580. George Sansom echoes Murdoch: "The disintegration of the old warrior society . . . was hastened by the war between the Courts, when . . . a warrior's loyalty to his overlord was weakened to such a degree that the turncoat became a common phenomenon." See Sansom, *A History of Japan 1334–1615* (Stanford: Stanford University Press, 1961), p. 205.

4. Peter Judd Arnesen, "The Provincial Vassals of the Muromachi Shoguns," in Jeffrey P. Mass and William Hauser, eds., *The Bakufu in Japanese History* (Stanford: Stanford University Press, 1985), p. 115.

either an enormous toleration for cynicism on behalf of the fourteenth-century Japanese or a system of obligation in which loyalty was limited.

Words such as "treason" or "loyalty" should be used with caution for they imply the existence of a coherent and widely recognized ethos of encompassing devotion to a political or institutional entity that is capable of transcending personal interest. Such an ethos seems to have been lacking in fourteenth-century Japan. The term *chūsetsu*—generally defined as loyalty—appears in a bewildering variety of circumstances, most of which are only tenuously related to an abstract notion of loyalty. One can find references to *kitō chūsetsu*, or *chūsetsu* through prayer; *chūsetsu* for divine matters and festivities; and even the *chūsetsu* of upright temple administration![5] Warriors were rewarded for "battle *chūsetsu*"; "wound *chūsetsu*"; the *chūsetsu* of dismembering an opponent; the *chūsetsu* of taking prisoners; the *chūsetsu* of arriving at an encampment; the *chūsetsu* of causing others to surrender; the *chūsetsu* of defecting; and the *chūsetsu* of building an arrow storehouse.[6] A few enterprising sorts could even receive nearly simultaneous recognition for *chūsetsu* by both the Northern and Southern Courts.[7] The one common denominator is that *chūsetsu* refers to tangible, meritorious services worthy of compensation, such as prayers for victory, participation in battle, temple administration, or the construction of fortifications. The term *chūsetsu* is less an abstraction than a description of services rendered.

The meaning of the term *chūsetsu* is critical in comprehending the nature of military service in fourteenth-century Japan. If *chūsetsu* is conceived of as "loyalty," then one would assume that military service was obligatory; in other words, a warrior was ideally bound to fight for some lord, and his failure to do so would constitute treachery. If *chūsetsu* is understood as being roughly analogous to "service," however, then the autonomy of those rendering *chūsetsu* should be seen as normative; warriors who rendered *chūsetsu* labored under no encompassing obligation. *Chūsetsu*, predicated upon the receipt of adequate remuneration, constituted a narrowly defined commitment to fight or to provide some other service, which could not be equated with

---

5. For *kitō chūsetsu*, see NBIK 831 (*kitō chūkin*); 1473 (*kitō chūsetsu*); 2090 (*kitō chū*); NBIC 4518 (*kitō chūsetsu*); for the *chūsetsu* of festivities, NBIK 4159; for *jimu kōkō chūsetsu*, NBIC 4489.

6. For *kassen chūsetsu*, see NBIK 945 and NBIC 1976–77; for wound *chūsetsu*, NBIK 3724; for the *chūsetsu* of the capture of an enemy's head, see NBIK 3723; for the *chūsetsu* of one prisoner and two heads taken, NBIC 400–1; for the use of *chūsetsu* for those who had arrived at an encampment, NBIC 4130; for those praised for persuading other warriors to become allies, NBIK 2633; for those who recently switched sides, NBIK 2633; for the *chūsetsu* of building an arrow storehouse (*yagura*), see *Kanagawa kenshi shiryōhen, Kodai-chūsei*, vol. 3, no. 1, document 3481.

7. See NBIK 2289–90, 2309, 2313, and 2315 for documents issued to Aso Koretoki. In a period of eight days during the third month of 1347, Koretoki was praised by Ashikaga Tadayoshi and Emperor Go-Murakami for his military service (*chūsetsu* and *gunchū*, respectively).

unconditional obedience. Instead of transcending personal or familial interest, *chūsetsu* was synonymous with it.

Of course, not all of those who fought received recognition for their service (*chūsetsu*). Only those warriors possessing homelands and the capa-
bility to fight with autonomy could request that their service be compensated.
And, as we shall see, these warriors resisted serving under the command of
local warriors of like status. Instead they preferred to fight under the command of socially distant, prestigious men of Ashikaga or imperial lineage.

A corollary to this absence of any overriding devotion to a higher cause
is that those who aspired to rule Japan labored under an intense, lordly obligation to compensate the *chūsetsu* of their followers. Those such as Imagawa
Ryōshun who behaved too strictly, demanding a degree of devotion that simply did not exist at this time, or who were too intent upon amassing personal
lands and power, suffered the defection of these warriors, which resulted ultimately in their own military defeat.

No single system of lordship could encompass such disparate warrior
interests. Those who aspired to regional lordship—a lordship over land—
attempted to amass lands and increase their bands of hereditary followers.
In contrast to these regional magnates, national hegemons achieved the support of autonomous warriors through confirmations, grants of lands rights,
and other gifts: they constructed, in short, lordships over men. A hegemonic
lord was obliged to keep his supporters content through the magnanimous
distribution of rewards. If he failed to offer adequate compensation, or if his
promises were unreliable, then his followers would desert him. In other
words, land grants were offered in exchange for service (*chūsetsu*); no further obligation was entailed. Land was merely a conduit which linked a hegemon's promises and legitimating authority to the interests of autonomous,
free-spirited warriors. He who offered the most reliable compensation secured
the support and conditional allegiance of autonomous warriors. Only when
such a system of lordship is understood can one judge whether the fourteenth
century constituted an age of "turncoats and mediocrities."

THE LIMITS OF LANDED LORDSHIP

Prior to the onset of protracted warfare in the 1330s, no stable method of
regional lordship existed. The only extant pattern of lordship, that of a land-
holding autonomous warrior (*tozama*) and his hereditary followers (*miuchi*),
became inherently unstable as the *tozama*'s power increased and his *miuchi*
also became landholders. No mechanism existed for incorporating landed
miuchi, or for that matter *tozama*, into an institutionalized system of regional
control or military organization.

Tozama were loath to serve under any figure of similar social status.[8] The Kawano, a powerful *tozama* family which had been established in Iyo province for centuries, could not readily mobilize other *tozama*.[9] In the sixth month of 1336 Ashikaga Tadayoshi ordered the Kawano to lead the *jitō gokenin* of Iyo Province.[10] Judging from the frequency of this order's reiteration, the Kawano were singularly unsuccessful. Some orders of mobilization (*saisokujō*) contained injunctions to lead the *jitō gokenin* of Iyo Province and to punish those who did not obey orders;[11] while others cajoled the *jitō gokenin* of Iyo Province to follow Kawano Tsushima Nyūdō with promises of reward for their *chūsetsu* and threats of punishment for those who remained.[12] In fact, the Kawano were unable to lead even their own collateral lineages.[13] Instead Southern Court forces, composed of Iyo *tozama*, kept the Kawano on the defensive and even managed to capture and occupy the Seta castle, the main fortifications of the Kawano.[14] Ashikaga Tadayoshi eventually dispatched the commander (*taishō*) Hosokawa Yoriharu to help subdue the "rebels" of Iyo in 1342.[15]

Hosokawa Yoriharu was more successful than the Kawano, because *tozama*, or *jitō gokenin*, were more amenable to serving under him. Kobayakawa Ujihira of Aki Province, for example, fought under Yoriharu's command.[16] *Tozama* refused to serve under the Kawano in spite of Kawano Michimori's appointment as *shugo* of Iyo Province in 1350.[17] Even as late as 1380 it was still necessary for Ashikaga Yoshimitsu to issue the following proclamation: "*Jitō gokenin*, those exercising administrative authority over homelands (*honshoryō azukaridokoro satanin*) and *myōshu* shall obey the commands of the *shugo* and render *chūsetsu*. . . ."[18] Ashikaga *bakufu*

---

8. An analogous situation in which aristocratic leaders could lead their peers with great difficulty is admirably elucidated in Karl Leyser, *Rule and Conflict in an Early Medieval Society* (Oxford: Basil Blackwell, 1989).

9. The Kawano have frequently been known as the Kōno, but a phonetic representation of the pronunciation of their name found in Takezaki Suenaga's scrolls depicting the Mongol invasions reveals that Kawano is the correct pronunciation. See Conlan, *In Little Need of Divine Intervention*, pp. 115–16

10. NBIC 376, 6.14.1336 Ashikaga Tadayoshi *gunzei saisokujō an*.

11. NBIC 440, 8.4.1336 Ashikaga Tadayoshi *gunzei saisokujō an*.

12. NBIC 530, 10.1336 Ashikaga Tadayoshi *gunzei saisokujō an*; also document 531. This order was duly repeated two months later; NBIC 562–63, 12.1336 Ashikaga Tadayoshi *gunzei saisokujō an*.

13. The Tokuno, for example, fought for the opposing Southern Court.

14. For the actions of the Kutsuna, see NBIC 1190, Kutsuna *ichizoku gunchū shidai*. The Ōtachi led the forces which captured Seta. See *Taiheiki*, maki 22, "Bingo Tomo ikusa no koto," p. 713.

15. NBIC 1167.

16. NBIC 1203, 10.20.1342 Kobayakawa Ujihira *gunchūjō an*. See also NBIC 1205, 1280–81. From this point onward, tensions between the Kawano and the Hosokawa increased, culminating in the Kawano's allegiance with the Southern Court. With the fall of Hosokawa Yoriyuki, the Kawano again allied with the Northern Court.

17. NBIC 1789.

18. NBIC 4627, 8.6.1380 Ashikaga Yoshimitsu *migyōsho an*.

authority and prestige constituted an important bulwark for Kawano efforts to mobilize *tozama* warriors; their own power and prestige were otherwise insufficient.

The power of local warrior lordship paled in comparison to that wielded by upstart warriors of Ashikaga blood. Much of the success of Ashikaga collaterals stemmed from the fact that they, more than magnates such as the Kawano, could readily ensure that *tozama* would receive rewards.[19] The Isshiki, Shibukawa, Shiba, Momonoi, Kira, Hosokawa, Niki, and Imagawa, little more than weak *gokenin* possessing minuscule landholdings in Mikawa province during the Kamakura period, suddenly became leaders of great armies as the Ashikaga amassed power and prestige.[20] Ancient local warrior families such as the Kawano could not compete with these former Mikawa *gokenin*.

Social stratification profoundly influenced institutional developments as well. Ashikaga collaterals were appointed military commanders (*taishō*), who could mobilize *tozama* from several provinces. *Shugo* offices were less powerful.[21] During the first two decades of the Nanbokuchō period *shugo* were unable to mobilize *tozama* from their appointed provinces readily.[22] Even when a powerful *tozama* such as Kawano Michimori was appointed *shugo* of his native province, he remained unable to call up other *tozama*. When men who had served as commanders (*taishō*) were concurrently appointed *shugo*, however, the office of *shugo* became virtually indistinguishable from that of a commander (*taishō*). This institutional amalgamation arose from the prominence of personality vis-à-vis position. *Tozama* were more concerned with the social status of a military leader than his office; collaterals exercised similar power whether *taishō* or *shugo*. The office of *shugo* was coveted by *tozama*, however, because it enabled them to distinguish themselves from other *tozama*.

Tozama who did not become *miuchi* of powerful men remained amenable to serving under Ashikaga collaterals because such men occupied a newly extant social strata superior to *tozama* status. For *tozama*, service under collaterals (be they *shugo* or *taishō*) in no way compromised their autonomy, nor lessened their status vis-à-vis other *tozama*. By contrast, service under the command of *tozama*, even those appointed *shugo*, was fundamentally undesirable for *tozama*. For example, the *tozama* Kutsuki Yoriuji willingly

---

19. For outright grants of lands as rewards by the Hosokawa in Tosa province, for example, see NBIC 933, 966. Most surviving Kawano documents are mere commendations. For six commendations (*kishin*) to Zennōji temple, see NBIC 3194–95, 3228–29, 3277, 3281.

20. See Ogawa, *Ashikaga ichimon shugo hattenshi no kenkyū*, pp. 29ff. and 333ff.

21. For further evidence of the refusal of *tozama* to obey the Shimazu in Ōsumi and Satsuma Provinces, see NBIK 3831, 3845, and 3883. See also *Taiheiki*, maki 38, "Miyakata hōki no koto," pp. 1130–34.

22. Urushihara Tōru, "Nanbokuchō shingi ni okeru shugo kengen no ichi kōsatsu," *Komonjo kenkyū* 27 (July 1987): 57–72.

fought under the command of Ashikaga collaterals such as the Imagawa in 1336, the Ishibashi in 1339, and Hosokawa Akiuji in 1347, but resisted serving under the command of the *shugo* Sasaki Dōyo, a non-Ashikaga magnate and *shugo* of Ōmi Province, in 1338.[23]

The power of Ashikaga *taishō* could be ephemeral. While imposing for a few weeks, armies composed of *tozama* suffered from inherent instability, and could, if defeated or stalemated, disintegrate with astounding rapidity.[24] Ashikaga collaterals had to rely upon other means, namely the creation of a local band of *miuchi*, to amass power and build a regional lordship. Some were successful; others were not. After the Kannō disturbance of 1350–52, several families of the Ashikaga lineage 0(*ichimon*) were destroyed or severely weakened.[25] On the other hand, the Hosokawa had no notable historical base in Shikoku but were able rapidly to recruit or absorb a number of Shikoku warriors as *miuchi*. This was a relatively easy task for the Hosokawa, because warriors of no great means preferred serving under a *taishō*, rather than a run-of-the-mill *tozama*. A *miuchi* of the Hosokawa occupied a superior social and political position to the *miuchi* of local *tozama*; those who linked their fortunes to a rising lord amassed derivative power, prestige, and quite possibly an opportunity for autonomy.

Social equality created an situation inimical to the creation of a local lordship. *Tozama* who amassed a degree of local power or prestigious titles incurred the hostility of other *tozama*. Furthermore, any *tozama* who expanded his local sphere of influence was forced to entrust castles and other lands to subordinates, thus providing them with an opportunity to achieve autonomy. In short, local magnates labored under severe difficulties when attempting to dominate a particular area. By comparison, Ashikaga collaterals dispatched to localities occupied a position of manifest social superiority to local *tozama* and easily forged a network of regional support.

Considerations of lineage, status, and personality influenced the sort of lordship a magnate would attempt, and the relative ease, or lack thereof, with which he would achieve his goals. Those who attempted to dispossess neighboring warriors generated the concerted opposition of local *tozama*, which ultimately crippled their attempts of regional consolidation. Of course, the creation of a regional lordship was not impossible; it was merely a labored,

---

23. Yoriuji served under Sasaki Dōyo early in 1338 (see chapter 2, p. 51) but refused to join Dōyo's Nara campaign later in the year. *Kutsuki monjo*, vol. 1, documents 7–9, 11. For Yoriuji's service under Hosokawa Akiuji, see ibid., document 14, 8.9.1347 Ashikaga Tadayoshi *migyōsho*; for his reluctance to serve under the Sasaki, see ibid., documents 56–58, 8.16.1338, 8.27, 9.3 Kyōgoku Dōyo *kakikudashi*; and document 10, 10.2.1338 Ashikaga Tadayoshi *migyōsho*.

24. For examples of *tozama* abandoning forces, see *Taiheiki*, maki 19, "Nitta Yoshisada Echizen no fu o otosukoto," pp. 598–602, and maki 38, "Miyakata hōki no koto," pp. 1130–34.

25. These included the Momonoi, Kira, and Ishibashi. See Ogawa, *Ashikaga ichimon shugo hattenshi no kenkyū*, p. 5.

piecemeal process most effectively accomplished over a span of several decades. *Taishō* who held powers of gift-giving had a significant advantage over their indigenous *tozama* competitors because they occupied a clearly superior social strata. Their largesse generated goodwill and prestige which, if they so chose, could be more readily transformed into a landed lordship. During the fourteenth century, however, the ephemeral qualities of prestige, awe, and reliability, generated by magnanimous rewards, were a sufficient basis for attracting *tozama* support.

Those tozama magnates most successful, such as the Ōuchi, were those who took advantage of the turmoil of the Kannō era to usurp hegemonic powers of largesse. Ōuchi Hiroyo first used the disturbances of the 1350s to occupy (*ōryō*) shrine lands.[26] More remarkably, in 1352, the Ōuchi started granting small amounts of lands to followers.[27] Ōuchi documents increased dramatically in scope and frequency during the ensuing decades. Disputes were adjudicated, indicative of the establishment of a local judicial apparatus; lands and *jitō shiki* were granted or entrusted to warriors for the sake of provisions; transfers of *jitō shiki* were confirmed; warriors were recommended to the *bakufu* to receive rewards, and even *tozama* holdings were confirmed.[28] In addition, the Ōuchi issued prohibitions for temples and undertook an extensive campaign of shrine rebuilding.[29] Through these myriad efforts the Ōuchi attempted to increase the social distance between themselves and other *tozama* by adopting a munificent policy of local patronage and largesse. Unsurprisingly, the Ōuchi usurpation of hegemonic prerogatives led to the *bakufu*'s campaign against them in 1399.[30] *Tozama* remained, however, unwilling to serve under him. For example, when Ōuchi Yoshihiro crossed into Kyushu in 1375, he led only three hundred family members and *miuchi*.[31] By contrast, Imagawa Ryōshun's army exceeded four thousand men.[32]

Ashikaga collaterals, such as Imagawa Ryōshun, led armies composed of *tozama* drawn from Northern Kyushu and Western Japan, but they could maintain a force for only a brief period of time. Indeed, even prior to his murder of Shōni Fuyusuke in 1375, Imagawa Ryōshun's problems were considerable. According to a petition by Mōri Motoharu of Aki Province,

---

26. NBIC 4572.
27. NBIC 2324.
28. For a sampling of the Ōuchi documents, see NBIC 4054, 4266, 4370, 4581, 4601–2, 4607–9, 4621, 4641, 4647–48, 4726, 4736, and for confirmation of some Kumagai holdings, 4731.
29. For the prohibitions, see NBIC 4734. Documentation for the rebuilding of shrines appears in NBIC 3543, 3785.
30. This campaign is chronicled most fully in *Sakaiki*.
31. NBIC 4252. The term *ichizoku kenin*, or family members and housemen, is used in this document.
32. For this estimate of the Imagawa forces, see *Sakaiki*, pp. 47–48, and Satō, *Nanbokuchō no dōran*, p. 450.

The *jitō gokenin* of the two provinces of Bingo and Aki either sent a representative (*daikan*) or arrived late or returned to their provinces. Only Motoharu alone, bringing along his sons served together [with Imagawa forces] since the very beginning [of this campaign] four years ago. In various encampments in various areas, not once have I been negligent. My service (*chūsetsu*) has been outstanding.[33]

Motoharu depicted his *chūsetsu* of remaining in Kyushu as truly exceptional; *jitō gokenin* acted as they pleased, joining and departing Ryōshun's army according to whim. After Ryōshun's debacle of 1375, Ashikaga Yoshimitsu dispatched his younger brother to lead *jitō gokenin* from Tōtōmi, Suruga, Bingo, and Aki Provinces to Kyushu to aid the beleaguered remnants of the Imagawa army.[34] Only a younger brother of the Ashikaga shogun had the prestige to lead a force of *tozama* drawn from such diverse areas.

Nearly all documented rewards were granted to fickle *tozama*, and not their *miuchi* counterparts. This apparent irony, that those who were least reliable received the most rewards, indicates that national, hegemonic lordship operated according to a different set of norms than regional lordship. National leadership, in other words, did not entail obligatory *tozama* subservience. Hegemonic lordship was based on land grants, not land per se. The act of granting lands and other rewards to disinterested *tozama* enabled a hegemon to create a reservoir of symbolic capital which formed the cornerstone of his political power. In order to rule the realm, one had to first give it away.

LAND, LARGESSE, AND LORDSHIP

After reading the above, one might be inclined to conclude that Murdoch was essentially correct—it was an age of turncoats if not, perhaps, mediocrities. *Tozama* warriors apparently exemplified men of mean scruple, demanding excessive rewards and offering niggardly services. Kitabatake Chikafusa certainly believed so, stating, "These days a popular saying has it that if a warrior should enter into a single battle or suffer the loss of a vassal he will demand that 'My reward should be all of Japan; half the country will not be enough!' Of course, no one is really apt to make such an absurd demand, yet the saying is a first step to disorder."[35] Chikafusa's criticism is founded on

---

33. NBIC 4065, 4665. For a later confirmation by Hosokawa Yoriyuki, see NBIC 4112.
34. NBIK 5332.
35. Paul Varley, trans., *A Chronicle of Gods and Sovereigns: Jinnō Shōtōki of Kitabatake Chikafusa* (New York: Columbia University Press, 1980), pp. 260–61.

the belief that warriors should not overly boast of their services or demand compensation.

Kitabatake Chikafusa posited the root of disorder as the failure of warriors to serve their "lords." He lamented, "Today . . . there are only people who, in all matters, disdain their lords and trumpet their own merits."[36] Chikafusa believed that a powerful central government, capable of serving as a focus of a transcendent notion of loyalty, served as the basis of social and political order. And yet, as should be evident, most *tozama* did not perceive the central government as consisting an obligation which transcended narrow self-interest. To the contrary, most *tozama* implicitly believed that the onus of responsibility rested not on themselves, but on the competing regimes to secure support by granting rewards. Instead of land grants guaranteeing obligation, service (*chūsetsu*) demanded adequate compensation.

Confirmations and land grants bestowed upon autonomous warriors forged social bonds but did not entail additional obligations of military service. A regime whose promises were generous and reliable established credibility and accumulated power in the form of symbolic capital directly proportional to its largesse.[37] This symbolic capital enabled Ashikaga shoguns and collateral generals of the Ashikaga lineage to formalize their superior status and concurrent power through the establishment of distinct social strata which monopolized the ability to distribute rewards. Their largesse generated support, and ensured that their social and political position of superiority did not openly threaten or challenge *tozama* control of lands. The resultant social division between those of Ashikaga blood and *tozama* correspondingly enhanced Ashikaga ability to mobilize, direct, and lead forces composed of regionally based warriors. The seeming selflessness of refusing to amass lands enshrined an inequality of power relations which enabled warriors who had no lands to direct armies and to exercise considerable military force. Lords of men, not land, ruled the realm.[38]

"Then was then; now is now—rewards are lord!"[39] This slogan is less a cynical commentary on warriors—as it might initially seem—than a metonymic recognition of the centrality of rewards for lordship.[40] Of course, rewards came

---

36. Ibid., p. 263.

37. For more on the nature of symbolic capital, see Pierre Bourdieu, *Outline of a Theory of Practice* (Cambridge: Cambridge University Press, 1977).

38. For an important article on the personal nature of lordship see Walter Schlesinger, "Lord and Follower in Germanic Institutional History," in Fredric L. Cheyette, ed., *Lordship and Community in Medieval Europe* (New York: Holt, Rinehart, and Winston, 1968), pp. 65–99. See in particular p. 75: "[T]he man who sought to erect a royal lordship depended on his followers; these were the chief props of his future power."

39. *"Mukashi wa mukashi ima wa ima on koso nushi yo,"* from *Genpei jōsuiki* (Miyai Shoten, 1991–), vol. 4, maki 20, "Ishibashi kassen no koto," p. 60.

40. This slogan likewise represents a parody of the *History of the Later Han Dynasty*.

in many guises. One character on one's name could be bestowed upon a deserving warrior; battle flags could be given; swords could be granted to a valorous warriors; homelands (*honryō*) could be confirmed; new land rights, or *shiki*, could be granted; and lands and revenues could be provisionally entrusted to warriors for the sake of military provisions.[41] Regardless of the form of rewards (*on*), largesse was an essential component of hegemonic lordship.

Although neither the *Baishōron* or the *Taiheiki* is a model of historical objectivity, both chronicles reveal that magnanimity was the hallmark of an ideal leader. Ashikaga Takauji received extravagant praise for his generosity. "Ruling the realm was his prime motive, so he placated bitter enemies by confirming their homelands (*honryō*) and bestowed grand rewards on those who had performed acts of merit (*chūkō*)."[42] Go-Daigo, on the other hand, was admonished for his parsimony:

> Since the great disturbance of Genkō (1331–33) all the soldiers (*shisotsu*) of the realm joined the imperial army (*kangun*) in order to receive rewards (*shō*) for military merit (*gunkō*). . . . These countless warriors hoped for a token of appreciation for their exploits after peace returned to the realm. Nevertheless, because only nobles and rank officials (*hikan*) have been granted rewards (*onshō*), each warrior, resentful that his acts of merit (*chūkō*) have received no recognition, has discarded his petitions (*mōshijō*), abandoned his suits . . . and returned to his home province.[43]

Go-Daigo granted rewards in order to demonstrate his authority over the court, but did not conceive these grants as a vehicle to compensate warriors for their *chūsetsu*. For example, two days after returning to the capital in triumph in 1333, he confirmed the holdings of the rival imperial lineage.[44] This served to establish his supremacy, because the right to give and confirm

---

41. In a particularly well-known case, Go-Daigo bestowed the "taka" of Takaharu (his name as imperial prince) to Ashikaga Takauji in recognition of the latter's service. For a more general reward of names, see NBIK 3723 (1354/9/3 Ashikaga Takauji *kanjō an*). The 3.29.1351 entree of the *Jizōin nikki* (most readily accessible as the *Kannō ninnen hinami ki*, pp. 364–65) tells of the grant of a battle flag (*mihata*) from Ashikaga Takauji to a deserving warrior. According to p. 79 of *Baishōron*, two housemen (*kenin*) of the Yūki fought so valiantly at Tenryūgawa in 1335 that Ashikaga Takauji gave each a sword in appreciation. Although rewards for *jitō shiki* were perhaps most common, warriors were also rewarded *ryōke shiki* for their efforts. See NBIC 2118, 2123, and 1354 (8.7.1344 Ashikaga Tadayoshi *saikyojō*). Although some later documents offer *jitō shiki*—see NBIK 5008, and NBIC 2119, 2128—others simply offer lands to be entrusted an make no distinction between *jitō*, *ryōke*, or any *shiki* at all for that matter. See NBIK 5001.

42. *Baishōron*, p. 140.

43. *Taiheiki*, maki 13, "Ryūme shinsō no koto," p. 351.

44. DNSR, vol. 1, 6.7.1333 Go-Daigo tennō *rinji* pp. 90–91. See also Tanaka Yoshinari, *Nanbokuchō jidaishi* (Kōdansha Gakujutsu Bunko, 1979), pp. 108–9.

affirmed a position of ultimate authority.[45] Nevertheless, Go-Daigo's Kenmu regime only grudgingly rewarded those who fought in battle; warriors merely reporting for duty were not rewarded because such action was considered obligatory.[46] By contrast, no such constraints hindered the Ashikaga, who praised warriors for arriving at an encampment.[47] Even in 1336 the Ashikaga seem to have had lower expectations regarding the obligation of their followers. Or, phrased positively, they provided compensation for a wider variety of military services than did Go-Daigo.

Go-Daigo could not countenance delegating his gift-giving authority even though this prerogative had been assumed by his son, Prince Moriyoshi, before Go-Daigo had even established his Kenmu regime. Moriyoshi had led the rebellion against Kamakura in 1332, while Go-Daigo languished in exile, and had enticed warriors to fight against Kamakura by issuing calls to arms and, as we shall see, bestowing grants of land.[48] Once the *bakufu* collapsed, however, the triumphant Go-Daigo refused to recognize rewards that had been granted by Moriyoshi, and instead chose to jail his "treasonous" son, who would be killed in 1335. For Go-Daigo, the desire to establish a centralized imperial state superseded the need to compensate those who had been rewarded by Moriyoshi. Nevertheless, the tenacity of the *Taiheiki* critique of Go-Daigo suggests that generous compensation of military exploits was widely recognized as an integral component of national lordship.

Go-Daigo's treatment of Moriyoshi partisans from Harima, the Akamatsu, reveals that his revocation of land grants generated considerable enmity. Go-Daigo dismissed Akamatsu Enshin from his post of *shugo* of Harima because he failed to order his son, Norisuke, to desist from despoiling lands.[49] The disgruntled Akamatsu Enshin is purported to have said,

45. The pioneering study on "gift giving" and authority is Marcel Mauss, *The Gift* (New York: W. W. Norton, 1990).

46. NBIK 93–94, 199–2000 reveal that warriors repeatedly submitted reports of arrival, but received no compensation for this service. For a warrior's complaint regarding his lack of compensation in 10.1335, see NBIK 330.

47. A Ryūzōji Ieyasu document contain references to his military service (*gunchū*), yet the only tangible service Ieyasu seems to have accomplished was to arrive at an encampment; NBIK 435. For another document which equates encampment with military service, see NBIK 421–22.

48. Prince Moriyoshi issued numerous calls to arms which proved instrumental in leading to the Kamakura *bakufu*'s downfall. For extensive coverage of Moriyoshi, see Mori "Ōtōnomiya Moriyoshi shinnō ryōji ni tsuite," pp. 210–13.

49. For the dispute, see KI 32319 and 32474, and *Hyōgo kenshi shiryōhen chūsei*, vol. 8, Kujō ke *monjo*, document 53, 2.9.1334 Abe Chikakatsu *keiyakujō an*. See also *Hyōgo kenshi shiryōhen chūsei*, vol. 8, documents 54–64. KI 32573 provides proof that Enshin served as *shugo*. For exhaustive treatment of this incident from Go-Daigo's perspective, see Andrew Edmund Goble, *Kenmu: Go-Daigo's Revolution* (Cambridge: Harvard University Press, 1996), pp. 146–47.

Although of no great stature, Enshin managed to turn back a great enemy during the initial dispute of Genkō (1331–33). In all, I believe that my merit was first [in all of Japan]. Nevertheless, my lands of reward (*onshō no chi*) were less than those unjust men who surrendered [from Kamakura]. Due to this particular resentment, I threw away the merit of many days.[50]

Although this passage may have been fabricated by the authors of the *Taiheiki*, other evidence suggests that the Akamatsu had been rewarded by Moriyoshi. Enshin is purported to have said, in the continuation of the above passage, that he could not forget the rewards granted by Prince Moriyoshi,[51] while his son, Norisuke, claimed to be a "newly appointed *jitō* as the result of the court's benevolence (*chō'on shinpo jitō*)" to Wada estate in Settsu Province.[52] As Go-Daigo refused to recognize Norisuke's appointment, one can infer that this "courtly benevolence" stemmed from Moriyoshi's largesse.[53]

The notion of compensating acts of merit proved essential in securing the allegiance of *tozama*. Inadequate compensation forced warriors to throw away their merit, and secure another source of compensation. The Akamatsu episode led to a fundamental critique of the Kenmu regime, which reveals that the notion of lordly largesse had become an unquestioned vehicle of legitimation. As the author of the *Taiheiki* would then comment, "For what crime did Enshin alone have only his single homelands confirmed, and his appointment as *shugo* [of Harima] revoked? Those who performed service should be promoted; those who have committed crimes should be punished."[54] In short, most *tozama* believed that even emperors were obligated to compensate the *chūsetsu* of their followers.

Promises of reward underpinned fourteenth-century military power. For example, once the breach between Go-Daigo and Ashikaga Takauji became manifest in the ninth month of 1335, Takauji immediately began confirming and bestowing lands. These rewards exceeded the narrow bounds of legality—for indeed Go-Daigo had already issued orders to attack the

---

50. *Taiheiki*, maki 16, "Saigoku hōki Kangun shinpatsu no koto," pp. 465–66.
51. Ibid.
52. *Hyōgo kenshi shiryōhen chūsei*, vol. 8, document 64, 4.1335 Settsu no kuni Wada no shō *jitō* Akamatsu Norisuke *chinjō an*.
53. Further evidence of the close ties between the Akamatsu and Moriyoshi are evident in the *Taiheiki*, where one sees that Enshin accompanied Prince Moriyoshi on his triumphant return to the capital in 1333. See maki 12, "Kuge onittō no koto," p. 311, for the Akamatsu serving with Moriyoshi. Likewise, for the possibility of Akamatsu Enshin's rebellious intentions after Prince Moriyoshi had been arrested, see Kōsaka, *Akamatsu Enshin Michisuke*, pp. 39–48.
54. *Taiheiki*, maki 13, "Ryūme shinsō no koto," p. 352.

Ashikaga brothers—but this did not infringe upon their legitimacy.[55] Promises were honored even when lands had been mistakenly granted; warriors were simply promised other lands. For example, Ōi Kishiro Takatsuna and eight other men interfered (ōbō) with the administration of Zōta no shō in Sanuki Province because they had apparently been promised the ryōke shiki of this shōen as a reward for military valor. The proprietor of this land, Daisō Shōbō of Zuishin'in, staunchly supported the Northern Court, so Ashikaga Tadayoshi ruled that Daisō Shōbō's manager was to take control of Zōta no shō, and Takatsuna and others were to receive (yodatsu) other lands from the onshōgata.[56] Far more important than the lands which composed a reward was the promise of a reward; rewards were irrevocable although the particular lands comprising them could easily shift.

Lands became appropriable (kessho) when the proprietor aided a competing political entity, which essentially destabilized the validity of all land rights. As land rights became insecure, the need for a protector or guarantor increased. Confirmations or rewards of lands most valued were those issued by a hegemon who had a reputation for reliability; the more prestigious and reliable the edict, the easier it was for a local to maintain (or seize) lands. All lands could be declared appropriable. Kessho claims originated from the local regions; central authorities frequently relied on oaths to determining their veracity.[57] Of course, the potential for abuse was considerable. For example, Miyoshi Michihide took advantage of Yamanouchi Michitada's absence—Michitada was fighting in Kyushu under the direction of Imagawa Ryōshun in 1375—and claimed that the hereditary lands (honryō) of the Yamanouchi, Jibi no shō, were kessho. After receiving an edict (kudashibumi) legitimating his claim, Michihide proceeded to forcibly enter (rannyū) and

55. For the initial grants by Ashikaga Takauji on 9.27.1335, see NBIC 167–68 (9.27.1335 Ashikaga Takauji kudashibumi); and NBIK 304, 9.27.1335 Ashikaga Takauji kudashibumi, granting Mutsu, Kawachi, Sagami, Settsu, Shinano, Bungo, and Kōzuke lands to the Miura. The first edicts demanding the chastisement of the Ashikaga brothers were issued on 9.25.1335. See NBIC 165–66. Although the Taiheiki claims that Ashikaga Takauji began awarding hereditary Ashikaga and Nitta lands to their followers immediately after defeating Hōjō Tokiyuki during the eighth month of 1335 (see Taiheiki, maki 14, "Nitta Ashikaga kakushitsu koto," p. 377), the first surviving records of Ashikaga grants appear after Go-Daigo's regime began issuing orders for the chastisement of the Ashikaga. For a grant by Ashikaga Tadayoshi to the Nagai in Harima (which was a proprietary province—bunkoku— of the Nitta) see NBIC 210, 12.26.1335 Ashikaga Tadayoshi kudashibumi.

56. NBIC 1354 (8.7.1344 Ashikaga Tadayoshi saikyojō). The onshōgata was the administrative organ of the Muromachi bakufu responsible for rewards. Bettō shiki had been previously granted to Daisō Shōbō of Zuishin'in on 5.14.1341, and this was translated into management (kanri). See NBIC 1078, 1082. Daisō Shōbō was able to maintain his bettō shiki rights, which were later transferred to another temple. See Kadokawa Nihon chimei daijiten (Kadokawa Shoten, 1978–1990), vol. 37, p. 466. The ultimate fate of Takatsuna and his companions is unknown.

57. See, for example, NBIC 4521.

plunder the *shōen*.[58] Although the Yamanouchi were ultimately able to maintain their lands, Miyoshi's plot failed merely because of Imagawa Ryōshun's staunch support for Yamanouchi Michitada. Even after forty years of warfare, an edict could legitimate the seizure of lands.

The relationship between hegemons and *tozama* was in many ways symbiotic. A magnanimous hegemon could confirm autogenic *tozama* rights, which although durable, were insufficient, for it was exponentially more difficult, although not impossible, for a *tozama* to maintain his lands without a prestigious edict of confirmation. Correspondingly, *tozama* aggrandizements at the expense of their neighbors were best achieved through receiving a prestigious confirmation which could overrule, if not fully erase, autogenic *tozama* rights. *Tozama*, in order to bolster their local power, preferred to serve under the hegemon most reliable and able to guarantee his promised rewards. A hegemon attempted to attract those *tozama* who were most powerful because they could protect their rights and attain, through force if necessary, those lands promised them. As for those who were relatively weak, their lands were generally destined to become "appropriable" (*kessho*).

Lordship was predicated upon the ability to procure rewards for allies and followers. This is most evident during the Kannō era (1350–52) when warfare erupted, precipitated by a dispute between the Kō brothers—Ashikaga retainers—and Ashikaga Tadayoshi. Ashikaga Takauji fought with the Kō brothers against his younger brother Tadayoshi, but suffered a string of defeats. Peace was restored on the twenty-seventh day of the second month of 1351 after the two Kō brothers had been ambushed and killed.[59] According to the *Entairyaku*, "The shogun, through tremendous effort, secured rewards for forty-two warriors."[60] He achieved this even though he had been worsted in battle by his younger brother. Furthermore, Takauji extracted an oath from Tadayoshi to honor his rewards. This concession was significant because Tadayoshi had already declared the lands of these forty-two appropriable (*kessho*) and rewarded them to his followers.[61] Tadayoshi's victory enhanced Takauji's power and prestige, and Takauji by first awarding his followers was able to consolidate his dominant position in the *bakufu* and reiterate his power as the ultimate giver of gifts. In spite of their military superiority, allies of Tadayoshi were not treated favorably. When Hosokawa Akiuji arrived in the capital at the head of an army drawn from Shikoku, he

58. NBIC 4260.

59. The best account of this incident appears in the *Kannō ninnen hinami ki*, pp. 361–62.

60. See *Entairyaku*, vol. 3, 3.3.1351, p. 426. Supporting documentary evidence can be found in NBIK 3021–22, 3.1.1351 Ashikaga Takauji *kanjō*, which refers to an oath by Tadayoshi guaranteeing that Takauji's followers would be rewarded.

61. Satō, *Nanbokuchō no dōran*, pp. 248–49.

requested an audience with Takauji but was rebuffed; the shogun had no
desire to meet a man who had surrendered (*kōsannin*). Tōin Kinkata wryly
commented that Akiuji showed fear for the first time since coming to the
capital.[62] In other words, once the indefatigable Takauji had established primacy in granting rewards, he could punish those who fought against him by
claiming that they surrendered; accordingly their lands were potentially
appropriable (*kessho*). Takauji's promise, more binding than Tadayoshi's,
ensured the supremacy of his authority. Those who fought with him invariably benefited; those who fought for Tadayoshi were less sure of adequate
compensation. It should come as no surprise that when warfare resumed a
few months later, Takauji easily defeated his brother.[63]

Close relatives were most liable to compete in asserting powers of hegemonic lordship. Ashikaga Takauji jealously guarded his prerogatives, and
even attacked one of his own sons, Ashikaga Tadafuyu, who began granting
lands to Kyushu warriors and mobilizing them to fight under his command,
instead of entering religious orders as he had promised.[64] Even though Tadafuyu claimed to be "acting in accordance with the wishes of both Ashikaga
Takauji and Tadayoshi,"[65] his father Takauji issued a stream of mobilization
orders to Kyushu warriors as soon as he was aware of the "clear rebellion"
of his "unfilial" son.[66] Tadafuyu continued granting lands to Kyushu warriors and mobilizing them to his cause. Takauji dispatched an army in the
fourth month of 1350,[67] but he met with a crushing defeat. In contrast to
Takauji, who limped back to the capital with only forty-two followers, Tadafuyu managed to dominate Kyushu and western Japan during most of the
1350s and 1360s.

Hegemonic lords amassed considerable power even though they knew next
to nothing about the lay of the land. For example, Ashikaga Tadafuyu promised
a certain Yasutomi Yasushige lands but mistakenly identified the province![68]
In order to avoid such misunderstandings, Tadafuyu often issued *uragaki ando*:

---

62. *Entairyaku*, vol. 3, p. 426 of 3.3.1351.

63. Tadayoshi was defeated, imprisoned in a Kamakura temple, and poisoned exactly one year after his
    triumph over the Kō brothers.

64. Ashikaga Tadafuyu chose to travel to Kyushu prior to 10.11.1349 instead of becoming a priest. NBIK
    2647–48. Once he arrived, he began granting lands to regional warriors and mobilizing them to fight
    under his command. For his first grants of lands to Kyushu warriors, on 11.19.1349, see NBIK 2661,
    and also NBIK 2663–64 and 2676; for his first mobilization order, on 11.9.1349, see NBIK 2657.
    For other orders issued by Tadafuyu in 1349, see NBIK 2665, 2669, 2679.

65. See NBIK 2657, 2665, 2669, and, for a prayer for both Takauji and Tadayoshi, see NBIK 2649.

66. NBIK 2680–83 for Takauji's mobilization orders; and NBIK 2685 for a letter of invective directed
    against his son.

67. NBIK 2739.

68. NBIK 3095, 3220. Yasutomi suggested that it was distance which had led to Tadafuyu's mistaking
    Buzen for Chikuzen Province. Tadafuyu duly corrected his error.

he confirmed a petition which had been submitted to him by adding a brief notation to the reverse side of the request.[69] In other words, Tadafuyu responded to *tozama* requests and granted whatever they desired. Tadafuyu's grants of land would be revoked, however, if the original owner joined his forces; hereditary homelands (*honryō*) were inviolable. As he stated, "If the original owner of [previously rewarded] lands allies himself with [our] forces, then [his lands shall be returned and] other lands shall be exchanged for rewards."[70] Tadafuyu's respect of *honryō* rights ensured that he would develop no mortal enemies. Unfortunately for him, a great number of western warriors, impressed by his generosity, flocked to his banner. Those who had previously served with Tadafuyu lost their rewards as all lands were returned to the original owners. The hapless Yasutomi Yasushige lamented, "Although I was rewarded various lands for military merit (*gunkō no chi*), I have become virtually landless (*musoku*) as the original owners (*honshu*) have joined our forces. This turn of events is unbearable (*nankan no shidai nari*)."[71] Tadafuyu became a victim of his own success. Because nearly every local warrior joined his forces, appropriable lands (*kessho*) became virtually nonexistent. Tadafuyu exhausted his supply of "gifts"; as his promises became less dependable, his forces withered.

Tadafuyu's initial military strength contrasts sharply with the legendary tribulations of Isshiki Dōyu.[72] Dōyu threatened to confiscate one fifth of the holdings of warriors who did not render military service.[73] He eventually confiscated the homelands of the Ryūzōji, who quickly abandoned such an "unprincipled" (*mudō*) leader, and instead joined Ashikaga Tadafuyu with the hope of receiving a confirmation of their homelands.[74] Tadafuyu obliged with an *uragaki ando* to Ryūzōji Ietane in 1350.[75]

By penalizing warriors who fought neither for nor against him, Isshiki Dōyu became increasingly unable to mobilize adequate forces. A comparison between Isshiki Dōyu and Ashikaga Tadafuyu reveals that magnanimity and largesse allowed a hegemon to gain the support of *tozama* warriors, while punitive measures spawned deep-seated grudges on the part of warriors who felt unfairly treated. Isshiki Dōyu acted too much like a regional magnate, attempting to build a base of lands, and not enough like a "gift-giving" supraregional hegemon. By confiscating lands of warriors who arrived in

69. For more on Tadafuyu's *uragaki ando*, see Kawazoe Shōji, "'Chinzei tandai' Ashikaga Tadafuyu: Kyushu ni okeru Kannō seihen," in *Kyūshū chūsei kenkyū* 2 (Bunken Shuppan, 1980): 187–242.
70. NBIK 2802, 2829. See also Yamaguchi Takamasa, *Nanbokuchōki Kyūshū shugo no kenkyū* (Bunken Shuppan, 1989), p. 21.
71. NBIK 3095.
72. Isshiki Dōyu suffered from confused jurisdiction, few lands, and little support. See NBIK 1475, 1481.
73. NBIK 840. For more on Dōyu, see chapter seven.
74. NBIK 3304–5.
75. NBIK 2903. By the first month of 1351, Ryūzōji Iehira received the same. See NBIK 2982, 3292.

encampments but refused to fight, Isshiki Dōyu seemed arbitrary and unreasonable to *tozama*. Tadafuyu's failure stemmed from the opposite flaw—his promises exceeded the bounds of reliability.

Kitabatake Chikafusa's relations with the Ishikawa family of Mutsu Province illustrates that Southern Court leaders were cognizant of the importance of rewards, but less aware of the significance of autogenic rights of homeland to *tozama* warriors. Even though the Ishikawa family had helped Nitta Yoshisada sack Kamakura in 1333, the governor of Mutsu under the new Kenmu regime, Kitabatake Akiie, granted Ishikawa lands to Yūki Munehiro in 1334.[76] Ashikaga Takauji confirmed, however, the land holdings (*hon chigyō*) of one Ishikawa collateral, Ishikawa Kabata Gorō Tarō, in 1335, but the main line of the Ishikawa received no confirmations.[77] Unsurprisingly, both Ishikawa Kabata Gorō Tarō and the other Ishikawa warriors fought for Takauji, participating in both the epic battle of Minatogawa and the attack on Mt. Hiei in 1336.[78]

Because their neighbors, the Yūki, were staunchly allied with the Southern Court, the Ishikawa came under intense pressure to defect. Kitabatake Chikafusa tempted them: "The Ishikawa have generally been enemies (*onteki*) but those who regretting their past actions shall join our forces will have their homelands (*honryō*) confirmed; later merit (*kō*) will be subsequently rewarded."[79] The Ishikawa responded by asking for their homelands, which had been granted to the Yūki in 1334. This incensed Kitabatake Chikafusa, who berated them:

It has been customary for those who regret their prior inaction [i.e., those who refuse to respond to a call to arms] to have only one half or one third of their land holdings (*shoryō*) confirmed. Confirmation of [all] your homelands (*honryō*) exceeds the bounds of benevolent rule (*zensei*). In recent years you have been deeply [tainted] with [association with] the enemy (*onteki*); now prior to joining our forces you present a list of desired lands. Is that not an insult to warriors (*yumiya no chijoku*)? . . . How can [people] who tend to have the outlook of a merchant (*shōnin*) be of use to the Court? Nevertheless, as previously promised, your homelands

76. *Fukushima kenshi* 7, Ise Yūki *monjo*, doc. 17, 4.6.1334 Mutsu Kokushi *kudashibumi an*, p. 371. Three districts (*gō*) of Ishikawa no shō were granted to Yūki Munehiro.

77. Ibid., Endō Ishikawa *monjo*, doc. 1, 8.1335 Ashikaga Takauji *kudashibumi*, pp. 456–57.

78. Ibid., Kakuda Ishikawa *monjo*, doc. 2, 7.1336 Ishikawa Yoshimitsu *wakatō* Yabukigawa Yorimichi *gunchūjō*, p. 532. Ishikawa Yoshimitsu was cut down in front of the Jizō-dō on the western slopes of Mt. Hiei.

79. Ibid., Matsudaira Yūki *monjo*, doc. 5, 12.3.1338 Kitabatake Chikafusa *migyōsho*, p. 503. The passage cited was a quote from a document of the previous month. See Ibid., Matsudaira Yūki *monjo*, doc. 3, 11.11.1338 Kitabatake Chikafusa *sodehan* Sōshin *shojō*, p. 501.

(*honryō*) shall be confirmed; later acts of service shall be correspondingly rewarded.[80]

Kitabatake Chikafusa had no qualms about enticing warriors with rewards for tangible acts of merit. He could not countenance the invalidation of earlier decrees; a reward was a reward. Lands granted to the Yūki could not be returned to the Ishikawa. Instead of finding other suitable lands to compensate the Ishikawa (or the Yūki), as Takauji might have done, Chikafusa castigated the Ishikawa as having "the outlook of a merchant" for daring to request additional lands prior to joining his forces. The impasse between Kitabatake Chikafusa and the Ishikawa stemmed from the perhaps inevitable uncertainty regarding the delineation of a family's homelands. From the Ishikawa's perspective, homelands constituted the fullest extent of their holdings—all the lands under their control prior to 1334. For Kitabatake Chikafusa, however, Ishikawa homelands were composed solely of current holdings. The Ishikawa demanded the full restoration of their homelands in order to rehabilitate their warrior honor (*yumiya no menmoku*), but to Kitabatake Chikafusa the desire for pre–1334 homelands constituted an unreasonable request (and reward) for surrendering. Without a full confirmation of their lands, the Ishikawa ultimately chose not to shift their allegiances.

Yūki Chikatomo abandoned the Southern Court cause in 1343 after receiving the enticing offer from Ashikaga Takauji that, "there shall be no disturbances regarding holdings (*chigyō*) [awarded] prior to Kenmu 2 (1335)."[81] With this edict Takauji was able to keep his promise to Ishikawa Kabata Gorō Tarō and entice the Yūki by allowing them to maintain their ex-Ishikawa lands.[82] Once the Yūki allied themselves with the Ashikaga, the hapless main line of the Ishikawa had no choice but to grudgingly support the Southern Court. The Kabata Ishikawa, however, remained allied with the Northern Court.[83] The main line Ishikawa lost out in the competition over lands; they suffered the ignominy of losing their homelands and disappeared

---

80. Ibid., Matsudaira Yūki *monjo*, doc. 4, 11.26 [1340] Kitabatake Chikafusa *sodehan* Sōshin *hōsho*, pp. 501–3.
81. DNSR, series 6, vol. 7, 2.25.1343, p. 573. This was reconfirmed on 2.27.1351. See ibid., series 6, vol. 14, p. 850.
82. A will (*yuzurijō*) dating from 6.19.1369 lists villages and counties (*go*) of Ishikawa no shō. See *Fukushima kenshi* 7, Shirakawa *koji kōshoshūmonjo* 1, doc. 3, Yūki Akitomo *yuzurijō an*, pp. 522–23. The members of the Ishikawa who had received rewards from Ashikaga Takauji fought with Yūki Chikatomo. See DNSR, series 6, vol. 7, 8.19.1343 Ishidō Nyūdō *migyōsho an*, and 9.1343 *chūshinjō*, pp. 705–8.
83. The Kabata Ishikawa fought against their brethren who joined the Southern Court. See *Fukushima kenshi* 7, Endō Ishikawa *monjo*, doc. 7, 11.17.1343 Ishidō Yoshimoto *kanjō*, p. 458. Between 1346 and 1353 some members of the mainline Ishikawa apparently supported, once again, the Northern Court. Because documents of this Ishikawa lineage do not survive, it remains difficult to chronicle their actions during the fourteenth century.

from the historical record. The Yūki, however, increased their holdings; some *tozama* prospered at the expense of others. One can also surmise that the most effective manipulator of this system was Ashikaga Takauji; he was able to preserve the value of his promises, keep his partisans satisfied, and expand his base of support. In contrast to Kitabatake Chikafusa, who pontificated profusely but only grudgingly granted rewards, Takauji's promises carried great weight and his largesse was unsurpassed.

Yūki Chikatomo timed his transfer of allegiance well and profited accordingly. The Ishikawa were not so fortunate, but still presumably received a confirmation of their homelands as delineated by the Southern Court. According to the "law of surrender" (*kōsan no hō*), a warrior was to be subjected to the confiscation of half his lands.[84] Or, to be more precise, "according to the set rule, half of the homelands (*honryō*) of those who had surrendered (*kōsannin*) were returned."[85] This "set rule" seems to have been observed more in breach than in practice. Powerful *tozama* rarely suffered such ignominy. Aso Koresumi, distressed by the liberal treatment of his father-in-law, Aso Koretoki, complained "it is a set rule that those who surrender should have only half [their holdings] confirmed. . . . How can [Koretoki] possibly wish for a full confirmation (*ichien ando*)?"[86] Koresumi went so far as to complain about "the set rule, whereas, irrespective of merit (*rihi o ron-sezaru*), all those who ally themselves will receive a full confirmation of their current lands."[87] Koretoki was powerful enough to switch sides without any ill effect.[88]

How can one account for the difference between warriors who lost half their lands and those who suffered not at all? Timing was crucial. One warrior's comment after another had surrendered in the field proves illuminating:

> I have never heard of such a thing! Norinaga, if you had intended to surrender (lit. become a *kōnin*) you should have done it when the shogun [Takauji] . . . invited you to join his forces with a communiqué (*migyōsho*)! After burning your expressly delivered communiqué, [why did] you come here to surrender? It is too much for words.[89]

---

84. Satō, *Nanbokuchō no dōran*, p. 181. An instance where a defeated warrior surrendered half of his holdings can be found in *Fukushima kenshi* 7, Kudama *monjō*, documents 7–8, 3.23.1339 Satake Katsuyoshi Hōgan Gyōkei *rensho uchiwatsejō*, pp. 211–12.

85. NBIK 4437, 5426.

86. NBIK 3880. The Southern Court promised to confirm only one half of Aso Koretoki's holdings upon his death in 1356, which helps explain why the Aso sided with the Ashikaga in the 1360s. See NBIK 4437.

87. NBIK 4281.

88. NBIK 2651.

89. *Taiheiki*, ed. Gotō Tanji, et al (Iwanami Shoten, 1961), vol. 2, maki 16, "Bitchū no Fukuyama kassen no koto," pp. 146–47. This passage does not appear in the oldest texts.

In other words, warriors responding to a request for service could switch sides and suffer no punishment. Those who arrived at an encampment with a request to join allied forces were actually eligible for further rewards.[90] If defeated in battle, however, a warrior had to hand over his weapons and unstring his bow, the customary practice in surrendering.[91] Thus the most powerful possessed ample opportunities to transfer their allegiances. Those unfortunate enough to suffer defeat were in a position of such weakness that the loss of some of their lands became inevitable.

This distinction was lost on some. Imagine a warrior's consternation if, instead of receiving rewards for service, he had only half his lands confirmed! Such was the unhappy lot of Sōma Tanehira. He expressed indignation in 1348 because he had been confirmed with only one half of his holdings in spite of the service (chūsetsu) rendered on his behalf by his son, who helped attack the Southern Court fortress of Reisan. To add insult to injury, according to Tanehira, his younger brother had fought at the same battle and received a full confirmation of lands.[92] Sōma Tanehira asserted that such a difference in treatment was incomprehensible. He failed to mention, however, that during 1336–37 he fought for the Southern Court.[93] Tanehira seems to have waited too long to switch sides. Five years after Yūki Chikatomo had defected, Southern Court supporters were hard-pressed by Ashikaga armies. In all probability Tanehira had not received an invitation to fight but, on the other hand, he had not surrendered his weapons in accordance with the custom of kōsan no hō. Surrender could be an ambiguous process.

The attitude of Sōma Tanehira, and the Aso, indicates that although familial unity existed as an ideal, highest loyalty was to the "family" controlled by each particular tozama, rather than the lineage (ichimon). Upset that his brother was rewarded far more than he, Tanehira's primary concern was not the welfare of all the Sōma. The Ishikawa's divisions likewise stemmed from divided interests: Ishikawa Kabata Gorō Tarō staunchly supported the Ashikaga while the main line, whose lands had been granted to the Yūki, fought with whomever opposed the Yūki. As interests diverged, so too did loyalties.

The success of intraregional hegemons depended upon weaving as many competing strands of tozama self-interest as they could into a fabric of guarded satisfaction. Popularity and military power were inexorably linked; by legitimating increasingly autogenic tozama rights a regime was able to establish a degree of support commensurate to its ability to protect promised

90. KI 32125.
91. For more on the kōsan no hō, see Taiheiki, maki 14, "Shōgun onnyūraku no koto," pp. 417–18.
92. Sōma Monjo, document 61, 9.1348 Sōma Tanehira mōshijō an, pp. 49–50.
93. Ibid., document 42, 8.26.1336[8?] Sōma Tanehira gunchūjō, pp. 35–37.

rights and rewards. A lack of foresight or flexibility in resolving the myriad of *tozama* claims weakened a hegemon's basis of support; a failure to honor one's promises ensured that the laboriously intertwined interests would unravel. Those who overtly attempted to aggrandize lands incited the opposition of *tozama* determined to retain holdings which were theirs by right. Only a hegemonic lord keenly aware of the interest of men and of his own fragile basis of support could devote himself to providing adequate compensation for his followers; his edicts of confirmation further secured and legitimated autogenic *tozama* rights in an unstable age of competing claims. By balancing the myriad of *tozama* interests and respecting as many rights as possible, a hegemon cobbled together a coalition of disparate warriors even as his position remained precarious. The fourteenth-century political terrain was unforgiving of missteps and ill-suited for mediocrities.

CONCLUSION

Individual warriors exhibited conflicting attitudes, which were inexorably linked to the particulars of their social and political position. *Tozama* exhibited autonomy in war and fought according to personal and narrowly defined familial interests, not out of a sense of allegiance to any "lord."

During the age of the Northern and Southern Courts political stability hinged upon social stratification. Of course, some men took advantage of the inherent instability of the age to obfuscate their social position. Those who were less fortunate clung to the privileges of their increasingly precarious social position, and either attempted to quash upstart *miuchi* or, fearful of losing their status, refused to serve under *tozama* magnates. Armies and polities were most effectively led, however, by men who were socially distant from their compatriots.

The crucial divide in fourteenth-century lordship was between those who could offer grants to followers, and those who could not. The former were national or supraregional hegemons, the latter provincial magnates. Supraregional hegemons' powers were great, although unstable. Some, such as Ashikaga Tadafuyu or a few Ashikaga collaterals, precipitously descend into obscurity. Others, such as the Hosokawa, were gradually able to attract locals as *miuchi*, and eventually established a landed lordship. Ashikaga Takauji proved most successful in his political endeavors because he granted generous rewards to followers, guaranteed his promises more than any of his competitors, and provided the most comprehensive compensation. In contrast, those who aspired for an intrusive national or regional lordship, such as Go-Daigo or Isshiki Dōyu, could not countenance such a diffusion of power and accordingly achieved less *tozama* support. Above all else, successful hegemons relied upon intangible powers—the good will generated from largesse and, as we shall see, powers associated with ties to the "other world"—in order to assert their authority over the fractured realm.

During the period from 1336 until 1350, only members of the Ashikaga lineage (*ichimon*) and a few *shugo* closely related to the Ashikaga maintained the ability to lead armies drawn from several provinces. Only after the turmoil of the Kannō disturbance (1350–52) were some *tozama* magnates, such as the Ōuchi, able to grant gifts of confirmations. In spite of this, the power of most *tozama* magnates, even those appointed *shugo* such as the Kawano of Iyo, generally remained limited. Because supraregional hegemons were able to harness the dissatisfaction and resentment of less fortunate *tozama* warriors and also liberally reward their more prosperous brethren, they could displace or dominate *tozama* lords who attempted to become regional magnates.

Military leaders could only mobilize *tozama* after respecting and confirming their homelands and after promising adequate remuneration for those who chose to participate in battle. Hegemons, lords of men, compensated *tozama* instead of competing with them. In the process they accumulated symbolic capital, which was the foundation of their lordships. Accordingly, the military leaders remained bound to keep their promises, to reward acts of merit, and to forgive *tozama* lapses of loyalty. In short, the warriors of the fourteenth century have been unfairly castigated as "turncoats" since, contrary to the assumptions of most historians, they owed service to none.

When Imagawa Ryōshun killed Shōni Fuyusuke, he seemed to have behaved in an unreasonable and excessively brutal manner to most *tozama*. In fact, Fuyusuke's behavior was neither egregious nor particularly unusual, though the same could obviously not be said for Ryōshun's cowardly act. And yet, although his forces disintegrated in 1375, the indomitable Imagawa was able to regroup and eventually to dominate most of Kyushu. Ryōshun's ultimate success indicates that the locus of power had already begun to shift toward regional magnates. One remarkable oath, signed in 1392 by the Shibuya, a *tozama* of southern Kyushu, reveals the increasingly precarious nature of *tozama* autonomy:

> Concerning those allied with the Shimazu: at all times . . . we shall protect the shogun (*shōgun-ke*). When we are not in accord with the [Shimazu] *shugo*, we shall, of course, all follow the wishes of the *Kubō* [Imagawa Ryōshun]. . . . There must be no dissension. The members of this *ikki* must be in accord. [If we] lack in right (*ri*), we lose [the right of] service (*chū*). In order for our sons and

grandsons to remain able to render military service (*gun'eki*) and
[to maintain our] land holdings (*chigyōbun*), together, we shall rely
upon the *Kubō* to determine the merit (*rihi*) [of all matters].[94]

It was at this stage that the many were starting to become the *miuchi* of the
few. *Tozama* such as the Shibuya preserved their autonomy from the Shimazu by subordinating themselves to a supraregional figure like Imagawa
Ryōshun. Although service in an *ikki* organization was not particularly desirable to a *tozama*, it was preferable to *miuchi* status vis-à-vis a regional magnate. But this is a story more of the fifteenth century than the fourteenth.
The age of limited loyalty was coming to an close. Perhaps, in the end, Imagawa Ryōshun's assassination of Shōni Fuyusuke was not such a grave
misjudgment after all.

94. NBIK 6251.

CHAPTER
6

Sacred War

For later on, that very powerful king of the English . . . collected a great army against the city of the legions. . . . When he was about to give battle and saw their priests, who had assembled to pray to God on behalf of the soldiers taking parting in the fight . . . [The king] said: "If they are praying to their God against us, then, even if they do not bear arms, they are fighting against us, assailing us as they do with their prayers for our defeat." So he ordered them to be attacked first.

Bede's Ecclesiastical History of the English People

In all affairs the divine was close and encompassing. It permeated the fabric of life throughout the fourteenth century; its familiarity obliterated the fear that often accompanies the unknown. The gods were not cruel and capricious beings, unknowable and unseen; instead, their behavior could be observed and their motives deduced. Omens, dreams, and an unusual configuration of stars were recorded with scientific precision, for it was believed that such phenomena were evidence of divine disorder or displeasure. Careful analysis of these signs could lead to the discovery of an "ultimate" cause, which in turn could be rectified or mitigated through prayers and ritual.[1] Religious institutions served as conduits to these gods, and their prayers were believed to alter the chain of causality.

"Religion" as it existed in fourteenth-century Japan cannot be conceived as a refuge from the "baser" endeavors of politics and war, nor can religious institutions be portrayed as bastions of peaceful sentiment that remained somehow impervious to the vicissitudes of the political order.[2] Rather than remaining outside the jurisdiction of the state, temples and priests were firmly embedded within it: they fractured their allegiances according to a litany of political particularities. The relative ascendancy of each temple functioned as a barometer of its patron's success. Conversely, "enemy" institutions and individuals were brutalized precisely because their destruction "proved" that the gods supported one's own cause. Control over these conduits to the gods, and assertions of divine favor, constituted essential prerequisites for the successful demonstration of hegemonic political authority.

The behavior of priests or, for that matter, the actions and policies of religious institutions constituted merely one component of "religion" in medieval Japan. Not only did "religious" beliefs—that is, the responsibility to mediate with the "otherworld"—underpin the power of religious institutions, but they also propelled behavior in the seemingly unrelated arenas of political legitimacy and war. To confine one's analysis to religious institutions is to present a desiccated view, lacking in the spirit that animated behavior, much the way a taxonomist's specimen cannot compare to a living creature. Better to study how such a system of beliefs influenced seemingly unrelated acts, such as those of war, in order to understand both the pervasive nature of "religion" and how these encompassing beliefs gradually became rarefied during the indeterminate process of fourteenth-century war.

The battlefield was conceived as a realm where gods and buddhas mingled with men. "Physical battle" and the "power of the gods" (*kami*) were not, as some authors assume, mutually exclusive; rather, "religious" attitudes informed

---

1. In times of drought or war, for example, political leaders interceded with the gods because the gods were responsible for order and prosperity in their domains. For the prayers and sutra copying of Ashikaga Tadayoshi in response to a drought, see Uwayokote Masataka, *Rekishi no kairaku* (Kōdansha, 1996), pp. 192–94, and DNSR, series 6, vol. 6, 8.7.1340, pp. 259–61.

2. Neil McMullin has convincingly argued that the modern idea of a separation between religion and politics has implicitly and anachronistically shaped historical narratives. See his "Historical and Historiographical Issues in the Study of Pre-Modern Japanese Religions," *Japanese Journal of Religious Studies*, vol. 16, no. 1 (1989): 3–40. Conversely, Amino Yoshihiko asserts that temple compounds were outside the jurisdiction of the state and that priests were "invisible" to political authority because of their "unattached" (*muen*) status. See his *Muen kugai raku*, particularly pp. 159–60 for priests being able to travel freely through battle areas.

the very act of war.[3] Prayers were considered to be lethal weapons, and arms and armor were emblazoned with religious motifs. Battles, too, were waged in sacred spaces. Some warriors fought in temple compounds, while others initiated insurrections within shrine precincts. Finally, both priests and shrine attendants requested rewards in a manner indistinguishable from warriors.

According to the mindset of the fourteenth century, victory revealed divine favor and thus was translated into the teleological notion that those who triumphed in war were destined to rule the realm. Because military prowess indicated "otherworldly" support, the Ashikaga were able to cast themselves as Buddhist kings and to foster an ideology, nurtured by their success in war, that their control over the fates superseded that of all others. The sacerdotal kingship that came to characterize shogunal authority helped to legitimate *bakufu* rule, but it ultimately led to a transformation of "religious" beliefs in the process. The "divine" became increasingly conceived as a distant, impersonal realm, accessible to Buddhist kings who patronized Zen temples and promulgated esoteric rituals, and to their priests, but no longer intimately bound to the patterns and rhythms of ordinary life.

THE PREMISE

Potent Prayers

To start a war one first needed to pray. Prayers were conceived as weapons that could focus the awesome powers of the gods in aiding one side and annihilating the other. This belief had a venerable ancestry—one even finds a reference in an eighth-century chronicle to curses initiating rebellion.[4] Likewise, generals customarily prayed at shrines before embarking on a campaign.[5] The establishment of Buddhism did little to hinder this ardor; instead, as we shall see, Buddhism provided an impressive liturgy of cursing.

Although the identity of the gods of war remained nebulous, belief in their powers was not. Because prayers mobilized these gods of war, who determined military success, wielding maces and chanting maledictions were

---

3. Mikael Adolphson has illustrated how religious institutions furthered their interests through a formalized process of demonstration. Adolphson nevertheless assumes that recourse to military force ipso facto discredited Buddhist schools and institutions. See *The Gates of Power: Monks, Courtiers and Warriors in Premodern Japan* (Honolulu: University of Hawaii Press, 2000), pp. 240–87, particularly pp. 273–80 and 286–87.

4. These curses occurred during the formative period of the Japanese polity, probably sometime in the fourth century. W. G. Aston, trans., *Nihongi: Chronicles of Japan from the Earliest Times to A.D. 697* (Rutland, VT: Charles E. Tuttle, 1972), pp. 156–57.

5. See, for example, a general praying at Ise prior to embarking on a campaign to conquer the north. *Ruijū kokushi* (Kokushi Taikei Kankōkai, 1965), 11.6.800. For Buddhist prayers prior to a campaign, see 1.28.804 and 12.7.805.

considered to be functionally indistinguishable.[6] A Japanese Clausewitz might even have characterized prayers as an extension of war by other means. Prayers were conceived as potent weapons. For example, the priest Rai'in was ordered to camp, where he set up an altar, initiated his maledictions, and was praised for "the most wondrous power of his prayers."[7] Rai'in complained, however, of inadequate compensation for his efforts:

> Whenever [the enemy was defeated], I received a document of praise. Nevertheless, those members of the 'white flag' unit (*ikki*) who were killed and wounded received rewards for the service of risking their lives in battle (*gaibun chūsetsu no shō nari*). They destroyed the enemy due to the efficacy of my three prayers. [Victory] was caused by the power of my prayers . . . and not the luck [of the Ashikaga]. How can it be that my service is not rewarded? If the office (*shiki*) [of the *bettō* of Kamakura's Myō-ōin temple] is not available, grant me other rewards so that [I can] continue my outstanding prayers.[8]

Rai'in believed that his prayers caused victory while the members of the white-flag *ikki* merely enacted a cosmologically determined outcome.

From the tenth century onward, the court monopolized "prayers of destruction" (*chōbukuhō*) that were offered to five potent Buddhist deities (Fudō, Gozanze, Gundari, Dai-i-toku-ten, and Kongō), whose function was to protect the state (*chingon kokka*).[9] (See figure 32.) These prayers were performed by five ranking priests, from noble families, who individually burned offerings (*goma*, or wooden sticks scribbled with prayers) and chanted prayers

---

6. Young priests (*wakashū*) rushed into battle while their elders performed maledictions. *Taiheiki*, maki 20, "Yoshisada kasanete moyosu Kuromaru kassen no koto," p. 630. For commands where "young priests (*wakashū*) were to fight and the old were to pray," see NBIC 236 and *Kuramaderashi*, ed. Hashikawa Shō (Kyoto, 1926), pp. 76–93.

7. The originals appear in *Kamakura shishi shiryōhen*, comp. Kamakura Shishi Hensan Iinkai (Kamakura, 1956–58), vol. 1, Myō-ōin *monjo*, documents 636–38. Some documents have been lost, but copies appear in "Rai'in Daisōjōgyōjo ekotoba," *Zoku gunsho ruijū* 9.1, *Denbu* (Zoku Gunsho Ruijū Kansekai, 1975), pp. 225–72.

8. *Kamakura shishi shiryōhen*, vol. 1, Myō-ōin *monjo*, document 638, 7.1387 Rai'in *mōshijō*. Rai'in demanded the *bettō shiki* of Kamakura's Myō-ōin temple. Nevertheless, the *bettō shiki* had belonged to priests affiliated with Jizōin, a subtemple of Daigoji, until Sūjo of Rishōin was appointed to this post. For more on the Jizōin priests, see *Daigoji shinyōroku*, ed. Akamatsu Toshihide (Kyoto, 1951–53), vol. 1, p. 167. Rishōin's Sūjo was an influential priest who helped celebrate the "spiritual victory" over the Southern Court in 1392. See chapter eight.

9. These five deities are mentioned in the influential *Ninnō-kyō* sutra. Dai-i-toku-ten was particularly prized for its efficacy in battle. Another deity, Aisen, was also believed to smite evil. The precedent for these so-called "five altar rituals" lay in the court's response to Taira no Masakado's rebellion. For a fourteenth-century reference to a reenactment of the Masakado curses (the "Masakado chobuku Fudō-myō-o"), see *Izumi shishi 1, Honpen shiryōhen*, Izumi Shishi Hensan Iinkai, comp. (Osaka, 1960), 5.1334 Matsuoji *jurora gonjōjō an*, pp. 631–33 and KI 32316.

Figure 32. *Dai-i-toku-ten* illustration, from *Go-dai myō-ō*, possession of Kiburuji. Photo courtesy Nara National Museum.

to these deities, each of which was believed to destroy malevolence—be it hostile emotions, "evil spirits," or inhospitable aspects of the natural world.[10] To pray to them was to magnify one's strength when fighting "evil."[11] Of course, it takes no great leap of the imagination to shift one's prayers to more earthly "evil" adversaries. The shape of the altar where *goma* were burned proved to be of critical importance in directing otherworldly energies. According to a gloss from a Buddhist text,

> a ring-shaped altar is used to prevent disasters; an elongated rectangle is used to increase one's wealth and longevity; a lotus shape is for love and respect; and a triangular-shaped altar is for maledictions. . . . When maledictions are performed, the triangular altar should be painted and a picture of armor drawn on each side.[12]

Five altar rituals were carefully monitored because they were believed to fatally undermine one's opponent. It should be no surprise that rebels relied heavily upon them. Minamoto Yoritomo, for example, initiated them shortly after his 1180 uprising.[13] Once the Kamakura *bakufu* was established, its officials attempted to monitor all spiritual activities because they believed that maledictions were instrumental in fomenting disorder.[14]

Once the ambitious emperor Go-Daigo decided to annihilate the Kamakura regime, he initiated five altar rituals.[15] Go-Daigo ostensibly ordered them for the safe birth of his progeny in 1325, but he had triangular altars substituted for oval ones, and thus surreptitiously cursed Kamakura

10. Kume Kunitake, *Nanbokuchō jidaishi* (Waseda Daigaku Shuppan, 1907) p. 126. Dai-i-toku-ten was the deity particularly favored in war. Others, such as Gundari, excelled at "conquering" nature.

11. For an account of praying to Dai-i-toku-ten and Bishamon in order to defeat demons, see "Jui ōjōden," *Kuramaderashi*, pp. 20–21.

12. *Monyoki*, in *Taishō shinshu daizōkyō* 78 *Zoku shoshūbu* 9 (Taishō Issaikyō Kankōkai, 1932), maki 170, ho 93, *gongyōhōho* 5.1, *Shuhō goma kutō yōshin toro no koto*, pp. 561–62. According to Shingon manuals, whether a prayer was felicitous or not depended upon which direction its priests faced while performing it. Ibid., pp. 549–59.

13. If the *Azuma kagami* is to be trusted, Yoritomo initiated prayers for the "protection of the state" on 10.16.1180. See also Martin Collcutt, "Religion in the Formation of the Kamakura Bakufu: As seen through the Azuma Kagami," *Japan Review*, 5 (1994): 71-2.

14. The court monopolized these five altar rituals through the mid–fourteenth century. For reference to the supporters of the court cursing the Kamakura *bakufu* during the Jōkyū war of 1221, see KI 6969, 5.16.1248 Kantō *gechijō*. For a good overview of the religious policies of Go-Daigo, see Andrew Goble, *Kenmu*, particularly pp. 185–99.

15. For surviving orders, see KI 29726 and 29742. Kannonji prayed for Go-Daigo in 1325 and also performed maledictions on his behalf in 1333. See *Santō chōshi, shiryōhen* (Shiga Prefecture, Santō chō, 1986), Kannonji *monjo* document 413, Kannonji Gokokuji shūto *moshijō*. Much of the following analysis is based upon Momose Kesao, "Gentoku gannen no 'chūgū onkainin,'" *Kanazawa bunkō kenkyū*, no. 274 (March 1985): 1–14. For more on the political context of this time, see Goble, *Kenmu: Go-Daigo's Revolution*, pp. 100–4, and Mori Shigeaki, *Go-Daigo tennō* (Chūkōshinsho, 2000), pp. 144–50.

for four years before alarmed *bakufu* officials belatedly discovered his "deplorable act."[16] Kamakura's henchmen arrested and tortured the priests involved, but in the mind of Go-Daigo, at least, they were already too late. Go-Daigo attributed the success of his second rebellion in 1331–33 to these maledictions and lavished praise on the priest Monkan, who "performed prayers of destruction against the Kantō [Kamakura] since the very beginning."[17] After Kamakura lay in ruins, the "deeply trusted" Monkan performed numerous "secret, great rituals and was appointed head of the [powerful esoteric (*Shingon*) Buddhist temples] Tōji and Daigoji."[18] Prayers used to destroy one regime could also be used to bolster the next.

Go-Daigo's belief in the efficacy of these prayers is most clearly expressed in a letter he wrote in the summer of 1335 in which he proclaimed, "The Dai-i-toku-hō, performed for the sake of the court (*ōdō*), has caused the eastern barbarians to be crushed. . . . That decisive victory occurred while [priests were] chanting [the Dai-i-toku-hō] . . . clearly reveals its remarkable power."[19] Go-Daigo, unwavering in his belief, once again had the Dai-i-toku-hō performed in his palace when Ashikaga Takauji turned on him two months later.[20]

Emperors were not alone in attempting to secure spiritual support. Warriors also requested otherworldly assistance. Generals granted lands to temples so that they could continuously burn wood prayer strips (*goma*) during campaigns.[21] This need for spiritual succor might even override the demand for supplies, for beleaguered authorities were known to order emergency prayers at times of supreme crisis.[22]

When Ashikaga Takauji broke with Go-Daigo in the fall of 1335, he attempted to garner as much otherworldly support as possible. One of his first acts was to have a powerful temple in Ōmi pray for him.[23] Takauji also worshipped at Iwashimizu Hachiman shrine in order to "add divine power to his cause, and succeed in the great enterprise" of ruling the realm.[24] In an attempt

---

16. Words of the high-ranking official Kanazawa Sadaaki. *See Kanagawa kenshi shiryōhen, Kodai-chūsei*, vol. 2, documents 2748 and 2646, and *Taiheiki*, maki 1, "Gosan o-inori no koto," pp. 9–10.

17. *Daigoji shinyōroku*, vol. 3, "Zasu shidai," p. 919. See also Amino Yoshihiko, *Igyō no ōken* (Heibonsha, 1986).

18. Ibid.

19. DNSR, series 6, vol. 2, 9.2(1335) *rinji*, p. 592.

20. Ibid., p. 721.

21. *Ibaragi ken shiryō, Chūseihen* 1, comp. Ibaragi Prefecture (Mito, 1967), Gokokuin *monjo* 1–2, p. 321.

22. For example, see DNSR, series 6, vol. 4, 3.14.1338, p. 764, and *Shibunkaku kosho shiryō mokuroku* 150, comp. Shibunkaku (Kyoto, June 1996), document 87, 3.14.1338 Ashikaga Tadayoshi *migyōsho*.

23. DNSR, series 6, vol. 2, pp. 859–60 for prayers to Jōshinji.

24. *Hyōgo kenshi chūsei shiryō*, vol. 7, Iwashimizu *monjo* document 30, 1.8.1336 Ashikaga Takauji *jitō shiki kishinjō*, p. 33. Takauji "offered praise to the god's glory on the battlefield" and commended *jitō shiki* to the shrine so that the *hannya shinkyō* sutra to be "turned and read" every day. His son Yoshiakira would also grant lands to Iwashimizu for "stability in the realm and [Ashikaga] prosperity." Ibid., document 36, p. 35.

to diminish Go-Daigo's spiritual base at Mt. Kōya, Takauji patronized Kongō Sanmaiin, a subtemple in the Kōya hierarchy that had been closely associated with the Kamakura regime.[25] Kongō Sanmaiin received praise and compensation for breaking ranks with the Kōya conglomerate.[26] The Ashikaga also neutralized Go-Daigo's support at Tōji and Daigoji by expelling Monkan, Go-Daigo's trusted appointee, and replacing him with an ally named Kenshun.[27] Those contesting political hegemony strove to monopolize prayer centers in order to consolidate their authority and prosecute the war.

Fate and the Gods of War

A pervasive, ironclad fatalism infused the intellectual universe of the fourteenth century. Every success and failure; life and death; victory and defeat unfolded according to divine plan. Hence each was comforted with the knowledge that his fortune—for better or worse—constituted one aspect of a larger, more comprehensive whole. For example, the veteran commander Nitta Yoshisada was killed after stumbling into an enemy patrol. No one could believe that Yoshisada would risk venturing onto the battlefield without the covering fire of skirmishers. As incompetence did not exist in the fourteenth-century lexicon of causality, most instead attributed his demise to the anger of the gods.

The ultimate responsibility for Yoshisada's death was credited to Eiheiji, the temple that performed maledictions against him. Their curses influenced the gods who communicated their intentions through a dream and then caused a "white feathered arrow" to be buried into his brow.[28] War, in other words, was perceived to be a manifestation of divine will.

The physical and spiritual realms were believed to be so permeable that some, such as the priest Kakushin, vowed to become an evil spirit (*onryō*) if anyone were to interfere with his testament.[29] Death did not bring with it a

25. Hōjō Masako had a pagoda (*tahōdō*) built for Minamoto Yoritomo which survives today. See *Kōyasan monjo*, vol. 5, *Kongō Sanmaiin monjo*, documents 1–3. In spite of its ties to the Kamakura *bakufu*, Go-Daigo designated this subtemple as an official prayer center. See ibid., document 289 of 6.24.1333. Nevertheless, Go-Daigo apparently confiscated Shinkai estate, which explains this subtemple's dissatisfaction with his regime. For the 1334 holdings of Kongō Sanmaiin, see ibid., document 150 of 10.5.1334, p. 424. Ashikaga Takauji promised to restore "all of the lands which had been confiscated since 1333" when wooing Kongō Sanmaiin. Ibid., document 155.
26. According to a document written by Ashikaga Tadayoshi: "I am overjoyed that you are performing the *Daishō kongō rokuji myō-ō hō*. . . . Continue praying for peace and stability in the realm." *Kōyasan monjo*, vol. 5, *Kongō sanmaiin monjo*, document 153, 9.9.1336 Ashikaga Tadayoshi *gohan migyōsho*. Rights to Kawachi's Kishiwada estate were commended to Kongō Sanmaiin in 1346. Ibid., document 160.
27. *Daigoji shinyōroku*, vol. 3, "Zasu shidai," p. 919, and DNSR, Series 6, Vol. 3, pp. 467–68.
28. A sequence of dreams, premonitions, and signs of divine handiwork was woven into the *Taiheiki*'s narrative of his death. *Taiheiki*, maki 20, "Yoshisada kasanete moyosu Kuromaru kassen no koto," p. 630, "Yoshisada musō no koto," pp. 630–33 and "Yoshisada ason jigai no koto," pp. 635–37.
29. *Santō chōshi*, Kannonji *monjo* document 13, 2.17.1299 Sō Kakunichi *shūriden kishinjō*, pp. 70–71. For the example of Nitta Yoshioki, who was tricked and killed and later reproached his murderers

sense of finality. Those who had passed away might still exert a protective (or malevolent) influence from the otherworld. The deceased could even become an "evil spirit" in cases where they had been wronged, tricked, or humiliated.[30] Thus, to succeed in any endeavor, one had to thwart "evil spirits" and gain the support of the "gods of war."

The "gods of war" were never authoritatively identified. Recountings dating from the twelfth century include the deities of Itsukushima, Kibitsumiya, Hiromine, Sumiyoshi, Suwa, Kashima, Takemikazuchi, Kantori, and Futsumeshi shrines.[31] Worship of these deities continued unabated. For example, when Ashikaga Takauji advanced on Kyoto during the fifth month of 1336, he halted his army at Kibitsumiya and had six hundred attendants dance for the gods while he enacted a ritual of destruction.[32] Buddhist deities increasingly became amalgamated under the rubric of the "gods of war." Later lists of these gods included members of the Buddhist pantheon such as Hachiman bodhisattva (*bosatsu*), Marishiten, Shōgun Jizō, and Fudō-myō-ō, while still others claimed that the semilegendary Prince Shōtoku was one as well.[33] As confusion reigned regarding the identity of these gods, some simply assigned the fantastic number of 98,000 to cover all possible contenders.[34]

The parameters of "Buddhism" and "Shinto" remained protean. Temples were believed to cause Buddhist avatars to shower arrows on their adversaries,

---

in their dreams, see *Taiheiki*, maki 33, "Nitta sahyōe no suke Yoshioki jigai no koto," pp. 1005–6. In an attempt to pacify his spirit, a shrine was built near the site of his death.

30. Men begged for the heads of comrades in order to ensure their rebirth in the afterlife. *Taiheiki*, maki 32, "Kōnan ikusa no koto," p. 973-4. See also ibid., maki 6, "Akasakajō kassen no koto," pp. 150–51, where a "priest who had conducted the last rites [e.g. chanted the *nenbutsu* ten times] requested the head of Honma and took it to Tennōji." For reference to the massacred defenders of Kanegasaki castle becoming "evil spirits (*onryō*)," see *Taiheiki*, maki 18, "Kanegasakijō ochiru koto," pp. 571–72.

31. *Ryōjin hisshō*, ed. Sasaki Nobutsuna (Iwanami Shoten, 1933), maki 2, "Shiku no kami uta," p. 50, for references to war gods that were worshipped at the Kashima, Kantori, Suwa, Atsuta, and the Tado no miya shrines in the east, and the Itsukushima, Kibitsumiya, Hiromine, and Sumiyoshi shrines in the west.

32. NBIC 365.

33. *Teijō zakki*, vol. 4, pp. 207–8, and *Koji ruien*, vol. 29, *Heiji bu*, vol. 1, p. 876. The encyclopedia compiled by Ise Teijō offers three glosses for the identity of the gods of war: they are either the "Shintō" deities, Takemikazuchi, Futsumeshi *mikoto*, and Kashima *daimyōjin*; an amalgamation of "Shintō" deities and historical personages such as Hachiman *daijin*, Empress Jingū, and Takeuchi sukune; or the Buddhist deities Marishiten, Daikokuten and Benzaiten. For a fourteenth-century reference to the "gods of war" referring solely to Hachiman *bosatsu*, see *Heihō reizuisho*, p. 58. According to Hyōdō Hiromi, Prince Shōtoku became worshipped as a god of war in the medieval period as well. See Hyōdō Hiromi, *Taiheiki 'yomi' no kanōsei* (Kōdansha, 1995), p. 115.

34. See *Teijō zakki*, vol. 4, pp. 207–8. Teijō characterizes this belief as "vulgar"; nevertheless it was already well established in the fourteenth century. For a reference to these deities in the fourteenth- century military manual, see the *Heihō reizuisho*, p. 60. In the *Soga monogatari*, "Kojirō Katara hiezaru koto," one sees a reference to a "blood festival" (*chi matsuri*) dedicated to the 99,000 gods of war. The *Soga monogatari* apparently suffers from a copyist's error. All other texts refer to 98,000 gods of war.

while shrines such as Tsurugaoka Hachiman also used "Buddhist" rituals to mobilize their gods.[35] A functional distinction existed, however, in that warriors invariably launched their rebellions within shrine rather than temple precincts. These men did not, however, instinctively appeal to "Shintō" deities. Ashikaga Takauji, for example, dedicated his oath to his "divine ancestor," the Buddhist deity Hachiman *bosatsu*, when he rebelled at Shinomura Hachiman shrine.[36]

Offerings to the Gods and Buddhas

A belief in reciprocal obligations between this world and the other influenced fourteenth-century behavior. Those aspiring to launch an attack restored shrines "out of both religious fervor and a desire to achieve [their political] ambitions," for they expected the gods to provide aid in exchange for their own "service to the gods" (*kami ni chū o itasu*).[37] In times of victory, shrine attendants conversely boasted of their god's "divine service" (*shinchū*).[38] Unsuccessful rebels, peeved by a patron god's indifference to these rules of reciprocity, destroyed the shrine where they had only recently rebelled, before committing suicide.[39]

The fatalistic belief that all was determined in the other world was matched with the optimistic notion that one could still influence the gods through either prayer or more tangible gifts. The demands of war gave warriors ample causes to pray for, but at the same time these men attempted to please the gods through unusual offerings. For example, captured prisoners might be decapitated as "offerings to the gods of war,"[40] and their severed

35. For Tōji, DNSR, series 6, vol. 3, pp. 525–26, 10.1339. Ashikaga Takauji would later grant lands to Tōji so that the Hannya sutra could be read unceasingly for Tōji's Chinju Hachiman. See DNSR, series 6, vol. 5, pp. 773–74, 10.27.1339. For Tsurugaoka Hachiman, see DNSR, series 6, vol. 4, p. 376. The Dai-i-toku-hō ritual, designed to "chastise Yoshino rebels," continued for seventeen days.

36. KI 32120. Claims such as those advanced by Takauji did not originate in 1333. The Iwashimizu Hachiman shrine was created by the Seiwa Emperor in 859, and the Seiwa Genji (including the Ashikaga) were descended from him.

37. So quoted in the case of Yamana Ujikiyo for his reconstruction of the Kamo shrines. See *Meitokuki*, "Kobayashi Yoshishige Ujikiyo ni zangen su," pp. 36–38.

38. *Ibaragi ken shiryō chūseihen* 1, p. 396, Hitachi no kuni Sōsha no miya *monjo* 28, 1.1344 Kiyowara Morouji *meyasu*. The phrases used to describe the gods' services mirrored those used by warriors in their petitions. This has been pointed out by Tomita Masahiro, "Chūsei Tōji no kitō monjo ni tsuite," *Komonjo kenkyū* 11 (November 1977): 24–59, particularly pp. 32–33.

39. *Taiheiki*, maki 3, "Sakurayama jigai no koto," p. 78. For the reciprocity between men and saints in medieval Europe, see Patrick J. Geary, "Humiliation of Saints," in his *Living with the Dead in the Middle Ages* (Ithaca, N. Y.: Cornell University Press, 1994), pp. 95–115.

40. *Taiheiki*, maki 6, "Akasakajō kassen no koto," p. 156. A commander also spurred his troops by saying "Kill the enemy and give an offering to the gods of battle (*ano teki are utte mazu gunjin ni matsure*)." *Taiheiki*, maki 32, "Kōnan kassen no koto," p. 968. In *Genpei jōsuiki* (Kokumin Bunko Kankōkai, 1911), maki 37, Minamoto Yoshitsune is purported to have ordered his troops to cut off the heads of miscellaneous captured troops (*zōhei*) and offer them to the gods of war. See p. 922.

heads could also be used to curse an enemy through a grisly form of black magic.[41]

Warriors also solicited divine support by writing poems. Ashikaga Takauji and his generals composed linked verse celebrating the Kannon bodhisattva during their 1336 summer offensive to retake the capital.[42] Shortly after this session, Takauji had a dream in which

> a brilliant light gleamed from the south and an image of the Kannon appeared on the ship's bow. Twenty-eight attendant deities also appeared to offer [him] protection, each wearing armor and carrying bows and swords. As soon as Takauji awoke, he said, "The Kannon has added its protective power to our forces. My auspicious dream portends certain victory." Thereupon he took some Sugihara paper, cut it so as to make a small book, penned "Praise the Kannon boddhisattva (*Namu Kannon bosatsu*)" and pasted one sheet on the sail of each boat. A fine wind then took the shogun's fleet to Bizen [Province].[43]

Imagawa Ryōshun likewise wrote poetry at several shrines while in the midst of his campaign to subjugate Kyushu. Ryōshun's army was soon buoyed by a favorable wind which, when coupled with a sighting of mysterious ships, compelled him to proclaim that "[these events] could only indicate the actions of the gods. My foolish poems moved [them]."[44] Poems were, in other words, secret weapons that could enlist divine support, which helps explain why Imagawa Ryōshun carried poetry manuals with him to battle.[45] On the other hand, a poorly composed poem could have disastrous consequences. During one siege, a warrior composed linked verse in which he inauspiciously compared his army to cherry petals and the enemy to a tempest.[46] Contemporaries attributed the ultimate destruction of his force to this ill-conceived poetic metaphor.

Because poems were believed to influence fate, Ashikaga Takauji sought poetic advice while on a campaign, and his son Yoshiakira solemnly examined a poetry compilation before going to battle.[47] At times of supreme

---

41. The head of one who had died an unnatural death could be mixed with water and ash. If it did not bleed when cut, then one's enemy would die without a visible wound. *Heihō reizuisho*, p. 73.

42. For the poems composed at Jōdoji, see NBIC 346.

43. *Taiheiki*, maki 16, "Takauji kō jōraku no koto," pp. 473–74. Many legends are associated with this campaign. For Takauji's encounter with the "arrow-grabbing Jizō," see *Hyōgo kenshi shiryōhen chūsei*, vol. 4, document 8 Settsu no kuni Hachibegun shason Zenpukuji *raireki no koto*, pp. 25–27. This copy (*utsushi*) dates from the Warring States period.

44. Imagawa Ryōshun, *Michiyukiburi*, in Nagasaki Prefecture, ed., *Chūsei nikki kigyō shū* (Shōgakkan, 1994), particularly p. 420.

45. Kawazoe Shōji, *Imagawa Ryōshun* (Yoshikawa Kōbunkan, 1964), p. 96.

46. *Taiheiki*, maki 7 "Chihayajō kassen no koto," pp. 166–67. See also McCullough, *The Taiheiki*, p. 184.

47. For the former, see Tsuda Sōkichi, *Bungaku ni arawaretaru kokumin shisō no kenkyū* 2, in *Tsuda Sōkichi zenshu* 5 (Iwanami Shoten, 1964), p. 180; for Yoshiakira's deeds, see *Entairyaku*, vol. 6, p. 313.

crisis, commanders sometimes found it propitious to compose poetry. For example, when Ashikaga Takauji's brother rose up in arms against him, Takauji, "unperturbed, said, 'fate (*un*) is determined in the heavens. You cannot prepare for it,' and took out a book of poetry and quietly composed verse."[48] Takauji was not as fatalistic as this passage might indicate, because he believed that poetry could influence the outcome of battle. At times, it was better to try to influence fate than to exhaust oneself in the minutiae of military preparation.

WORLDLY ASPECTS OF RELIGIOUS INSTITUTIONS

Priests and Shrine Attendants

Priests were firmly embedded in the fabric of political life. Although Pure Land priests (*jishū*) might act as messengers or spies, they were neither exempt from the vicissitudes of war nor invisible to hostile armies because of their "unattached" (*muen*) status.[49] For example, one Ishiyama priest managed to skirt enemy lines and report to the capital, but he relied upon his wiles, not his *muen* "invisibility," to do so.[50] Other frocked messengers might be bound and imprisoned upon capture, or even suffer decapitation.[51] The purported *muen* immunities of Pure Land (*ji*) priests likewise did nothing for Bun and Sei Amidabutsu, who were slaughtered in an ambush.[52] *Muen* had its limitations!

In fact, most priests were virtually indistinguishable from warriors. One fourteenth-century picture scroll, the *Aki no yo no nagamonogatari*, depicts a battle between Mt. Hiei and Miidera priests, and yet the combatants wore the same armor as warriors.[53] (See figure 33 = pl. 22.) Not only did *ji* priests accompany armies, sometimes in the hundreds,[54] but some, such as Hitomi

---

48. *Taiheiki*, maki 30, "Nishikikōjidono Kyōto taishitsu no koto," p. 891.

49. For priests as messengers, see *Sekijō chōshi*, document 74, 11.1341 Shirakawa Yūki Chikatomo *ate* Hōgen Senshū *shojō utsushi*, and document 79, Shirakawa Yūki Chikatomo *ate* Kasuga Akikuni *shojō utsushi*. For priests reporting sensitive information, see *Entairyaku*, vol. 3, 8.18.1350, p. 299; 12.10.1350, p. 379; and *Kitabatake Chikafusa monjo shūko*, pp. 316–17. For Amino's contrary viewpoint, see *Muen kugai raku*, pp. 153–63.

50. *Entairyaku*, vol. 3, 12.5.1350, p. 376.

51. For the capture of priests, see *Entairyaku*, vol. 3, 11.29.1350, p. 374. Only the heads of "the mountain priest Dankōbōsan'i rissha and kugyō of Kurama temple" were "captured" by Tairanogo Shigetsugu. NBIC 400.

52. *Entairyaku*, vol. 3, 2.27.1351, pp. 422–23.

53. I am indebted to Asakura Takako of the Idemitsu Museum of Arts for initially providing me with pictures of this scroll.

54. "Kusunoki kassen chūmon," 2.28.1333. The *ji*, one faction of Ippen's Pure Land sect, were composed of itinerant priests who prayed for the souls of all who were killed in battle. See Amino, *Muen kugai raku*; Akamatsu Toshihide, *Kamakura bukkyō no kenkyū* (Kyoto: Heirakuji Shoten, 1957), pp. 173–212; and Ōhashi Toshio, *Jishū no seiritsu to tenkai* (Yoshikawa Kōbunkan, 1973), pp. 188–213.

Figure 33. Warring priests. Source: *Aki no yo no nagamonogatari*. Possession of the Idemitsu Museum of Arts.

On'a, even launched suicidal charges in order to attain the "honor" of being the first to die in battle.[55]

Those who took the tonsure did not forget their social origins. According to one frank acknowledgment, "a priest who comes from the warrior order (*buke*) remains part of that order."[56] Priests maintained considerable interest in familial matters. Although their ultimate obligations remained with their affiliated institution, some tried to be loyal to both. One Katsuoji priest of Sugano stock persuaded his temple to occupy contested lands in support of his brother.[57]

Status distinctions between priests mirrored those of hereditary warriors. High-ranking priests skilled in the maledictory arts, such as Rai'in, might be appointed to temple offices, but lower-ranking priests could not personally receive rewards. Tellingly, lands granted to weapon-wielding priests were administered by the temple instead of those who earned them.[58] Both ranking priests and *tozama* warriors were thus personally compensated for their efforts, but their less exalted brethren were not. Warring priests were no different from the typical retainer in this regard, save that their "lord" was an institution instead of a man.

55. Tachibana Shundō, "Taiheiki ni arawareta jishū no katsuyaku," *Jishūshi ronkō* (Kyoto: Hōzōkan, 1975), pp. 214–37, and *Taiheiki*, ed., Okami Masao, vol. 2, note 11.26, pp. 461–64.

56. KI *hoi* 1792, 8.1298 Bō *moshijō*.

57. The priest's older brother was a powerful *myōshu*. See *Minoo shishi shiryōhen*, vol. 2, document 574, 2.1334 Konoe *karyō kyojū jisō kōmyō chūmon an*, and 578, 8.1334 Jōdoji Sōshōbō Kumonjo Gyōshin *moshijō an*, pp. 1–3.

58. For example, one Awaji asshari was awarded *jitō shiki* for military valor, but these lands were administered by his temple. *Minoo shishi shiryōhen*, vol. 2, document 608, 10.21.1337 Katsuoji Shūgijō, p. 16. For another, see Gamō *monjo* document 35, 6.3.1353 Ashikaga Yoshiakira *sode kudashibumi*, in *Minakuchi chōshi*, vol. 2, p. 278. After this priest's death his lands were transferred to another priest. See ibid., document 40, 6.2.1363 Sō Enshin Kōen *rensho shōmon*, p. 279.

Shrine attendants, on the other hand, did not belong to any such cohesive organization. They were simply warriors who were concurrently invested with shrine office. Identified as both "shrine attendants and *gokenin*," these men were called into actual battles and fought indistinguishably from other warriors.[59] In conclusion, although priests and shrine attendants were socially distinct, they remained more of the world than apart from it.

Temples and Shrines

Temples, too, were firmly embedded in the political landscape of Japan. Tarashima Satoshi has shown that temples which prayed for military success received special protection from encroachments and were granted tax exemptions.[60] Conversely, enemy "prayer centers" were military targets. Their destruction bolstered claims that their clients were "enemies of the gods and buddhas."[61] For example, Go-Daigo designated Kōjōji of Hizen province as an imperial prayer temple in 1333, but it was torched by his opponents approximately twenty years later.[62]

Shrines were ideal locales to initiate rebellion because obligations to one's lord held less immediacy within their confines. For example, Ashikaga Takauji appealed to both imperial and divine authority in 1333 when he turned against his Kamakura lords at the Shinomura Hachiman shrine.[63] The potentially revolutionary consequences of divine legitimation were denied by conservative critics, who asserted that those who expected compensation from the gods would not be heeded if "their appeals lacked propriety (*hirei o ukezu*),"[64] but such excuses merely highlighted the principle that "divine support" abetted war and rebellion.

---

59. NBIK 2754. See also *Hiraoka shishi shiryōhen* 1, 2.4.1332 Fujiwara Yasumasa *yuzurijō utsushi*, 2.1332, pp. 408–10. See also Kuroda Toshio, *Jisha seiryoku* (Iwanami Shoten, 1980), pp. 150–51 and DNSR, series 6, vol. 3, pp. 846–47. Mobilization orders were commonly issued to the heads (*daigūji*) of prominent shrines. See for example, NBIK 494, 610, 670, 758 (the *daigūji* of Takao shrine); KI 31994, 32105, 32284, NBIC 121, 146, 290 (the Ōhōri of Ōyamazumi shrine); and *Ino Hachimangū monjo*, "kaisetsu," p. 155 for the Iga of Mutsu. Iga Morimitsu refers to himself as both a shrine attendant (*kannushi*) in document 78 and as a *gokenin* in document 134. For shrine attendants submitting reports of arrival, see *Shizuoka kenshi shiryōhen*, vol. 6, *Chūsei*, no. 2, document 422.

60. Tarashima Satoshi, "Nanbokuchō jidai no seisatsu to kinsei," *Komonjo kenkyū* 35 (December 1991): 1–10. For supporting evidence, see NBIK 557 and 574.

61. For such a characterization, see *Taiheiki*, maki 17, "Yama seme no koto," p. 514.

62. NBIK 3497. For Go-Daigo's original confirmation, see *Saga-ken shiryō shūsei*, comp. Saga Prefecture (Saga, 1956), vol. 2, Kōjōji *monjo*, documents 44–45. This document does not appear in KI, vol. 42, but see document 32591, Kōjōji *monjo*, documents 47–48, and NBIK 119–20 for Kōjōji's designation as an imperial prayer temple.

63. For his prayers, see KI 32120 and 32140. Another rebel, Nitta Yoshisada, also "raised his flag [of rebellion] in front of the Ikushina deity." *Taiheiki*, maki 10, "Nitta Yoshisada muhon no koto," p. 251.

64. See *Meitokuki*, p. 38, and *Taiheiki*, maki 3, "Sakurayama jigai no koto," p. 78.

SACRED WAR

Buddhist symbols and imagery pervaded nearly every aspect of warfare. Banners of war were emblazoned with Hachiman *daibosatsu*, a god of war; some warriors wrote the name of Jizō *bosatsu* on their armor, while others inserted Buddhist *mandalas*—identical to those used in funeral ceremonies—into their capes (*horo*) in order to "provide for safety in this life and salvation in the afterlife."[65] The bright, billowing capes (*horo*) that warriors wore into battle physically protected them from stray arrows, caused them to stand out in battle, and ensured the safe repose of their soul.[66] (See figure 34.) Religious imagery also helped boost morale. Before the battle of Tadarahama, a shrine attendant festooned the shoulder boards of Ashikaga Takauji with cedar branches (*sugi*), and members of his army inserted that symbol in their helmets to ensure divine support.[67]

The gods were believed to roam the battlefield and fight in a manner indistinguishable from warriors. According to one petition,

> when [general Ashikaga Tadafuyu] offered a prayer . . . the deity appeared. In response to this apparition, [Tadafuyu] granted lands to Takeo shrine. . . . The shrine attendants then fervently prayed for his military success. Accordingly during the . . . battle of the twenty-third, the god [again] appeared.[68]

Ashikaga Tadafuyu also requested that "divine soldiers" (*shinhei* [神兵]) be incorporated into his corporeal armies.[69] Both Tadafuyu and sober battle administrators believed that they had actually witnessed the gods and their handiwork in battle. One of the latter reported that "the enemy had already

---

65. "Kyūsen kiroku" in *Zoku gunsho ruijū bukebu* 52, pp. 88–102, describes the physical and spiritual protection provided by *horo* and contains a copy of one such *mandala*. Also see *Baishōron*, p. 121, and Itō Masako, "Chūsei no mihata," *Rekishi Hyōron* 497 (September 1991): 25–36, for references to battle flags emblazoned with the names of Amaterasu and Hachiman. For a warrior writing the name of Jizō *bōsatsu* on his armor, see *Taiheiki*, maki 20, "Yūki Nyūdō jigoku ni ochiru koto," pp. 371–72.

66. For warriors who placed *mandala* in their *horo* when they expected to die in battle, see *Taiheiki*, maki 24, "Bingo Tomo ikusa no koto," Izumi Shoin, p. 713, and maki 3, "Tōgoku sei jōraku no koto," p. 65. When heads were taken they were wrapped in the deceased's *horo*. See *Taiheiki*, maki 32, "Miyako kassen no koto," p. 976. Surplices borrowed from priests were sometimes used as *horo* in order to "mitigate one's evil deeds in the afterlife." Ibid., maki 34, "Futatabi Ryūmonzan ikusa no koto," p. 1020. Finally, for genealogical references to Kii warriors who always wore crimson *horo* in battle, see *Kōyasan monjo* 10, pp. 256–57 for Suda Yoshikata and Tadamitsu.

67. According to the *Baishōron*, this shrine attendant was in fact a manifestation of the shrine's deity. See p. 103.

68. NBIK 2754.

69. NBIC 2704. Such a belief is hardly unique to Japan. For references to saints fighting in ninth-century France, see Carl Erdmann, *The Origin of the Idea of Crusade* (Princeton: Princeton University Press, 1977), p. 27.

Figure 34. A *horo*. From *Horo isuikō* (保侶衣推考). Manuscript edition copied by Taira Sada-fumi in 1775. Possession of author.

breached the castle walls, when from the Hachiman Nitta shrine we heard two or three humming arrows (*kaburaya*) that fell among the enemy."[70] The combination of arrows fired from the shrine and the repelling of the enemy convinced these administrators that Hachiman had successfully intervened on their behalf![71] So ingrained was this belief in gods physically fighting that some devout warriors donated swords and suits of armor to shrines for the gods' exclusive use.[72]

The inherent uncertainty of the battlefield caused men to be particularly receptive to divine revelations, manifestations, and omens. Each was considered prophetic, but many of these prophecies were concerned less with predicting the future than in isolating selected moments of the present that had appeared in predictions of the past.[73] Dreams, perhaps the most common sign, were objectively believed to confirm otherworldly succor. For example, Isshiki Dōyu had an auspicious dream while embarking on an offensive. He thereupon granted thirty acres (*chō*) of Iwada no shō as "poem fields" (*waka tokoro*).[74] In this case, Dōyu responded to a divine message (dream) by providing a continuous response of poetic thanks for the gods' expression of support during his campaign. Conversely, generals attributed their abandonment of military campaigns to inauspicious dreams. Thus Akamatsu Tomonori had a dream where " a flock of thousands of mountain doves" appeared. According to contemporary military manuals, this was a sign of divine support for the Akamatsu's adversaries.[75]

Dreams were also believed to be a phenomenon through which a future course of events could be inductively comprehended. This view was reflected in the *Taiheiki*, which states, "although in the Diamond sutra the reality of dreams is compared to the shadows of foam[, dreams are in fact real]. If you see someone's head chopped off, then his decapitation will inevitably come

---

70. NBIK 1382.
71. See NBIK 1374, 1382.
72. One magnificent suit of armor dedicated to the Kasuga deity remains at Kasuga shrine. *Kasuga Shrine Art Masterpieces and Treasures*, (*Kasuga taishako shinhō takaramono zuroku*), comp. Kasuga Taisha (Nara, 1987), exhibit 77, *Akai odoshi ōyoroi taketora suzume kazari*. Nitta Yoshisada, when fleeing the capital, solemnly presented his sword "demon cutter" to the Hiei shrine. *Taiheiki*, maki 17, "Yoshisada botsuraku no koto," p. 536.
73. For more on this, see David Potter, *Prophets and Emperors* (Cambridge: Harvard University Press, 1994), particularly pp. 1–22.
74. NBIK 2773.
75. *Taiheiki*, maki 29, "Kōmyōji kassen no koto," p. 867–68. For interpreting this dream, see *Heihō reizuisho*, p. 60. Another manual states that if mountain doves soar above one's army, then victory is assured. If they fly from one's encampment to the enemy, then victory is likely, but if they fly in the opposite direction, then defeat is inevitable. See "Hyōsho jinkun yōryaku shō," in *Zoku gunsho ruijū* 25.1 *bukebu* (Zoku Gunsho Ruijū Kanseikai, 1975), pp. 80–81. This motif appears in literature as well. See *Genpei jōsuiki*, maki 21, pp. 509–10.

to pass, even if he has committed no crime."[76] Hence, dreams were some-times scrutinized like valuable intelligence because they were believed to reveal divine favor, which was, after all, the basis for political legitimacy. For example, when a rift developed between Ashikaga Takauji and Tadayoshi in 1350, a Kōfukuji priest sprinted to the capital bearing news that the younger brother had "the most mysterious (*fushigi*) and auspicious dream in which he was protected by Hachiman."[77] Tadayoshi thus became a legitimate contender for the shogunate, for he "proved" that he too could personally communicate with the gods and buddhas.

Observations tended to support preconceived notions of causality that only slowly shifted through time. Some omens appear as self-fulfilling prophecies. For example, the courtier Tōin Kinkata ascertained that the "insignificance" of Ashikaga Takauji's army in 1350 was emblematic of divine disfavor.[78] Kinkata also recorded how the standard bearer of Takauji's chief of staff fell from his horse, a portent of doom.[79] A modern observer would have probably arrived at the same conclusions as did Kinkata, but for utterly different reasons.

Dreams and omens were valued as signs that "otherworldly powers allied themselves to [one's] cause."[80] The motif of flying birds, for example, appeared in the diary of the courtier Tōin Kinkata: "While pursing the enemy, a flock of birds suddenly flew above enemy forces, and a great wind arose, billowing enemy flags. [The pursing army] decided that they should hold off [the attack]. Instead, they would achieve victory through the fervency of their belief and through granting a virtuous government (*tokusei*) edict."[81] Thus, both dreams and omens influenced the waging of war. The course of war was likewise thought to reveal the contours of divine will.

ASHIKAGA APOTHEOSIS: THE CREATION OF AN IDEOLOGY OF KINGSHIP

In order to bring peace to the worldly realm, one had to pacify the spiritual realm and quell the spirits of those who died in battle by promoting Buddhist works. Since the twelfth century, the initiative for ordering memorial services for the spirits of those warriors who had perished in battle had remained the preserve of either reigning or retired emperors. For example, in

---

76. *Taiheiki*, maki 35, "Kitano mode hito sejō zatudan no koto," p. 1057.
77. *Entairyaku*, vol. 3, 2.10.1350, p. 379. For another example of an important dream, see ibid., pp. 408–9.
78. *Entairyaku*, vol. 3, 10.29.1350, p. 362.
79. *Entairyaku*, vol. 3, 10.28.1350, pp. 360–61. According to contemporary military manuals, "if a banner man falls off a horse from his left side, it is unlucky, but from his right side it is auspicious . . . and if the flag pole breaks, it is inauspicious." *Heihō reizuisho*, p. 61.
80. NBIC 306 and 394.
81. *Entairyaku*, vol. 4, 8.1.1353, p. 349.

1186 the emperor Go-Toba ordered a memorial service for those who perished during the Genpei war (1180–85), and in the following year the retired emperor Go-Shirakawa offered a service for the dead of the Hōgen (1156) and Heiji (1160) disturbances.[82]

Until the Ashikaga established their shogunate, only reigning or retired emperors mediated with the otherworld by offering prayers for the sake of the realm. Go-Daigo, always an astute wielder of political power, likewise ordered prayers performed in his palace and apparently enacted some rituals himself, which undoubtedly contributed to his majesty.[83] Perhaps Go-Daigo had an ideological agenda as well. In one of the most remarkable portraits of the age, he, alone of all emperors, is represented as a Buddhist deity.[84]

Nevertheless, Ashikaga Takauji began offering memorial services and constructing temples in order to placate the "evil spirits" of the Hōjō dead in the spring of 1335, well before he attempted to topple Go-Daigo's Kenmu regime.[85] Takauji's acts represent a significant infringement on imperial sacerdotal authority, for with these offerings, the Ashikaga were making claims that they could mediate with the otherworld, even though Go-Daigo still remained the nominal focus of all temporal and sacerdotal authority. In this atmosphere of contested otherworldly authority, Go-Daigo's supporters went to such great lengths to portray him as a Buddhist deity.

Ashikaga Takauji asserted his personal ability to mediate between gods and men once he "rebelled" against Go-Daigo late in 1335. After driving Go-Daigo's forces from the capital in the summer of 1336, he wrote the following prayer to the Kannon boddhisattva:

> This world is nothing but a dream. I, Takauji, feel compelled to enter religious orders. Please let my later incarnations achieve enlightenment. Now, as I desire to take the tonsure, please let me

82. In 1186, the emperor Go-Toba ordered a memorial service for those who perished during the Genpei wars (1180–85), and in the following year the retired emperor Go-Shirakawa offered a service for the dead of the Hōgen (1156) and Heiji (1160) disturbances. For the former, see the Go-Toba *tennō senji* of 4.23.1186. Although this document is missing from KI, a picture of it appears on p. 109 of the *Kōyasan senhyakunenshi*, Kōyasan Kongōbuji Kinnen Daihō-e Jimukyoku, comp. (Kōyasan, 1914); for the latter, of 3.6.1187, see KI 217.

83. For references to Go-Daigo ordering five altar rituals performed in the palace in 1335, for example, see DNSR, series 6, vol. 2, p. 510–12.

84. This is the only known overt claim of an emperor as a Buddhist deity. See Goble, "Visions of an Emperor," in Jeffrey P. Mass, ed., *The Origins of Japan's Medieval World: Courtiers, Clerics, Warriors, and Peasants in the Fourteenth Century* (Stanford: Stanford University Press, 1997), pp. 124–27. For a discussion of how this portrait bolstered Go-Daigo's disputed claims to sole imperial legitimacy, see Kuroda Hideo, *Ō no shintai, ō no shōzō* (Heibonsha, 1993).

85. For a grant of land by Ashikaga Takauji to Hōkaiji in order to pacify the evil spirit of Hōjō Takatoki, see *Kamakura shishi shiryōhen*, vol. 1, 3.28.1335 Ashikaga Takauji *kishinjō an*, Hōkaiji *monjo* document 413, pp. 287–88. See also NBIK 223 (to placate the "evil spirits of Kamakura officials") and NBIK 507 (for the spirits of those who had died in battle).

have the peace of mind (*dōshin*) to do so. As for the karma of this world, please transfer it to later incarnations. As for the karma of my life, please transfer it to [my brother] Tadayoshi. Protect him in all ways.[86]

Historians have misinterpreted such prayers as a desire to withdraw from the world, but Takauji was in fact far more ambitious—he attempted to channel the course of fate. Regardless of his success (or lack thereof) in this endeavor, Ashikaga rule was ultimately legitimated by the trappings of a Buddhist kingship.[87]

Once Go-Daigo's support began crumbling in 1337, Takauji's brother Ashikaga Tadayoshi initiated the construction of a temple and pagoda in each of the sixty-six provinces of Japan, calling them "Temples of Peace in the Realm (*ankokuji*) and Pagodas of the Buddhas Favor (*rishōtō*)."[88] In one of the earlier examples, Ashikaga Tadayoshi established the strategically important temple Kumedadera as a *rishōtō* in the 5.17.1338.[89] Ultimately, "Temples of Peace in the Realm and Pagodas of the Buddhas Favor" were constructed in all of the sixty-six provinces and two islands which comprised the administrative regions of Japan, with the possible exception of the central province of Yamato.[90] Once the Ashikaga established this nationwide system, temples from each province competed for the "honor" of receiving this designation.[91] The priests of Myōtsūji, for example, requested funds so that a Pagoda of the Buddhas Favor be built in their compound, but a rival temple was granted the honor instead.[92] The Ashikaga were able to create an

---

86. DNSR, series 6, vol. 3, *hoi*, p. 3, and Tsuji Zennosuke, *Nihon bukkyōshi* 4, *Chūsei* 3 (Iwanami Shoten, 1949), pp. 165–66.

87. For an informative essay on Buddhist kingship, see Stanley Tambiah, "A Reformulation of Geertz's Conception of the Theater State," in *Culture, Thought and Social Action* (Cambridge: Harvard University Press, 1985), pp. 316–38. For another study of the Ashikaga as "warrior kings" through the lens of their attitudes toward relic worship, see Brian D. Ruppert, *Jewel in the Ashes: Buddha Relics and Power in Early Medieval Japan* (Cambridge: Harvard University Press, 2000), particularly pp. 254–60.

88. *Baishōron*, pp. 138–39. Although one was established for each province, the names "Temples for Peace in the Realm" and "Pagodas of the Buddhas Favor" were not established until 1344. Tsuji, *Nihon bukkyōshi* 4, *Chūsei* 3, p. 102.

89. NBIC 802. Structures were to be built "in order to pray for ten thousand generations." By the ninth month, Jōdoji, where Ashikaga Takauji had stopped when he was advancing the capital from Kyushu in the spring of 1336, was established as well. This temple appears in figure 10.

90. Yamato Province was both a stronghold of the southern court, and Kōfukuji, both of which resisted the creation of this new system of temples. See Imaeda Aishin, *Chūsei zenshūshi no kenkyū* (Tōkyō Daigaku Shuppankai, 1970), pp. 77–138, and Tsuji, *Nihon bukkyōshi* 4, *Chūsei* 3, p. 104. For English summaries of *ankokuji* and *rishōtō*, see Martin Collcutt, *Five Mountains* (Cambridge: Harvard University Press, 1981), pp. 106–9, and Ruppert, *Jewel in the Ashes*, pp. 254–59.

91. For the characterization that a temple "lost honor" because of inadequate compensation, see *Minoo shishi shiryōhen*, vol. 1, document 563, 8.16 Katsuoji Nengyōji *shojō an*.

92. *Fukui kenshi shiryōhen* 9, *Chū-kinsei* 7, Myōtsūji *monjo* document 27, pp. 577–78, and Jingūji *monjo* document 10, p. 310. The Northern Court's Kōgon Emperor designated Jingūji as the *rishōtō* of

imposing religious edifice and, in the process, consolidate their rule by tying the interests of a myriad of temples to their own through a complex web of patronage.

The Ashikaga creation of this system of *ankokuji* temples and *rishōtō* pagodas represents the first time that of a network of temples had been constructed throughout the land that was not entirely an imperial undertaking. To be sure, Kōgon, the retired emperor of the Northern Court, was closely involved with the selection of *rishōtō* and the creation of *ankokuji*, but as the polemics of chronicles such as the *Baishōron* reveal, these structures represented above all a component of an Ashikaga ideological edifice.

Go-Daigo's sudden death in 1339 provided the Ashikaga with their next opportunity to assert otherworldly powers. Ashikaga Takauji dedicated the temple of Tenryūji to the souls of the deposed emperor, Go-Daigo. And, in addition to constructing a network of temples throughout the realm, the Ashikaga also copied the Buddhist canon in order to "pacify those killed in battle since 1331." [93]

The Ashikaga usurped several prerogatives of Buddhist kingship that had been hitherto reserved for the court as they consolidated their authority. "Protector" priests (*gojisō*), who had been appointed to protect the emperor since late in the eighth century, were now appointed to pray for Ashikaga prosperity as well.[94] The esoteric specialist Kenshun described his appointment as a *gojiso* for both the emperor and the Ashikaga as an "extreme honor"— which concurrently marked a blurring in imperial sovereignty.[95]

Sometime late in 1345 or early in 1346, the Ashikaga co-opted another symbol of imperial authority when they issued the unprecedented command that their "protector priest" Kenshun perform five altar rituals in their own residences.[96] Previously, such rituals had only taken place at the palace or in major temples at imperial bequest. The Ashikaga could now enact rituals of

---

Wakasa Province. Nevertheless Jingūji's finances were strained as the war dragged on and in 1353, its priests submitted a request for more remuneration in 1353. For Jingūji's holdings, see document 20, pp. 312–13, 6.1457 Jingūji *jiryō mokuroku an*.

93. The Buddhist canon was copied by the Ashikaga for the spiritual repose of all those who died in battle since 1331. *Shizuoka kenshi shiryōhen* 8, *chūsei hōi* 1 4, document 95, and *Baishōron*, p. 138. It was commonly believed that all those who died in battle became "evil spirits." *Taiheiki*, maki 24, "Masashige onryō tsurugi o kō koto," p. 707.

94. For a recent study of the relationship between the emperor and protector priests, see Hori Yutaka, "Gojisō to Tennō," in *Nihon kokka no shikteki tokushitsu kodai chūsei*, ed. Ōyama sensei taikan kinen ronshū kai (Kyoto: Shibunkaku Shuppan, 1997), pp. 385–410.

95. This first reference to Ashikaga *gojisō* appears in the 4.4.1338. See DNSR, series 6, vol. 4, pp. 788.

96. This happened between 1345 and 1346. See Mori, *Taiheiki no gunzō*, p. 184. Kenshun of Sanbōin was first ordered to perform this by Ashikaga Tadayoshi. See Kenshun's diary, in *Ichinomiya shishi shiryōhen* 6, comp. Iyanaga Teizō and the Ichinomiya Shishi Hensanshitsu (Ichinomiya, 1970), p. 887, 9.26.1346.

considerable military importance which concurrently implied that they possessed at least a fragment of sovereign authority.

The Rinzai Zen priest Musō Kokushi reserved special criticism for Shingon priests, such as Kenshun, who engaged in rituals on behalf of the Ashikaga. He criticized the intensely political role of these priests, and Esoteric Buddhism, in the following passage:

> Shingon esoteric (*kaji*) rituals and ordinary *kaji*-style prayers to avoid disaster or increase wealth are all expedient devices to guide foolish persons. . . . These days people still have faith in the esoteric verbal formulas, but rare indeed is the aspiration to penetrate the innermost secret teachings, pass through the true *kaji* gate, and actualize the principle of attaining Buddhahood in this very body. Instead, people devote themselves exclusively to worldly prayers. Even though the venerable monks who must uphold the esoteric tradition do not consider these prayers to be their proper purpose, they are compelled to direct their ceremonies and secret practices to worldly ends. There are also Shingon priests, ignorant of the inner teachings of esotericism, who construe these worldly activities as their proper vocation. They seem to be praying for patrons and soliciting donations in order to advance their own fame and gain. This is why esotericism has gradually declined and changed into something resembling the methods of the yin-yang teachers.[97]

Musō criticizes the emphasis by esoteric priests on ritual, and implies that worldly motives influenced their behavior, which, in fact, reveals that they lacked a profound understanding of Buddhist principles. Such critiques proved significant by drawing a sharp distinction between "worldly" and "religious" behavior, but Musō's notion of a "pure" religious tradition was ignored by both Shingon priests and, more significantly, the Ashikaga shoguns.

The integral relationship between prayer, military success, and a Buddhist ideology of rulership is most clearly revealed in the *Gen'ishū*'s panegyric:

> The shogun's house supersedes all others in their patronage of Buddhist works. . . . [As the enemy advanced on the capital] one person . . . said: "Regarding Buddhist [matters] . . . the way of heaven is intertwined with the way of justice (*seiri*) because there is nothing private in Buddhist affairs. [Thus] if one copies the Buddhist canon in order to achieve a great vow and that comes true

97. Kenneth Kraft, trans., "Musō Kokushi's Dialogues in a Dream Selections," *The Eastern Buddhist* n. s. 1 (The Eastern Buddhist Society, Kyoto, Japan): 82–84 and *Muchū mondō*, ed. Satō Taishun (Iwanami Shoten, 1934), dialogue 15, "Kaji kitō no shin'i," pp. 52–53.

then it is a cause for joy. . . . Even if the enemy were to attack, [Buddhist services should continue to be performed.] We all have achieved success, control over the land, and [political] support through divine largess. The otherworld shows no partisan favor. Hence rebels lacking just cause will inevitably endure the punishment of heaven. Even if the enemy advances on the capital, Buddhist services must be [our] first priority.[98]

Military success was taken as proof of divine favor, which in turn accrued to the most just. This self-legitimating doctrine of war (victory = divine support = a just cause) obviously found correspondingly less favor as Ashikaga rule solidified. Hence a belief was fostered that the Ashikaga were close to the gods, due in no small part to their diligence in performing Buddhist rituals. Some went so far as to assert that Takauji was in fact an incarnation of the gods.

Ashikaga Takauji claimed to be particularly favored by Jizō *bosatsu*, a Buddhist avatar of compassion. Not only did he carry a small statue of the Jizō as a prized possession,[99] but he communicated with Jizō through dreams. For example, when war erupted between Takauji, his loyal retainers the Kō brothers, and Ashikaga Tadayoshi,

> . . . Takauji had a dream in which he was pressed by enemy forces. He fled to the mountains. At the peak, the road came to an end and he was in danger of falling. He looked back and was grabbed by [his brother Ashikaga] Tadayoshi, who exerted all his strength in trying to plunge Takauji into the abyss. Then, suddenly, Takauji saw a single priest (*bikuni sō*) in the form of the Jizō *bosatsu*, who took him by the hand, and led him to the safety of the plains [below], where the Kō brothers and an army of thousands greeted him. Later, when reaching Kyushu, he encamped at just such a plain, proof of his dream. Thereupon Takauji drew a picture of the Jizō in which he praised being able to sense [Jizō] through dreams.[100]

Dreams of Jizō helped further Ashikaga Takauji's political image. Starting in 1349 and continuing until shortly before his death, Ashikaga Takauji repeatedly drew Jizō and boasted of his "ability to sense [Jizō] while dreaming

---

98. *Gen'ishū*, pp. 232–33.
99. *Inryōken nichiroku*, quoted in Hayami Tasuku, *Kannon Jizō Fudō* (Kōdansha, 1996) p. 149.
100. *Kūge nichiyō kufū ryakushū*, ed. Tsuji Zennosuke (Kyoto: Taiyōsha, 1939), 10.1.1382, pp. 175–76. This dream was remembered by Aiba Ujinao, a close favorite of Takauji, thirty-three years after the event.

(*muchū kantsū ari*) (夢中有感通)."[101] (See figure 35.) These drawings came to "prove" that Takauji superseded other mortals and was therefore destined to rule the realm. Indeed, Akamatsu Norisuke would proclaim, "the one who draws Jizō and worships it will be reborn in the thirty-third level of heaven. If the grace of the heavens is exhausted and he is reborn as a person, he will become king of the realm (*nao kokuō to naru*)."[102]

The religious aura that accrued to Takauji was enhanced by his success in battle. So great was his divine favor, or so it was reasoned, that Ashikaga Takauji began to be characterized as a manifestation of the Jizō bodhisattva. According to some legends, Takauji carved statutes of the Jizō that were exactly the same height.[103] If we are to trust Buddhist chronicles, he even made explicit comparisons between himself and Jizō, stating, "With my three-foot sword, I have conquered the realm on horseback. Although many have been killed, they do not exceed 100,000"—the maximum number of souls that Jizō could save.[104] Buddhist pictures drawn by Takauji likewise became invested with a holy aura, and even helped institutionalize the charisma of Takauji after he had passed away. For example, during the political instability of 1361, the soon-to-be third shogun Ashikaga Yoshimitsu had a dream. He pointed to a picture of Jizō that had been drawn by his grandfather Takauji, and said, "This person promised never to leave my side."[105] Whether Yoshimitsu communicated with Jizō or Takauji in his dreams is not clear, but the matter was moot, for one (Takauji) was believed to be an incarnation of the other (Jizō).

Parallels were conveniently drawn between Ashikaga Takauji and the saintly leaders of the past. According to the *Baishōron*,

> Prince Shōtoku built forty-nine temples and promoted days of abstinence in the realm. Emperor Shōmu built Tōdaiji and

101. The earliest one dates from the first month of 1349, when tensions between Takauji and his brother were mounting. For a color reproduction of this document, belonging to Jōmyōji in Kanagawa Province, see Seno Sei'ichirō, ed. *Bunretsu to dōran no seiki: Nihon rekishi tenbō 5 Nanbokuchō* (Ōbunsha, 1981). For photographs of another, dating from 7.6.1350, see *Shizuoka kenshi shiryōhen 6, Chūsei 2*, document 416, and plate 16. For a later sketch dating from 7.24.1355, see DNSR, series 6, vol. 19, pp. 860–61.

102. *Kanringoroshū*, in Uemura Kankō, ed., *Gozan bungaku zenshū*, vol. 4 (Gozan Bungaku Zenshū Kankōkai, 1936), pp. 672–3. This account was written by Keijo Shūrin, a grandson of Akamatsu Norisuke, and is also quoted in Usui Nobuyoshi, *Ashikaga Yoshimitsu* (Yoshikawa Kōbunkan, 1960), pp. 15–16.

103. *Hyōgo kenshi shiryōhen chūsei*, vol. 4, document 8, "Settsu no kuni Hachibe gun Kuruma mura Zenpukuji *raireki no koto*," pp. 25–27.

104. DNSR, series 6, vol. 5, 7.6.1339, p. 600.

105. *Kanringoroshū*, pp. 672–73 and Usui, *Ashikaga Yoshimitsu*, pp. 15–16 (*kono hito ga ware ni katari, ware nanji to nagaku hanarezu to itta*).

Figure 35. A Jizō drawn by Ashikaga Takauji in 1349. Possession of Jōmyōji. Photograph courtesy of Kamakura Kokuhōkan.

Kokubunji temples in each province. Fujiwara no Fubito built Kōfukuji. These events of long ago were due to the Buddhas manifesting themselves as mortals. Now, both generals (Ashikaga Takauji and Tadayoshi) cannot be likened to typical mortals, for they promote Buddhism, had Musō Kokushi found Tenryūji [temple] and copied the complete Buddhist canon. They even monogrammed pictures of the Buddhas that they personally drew and annotated.[106]

From this passage, one can infer that the Ashikaga relied upon elements of both esoteric Buddhism and Zen to legitimate their rule. According to this formulation, the Ashikaga transcended the various factions of Buddhist thought. In addition to performing considerable acts of Buddhist merit, Takauji also asserted another link with Prince Shōtoku by alluding to his knowledge of an important oracular text, the "Chronicle of the Future" (*Miraiki*), written purportedly by the perspicacious prince himself, which provided a prophecy of all future political events in Japan.[107] It was widely believed that such a text was could only be viewed by one particularly favored by the now-deified Shōtoku himself.

These comparisons between Ashikaga Takauji and the saintly seventh-century Prince Shōtoku helped legitimate the Ashikaga's use of force as being impersonal and transcendent. Musō Kokushi noted that Prince Shōtoku's slaughter of his rival Mononobe Moriya was in accordance with the wishes of the Buddha and thus truly a source of merit.[108] The implications of his polemic regarding the legitimacy of Ashikaga military might were lost on none. Because the Ashikaga copied the Buddhist canon and did other exemplary activities, they possessed a special affinity to deities of the otherworld. Accordingly, their enemies were destined "to endure the punishment of

---

106. This final passage is a reference to Takauji's drawings of Jizō. Ashikaga Tadayoshi was not apparently so inclined. *Baishōron*, pp. 138–39. As should be evident in this passage, both Ashikaga Takauji and Tadayoshi aspired to becoming Buddhist kings, which helps explain why war erupted between them shortly after this panegyric was completed. One can also find similar references to European monarchs engaging in similar activities. Charlemagne devoted considerable attention to correcting the Bible while Byzantine emperors such as Constantine VII painted icons. See Heinrich Fichtenau, *The Carolingian Empire* (Toronto: University of Toronto Press, 1978), p. 36, and Michael McCormick, *Eternal Victory* (New York: Cambridge University Press, 1986), pp. 142–43 and 245–47.

107. NBIC 678. For an interpretation of these poems, see *Ōsaka fushi* 3, *Chūsei* 1 (Osaka, 1981), pp. 673–74. This text also appears prominently in the *Taiheiki*, and was purportedly viewed by Kusunoki Masashige as well. See *Taiheiki*, maki 6, "Kusunoki miraiki o nozumu koto," pp. 143–48, which links this chronicle to the death of an anti-Buddhist proponent named Mononobe Moriya. For more on the "Chronicle of the Future" (*Miraiki*), see Akamatsu, *Kamakura bukkyō no kenkyū*, pp. 267–316.

108. *Muchū mondō*, "Inori no kokoro no koto," pp. 42–43. Shōtoku is depicted slaughtering Mononobe Moriya in figure 9, pl. 7.

heaven," for to rebel against the Ashikaga was to rebel against the gods and Buddhas as well.[109]

THE ORDERLY RETREAT OF THE GODS AND BUDDHAS

A religious aura accrued to those who triumphed in battle, for they were believed to possess the ability to influence fate and intercede with the gods. According to the teleological mind-set of the age, the victorious were best suited for governance because they were closest to, and most favored by, the gods.

Military victory thus brought with it the seeds of ideological control. The outcome of battle, instead of being influenced by the gods or the prayers of Buddhist monks, became directly linked to the "luck" of the Ashikaga.[110] Ashikaga Takauji succeeded in demonstrating that he and his descendants could intercede with the gods and influence fate.

The Ashikaga ideology of Buddhist kingship nevertheless remained inherently unstable at the pinnacle of authority, for anyone who sprang from the Ashikaga lineage could potentially appropriate the Ashikaga spiritual edifice. Ashikaga authorities vigilantly monitored the spiritual behavior of their collaterals because maledictions constituted the inevitable first step to rebellion.

Despite this vigilance, Ashikaga rule would be racked with succession disputes, starting with Ashikaga Tadayoshi's failed attempt to supplant Takauji in 1350 (the Kannō disturbance). Another major revolt occurred in 1361, when Hosokawa Kiyouji, the chief of staff (*kanrei*) of Ashikaga Yoshiakira, the second shogun, was framed by a forged curse,[111] by which he was portrayed as praying for the deaths of Ashikaga Yoshiakira and Motouji in order to "control the realm and [allow for Kiyouji's] descendants to bask in glory."[112] This malediction succeeded in discrediting Kiyouji precisely

---

109. *Gen'ishū*, p. 233.

110. An honorific prefix is attached to the word "luck," which indicates that it became the preserve of those exercising hegemonic authority. For other examples regarding signs of the Ashikaga's "honorable luck," see *Taiheiki*, maki 31, "Musashino kassen no koto," p. 919.

111. Imagawa Ryōshun would later claim that Kiyouji had been framed, for "the prayer was not written by Kiyouji and the monogram was suspicious." "Nantaiheiki," pp. 305–21. Kiyouji's ruin was precipitated by a pilgrimage to a temple where he fasted for three days, ostensibly to pray for the shogun's return to health. *Gukanki* (Konoe Michitsugu), ed. Tsuboi Kumezō, Kusaka Hiroshi, and Takeuchi Rizō, in *Zōho shiryō taisei* 1–4 (Kyoto: Rinsen Shoten, 1965), 9.23.1361 and Ogawa, *Ashikaga ichimon shugo hattenshi no kenkyū*, pp. 115–25. Although he appears to have prayed for three days, the *Taiheiki* claims it was three weeks, a time span typical for curses.

112. *Taiheiki*, maki 36, "Sagami no kami Kiyouji inbō rōken no koto," pp. 1089–90. Kiyouji supposedly offered a prayer to Dakini, originally a Hindu deity that took the form of an old woman noted for eating the hearts of those who were about to die. Dakini, if placated, could bring prosperity. For more on Kiyouji's prayer, see Hayami Tasuku, *Shujutsu shūkyō no sekai* (Hanashinsho, 1987), pp. 190–94.

because its treasonable nature was unquestioned.[113] The Ashikaga were nevertheless successful in asserting the supremacy of Takauji's lineal descendants, in part through the auspicious dreams of his grandson, Yoshimitsu.

A spiritual transformation arose concurrent with the establishment of this ideology of Ashikaga kingship. Some began to conceive of fate as being most responsive to those in authority—a belief that inevitably undermined the spiritual (and political) autonomy of religious institutions. Priests and shrine attendants disputed this new belief. Rai'in, for example, explained that military victory "was determined by the power of my prayers . . . and not by the honorable luck (*on'un*) [of the Ashikaga],"[114] while a shrine attendant explained, "although one might believe that our victory stemmed from fate as determined by the heavens (*ten'un on onkaho*), it is in fact solely due to the protection of this shrine's deity."[115] In short, those affiliated with religious institutions struggled to maintain political leverage by emphasizing their own role in influencing causality, but their argument became increasingly untenable as the Ashikaga accumulated power and prestige.

Political authority was thus perceived as a "higher cause" whose needs overruled all other considerations. Some generals even risked personal damnation in order to fulfill military objectives. During one battle, Hosokawa Akiuji "consigned Gokurakuji . . . and numerous other shrines and temples to the flames. Fearful of divine punishment, or so the general opinion goes, Akiuji took the tonsure."[116] Generals might damage temples in the heat of battle but the fear of divine vengeance was still strong enough that they later regretted their behavior.

Some Zen priests promoted a distant, impersonal sense of fate and criticized the military service of religious institutions.[117] As Musō Kokushi observed,

> As the realm has recently been disordered, prayers from Kantō and Kyoto have been extremely common. . . . I wonder why such prayers are even offered. . . . All happenings stem from karma[118]—that is the teaching of Buddhism. . . . Because priests used the

113. For a similar situation in imperial Rome, see David Potter, *Prophets and Emperors* (Cambridge: Harvard University Press, 1994), pp. 171–82.

114. *Kamakura shishi shiryōhen* 1, Myō-ōin *monjo*, document 638, 7.1387 Rai'in *mōshijō*.

115. NBIK 2754.

116. *Entairyaku*, vol. 4, 7.5.1352, p. 152.

117. For an unusual early critique of warring priests, see *Kamakura shishi shiryōhen* 3, document 125, Nyōinan *monjo*, of 10.1332, which states that "Zen priests should refrain from leaving and entering military camps." "Ritual warring" (*hōsen*) (法戦) was likewise characterized as being incompatible with Zen.

118. Literally, the interplay between primary and secondary karma (*innen wagō*).

power of the Buddhist law as a kind of service, a provisional
prayer tax (*kayaku*) is levied on temples, making it no different than
vulgar [types of] service. When great secret prayers are enacted,
the funds (*kuryō*) for such prayers are not granted as they should
be. . . . At times offering are given, but most are pro forma rewards
lacking substance. This problem is not confined to prayer [levies].
Buddhism is treated in a similar manner which leads to a dimin-
ishing belief in the Buddha's law (*buppō*).[119]

Musō believed that karma could not be influenced by prayers; hence prayer
"service" came to be taken for granted, which diminished belief in Buddhism
and the efficacy of its prayers.

   Musō's critique resonated well with authorities. Zen institutions that
abandoned all claims to influence fate aided the Ashikaga in their ideological agenda. The fourteenth century also witnessed the quiet birth of a
belief that religious institutions were not "legitimate" political actors, at
least in tangible spheres. In 1367, Hosokawa Yorimoto admonished the
priests of Sanuki's Zentsūji not to be remiss in ceremonial matters. At the
same time, while reaffirming that warriors were not to enter temple grounds
or despoil tax-exempt paddies, Yorimoto demanded that temple priests
(*jisō*) no longer carry bows and arrows (*yumiya*) and other weapons of war
(*heijō*).[120] *Ji* priests devised a set of regulations which proscribed their military activity, limiting themselves to wearing helmets and armor, but not
carrying bows or other weapons.[121] Likewise the dual identity of shrine
attendants as religious figures and warriors began to collapse as physical
and spiritual behavior became reified.[122] Notions of the gods and signs of
their handiwork were becoming less concrete and more closely linked to
political authority.

   Once control over fate became monopolized by authority, then "religion"
gradually ceased to permeate society; instead it became more distant, distinct and identifiable. As was perhaps inevitable, once Buddhist kings ruled
the realm, the gods and buddhas began their slow and steady retreat from the
battlefield.

---

119. *Muchū mondō*, "Kokuō daijin no kigan," p. 44.

120. NBIC 3545.

121. *Iwate ken chūsei monjo* 2, document 35, Ta Ami *jishin jishū kokoro e no jō jō*, p. 11.

122. The Iga of Mutsu, for example, abandoned their warrior calling and solely became identified as a
     shrine attendant in 1499. See *Ino Hachimangū monjo*, "kaisetsu," and document 112, 7.1505 Iwaki
     Tsunetaka *ganmon*, p. 73.

CHAPTER 7

Law and the Legitimation of Judicial Violence

Tell you the Dauphin I am coming on
To venge me as I may, and to put forth
My rightful hand in a well-hallowed cause.

Shakespeare, *Henry V*

Modern societies are . . . fiercely attached to the doctrine that responsibility for any set of actions rests with the individual who undertakes them and not with his relatives or anyone else.

"Nepotism: A little more than kin," *The Economist*, Dec. 24, 1994–Jan. 6, 1995

Times of great violence possess a peculiar and particular order. Nevertheless, in our day we invariably associate violence with irrationality. Indeed, the very phrases and couplings of words commonly bandied about imply an intimate correlation between violence and unpredictability. "Random violence," "senseless violence," and "lawless violence" are all indicative of the modern belief that violence and mayhem cannot be sustained by a logical system of thought. The correlation between irrationality and violence has seeped into our consciousness to such an extent that words to the opposite effect—"logical violence" or "lawful violence"— seem absurd. And yet, as we shall see, violence wielded in the defense of rights constituted a defining aspect of the medieval in Japan.

Elizabeth Berry has described a "culture of lawlessness" that prevailed in Japan's middle ages. According to her, this culture constituted "the state of being without, or lacking, the host of social assumptions intimated by the word *law*. Rather than mere transgression against presumptively normative rules of conduct, lawlessness indicates suspension in a world where the rules have lost their cogency."[1] Berry's characterization of "rules" as constituting both legal codes and norms of conduct is problematic, however, for no correlation necessarily exists between the two. For example, a tendency to ignore codified laws can become a cultural norm. In the case of fourteenth-century Japan, unwritten, widely shared notions of justice coexisted with an almost congenital disregard for codified laws.

George Sansom characterized Japan in the fourteenth and fifteenth centuries as having "much law and little justice."[2] Historians who share Sansom's view that endemic violence invariably breeds injustice ignore the fact that rights and privileges must ultimately be *enforced* by coercive power.[3] Otto Brunner provided a more sophisticated frame of analysis by demonstrating that violence (specifically, feuds) possessed a precise judicial function.[4] Thus, rather than "destroying the expectations that had once governed daily life," violence could constitute one of the governing expectations of daily life.

Rising prosperity whetted the appetite of warriors for the liberty of alienating their "property" (generally in the form of *shiki*, or status-based rights of income) as they saw fit. The rules promulgated by the Kamakura *bakufu* bolstered and codified these rights. In the mid–1280s, however, the *bakufu* attempted to enforce the impartial application of its regulations by punishing administrative infractions. As bureaucratic process was only dimly

---

1. Berry, *The Culture of Civil War in Kyoto*, p. xxi.
2. George Sansom, *Japan: A Short Cultural History* (Stanford: Stanford University Press, 1931), p. 354.
3. This is exemplified by Grossberg, who states that "the age was characterized by as little law as necessary and as much justice as could be expected in the chaotic circumstances" Grossberg and Nobuhisa, *The Laws of the Muromachi Bakufu*, p. 3.
4. Otto Brunner, *Land and Lordship: Structures of Governance in Medieval Austria* (Philadelphia: University of Pennsylvania Press, 1992). Brunner's notion of the feud, first formulated in his 1939 monograph (and only translated into English fifty-three years later) has proved influential to Japanese scholars. See Haga Norihiko, "Kosen bōsen o megutte," *Ronshū Chūsei no mado* (Yoshikawa Kōbunkan, 1977), pp. 113–40, and Ishii Shirō, *Nihonjin no kokka seikatsu* (Tōkyōdō Shuppan, 1986), pp. 1–72.

perceived—and widely disregarded at that time—these penalties were thought to be "unjust."

By punishing intransigence and punitively confiscating lands, the *bakufu* began to be seen as a hostile and aggrandizing regime. Some warriors resorted to violence in order to defend their rights and prerogatives. Although recourse to violence was initially prohibited in codified law, it achieved de facto legitimation once civil war consumed the archipelago. Thereupon rights to the land became enforced more by individuals than by the state, and codified law correspondingly withered in importance. From the mid–fourteenth century onward, Japan can be best characterized as having a strong sense of justice, but little regard for the law.

DEVELOPING NOTIONS OF LAW AND JUSTICE

Japan in the late seventh and early eighth century had laws but no sense of justice. The law codes promulgated by the rulers of the early imperium consisted of universally applicable administrative codes and penal regulations (*ritsuryō*). These regulations ordered the realm by dividing it into administrative spheres.

Proprietary (*honjo*) rights gradually developed after the mid–eighth century as plots of land (*shōen*) were delineated and permitted to be hereditarily transmitted in principle. This process, which has been characterized by John Hall as "the return to familial authority,"[5] did not permeate the fabric of local society until the tenth century.[6] These coalescing proprietary rights were undermined in 1069 when Go-Sanjō, the emperor at the time, opened an office (the *kirokujo*) which systematically assessed the "legality of estates."[7] He and his successors successfully asserted ultimate authority in determining proprietary rights. Men from the provinces commonly commended a cut of their income in the form of status-based *shiki* to retired emperors in exchange for a confirmation of their land rights.[8] Retired emper-

---

5. Hall, *Government and Local Power in Japan*, pp. 99-128.

6. By 971 one sees disputes regarding the transmission of lands, and the oldest surviving testament dates from 1022. Mass, *Lordship and Inheritance*, p. 13, and HI 299 and 4605. For translations of mid–twelfth-century testaments, see Mass, *Lordship and Inheritance*, documents 1–4, pp. 123–26, and, for a patron's confirmation of these land rights, document 5, pp. 126–27.

7. For more on the significance of these measures, see Hall, *Government and Local Power in Japan*, p. 120, and, for a critique, see Keirstead, *The Geography of Power*, pp. 19 and 126. Both Hurst and Keirstead summarize the retired emperors' pattern of confiscations. See G. Cameron Hurst, III, *Insei: Abdicated Sovereigns in the Politics of Late Heian Japan* (New York: Columbia University Press, 1976), pp. 110–19; 232–36 and Keirstead, *The Geography of Power*, pp. 17–22.

8. For the precarious state of provincial proprietary rights, see Mass, "The Missing Minamoto in the Twelfth-Century Kantō," pp. 121–45, particularly pp. 135–42, and also Jeffrey P. Mass, "Patterns of Provincial Inheritance in Late Heian Japan," *Journal of Japanese Studies* 9.1 (Winter 1983): 67–95. Peter Judd Arnesen in his "The Struggle for Lordship in Late Heian Japan: The Case of Aki," *Journal of Japanese Studies* 10.1 (Winter 1984): 101–41, and his "Suō Province in the Age

ors thereupon amassed gigantic portfolios of rights to revenue, drawn from a myriad of estates. The imperial family managed to establish over a thousand estates in the century following 1090. In the case of Noto Province alone, over half of the land was converted into *shōen* between 1136 and 1150.[9]

War erupted in 1180 in part as a reaction to the arbitrary redistributive power of central authority. As a result, the newly established Kamakura *bakufu* upheld existing proprietary rights.[10] Imperial regulations thereupon became tempered by a guiding belief in justice (*dōri*) and bound by precedent.[11] From this point on, innovations became associated with "illegalities" (*hihō*)—a term that refers more to an unwritten, transcendent conception of "justice" than legality in the narrow sense of abiding by written laws.[12]

The Kamakura regime founded by Minamoto Yoritomo dispensed justice without any codified law for fifty years. Judgments were initially promulgated according to the broadly construed "will" of the "Kamakura lord."[13] Kamakura gradually developed sophisticated procedures for evaluating its judicial capabilities, but the main thrust of its decisions was to confirm or, on occasion, adjust local custom and hereditarily transmitted rights.[14]

---

of Kamakura," in Jeffrey P. Mass, ed., *Court and Bakufu in Japan: Essays in Kamakura History* (New Haven: Yale University Press, 1982), pp. 93–101, illuminates the impact the retired emperor's policies had on proprietary rights in western Japan. Not all commendations were to retired emperors. Some centrally based proprietors, such as major shrines and temples, were granted lands as well. For one example of "homelands" being created in 1167 when lands were commended to a major shrine, see KI 16780.

9. Keirstead, *The Geography of Power*, p. 16, and Hall, *Government and Local Power*, p. 120. See also Ishii Susumu, "Insei jidai," in *Hōken shakai no seiritsu, Kōza nihonshi* 2 (Tōkyō Daigaku Shuppankai, 1970), pp. 207–9. See also Nagahara Keiji, "Land Ownership Under the Shōen Kokugaryō System," *Journal of Japanese Studies* 1 (Spring 1975): 269–96.

10. This has been most eloquently expressed by Cornelius J. Kiley, "Estate and Property in the Late Heian Period," in John W. Hall and Jeffrey P. Mass, eds., *Medieval Japan: Essays in Institutional History* (Stanford: Stanford University Press, 1974), pp. 109–24, and Mass, "The Emergence of the Kamakura Bakufu," in *Medieval Japan*, pp. 127–56. Although the *bakufu* even protected estates that had only been recently established by retired emperors, it is worth noting that no new imperial portfolios of estates were created after 1185. Lecture by Ōyama Kyōhei at Kyoto University, May 1997. The *bakufu* attempted to limit its jurisdiction but subsequent reforms ensured that the court would adjudicate disputes according to the same legal principles. See Kiley, "The Imperial Court as a Legal Authority in the Kamakura Age," in Jeffrey P. Mass, ed., *Court and Bakufu in Japan: Essays in Kamakura History* (New Haven: Yale University Press, 1982), pp. 29–44.

11. Some authors have commonly made the distinction between "courtier," "warrior," and "proprietary" (*honjo*) law which existed in the Kamakura period. Nevertheless, as Kiley has observed in his "The Imperial Court as a Legal Authority in the Kamakura Age," all were based upon precedent and thus were functionally indistinguishable.

12. One sees many references to the phrase *shingi hihō*, "innovations and illegalities," which reflect this attitude. See for example, CHSS, vol. 1, *sankō shiryō* document 9, p. 328.

13. Nitta Ichirō, *Nihon chūsei no shakai to hō* (Tōkyō Daigaku Shuppankai, 1995), p. 49.

14. The best summary remains Mass, *The Development of Kamakura Rule*, pp. 61–159. Likewise, as Furusawa Naoto has pointed out, most of the early judgments were reserved for inheritance disputes between contending family members and did not concern land rights per se. See his *Kamakura bakufu to chūsei kokka* (Azekura Shobō, 1991), pp. 59–76.

Kamakura officials penned a law code in 1232, the *Goseibai shikimoku*, which rapidly became woven into the fabric of local governance due to the protection that it provided for extant rights.[15] Nevertheless, Kamakura did not enforce compliance to its edicts until half a century after this code had been promulgated. From the 1280s, authorities tended to treat all administrative infractions as criminal behavior, but punishments administered for a failure to abide by rules were believed by many to violate judicial norms.

When promulgating law, tension invariably exists between its divergent and at times conflicting functions. Most laws in fact are an amalgamation of: 1) administrative law, in which codified rules consistently applied in a uniform manner are used to regulate society and behavior; 2) penal law, in which those who fail to act in accordance with these regulations are punished; and 3) judicial law, in which law appeals to a system of rules that are communally regarded as binding and proper.[16] Denizens of the thirteenth century possessed a clear understanding of what could be characterized as "judicial" and "penal" aspects of the law, but were never able to fully grasp or, for that matter, identify "administrative" law.

LEGAL REFORM AND JUDICIAL VIOLENCE

The Subordinate Status of Administrative Law

The 1232 laws were seen as epitomizing justice because the *bakufu* was lax in enforcing administrative aspects of its laws. Kamakura's legal decisions were based upon a quest for justice, not obedience.[17] In cases where one of the aggrieved parties failed to follow regulations—such as ignoring a writ or summons—lands would be reassigned in principle. Nevertheless, administrative concerns were secondary to judicial ones.[18]

---

15. The law is first quoted in documents in 1239. For more on the promulgation of the "Jōei Formulary," see Mass, *The Development of Kamakura Rule*, pp. 102–12. The documents have been translated on pp. 232–33. For later examples, see KI 12792. The *Goseibai shikimoku*'s twenty year statute of limitations is frequently invoked in legal documents. For two more examples, see KI 18789, 3.28.1295 Kantō *gechijō*, and KI 23493, 12.25.1308 Kantō *gechijō*. Carl Steenstrup, in his *A History of Law in Japan until 1868* (Leiden: E.J. Brill, 1991) claims that this code represents the "beginning of "the rule of law." See p. 85. Finally, according to Kiley, law in the Kamakura period is best characterized as "customary law." See Kiley, "The Imperial Court as a Legal Authority in the Kamakura Age," p. 30.

16. Many of these insights into the nature of "law" I owe to a discussion with Martin Jay at the Stanford Humanities Center, November, 1997.

17. See Furusawa, *Kamakura bakufu to chūsei kokka*, pp. 59–76, and Nitta, *Nihon chūsei shakai to hō*, pp. 47–67.

18. If a plaintiff's complaint was considered to be just, he received the lands. If, however, the claim was spurious, the defendant's lands would be reassigned to an unspecified third party. CHSS, vol. 1, article 35, pp. 21. No references exist to this clause ever having been enforced.

Kamakura officials were initially reluctant to mete out punishments for administrative lapses. Hōjō Yasutoki, the driving force behind the *Goseibai shikimoku*, went so far as to criticize his Rokuhara branch office for "outrageously" ignoring administrative infractions such as a failure to obey summonses.[19] Rokuhara's reluctance stemmed from their subordinate judicial authority, which tended to be perceived as being nonbinding. In 1233, for example, the representative of a land steward (*jitō*) stated, "I do not intend to abide by Rokuhara judgments . . . because these lands were not bestowed by Rokuhara. Instead . . . [the *jitō*] received these lands from Kamakura. Unless Kamakura and *jitō* documents are appended [to the Rokuhara judgment] I will ignore them."[20]

Administrative documents likewise were perceived to possess a subordinate function to judicial edicts and tended to be disregarded. Many had no qualms about disregarding summonses. In one dispute, over fifty were ignored![21] In 1248, the *bakufu* issued an amendment to their laws which stated that if three summons were ignored, the plaintiff would automatically win his dispute, but no evidence exists to suggest that this provision was enforced.[22] The *bakufu* rarely enforced administrative infractions, going so far in 1264 as to recognize the "custom" (*bōrei*) whereby defendants had the "freedom" (*jiyū*) to disobey summonses.[23] Even as late as 1275, Kamakura chose not to punish a certain Kita Nagaie for "disobeying orders and committing outrages." Nevertheless, by 1287 its officials hardened their attitudes and confiscated Nagaie's lands according to the very charges that they had ignored twelve years before.[24]

Administrative Reform and Patterns of Judicial Violence

The *bakufu* started enforcing administrative regulations in the aftermath of the attempted Mongol invasions.[25] This period roughly coincides with Hōjō Sadatoki's appointment as Kamakura regent (*shikken*) and the promulgation

---

19. CHSS, vol. 1, amendment 30, pp. 75–76 and Furusawa, *Kamakura bakufu to chūsei kokka*, pp. 101–3.
20. KI 4534 and Furusawa, *Kamakura bakufu to chūsei kokka,* pp. 116–18.
21. For the fifty summons, see KI 12792. Such figures may seem like hyperbole, but twenty-six summonses and documents of inquiry (*toijō*) still survive in one cache of documents. See *Kujo ke monjo*, vol. 2 for documents relating to Ikushima estate. For references to seven summons (*meshibumi*), see KI 6167; for ten *meshibumi*, see KI 9305. Copies of five such *meshibumi* appear in KI 12927. See also Furusawa, *Kamakura bakufu to chūsei kokka*, pp. 119–23. For translations of such documents, see Mass, *The Development of Kamakura Rule*, docs. 86–88, pp. 235–37, and for examples of intransigence, docs. 110–24, pp. 251–61.
22. *Azuma kagami*, vol. 3, 5.20.1248, p. 409.
23. KI 9166, of 10.10.1264, where the failure to respond to four summons merits no punishment. See also Furusawa, *Kamakura bakufu to chūsei kokka.*
24. Compare KI 11945, the 7.5.1275 Kantō *gechijō*, with KI 16342, the 9.15.1287 Kantō *migyōsho.*
25. See Furusawa, *Kamakura bakufu to chūsei kokka*, and Nitta, *Nihon chūsei no shakai to hō*, particularly pp. 41–43.

of a new body of laws (*shin goshikimoku*) in 1284.[26] According to Furusawa Naoto, administrative infractions such as the crime of disobeying a summons were first punished in 1286. Punishments for such "crimes" were meted out with increasing frequency. From 1286 until 1301, eleven such cases occur in which a failure to obey a summons elicits punishment; from 1302 until 1316, the number rises to fifty-two and from 1316 until 1332, eighty-three! By the onset of the fourteenth century, a majority of judgments were determined according to whether administrative infractions had occurred rather than according to the judicial merits of a case.[27] Warriors who now failed to heed three summonses had their lands confiscated.[28]

Those who lost control of their hereditary parcels of proprietary rights resorted to violence to maintain their lands that had been "unjustly" seized. These men, known as "brigands" (*akutō*), tended to be drawn from dispossessed landholders and their cohorts.[29] Judicial and not economic factors underpinned most cases of violence.[30] Some resorted to violence as early as the 1220s in order to press claims while at the same time pursuing formal

26. These laws were formulated by Adachi Yasumori. For more on him, and the laws, see Conlan, *In Little Need of Divine Intervention*, pp. 2–3.

27. For the new laws, see CHSS, vol. 1, pp. 250–53. This process is clearly enunciated in Furusawa, *Kamakura bakufu to chūsei kokka*, pp. 134–75. The first reference to administrative punishments dates from the eleventh month of 1286. See KI 17062, 7.9.1289 Kantō *gechijō*. For the Rokuhara *tandai*'s first such enforcement of administrative edicts, see KI 17974, 8.2.1292 Kantō *gechijō*. Takeuchi Rizō mistakenly identifies this as a Kamakura *bakufu* document. For the correct designation of Rokuhara, see *Zōtei Kamakura bakufu saikyojō shū*, Seno Sei'ichirō, comp. (Yoshikawa Kōbunkan, 1994), vol. 2, document 24, p. 39. Finally, for the first such judgment concerning Chinzei (Kyushu), see KI 17087, 8.2.1289 Kantō *gechijō an*. Enforcement of administrative decrees accounts for nearly seventy percent of all Kyushu decrees, half of all Rokuhara decrees, and eighty percent of all Kamakura decrees from 1316 until 1332. Furusawa, *Kamakura bakufu to chūsei kokka*, p. 136.

28. KI 21689, 11.27.1303 Kantō *gechijō*. For references to a fourth summons leading to criminal charges, see KI 19769; for five such ignored summons spawning an outbreak of violence by "evil bands (*akutō*)," see KI 30164. For an example of lands confiscated in 1304 as a result of a failure to respond to summonses, see Mass, *Lordship and Inheritance*, doc. 134, pp. 270–71.

29. Goble, *Kenmu*, pp. 107–9 and p. 256. For a brief summary of *akutō*, and references to their deeds and origins, see Jeffrey P. Mass, "Of Hierarchy and Authority at the End of Kamakura," in Jeffrey P. Mass, ed., *The Origins of Japan's Medieval World: Courtiers, Clerics, Warriors, and Peasants in the Fourteenth Century* (Stanford: Stanford University Press, 1997), pp. 26–28. Much of my information concerning *akutō* is drawn from Lorraine F. Harrington's "Social Control and the Significance of Akutō," in Jeffrey P. Mass, ed., *Court and Bakufu in Japan: Essays in Kamakura History* (New Haven: Yale University Press, 1982), pp. 221–50. The conclusions are, however, my own.

30. Most postwar scholars of Japanese history have tended to emphasize economic factors. Ishimoda Shō claimed in his *Chūseiteki sekai no keisei* (Tōkyō Daigaku Shuppankai, 1957) that changes in economic production proved to be the catalyst for the surge in violence during the late thirteenth and early fourteenth centuries. Amino Yoshihiko, in a recent essay, continues this line of thought by asserting that "brigands" (*akutō*) were low-class people who engaged in protocapitalist activity. See *Nihon chūsei ni nani ga okita ka*, pp. 154–55. Likewise, in his *Igyō no ōken*, Amino asserts that these "evil bands" were largely composed of "commoners," based upon the "strange clothing" they wore.

legal appeals.[31] Others launched attacks and occupied "their" recently confiscated lands.[32] For example, Wakasa Tadakane, *jitō* of Tara estate, had his lands confiscated in 1302 as a result of his refusal to obey a Kamakura decision (*ongechi*).[33] He compounded his offense by "illegally" occupying lands with a force of fifty, beating and imprisoning temple representatives, and seizing crops—a flouting of authority that Kamakura branded an "outrage" (*rōzeki*).[34]

Those who resisted Kamakura did so in order to preserve their hereditary rights. Kamakura dispatched "over ten" summonses to the recalcitrant local officials from Iga province's Kuroda estate during the Kōan and Shō-ō eras (1278–93), but none were heeded.[35] The Ōe had been *gesu* of Kuroda estate for six generations, but Ōe Kanshun was dismissed from his post for what he believed to be "minor infractions" (i.e. a failure to obey summonses).[36] The indignant Ōe, firm in their conviction that this post was theirs by "hereditary right" (*sōden no dōri*), engaged in progressively more violent reprisals in order to recover it.[37]

Kamakura's punitive measures for administrative lapses were perceived as being fundamentally "unjust" to men such as the Wakasa and the Ōe.

31. For example, as Lorraine Harrington has shown, a dispossessed manager (*gesu*) proceeded through legal channels before resorting to violence. See her "Social Control and the Significance of *Akutō*," p. 225. See also KI 3658. For other examples, see KI 6167 for men resorting to arson in settling disputes, and 9305 for aiding in a jail break.

32. *Zōtei Kamakura bakufu saikyōjō shū*, vol. 2, *hoi* document 11, p. 327, of 7.27.1313. For another example of a violent response to lands confiscated as a result of a failure to respond to three summonses, see the 3.2.1320 Kanto *gechijō* of KI 27392.

33. KI 17125, v. 22, p. 296, 298–99.

34. KI 16286. Tadakane was the son of Tadakiyo, the previous *jitō* of the estate. For references to Tadakane, see KI 15863, v. 21, p. 85. Tadakane's grandfather Toshikiyo was also *jitō* of the estate since 1221. See KI 16442. Tadakane's *jitō* post was abolished in 1302 as a result of his infractions. See KI 18538, 18827, 18886, and 21469; Satō Kazuhiko, *Nanbokuchō nairan shiron* (Tōkyōdō Shuppan, 1979), pp. 132–33, and Harrington, "Social Control and the Significance of *Akutō*," pp. 239–40. For the characterization of "outrages," see KI 16286 and 17125. The Wakasa were not exceptional. Many who had used force to assert their rights to the land suffered confiscation as a result of their crimes. See KI 25665. For the case of Yano estate, see KI 24875, 24992, and 25581. See also Harrington, "Social Control and the Significance of *Akutō*," pp. 233–34, and Satō, *Nanbokuchō nairan shiron*, pp. 160–66.

35. KI 29986.

36. For this claim, see KI 20497. For proof that one of the major *akutō*, Kanshun, was *gesu* of Kuroda estate, see KI 18553.

37. The most detailed description of the violence is found in KI 30067. For related documents dating from 1327, see KI 29755, 29757, 29780, 29806, 29821, 29827, 29837, 29841, 29845, 29877–78, 29881, 29900, 29911, 29920, 29927, 29957, 29966–67, 29982, 29986, 29994, 30022, 30031, 30043, 30046, 30049, 30054–56b, 30059, 30072, 30120. See also Furusawa, *Kamakura bakufu to chūsei kokka*, pp. 152, 171. The Ōe's litany of evil deeds included building a castle, destroying homes, capturing the estate manager and stripping him of his holy robes, calling up comrades from nearby areas, raiding and plundering the estate with a band of hundreds, and imprisoning its "peasants" (*domin*).

Warriors did not believe that a failure to obey summonses constituted a punishable offense. One who had his rights so confiscated complained that "for lands bestowed as a result of merit to be confiscated as a result of no crime is most improper (*motto mo fubin no shidai nari*)."[38] Such indignation impelled some to perform violent acts. Nevertheless, of those who were willing to resort to violence, most had their henchmen ransack their former estates so as to be able to deny personal culpability for any disturbances.[39] Most maintained a healthy respect for Kamakura's coercive powers.

It is a measure of Kamakura's skill in settling disputes that outbreaks of violence remained fairly uncommon until the *bakufu* began rigorously enforcing administrative law. According to the reminisces of one priest from Harima province, "brigands" (*akutō*) started appearing during the Shōan and Kangen eras (1299–1302), precisely the time when Kamakura began widely enforcing administrative regulations.[40] Violence and a disdain for authority increased as result of Kamakura's criminalization of administrative lapses. According to a contemporary account, "edicts were issued but they have no effect," for "those who do not rely upon judicial edicts were not punished. . . . Throughout the provinces, over half of the men of high and low [statuses] sympathize [with the *akutō*].[41] Resentment of Kamakura's administrative inflexibility was such that when one or two thousand men were ordered to search for *akutō* at Kuroda estate, for example, they did so grudgingly and only managed to capture five or six individuals.[42] It is certainly ironic that the Kamakura regime which had provided unparalleled protection for land rights came to be perceived as being fundamentally unjust because of its administrative zeal.

Proxy Punishments and Penal Law

Judicial violence was not confined to those who resisted Kamakura's administrative authority; those who enforced its laws also relied on violence. Infractions tended to generate a curious chain of reprisals which ultimately accrued to unfortunates indirectly related to the original incident. For example, a young boy was thrown in jail because of a mischievous dog that he did not even

---

38. KI 25995. A failure to abide by administrative regulations was not perceived by Nomoto Tokishige of Hitachi to be a crime.

39. On 8.26.1291 a representative of Kanemochi Hirochika, partial *jitō* and *gesu* of the estate, led a force of approximately one hundred onto contested lands, where they seized crops, and killed five and wounded eleven. Hirochika nevertheless flatly denied allegations of brigandage. KI 19934, 1.27.1299 Kantō *gechijō an*.

40. *Hyōgo kenshi shiryōhen chūsei*, vol. 4, "Mineaiki," pp. 64–65. For the more on Kamakura's enforcement of administrative law at this time, see Furusawa, *Kamakura bakufu to chūsei kokka*, p. 150.

41. *Hyōgo kenshi shiryōhen chūsei*, vol. 4, "Mineaiki," pp. 64–65.

42. KI 29986.

own. The dog in fact belonged to Ōsumi Munehisa, the local law enforcement officer (*jitō*). It must have been a resourceful, albeit ill-behaved beast, for it somehow managed to creep into where Warabino Gorō was storing fermented rice, his stock for brewing saké, and lap up a considerable amount of the potent brew. Warabino Gorō was enraged to the point of hacking this inebriated dog to death when he discovered him. Gorō was perhaps justified in slaughtering this animal, but Ōsumi Munehisa thought that the punishment exceeded the crime. Demanding compensation for the "crime of killing dogs," Munehisa captured and bound Gorō's son and confiscated three *kan* of cash.[43]

This incident reveals that one needed to possess coercive force to defend one's rights and that the more force at one's disposal, the more sensitive one became to upholding these rights. Ōsumi Munehisa could unilaterally enforce dogs' rights to due process because, after all, he was a *jitō* who possessed considerable constabulary powers, while Warabino Gorō had no choice but to protest the impropriety of Munehisa's behavior to an institutional authority such as Kamakura's Chinzei office.

The patterns of violence that permeated such disputes were not arbitrary, nor did they continue indefinitely. As soon as each party achieved rough parity in damages, the violence ceased. The "parity" reached in this case clearly reflected Munehisa's preponderance in coercive force, but his demand that his dog's death be compensated was nevertheless not entirely without merit. Violence was thus both rationalized and constrained by a transcendent, unwritten notion of justice.[44]

The crux of Warabino's continued claim was not whether crimes merited violent reprisals,[45] but whether acts such as killing a dog constituted a "crime" (*hihō*). In another case, a *jitō* threatened *hyakushō* that "if you do not cultivate wheat on the fields that you abandoned, I will imprison your wives and children for your crimes, bind them from head to toe, cut off their ears and slice off their noses."[46] The *hyakushō* involved did not criticize the impropriety of these brutalities, but instead claimed that the tax levies were not justified.[47]

---

43. KI 20476, 7.2.1300 Chinzei *gechijō*, volume 27, page 180. This document is littered with other examples of hostages being taken to punish various infractions.

44. Hence characterizations that "the spirit of revenge" in feuds constituted "an intolerable menace" that might "initiate a chain reaction whose consequences will quickly prove fatal to any society of modest size" are overstated. For one such pronouncement, see René Girard, *Violence and the Sacred* (Baltimore: Johns Hopkins University Press, 1977), p. 15. For similar views, see Max Gluckman, "The Peace and the Feud," *Past and Present* 8 (1955): 1–14, and John Michael Wallace-Hadrill, *The Long-Haired Kings* (Toronto: University of Toronto Press, 1982).

45. All judgments hinged upon whether in fact a crime had been committed. The appropriateness of bloodshed was unquestioned. KI 22443, intercalary 12.12.1305 Kantō *gechijō*.

46. KI 12076, 10.28.1274 Kii no Kuni Ategawa no Shō Kamimura *hyakushōra gonjōjō* (*mōshijō*).

47. This point has been noted by Kasamatsu Hiroshi, "Mimi o kiri, hana o sogu," in Amino Yoshichiko, ed., *Chūsei no tsumi to batsu* (Tōkyōdō Shuppan, 1983), p. 32.

The need to enforce criminal or administrative lapses often superseded narrow concerns of individual responsibility. To be sure, ranking warriors were treated as individuals, but their dependents—their wives, children, or hereditary retainers—were not.[48] Criminal punishments were not invariably meted out to those who perpetrated particular crimes. "Substitutes" (*migawari*), particularly among those of the lower social orders, could be brutalized instead,[49] particularly in cases where "criminals" had absconded or were otherwise "difficult to punish."[50] Substitutes could even suffer for capital crimes. One murderer of *gokenin* rank dispatched a "double" (*geshunin*) to endure his punishment of exile,[51] while others were handed over to a wronged party and killed in order to atone for a committed murder.[52] One might conceive of hostages as a commodity given to the wronged party so as to end a dispute, but any such desires for social harmony were in fact superseded by the need to rigorously enforce penal and judicial norms of law. Violent means were often pursued in order to achieve judicial ends by both by those who opposed Kamakura's decisions and by those who enforced *bakufu* edicts. Even though unilateral recourse to violence was condemned, the principle of brutalizing people who had done nothing wrong was already embedded within thirteenth-century judicial practice.

Crimes were punished in direct correlation to the degree of force that could be brought to bear in a dispute. Both Kamakura and their regionally appointed land stewards (*jitō*) proved increasingly able to muster considerable coercive powers. Problems arose, however, because Kamakura's attempts to enforce its administrative authority collided with *jitō* who were increasingly able to assert their own rights to the land.

---

48. Indeed, Kamakura asserted repeatedly that family members were not to be punished for an individual's misbehavior. CHSS, vol. 1, article 4; amendments 21, 29, and 283, pp. 71, 74–75, and 172. According to amendment 21 of the *Goseibai shikimoku*, found in CHSS, pp. 3-322, punishments for rebellion and other crimes were to be meted out to those who performed them, and not to their wives, families, or followers. See *Azuma kagami*, vol. 3, 5.20.1248, p. 409. Kamakura made a few exceptions to the doctrine of individual responsibility. If a son or grandson killed another as part of a feud, for example, the grandfather was guilty, even if he was unaware of the deeds, because his anger had incited the conflict. See CHSS, vol. 1, article 10, p. 8.

49. KI 7091, 7.13.1249 Kantō *gechijō*, and, for an earlier case in which women were taken as hostages in a related dispute, see KI 6266, 12.23.1243 Kantō *gechijō*. Finally, for a later example of hostages being taken, see KI 18056–57.

50. CHSS, vol. 1, amendment 287, p. 173. For a case in which a man who stole three times incurred punishment for himself and his wife, see CHSS, vol. 1, amendment 286, p. 173. Finally, for a case in which a man, his wife, and family were slaughtered by rivals, see KI 6204, 7.19.1243 Kantō *gechijō*.

51. KI, *hoi*, vol. 3, document *ho* 1335, 3.28.1245 Kantō *gechijō*.

52. For example, a certain Sakon no shōgen was turned over as a *geshunin* to the relatives of a man who had been murdered in front of a temple. KI 27089, 7.7.1319 Kantō *gechijō*. For examples of *geshunin* being slaughtered by their captors, see CHSS, vol. 1 (*sankō shiryō*) document 74 and document 76, p. 366.

INNATE RIGHTS TO THE LAND

Status as a *gokenin*, or "houseman, " of the Kamakura *bakufu* became increasingly predicated upon the ability to assert "homeland" (*honryō*) rights.[53] As the early fourteenth-century law primer the *Sata mirensho*, explained, "a *gokenin* is a man whose ancestors held since time immemorial ownership of the land because they cleared it and received a *bakufu* edict (*kudashibumi*) confirming them as land-holding warriors."[54] Likewise "homelands" (*honryō*) were defined as "paddy or dry or other land which a man owns because his ancestors cleared it and obtained a *bakufu kudashibumi* confirming them."[55] Any such land so cleared and confirmed became the hereditary possession of its owners. An expansion in the amount of cultivated land during the thirteenth century caused the ranks of those asserting land rights to expand. According to a contemporary doctrine of land rights, "the clearer of the land is its lord—that is the standard law throughout all provinces [of Japan]."[56]

Honryō rights could circulate in the short term, although they were perceived as being inalienable in the long term. They might be passed to others through sale or commendation, but such conveyances were valid for only a generation and did not entail the cessation of fundamental *honryō* claims.[57] Lands reverted to the descendants of "original owners" after those involved in any particular transaction had passed away.[58] Because violence might erupt

53. The phrases "original lands" (*honryō*), hereditary holdings (*sōden ryōshu chigyō*), and "original holder" (*honryōshu* and *honshu*) are synonymous. See CHSS, vol. 1, amendment 602, p. 277. This has been already elucidated by Uwayokote Masataka, "Kōan no jinryō kōkōrei o megutte," *Kamakura jidai seijishi kenkyū* (Yoshikawa Kōbunkan, 1991).

54. Steenstrup, "*Sata mirensho*: A Fourteenth-Century Law Primer," article 46, p. 418.

55. Ibid., article 52, p. 419.

56. *Takaishi shishi 2, Shiryōhen 1*, document 174, Tashiro Mototsuna *chinjō an*, pp. 619–20, which states, "*kaihatsu o motte sono shu to nasu no jō shokoku heikin no tsūhō nari.*" Some areas, such as Kikugawa in modern-day Shizuoka Prefecture, witnessed substantial increases in cultivated lands as the thirteenth century progressed. Thus, the Mataga, warriors who had initially been forced to reside near a swamp, managed to prosper by reclaiming it into paddies. Nearly all of the development, which doubled the size of the estate, stemmed from their efforts. I walked this area in October 1995. For more information on the Mataga, particularly their dwellings, see *Takada ōyashiki iseki dai 8, Ji hakkutsu chōsa hōkokusho*, comp. Kikugawa Shi (Shizuoka: Kikugawa-chō Kyōikuiinkai, 1993). Finally, for documentary evidence of new paddy cultivation occurring sometime between 1237 and 1316, see KI 25995.

57. The residual strength of land rights was such that even as late as the fifteenth century, original owners appended quitclaims to bills of sale, thereby recording approval of the transaction. See *Chiba ken no rekishi*, 15, *Shiryōhen chūsei*, no. 2, comp. Chiba Ken Shiryō Kenkyū Zaidan (Chiba: Chiba Prefecture, 1997), Kantori Yōgai ke *monjo* document 63, 9.21.1449 Ōnakatomi Norifusa *soejō*, pp. 56–57, 538.

58. For an excellent summary of this process, see Nitta, *Nihon chūsei no shakai to hō*, pp. 71–74. Some laws stipulated that, in cases of sale, the transaction would only remain valid until the buyer's death, whereupon the lands would revert to the "original owner" (*honshu*) or his descendants. For 1334 regulations that were sent to the shrine families working at Kantori shrine, see *Chiba ken no rekishi*, vol. 15, *shiryōhen chūsei*, no. 2, Kantori Tadokoro ke *monjo* document 8, 5.3.1334 Kebiishichō *an*, p. 238. Although this shrine is now commonly known as "Katori," *kana* documents reveal that its name was pronounced as "Kantori" in the fourteenth century. See also ch. 6, p. 173.

in cases where the "original owners" perceived the sale of their lands to be a
"lease," while the buyers might interpret the transaction as be a more permanent alienation,[59] the *bakufu* maintained that *honryō* rights were ineligible to
be bought and sold.[60] Proof of several generations of hereditary transmission
had to be demonstrated in order for *honryō* rights to be successfully asserted.[61]

Special rights accrued to *honryō* property. Longstanding *bakufu* policy
stipulated that *honryō* rights could concurrently span several generations. In
cases where one who had only been entrusted with lands for a lifetime committed crimes, then his holdings would be transferred to the next generation's
designated heir.[62]

Honryō rights were thought to accrue "naturally" to lineal descendants
of an original owner. Some regulations prohibited the sale of *honryō* to others (*tanin*).[63] When more distant relatives were granted *honryō* in spite of
these prohibitions, they remained in continuous jeopardy of more lineal
descendants of the "original holder" asserting proprietary rights.[64] Lands sold
or pawned to "outsiders" of a different surname could on occasion be successfully "reclaimed" on the merits of a contending party's lineage, which
explains why landowners were reluctant to pass their properties to someone
with a different surname.[65]

The creation of a new surname enabled some members of a particular
lineage to assert rights to the land at the expense of their brethren. Relatives
with a different name were, according to this notion, ineligible to receive such
lands because they were "outsiders" (*tanin*). For example, the childless Shiga

59. CHSS, vol. 1, amendment 439, p. 228.
60. For the custom of being able to buy and sell all lands save those granted as a result of rewards, see
    CHSS, vol. 1, clause 48, p. 27, and amendment 433, pp. 225–26.
61. For some such claims, see KI 27089, 7.7.1319 Kantō *gechijō*, and *Zōtei Kamakura bakufu saikyojō
    shū*, vol. 1, *hoi* document 12, 9.18.1260 Kantō *gechijō*, pp. 437–38, for a record missing from KI.
    Hence, permanent quitclaims contained proof of possession through several generations. The heir
    of the next generation also signed the bill of sale in order to record his consent. See KI 32169.
62. CHSS, vol. 1, amendment 462, p. 237, and amendment 611, p. 280.
63. In one case, some lands were confiscated, while in others they were given to relatives of the original
    holders. KI 7211, 7.7.1250 Kantō *gechijō an*.
64. CHSS, vol. 1, clause 16, pp. 11–12; clause 19, pp. 13–14; and amendment 433, pp. 225-26. The "will"
    of the original owner, entailing the transmission of lands to direct lineal descendants, seems to have
    possessed particular legal weight. For one such example of the "will of the holder," see ibid., clause
    20, p. 14. This phrase commonly appears in judicial documents. See for example, KI 24928,
    7.20.1313 Kantō *gechijō*; KI 19196, 11.24.1296 Kantō *gechijō an*; KI 12792, Toba Kunishige
    moshijō an; and Mass, *Lordship and Inheritance*, doc. 119, pp. 253–55. This also explains why a
    wife who remarried must pass her husband's *honryō* to the son of her first match. CHSS, vol. 1,
    clauses 20–21, p. 14.
65. See *Zōtei Kamakura bakufu saikyōjō shū*, vol. 2, document 206, 7.16.1332 Chinzei *gechijō*, p. 298.
    In another example, an original owner tried to gain lands back by claiming that the person he sold
    them to was a non-*gokenin*. This claim was, however, false. Ibid., vol. 2, document 79, 4.16.1314
    Chinzei *gechijō*, pp. 183–84. For a difference in surname causing concerns regarding female inher-
    itance, see NBIC 1467.

1. The tedium of guard duty. Source: *Heiji monogatari emaki*. Individual Collection. Photograph provided by Chūōkōronshinsha.

2. The tedium of guard duty. Source: *Go-sannen kassen ekotoba*. Permission and photo granted by the Tokyo National Museum.

3. Warrior returning with head. Source: *Shōtoku taishi eden*, "Mononobe Moriya to no kassen" permission of Jōgūji. Photo courtesy Ibaragi Kenritsu Rekishikan.

4. Decapitated heads. Source: *Go-sannen kassen ekotoba*. Permission and photo granted by the Tokyo National Museum.

5. Aiding the wounded. Source: *Heiji monogatari emaki*. Individual Collection. Photograph provided by Chūōkōronshinsha.

6. Extracting an arrow. Source: *Go-sannen kassen ekotoba*. Permission and photo granted by the Tokyo National Museum.

7. The use of shields in battle. Source: *Shōtoku taishi eden*, "Mononobe Moriya to no kassen" permission of Jōgūji. Photo courtesy Ibaragi Kenritsu Rekishikan. Also note the prevalence of arrows, and how mounted warriors managed to decapitate their enemies.

8. Different coloring styles of armor. Note also the tiger skin saddle blanket. *Mōko shūrai eko-toba*, scroll 1, page 9, "The Encampment of Shōni Kagesuke." Possession of Kunaichō Sannōmaru Shōzōkan. Permission for reproduction granted by the Imperial Household Ministry.

9. Unhorsing an opponent. Source: *Kasuga gongen kenki e*, scroll 2, section 2 (partial). Possession of Kunaichō Sannōmaru Shōzōkan. Permission for reproduction granted by the Imperial Household Ministry.

10. Warriors setting off in boats. Source: *Aki no yo no nagamonogatari*. Possession of the Idemitsu Museum of Arts.

11. The inspection process. *Mōko shūrai ekotoba*, scroll 2, page 40, "Suenaga presenting enemy heads." Possession of Kunaichō Sannōmaru Shōzōkan. Permission for reproduction granted by the Imperial Household Ministry.

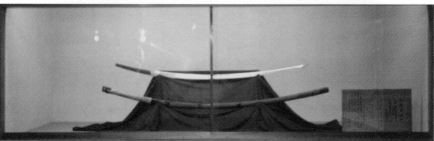

12. a. Warrior with an *ōdachi*. Illustration courtesy Futaarasan shrine. b. National Treasure Ōdachi mei Bizenshū Osafune Tomomitsu. Illustration courtesy Futaarasan shrine.

13. Warrior with a battle axe. Source: *Go sannen kassen ekotoba*. Permission and photo granted by the Tokyo National Museum.

14. Warriors fighting with swords, pikes and *naginata*. Source: *Aki no yo no nagamonogatari*. Possession of the Idemitsu Museum of Arts.

15. Leg armor of the late fourteenth century. Photograph and permission courtesy the Kyoto National Museum. This famous portrait of a mounted warrior has commonly been though to portray Ashikaga Takauji. Recent scholarship has revealed, however, that the illustration depicts a warrior from the mid-fourteenth century (probably the 1360s). The armor contains the Kō family crest, revealing that this warrior is a member of the Kō family. Kuroda Hideo has postulated that this warrior is Kō no Moroakira, a warrior who died defending the second shogun, Ashikaga Yoshiakira, whose monogram appears above the portrait.

16. Three warriors wearing *hōate*. Source: *Aki no yo no nagamonogatari*. Possession of the Idemitsu Museum of Arts.

17. Infantry fighting in poor terrain. Source: *Kasuga gongen kenki e*, scroll 19, section 1 (partial). Possession of Kunaichō Sannōmaru Shōzōkan. Permission for reproduction granted by the Imperial Household Ministry.

18. The market of Fukuoka. Source: *Ippen hijiri e den*, scroll 4, page 7. Jishū Sōhonzan Yūkōji. Photo courtesy Tokyo National Museum.

19. Fourteenth-century castle under attack. Source: *Rokudō-e*, "Jindō no kuso." Permission granted by Shōjuraikōji. Photo courtesy Nara National Museum.

20. Non-combatants fleeing the battlefield. Source: *Aki no yo no nagamonogatari*. Possession of the Idemitsu Museum of Arts.

21. Armed *hyakushō*? Source: *Konda sōbyō engi emaki*, scroll 1, "Ōjin tennō no misasagi o chikuzō suru dan." Possession of the Konda Hachiman shrine. Photo courtesy Habikino city, Bunka rekishi shiryōshitsu.

22. Warring priests. Source: *Aki no yo no nagamonogatari*. Possession of the Idemitsu Museum of Arts.

Zenki attempted to pass his lands to a nephew with the surname of Betsugi, but Zenki's brother opposed the transfer of Shiga lands to an "outsider," and ultimately forced Zenki to give them to his own son.[66] Surnames superseded biological relation as the denominator of warrior identity, and functioned as a means of limiting the number of possible heirs to an estate. The need to monopolize rights to a particular parcel of land explains why the warriors of the later Kamakura era created hundreds of new familial names.

The *bakufu* passed a law in 1297 that further bolstered *honryō* rights. Commonly known as the *tokusei* edict, it stipulated that as long as twenty years had not passed, an original owner could have his lands returned if he had sold them to a non-*gokenin*.[67] This act was passed in conjunction with a lesser-known regulation whereby Kamakura limited the rights of land-holders to file appeals.[68] While strengthening *honryō* rights on the one hand, the *bakufu* undercut them on the other by demanding that landholders comply with its commands. These new regulations only sowed more confusion regarding *honryō* rights. In response, some landholders mustered documents predating Kamakura's rise in 1180, while others copied five-hundred-year-old gazetteers (*fudoki*) in order to bolster claims of "original" ownership.[69] The number of legal cases (and instances of violence) accordingly skyrocketed in this uncertain legal environment.[70]

Bakufu reforms proved unsuccessful in resolving disputes because *honryō* rights were increasingly perceived as constituting comprehensive rights to the land, determined by physical occupancy, instead of simply status-based, overlapping rights to revenue (*shiki*). The ambiguity inherent in *honryō* was exacerbated by the fact that the earlier arrangement of partible *shiki* rights to income from the land had broken down. No one could readily determine which *shiki* rights translated into the "ultimate" claim of proprietary rights. In cases

66. See KI 10795, 3.5.1271 Sō Zenki *keiyakujō*, and document 12332, 4.1276 Shiga Yasutomo *chinjō an*. For Zenki bestowing this land to his brother's son, see NBIK 2303–4, 2.9.1347 Shiga Enjō *yuzurijō an*. The Shiga are described in more detail in Conlan, *In Little Need of Divine Intervention* pp. 210–13. For a contrary example of successfully asserted autonomy, see ibid., pp. 243–45. Finally, for a pioneering study of surnames in the Kamakura era, see Jeffrey P. Mass, *Antiquity and Anachronism in Japanese History* (Stanford: Stanford University Press, 1992), pp. 92–99.

67. CHSS, vol. 1, amendment 657, p. 295. For more on the *tokusei*, see Mass, "Of Hierarchy and Authority at the End of Kamakura," pp. 21–23.

68. CHSS, vol. 1, p. 296, and Gomi Fumihiko, *Kamakura to Miyako* (Shōgakkan, 1992) pp. 436–39.

69. See KI 19764, 8.10.1298 Kantō *gechijō an*; KI 24625, 7.23.1312 Kantō *gechijō utsushi*; and KI 26889, 12.12.1318 Chinzei *migyōsho an*, for references to pre-Kamakura documents. For the 1297 copying of an ancient gazetteer (*fudoki*), see Michiko Aoki, *Records of Wind and Earth: A Translation of Fudoki with Introduction and Commentaries*, Association for Asian Studies Monographs and Occasional Papers Series, Number 53 (Ann Arbor: Association for Asian Studies, 1997), p. 29. The record for an appeal to antiquity probably belongs to shrine attendants of Kantori shrine, who claimed unchanging shrine status since the time of Emperor Jinmu, some 1,959 years before. See Mass, "Of Hierarchy and Authority at the End of Kamakura," p. 30, and KI 25757.

70. The *bakufu* admits this in CHSS, vol. 1, amendment 730, p. 318.

where administration was divided between a *jitō* and a proprietor (*ryōke*), each believed his *shiki* rights superseded the other. For example, in a dispute concerning an estate that had been divided between the proprietor (*ryōke*) and the resident *jitō*, the *ryōke* claimed that all of the *jitō*'s holdings should be confiscated in accordance with the *tokusei*. The *jitō*, named Shiga, believed to the contrary that he possessed "original cultivation" (*kaihatsu ryōshu*) rights to lands reclaimed *after* the *shitaji chūbun* division. Kamakura ruled, however, that *all* lands were to be returned to the *ryōke*. In spite of the *bakufu*'s unfavorable judgment, the Shiga continued asserting their "basic" (*shitaji*) rights by occupying (*ōryō*) the contested lands.[71]

The Kamakura *bakufu* never succeeded in clarifying the legal ambiguity that pervaded *honryō* rights, but such a solution was neither necessary nor advisable. The inherent elasticity of *honryō* rights allowed for the notion of innate possession of land to exist in a time when land transfers became increasingly commonplace. Attempts to clarify *honryō* rights risked unleashing a cycle of violence even greater than that which had greeted Kamakura's attempts at administrative efficiency.

When Go-Daigo established his authoritarian Kenmu regime in the summer of 1333, he continued the Kamakura *bakufu* policy of protecting "original" rights. He went one step further, by stating that all homelands "unjustly" seized by Kamakura were to be returned to the original owner.[72] According to Go-Daigo's legal formulary, "the descendants of those who cleared the land or who had hereditarily transmitted their holdings shall have, upon a careful examination of their documents, their lands restored if they have been unjustly confiscated."[73] *Honryō* rights were immeasurably strengthened in that all "unjust" confiscations were to be rescinded, but by voiding bills of sale and rewards from Kamakura, Go-Daigo caused these rights to become more inflexible. Previously, the very act of exchange in no way hindered the ability to assert *honryō* rights, but Go-Daigo's judgments interfered with this process of land transfers by making actual possession a prerequisite for the successful assertion of *honryō* rights.[74]

---

71. NBIK 329. For more on the relationship of the Shiga and Usa Hachiman shrine (the *ryōke*), see KI 23565 and KI 24740 for reference to the original *shitaji chūbun* division. The Shiga possessed "the testament of the original owner and the partition" which carried particular legal weight. See KI, vol. 32, p. 218 for the relevant passage. At one point the *jitō shiki* had been confiscated by Kamakura as a result of the Shiga's failure to comply with a summons, but later "it was ascertained that no crime had been committed" and so the lands were returned. See also KI 25147, 25153, 25730–31, 26073, 28069-70, 28119-20, 28130, 28143, 30769, 30990, 31040, 31776, 31849, 32008, 32135, and 32732.

72. *Chūsei seiji shakai shisō*, *ge*, vol. 2, p. 70. For more on Go-Daigo's policy on land rights, see Goble, *Kenmu*, pp. 137–72.

73. *Chūsei seiji shakai shisō*, *ge*, vol. 2, pp. 68–69.

74. Ibid., pp. 77–78, which states, "All records of sale dating after 1221 are not binding. If the buyer has died, the "original owner" should [again] assert jurisdiction over his lands. In cases where the buyer and original owner both fought for us, then the case should be decided according to the particularities of the situation, but sales after 1331 should, in particular, revert to the original owners."

The Kenmu regime also continued the late-Kamakura tradition of demanding compliance to its edicts, and punished violations of its decrees even more severely than had previously been the case. In cases in which one failed to obey imperial edicts, all homelands and rewards stemming from military service were to be confiscated. Nevertheless, Go-Daigo's court could not readily assert much administrative or judicial authority in the political vacuum that greeted the fall of the Kamakura *bakufu*.[75] For example, Wakasa Tadakane, who had been dispossessed of his lands in 1302, led an army of "several hundred" and occupied "his" lands in Tara estate immediately after the Kamakura *bakufu* had been destroyed in 1333.[76] Such warriors continued to occupy "their" land in spite of imperial (administrative) authority.[77] *Honryō* rights were thus becoming synonymous with physical occupancy of the land.

Go-Daigo attempted to uphold the principle that original owners should have their lands restored, but determining the lineal descendants of original owners proved to be nearly impossible. Land disputes tended to be resolved in a seemingly arbitrary manner. Some, such as Yasutomi Yasushige, had their lands confirmed because a statute of limitations had run out.[78] Others had their suits dismissed because they had not "reclaimed the land" (*kaihatsu miru tokoro naku*)[79] which after all was the hallmark of "original" ownership. Those who had been "wronged" by Kamakura used Go-Daigo's claims courts to recover lands which were invariably classified as lost homelands. For example, the Sagara claimed that half of the lands that they had cleared in 1205 had been confiscated by Kamakura in the 1240s and granted to another warrior.[80] Conversely, others were successful in having their homelands restored as much through military prowess as through legal claims. The Tōyama had *honryō* lands that they had cleared confiscated by the Kamakura *bakufu* in 1272. Kamakura thereupon granted these lands to Nagai Tokihide. Once Kamakura was destroyed, the Tōyama reoccupied "their" lands, half of which were confirmed on 10.5.1333. On 12.26.1339, all of the Tōyama *honryō* were restored as a reward for exemplary military service at Hyōgo

---

75. For an early example of warriors no longer willing to toe the line of authority, see Goble, *Kenmu*, p. 234, and *Iwate ken chūsei monjo* 1, document 101 (1.10.1334), 103–4 (2.1334), 112 (3.1334), 118–19 (1334.6), and 141 (12.14.1334).

76. Wakasa Tadakane and his son Toshikane, who was characterized as an *akutō*, occupied Tara estate only after the Kamakura *bakufu* was destroyed in 1333. See KI 32771–72; 32814.

77. Thus forcing Go-Daigo's Kenmu regime to admonish that "if one claims his lands are homelands (*honryō to go shi*) or more recent rewards, and ignores imperial edicts, then his suit shall be abolished and he shall be summoned and charged with a crime, even if he has received rewards through military service or has properly inherited his home lands" (*Chūsei seiji shakai shisō, ge*, vol. 2, p. 72).

78. For cases in which "old holdings" were considered outside the jurisdictional boundaries of the Kenmu regime, see NBIK 116.

79. NBIK 27. See also Goble, *Kenmu*, p. 166.

80. KI 32842. For a similar complaint, see KI 32526.

Island in 1336.[81] Sixty years of occupancy by the Nagai did not necessitate a cessation of the Tōyama's *honryō* rights. Political instability and the seemingly arbitrary (and "unjust") nature of land confirmations during the 1330's impressed upon all the principle that homeland rights were best asserted by physical force.

"Inalienable Rights" in Times of War

The outbreak of war and the concomitant demands for rewarding followers and punishing enemies fundamentally destabilized *honryō* rights. Nevertheless, the concept of *honryō* inviolability remained absolute in spite of the fact that land ownership was not.

Assertions of *honryō* rights proved to be an effective strategy for restoring lands that had been granted to others. The language of respect for *honryō* rights constituted a key element of these exchanges. The Mutō, for example, had been granted rights to Shida district but returned them to Aso shrine once the latter asserted a claim of "original" ownership. Conversely, the Mutō desired the "honor" of having their "homeland" rights to Yoshida village in Buzen Province—"where their ancestors had cleared the land (*senzō kaihatsu shiryō*)"—restored.[82] Mutual recognition of "homelands" proved to be the vehicle for amiable transfers of lands. *Honryō* claims were even honored as the basis for exchanges long after they had been granted to religious institutions. In 1333, a Shami Gyōsai, fearing the "wrath of the gods" if he were to reoccupy shrine lands which had once been his family's *honryō*, requested other lands in lieu of those proprietary parcels that had been confiscated from his ancestors in 1221.[83]

In contrast to lands that had been granted to religious institutions, lands granted as rewards for military service were perceived as being a temporary gift that could be superseded by assertions of *honryō* rights. For example, a certain Shimazu Suō Gorō Saburō Tadakane complained that his hereditary lands (*honryō*) had been mistakenly rewarded to the "military forces of Shirahata castle." In due course his lands were restored.[84] In fact, the military commander Ashikaga Tadafuyu stated that *honryō* rights were supreme: "When the original owner of lands [that had been temporarily assigned to others] allies himself with [our] forces, then [his lands shall be returned and] other lands shall be exchanged for rewards."[85]

81. *Kanagawa kenshi shiryōhen, Kodai-chūsei*, vol. 3, no. 1, document 3976.
82. NBIK 330.
83. KI 32312. For more on the "permanent" nature of grants to shrines and temples, see Kasamatsu, *Hō to kotoba no chūseishi*, pp. 86–119.
84. NBIK 1128, 1231, and 1284.
85. NBIK 2802, 2829. Indeed, it was typical for warriors to promise to confirm the homelands of all warriors who joined their cause. See for example *Fukushima kenshi 7, Shiryōhen kodai chūsei*,

Men who respected innate rights to the land were portrayed as ideal—and just—leaders. Thus, the *Baishōron*'s panegyric praised Ashikaga Takauji for "placating bitter enemies by confirming their homelands."[86] Successful post-Kamakura hegemons recognized the limitations of the state's coercive power and respected *honryō* claims that were backed up with physical occupation.[87] Conversely, confiscation of *honryō* lands engendered violent opposition, similar to that which had greeted the Kamakura *bakufu*'s attempts to enforce its administrative authority. Isshiki Dōyu, for example, threatened to ignore the land claims of warriors who refused to join his army and, in addition, to confiscate one fifth of the lands of those who reported but did not fight.[88] Since Ryūzōji Rokurō Ietane chose not to serve, Dōyu eventually confiscated his homelands and granted them to Imagawa Tsuneyori. Ietane described this course of action as "an affront to warrior honor (*yumiya no menmoku*)."[89] Likewise, another Ryūzōji, Iemasa, excoriated Dōyu as being "unprincipled" (*mudō*) for such effrontery.[90]

Those in authority relied upon a rhetorical strategy of branding one's enemies as criminals in order to justify their confiscation of *honryō*. The Shimazu, for example, argued that the Shida could not reassert their *honryō* because of their "criminal" allegiances to "enemies of the court."[91] These claims of criminality functioned as a means of negating homeland rights, but did not lead to the physical punishment or incarceration of opponents.[92]

The enduring elasticity of *honryō* rights meant that even those who had their lands confiscated as a result of "criminal" associations with an "enemy" could still petition for the return of their land. So tenacious were these rights that relatives of Kamakura officials, whose lands were confiscated in the aftermath of the *bakufu*'s destruction in 1333, asserted their

---

Matsudaira Yūki *monjo* document 5, 12.3.1338 Kitabatake Chikafusa *migyōsho*, p. 503, and Matsudaira Yūki *monjo* document 3, 11.11.1338 Kitabatake Chikafusa *sodehan sōshin shojū*, p. 501.

86. *Baishōron*, p. 140.

87. Evidence can be mustered that lands had to be physically occupied and defended by force, particularly in the 1370's. For lands occupied (*ōryō*) while away on battle, *Tochigi kenshi shiryōhen chūsei*, vol. 2, Motegi *monjo* document 27, 2.27.1360 Ashikaga Yoshiakira *shojō*, and NBIC 4260 for the case of the Yamanouchi.

88. His document reads "those who do not report [to the Isshiki] (*fusan no tomogara*) will have all appeals for rewards (*onshō soshō*) ignored; those [who report but] render no military service (*gunchū*) shall have one fifth of their lands (*shoryō*) confiscated." NBIK 840. The Ryūzōji were *gokenin*. See KI 32633.

89. NBIK 3304–5.

90. NBIK 3304–5. Thus, it should come as no surprise that the Ryūzōji, who had nominally fought for the Isshiki, quickly joined Ashikaga Tadafuyu, who was allied with the opposing Southern Court, with the hope of receiving confirmation of their homelands. Tadafuyu obliged in 1350. NBIK 2903, for an appended confirmation (*uragaki ando*) to Ryūzōji Ietane. By the first month of 1351, Ryūzōji Iehira received the same. See NBIK 2982, 3292.

91. NBIK 221.

92. Those who instigated war or rebellion were, however, generally executed.

honryō rights only a few years later.[93] Particularly durable rights accrued to "name lands" (*myōji chi*), where members of a particular lineage adopted the name of a locale. In the event of a wholesale redistribution of lands, those who shared the same name as a locale were given precedence in having "their" lands restored, even if they had been previously confiscated as a result of their "criminal" behavior.[94] Accordingly, some adopted the name of contested lands in order to bolster their claims of "ownership," but this strategy alone proved ineffective in asserting rights to the office of *jitō*.[95] Nevertheless, that some could claim that their name and *jitō* rights were synonymous suggests that they believed their rights to homelands transcended all other considerations.

LEGITIMATING VIOLENCE THROUGH "PUBLIC WAR"

Violence, once something carefully delineated from the strictures of society by the weight of central authority, became integrally woven into the fabric of daily life during the fourteenth century. Prior to the onset of civil war, the unilateral recourse to violence outside of an institutionalized judicial framework remained a stigmatized act, liable to be punished. A nuanced vocabulary existed to describe violence, for the severity of each act hinged upon the degree to which it flouted authority. A continuation of simple acts of "violence" (*ranbō*) became classified as an "outrage" (*rōzeki*), a far more serious charge, if it continued unabated after a cease-and-desist order had been issued. The gradation between these terms is evident in the following passage: "On the twentieth day of the past month, [Okamoto Hikojirō Nyūdō] violently entered (*uchiiri*) the Kane oka higashi estate and committed *ranbō*. If true, this constitutes *rōzeki*."[96]

Late in the Kamakura era, "battles," were sometimes waged which apparently were synonymous with "outrages." For example, a certain Nakahara fought a battle (*kassen*) with Fujiwara Yasutane and killed Yasutane's father in a dispute over managerial rights (the *kumon shiki*) to Nagataki estate. Yasutane responded by entering the estate, illegally harvesting crops and com-

---

93. See *Kanagawa kenshi shiryōhen, Kodai-chūsei*, vol. 3, no. 1, document 3760.

94. See, for example, NBIK 6465. For a much later reference to "name lands," see *Kutsuki monjo*, vol. 1, document 31, Ashikaga Yoshiaki *sodehan migyōsho*, p. 16.

95. *Koga ke monjo 1*, comp. Kokugakuin Daigaku Koga Ke Monjo Hensan Iinkai (Zoku Gunsho Ruijū Kanseikai, 1982–87), document 61, 8.21.1342 Ashikaga Tadayoshi *saikyojō*, p. 87.

96. NBIC 4091 and 4109. Likewise, the term *muhon*, often translated as "rebellion," seems to designate a serious political disturbance that required the intervention of authority. How this term might have been distinguished from *rōzeki* is by no means clear. For more on *muhon*, see Tanaka, *Nanbokuchō jidaishi*, pp. 63–64. Tanaka refers to Go-Daigo's "honorable *muhon*." For the relevant document, see *Fukushima kenshi 7, Shiryōhen kodai chūsei*, 9.26 Yūki Munehiro *shojō an*, p. 453, and KI 28835.

mitting "outrages" (rōzeki). The proprietor decided to confiscate the shiki from both parties and commend it to the temple.[97]

In the absence of overarching political authority, only a semantic distinction existed between acts of "violence" (ranbō) or "battles" (kassen): each term reflected a particular region's political stability more than the intensity of the conflict per se.[98] Punishment for "criminal" acts was reserved for areas under secure political control. Thus, aiding an enemy might be construed as a criminal act, while becoming an enemy was not necessarily so.[99] Even during times of civil war, it often was a matter of interpretation whether hostile partisans were criminals or "honorable enemies" (onteki). Although some prisoners captured in battle were killed at Rokujō kawara—the common grounds for executions—[100] this was mainly a fate reserved for those who instigated rebellion and not for those who fought in an ongoing "public" war.[101] A tendency to treat "enemies" and their sympathizers as "criminals" arose in areas that witnessed an increase in coercive power concomitant with regional political stabilization.[102]

Most of the "criminal" acts that entailed the construction of castles represented in fact assertions of judicial violence.[103] A conflict over jitō rights to Takadahara, in Aki province, for example, caused hundreds of "bandits" (akutōnin) to build castles, trade insults, and wage war against each other. In response, the Ashikaga bakufu ordered those "criminals" who had violated their orders (ongechi o somuku) and had attacked officials to be banished, but these attempts to ensure administrative compliance failed.[104] Conversely, deeds such as theft which might seem to happen solely in the "civil" sphere could be associated with military actions. Thus the chancellor (dajō daijin) Tōin Kinkata described theft in the capital as either an "outrage (rōzeki) or perhaps the deeds of Southern [Court] partisans."[105]

---

97. KI 25927, 26027, and 26035. See also KI 26865 and 31234.

98. For "ranbō to ii, kassen to ii," see Shinpen Saitama kenshi shiryōhen 5, Chūsei 1, document 339, 7.8 (1341) Hōgan Senshū shojō utsushi, p. 260.

99. For the crime of aiding "imperial rebels," see NBIC 1148. Other examples include NBIC 4067 and 4260. At times, authorities treated acts of war—the building of castles and firing upon messengers—as crimes. See NBIK 928; Sōma monjo, document 97; and Fukushima kenshi 7, Endō Shirakawa monjo document 20, p. 460.

100. NBIC 775.

101. The perpetrators of an uprising in Mino were dispatched to the capital and then executed. Entairyaku, vol. 3, 9.28.1350, p. 307. Likewise, one can find references to the "crime of abetting the enemy" in describing a short-lived military conflict. KI 28532.

102. For example, the residents of Akanabe no shō complained that "we heard rumors that we were going to be classified as an 'enemy' and have hostages taken and our houses burned." Gifu kenshi, kodai-chūsei shiryō, vol. 3, document 367, p. 899.

103. See for example, NBIC 792, NBIC 4067, and Fukushima kenshi 7, Sōma monjo document 95, 12.11 Ashikaga Takauji gonaisho, pp. 134–35.

104. NBIC 3644. For a similar example, see NBIK 928.

105. Entairyaku, vol. 6, 11.11.1359, p. 307.

For those willing to engage in judicial violence, treatment as an enemy was preferable to that of a criminal. Those who had killed others and "surrendered" on the field of battle were immune from capital punishment, while in cases where a state of war did not exist, such actions might entail death. One man who killed eight, for example, claimed that he was immune from punishment because his deeds were part of a larger war.[106] Conversely, these "enemies of the court" could surrender and only suffer a partial confiscation of their lands, while those accused of criminal misbehavior were more likely to be jailed and executed.

One could avoid the criminal implications of unacceptable violence by claiming to be engaged in a "public" (*kōsen* 公戦) rather than a "private" (*watakushi no ikusa* 私の戦) war. Although "public war" had originally been the prerogative of court authority, no monolithic sovereignty existed for the ability to declare war. Any retired emperor, imperial prince, or, of course, reigning emperor could issue a communiqué and unleash a "public" conflict. A proliferation of competing emperors enabled many to declare that the resort to arms was a legitimate course of action. Whenever anyone received an edict from the court demanding the other party's "chastisement," the conflict then became a "public war."[107]

The process in which the recourse to violence became associated with the waging of "public war" is most evident when news of the outbreak of war reached a remote locale in southern Kyushu. One of the combatants, Tsuchimochi Nobuhide, stated,

> On the 13th day of the 12th month of 1335, I received news that warfare had erupted in the realm. Just as I was about to lead my family (*ichizoku*) to the capital, the rebel [forces of] Itō Tōnai Saemon Sukehiro . . . forcibly entered Kunitomi no shō and . . . committed repeated acts of violent outrage (*ranbō rōzeki*). . . . Thereupon on the 27th, we raised our battle flags as a family (*ichizoku*) and departed.[108]

---

106. He stated, "As is customary, enemies who surrender are pardoned for their crimes." KI 2025.

107. This was recognized by Jien in his *Gukanshō*. One warrior who received an edict demanding the chastisement of others stated, "I have joined battle many times, but I have always feared the [wrath] of the Imperial Court. . . . Having today received the imperial command to seek out and destroy [the enemy] I have peace of mind as I set off to engage him in battle." For an English translation, see Delmer Brown and Ishirō Ishida, trans., *The Future and the Past: A Translation and Study of the Gukanshō* (Berkeley: University of California Press, 1979), p. 102, and William R. Wilson, trans., *Hōgen Monogatari: A Tale of the Disorder in Hogen* (Sophia University, 1971), appendix A, pp. 13–14. Prior to this time, Yoshitomo is described as having engaged in "private wars" (*watakushi ikusa*). See Wilson, *Hōgen Monogatari*, p. 20 (which he unfortunately merely translates as "war"), and Ishii, *Nihonjin no kokka seikatsu*, pp. 8–9.

108. NBIK 408.

Nobuhide considered the "real" war to be the struggle for political supremacy being waged in the environs of the capital, while Itō Sukehiro's raid on Kunitomi estate was merely an "outrage" that prevented him from joining that conflict. Nobuhide did not realize for some time that his reprisals had in fact been legitimated by an imperial edict. When the Tsuchimochi became aware that Itō Sukehiro had received mobilization orders from Go-Daigo's allies, they treated Sukehiro's "outrages" as acts of war and recorded the ebb and flow of their conflict in a petition for rewards (*gunchūjō*).[109] In contrast to regions of Japan that witnessed the clash of armies and casualty rates approaching sixty percent (see chapter two), this dispute in Hyūga province appears to have been fought with less intensity. One sees reference to six damaged structures and two battle casualties.[110] Even the hyperbole of these documents is limited: Nobuhide only boasts of "tens" being killed. Both parties could ill afford severe casualties because their raids and reprisals constituted an intermittent, indeterminate process. Resistance met with rapid retreat. As Nobuhide reported, "We fought a battle, suffered severe casualties, our forces withered to nothing, and so we fled."[111]

Contemporary sources reveals that "public" wars were initially fought more fiercely than "private" judicial conflicts.[112] With the possibility of decisive victory and the political stability that it entailed, warriors would risk all or, conversely, quickly surrender. If the state proved capable of wielding sufficient military force, a modicum of peace was restored. Unsurprisingly perhaps, once an Ashikaga army was dispatched to southern Kyushu, Itō Sukehiro and his cohorts ceased all resistance.[113] Nevertheless, as the novelty of a "public war" abated and the prospect of a decisive settlement dimmed, the need to preserve local power became paramount. Accordingly, conflicts legitimated by court authority tended to be fought less fiercely. After the Itō had been vanquished, the Tsuchimochi resisted participating in the "public war" and ignored summonses to battle during the summer of 1338.[114] Rather than serving to prosecute the "public" war, Nobuhide preferred prosecuting the war to serve his own interests.

109. For the first references to this conflict, see NBIK 391. See also NBIK 407–8.
110. Five "castles" and one "estate headquarters" (*mandokoro*) were consigned to the flames, while one Itō partisan who had been taken prisoner was executed; Tsuchimochi Nobuhide's son was twice wounded in the leg. NBIK 408.
111. NBIK 408.
112. This sentiment is reflected in the *Genpei jōsuiki*, whereby Kumagai Naozane wanted to spare his prisoner, Taira no Atsumori, from death, but stated that he could not afford such leniency in a "public battle." *Genpei jōsuiki* (Kokumin Bunko Kankōkai, 1911), maki 38, p. 938. See also maki 21, p. 524, for similar references to "public war."
113. NBIK 1176. A member of the Ashikaga lineage, Hatakeyama Tadaaki, was dispatched to southern Kyushu.
114. NBIK 1255, 1261. By 1340, Nobuhide complained of exhaustion due to his "long and arduous service." See NBIK 1306–7.

Tsuchimochi Nobuhide now attacked local rivals with impunity. The war provided him with a pretext to settle scores and demand rewards for doing so in the process. As one survivor who had been defeated by Nobuhide and his allies lamented,

> In their defense statement, [our] enemies claim that they were ordered to kill (*uchikoroshi*) the deputy *jitō* [Kakuei]. Furthermore, they claim to have surrounded Kakuei's lodging . . . upon hearing a report that Kakuei had allied with enemy forces. However, [Tsuchimochi] Nobuhide first received an order (*migyōsho*) from the Satsuma encampment on the fifth day of the ninth month. He arrived at Hyūga [province] on the ninth day and entered Masaki estate on the twenty eighth. Nevertheless, the battle of Yoshida occurred on the sixth day of the ninth month. Kakuei was pursued and killed on the roadside [in distant Bingo province] This is clearly not the will of the shogun; instead it stems from the grudge of an old enemy. They plundered our crops, turned the estate into a wasteland, and killed Kakuei and his relatives. Such crimes are hardly minor.[115]

The distinction between claims of battle service or accusations of criminal behavior were ultimately settled by who could wield the most coercive authority. Nobuhide's latent military power ensured that he could determine and punish Kakuei's "criminal" behavior and receive rewards for military service in the process. In unsettled times, police powers constituted an integral component of "public" war.[116]

The Ashikaga *bakufu* grudgingly conceded the legitimacy of violence in its laws, although it stipulated that such violence had to be "defensive" in nature. According to a law promulgated in 1346,

> Even if one bears a clear grudge, he must respect the judgment [of authority]. To willfully commit murder will not be punished lightly. In the case of offensive warfare, even a justifiable cause will not be excused. If there is a good reason for defensive warfare it will be pardoned, but otherwise it will be punished as severely as offensive warfare.[117]

---

115. NBIK 2159.

116. Acts of war and "law enforcement" were at times indistinguishable. For example, one warrior was praised not for fighting in battle, but for capturing the "violent criminal and jailbreaker Katase Saburō Saemon no jō Sadaie." NBIK 1434. For another example, see NBIK 7019.

117. Grossberg, *The Laws of the Muromachi Bakufu*, pp. 33–34, and CHSS, vol. 2, pp. 16–17.

Ashikaga *bakufu* officials continued Kamakura's tradition of emphasizing proper procedure over just cause, but this distinction became progressively difficult to enforce.

The vocabulary used in these laws indicates a subtle but significant shift in the mentalities of violence. Instead of simply castigating "outrages," one sees reference to "offensive and defensive war"—(*kosen bōsen*). Likewise, the character for "offensive" war is not attack (*kō* 攻) but "justification" (*ko* 故). What initially appears to be a disavowal of offensive war instead supports a transcendent sense of "right" divorced from laws. One could resort to violence if "there is justifiable cause."[118] Later laws promulgated in the 1350s became even more ambiguous, stating simply that "punishment for offensive warfare . . . will depend upon how severe the offense has been. As for punishing defensive warfare, that will be decided upon after investigation of the details and weighing the situation."[119]

The Kannō disturbance of 1350–52, whereby the Ashikaga *bakufu* dissolved into two warring factions, coupled with the concurrent resurgence of the Southern Court, led to the disintegration of overwhelming hegemonic authority. Thereupon, the boundaries between "public" and "private" war grew arbitrary as groups used this dichotomy for their own ends depending upon their rhetorical need for legitimation. The unilateral application of judicial violence achieved unprecedented acceptance as a transcendent right. From 1350 onward, even high-ranking Ashikaga *bakufu* officials engaged in feuds in the capital. On 4.23.1355, Niki Yoshinaga and Hosokawa Kiyouji prepared to war against each other in order to settle a proprietary dispute. Ashikaga Takauji and his son Yoshiakira, acting as peace makers, managed to contain the violence but punished neither.[120] Hosokawa Kiyouji, whose house Niki Yoshinaga "occupied," bided his time until 1360, when he raised an army in order to oust his rival, who sensibly

---

118. Grossberg, *The Laws of the Muromachi Bakufu*, p. 40, and CHSS, vol. 2, p. 21. The relevant clause reads as follows: "Concerning offensive and defensive warfare. Even if one bears a clear grudge, he must appeal [to authority] and respect the ensuing judgment. No man can escape punishment if he willfully commits murder. In the case of offensive warfare, although one's original petition possesses merit one cannot escape the punishment. . . . Still more so, those who lack justification [for offensive warfare]. Henceforth, this will be strictly forbidden. If anyone disobeys this purport, he will have his homelands confiscated and he shall be banished. As for accomplices, their lands shall be confiscated. If they are landless, they shall be exiled as mentioned before. As for defensive warfare, if the perpetrator is not a landed lord (*hiryōshu taraba*) he shall be punished as if it were offensive war. If, however, he has justification (*riun*) then the case will be judged according to its merit."

119. Grossberg, *The Laws of the Muromachi Bakufu*, p. 50, and CHSS, vol. 2, pp. 30–31.

120. *Entairyaku*, vol. 5, 4.23.1355, p. 19.

fled.[121] Kiyouji was not punished for his deeds.[122] Violence was becoming embedded in the fabric of daily life.

The outbreak of warfare and the unprecedented legitimacy afforded to feuding ensured that neither could administrative fiat any longer be unquestionably obeyed, nor could administrative law be enforced by the center. Central authority's role in judicial matters correspondingly declined as well. Warriors instead asserted and defended their rights without relying upon authorization. Members of a military unit (*ikki*) summed up this attitude when they wrote in 1377, "if someone attempts to assert claims over our lands and a battle erupts we shall all rush to the disputed region and fight a defensive war (*bōsen*) and not wait for the judgment of authority (*Kubō* [*no*] *goi*)."[123]

Land rights came to be enforced more by violence from the periphery than by a government's codified laws. Local control became increasingly divorced from the pronouncements of public authority. For example, in 1338, Isshiki Dōyu granted the *jitō shiki* rights of Ishidō village to Takeo shrine for its "service" of providing prayers for victory.[124] Two men, Saru Shitarō and Yoshida Yajirō, were to go to Ishidō and assert Takeo's rights to the *jitō shiki*,[125] but they were rebuffed by Ishidō Hikosaburō, who claimed that he had been granted these lands as reward for his military service. Hikosaburō and his men, labeled by Saru Shitarō as *akutō*, constructed a castle on "their" lands and prevented the representatives of Takeo shrine from administering the estate.[126] Isshiki Dōyu demanded that they destroy their castles but Hikosaburō ignored him.[127] The Ishidō legitimated their lordship by allying themselves with the rival Southern Court, and even began issuing their own confirmations of rights for "ceremonial rice" on behalf of Dazai Hachiman.[128] For the next two hundred years the Ishidō managed to maintain their lands.[129] Disregard for central authority, coupled with a tendency to resort

---

121. See *Gukanki*, 7.6.1360 for Kiyouji leading his army, ostensibly to attack the Southern Court, and 7.13.1360 for Yoshinaga's hasty retreat to Ise. See also Ogawa, *Ashikaga ichimon shugo hattenshi no kenkyū*, pp. 115–25. For other examples of Kiyouji's bravery, see *Taiheiki*, maki 34, "Ryūsenji ikusa no koto," p. 1028, and maki 32, "Shujō Yoshiakira botsuraku no koto," p. 953; and *Gen'ishū*, pp. 209–10.

122. Nevertheless, as we have seen in chapter six, he was brought down a year later by a curse forged, in all probability, by Niki partisans.

123. NBIK 5422. For another example of one party in a dispute unilaterally seizing lands without waiting for the pronouncements of authority, see *Kanagawa kenshi shiryōhen, Kodai-chūsei*, vol. 3, no. 1, documents 5068, 5070, and 5107.

124. NBIK 1177.

125. NBIK 1184.

126. NBIK 1320, 1380, and 1405.

127. NBIK 1440, 1547, and 1616–17.

128. NBIK 3877. The Sugawara were another name for the Ishidō. See also *Kadokawa chimei daijiten*, vol. 41, p. 83. Even the Fukabori recognized Dazaifu's jurisdiction over five *chō* of land. NBIK 1547.

129. *Kadokawa chimei daijiten*, vol. 41, p. 83.

to bloodshed in solving disputes, became the dominant pattern of judicial recourse in medieval Japan.[130]

CONCLUSION

Rising prosperity and the increased cultivation of land solidified a notion of proprietary rights among the regional elites of Japan. The notion of alienating these parcels of land as one wished arose in the tenth century, but was not supported by a legal framework until Kamakura *bakufu* law was formulated in the thirteenth century. The protections offered by Kamakura fostered a sense that landholders possessed the right to control and dispose of their lands as they saw fit. Ironically, the *bakufu* succeeded all too well in imparting a notion of the inviolability of proprietary rights, for when Kamakura began meting out punishments for administrative lapses late in the thirteenth century, landholders perceived these punitive measures as being fundamentally unjust.

Violence remained stigmatized during the Kamakura era, suffering almost universal condemnation in written sources as "outrages" or acts of "brigandage," but it received tacit approval by local landholders as an acceptable recourse in defending of existing rights. Local warriors increasingly possessed both the will and the means to assert their rights to the land, and their compatriots, who were invested with policing powers, were loath to do anything to prevent such assertions of judicial violence. Nevertheless, the recourse to violence as a judicial end only received full sanction with the outbreak of civil war, when bloodshed became subsumed under the rubric of a "public war." Thereupon, codified law became divorced from judicial concerns, particularly after the crumbling of hegemonic political authority that accompanied the Kannō disturbance of 1350–52.

An episode that arose in 1355 reveals how the punctuated indeterminacy of judicial violence came to permeate nearly all struggles. At festivities at the Kamo shrine, children made armor out of iris reeds and participated in a mock battle. Other children joined in, as did adults—and warriors—and the battle became fought with greater intensity, leading to several wounds and fatalities.[131] The diarist Tōin Kinkata recorded this altercation in passing, but even he reflected that the incident "truly deserved no comment." None questioned the assumption that wrongs—even those caused by children—spawned "injustices" that had to be avenged.

From the mid–fourteenth century onward, the state abdicated its monopoly over coercive violence. Rather than impartially administering its laws,

---

130. For other examples, see NBIC 4144, 4680, and 4702.
131. *Entairyaku*, vol. 5, 5.5.1355, pp. 21–22.

even high-ranking officials attacked and killed each other in order to expiate injustices. Central authorities such as the Ashikaga shoguns tended merely to enforce parity by balancing body counts in feuds.[132] The aged courtier Tōin Kinkata characterized this milieu of violence as "a world of devils (*makai*)," a phrase that adequately expresses the frustrations of one who had lived most his life with the expectation that central authority should dominate, but which concurrently ignores that fact that these "devils" were fighting to preserve—or assert—rights that the center could no longer enforce.[133]

Once the unilateral recourse to violence became an untrammeled right, its successful prosecution tended to supersede all other concerns. Even state rituals that had previously been impervious to the vicissitudes of war began to be impacted by the consuming desire to destroy one's enemy.[134] This new order of transcendent violence is perhaps epitomized by the statements of Nagae Shigekage, who declared that prohibitions against killing within temple precincts were voided in cases of "night attacks, armed robbers, and battle." Nevertheless, Shigekage considered the temple grounds to be part of the "public realm" (*kugai*) for personal enemies (*shinteki*). Once violence was no longer monopolized by the state, then the unilateral application of uncodified norms of justice became associated with the "public" realm.[135] Such violence became a controlling aspect of daily life—one which neither official sanction, nor religious prohibitions, nor notions of sanctuary or defilement, could limit.

Military force applied in a predictable manner now provided the primary defense for fragile rights to the land. Although *shugo* proved ultimately most capable of enforcing judicial norms, they nevertheless did not amass enough coercive authority and hegemonic ambition to began codifying laws until the mid–fifteenth century.[136] These regional magnates attempted to bring

---

132. For example, in 1448, sixteen or seventeen young children were killed in the capital. Ashikaga Yoshimasa, shogun at the time, ordered the lord of the killers to dispatch a substitute (*geshunin*) to the wronged party in order to "solve" this dispute. See Ogawa Makoto, *Yamana Sōzen to Hosokawa Katsumoto* (Shinjinbutsu Ōraisha, 1994), pp. 84–85.

133. *Entairyaku*, vol. 5, 4.23.1355, p. 19.

134. For the example of Hosokawa Kiyouji, who opposed dispatching a new compilation of court poems to Sumiyoshi shrine because it was "currently an enemy encampment," see *Entairyaku*, vol. 6, 4.6.1359, pp. 159–60.

135. *Gifu kenshi*, vol. 2 no. 1, Myō-ōji *monjo*, 9.16.1384 Nagae Shigekage *sadamegaki*, pp. 479–80. For a brief commentary on this document, see Kasamatsu, *Chūseinin to no taiwa*, p. 233. From this point on, public and private battles elicited little outrage, comment, or stigma. See for example *Shinano shiryō*, vol. 7, *Ōtōnomiya monogatari*, p. 374, for references to "*kosen bōsen no gi*."

136. Although some early fourteenth-century law codes exist, their veracity demands further analysis. Seno Sei'ichirō has recently revealed that the codes pertaining to the Munakata shrine were in fact a copy written during the mid–fifteenth century. See Seno, "Kankō shiryōshū seiri no hitsuyōsei," in *Kamakura jidai no seiji to keizai*, comp. Kamakura Ibun Kenkyūkai (Tōkyōdō Shuppan, 1999),

peace to the realm through the application of overwhelming force: all perpetrators were brutally punished regardless of the justice (*dōri*) of their cause.[137] In order to exterminate judicial violence, rights to the land had to be abrogated. Only when these magnates reconstituted overwhelming state power could this blooded concept of transcendent, inviolate rights be consigned to fitful oblivion.

---

pp. 20–24. The first verifiable codes were penned by the Ōuchi in 1439 and amended continually thereafter, while the second was created by the Sagara in 1493. Codes for the Rokkaku, the Yūki, the Imagawa, the Takeda, the Chōsōkabe, the Asakura and the Hōjō were created in the sixteenth century. See CHSS, vol. 3.

137. For an early example, see CHSS, vol. 3, Imagawa *kana mokuroku*, p. 117.

8

The Order of Violence

Turning and turning in the widening gyre
The falcon cannot hear the falconer;
Things fall apart; the centre cannot hold

W.B. Yeats, "The Second Coming"

Hegel remarks somewhere that all great, world-historical facts
and personalities occur, as it were twice. He has forgotten to
add: the first time as tragedy, the second as farce.

Karl Marx, *The Eighteenth Brumaire of Louis Bonaparte*

On the twenty-eighth day of the tenth month of 1392, a motley procession
of Southern Court warriors, courtiers, and their emperor returned to Kyoto,
where they handed over their regalia to the Northern Emperor, thereby abdi-
cating their claims to legitimacy in exchange for a promise (hollow, it turned

out) to become next in line for the throne.[1] For three nights, dances dedicated to the gods (*kagura*) were performed at the palace, celebrating the return of the regalia. Sūjo, an influential priest of Rishōin, one of Daigoji's subtemples, participated in several rituals celebrating this "spiritual victory" (*myōshō*), thereby bringing six decades of war to a close.[2]

The Ashikaga had much cause to celebrate on this autumn day in 1392, for the frayed strands of legitimacy were once again rewoven. There was now one emperor and one shogun residing in the capital. To be sure, wars would continue to erupt—the next major conflict was in 1399—but these outbreaks were conceived as being mere "disturbances," posing little danger to the Ashikaga regime.

Even though the Southern Court held little sway over the whole of Japan, it exercised a disproportionate influence. As long as this sputtering source of legitimation remained, another nationwide conflagration was always possible. In this sense, warfare was above all a political act. Although the patterns of its waging might be culturally influenced, political considerations determined its scope, timing, and magnitude.

Surviving sources suggest the scale of battle during sixty years of war closely mirrored political developments. Nevertheless, the scale of battle appears to have been relatively small. During 1336, one can trace the activities of over sixteen hundred warriors, but for most years, fewer than two hundred can be verified as actively fighting.[3] Likewise, on average, only six or seven warriors are mentioned in each document. Nevertheless, the impact of war was greater than these aggregate numbers would imply. War was fought throughout the land by warriors from every province, from Mutsu to the north to Satsuma in the south. The war was general and endemic—at least 235 days of serious fighting can be traced during 1336 alone.[4] Every region experienced fighting; even those who attempted to remain aloof from the fray were affected by war levies and disruptions in trade.

Battles were fought with less intensity after the initial five years of civil war. After the peak year of 1336, warfare became localized into five major theaters of conflict. Throughout the 1340s the Southern Court's strongholds in the eastern (Kantō) plains and in north central Japan (the Hokuriku region) were systematically reduced through wars of attrition. Although resistance

---

1. For the surrender, see Mori Shigeaki, *Yami no rekishi, Gonanchō* (Kadokawa Sensho, 1997), pp. 51–63. The most convenient compilation of sources appears in *Murata Masashi chosakushū*, comp. Murata Masashi (Kyoto: Shibunkaku, 1986), vol. 7, pp. 479–86.
2. *Daigoji shinyōroku*, vol. 3, pp. 792, 800, 808–12, 1070, and 1232.
3. I compiled this data while conducting the research for chapter two.
4. Each month witnessed only, on average, slightly under nine days of peace. The first and eighth months only had four calm days, while the eleventh month witnessed seventeen days.

continued in both Kyushu and Shikoku to the west, the Southern Court was devastated when its capital of Yoshino was reduced to ashes during Kō no Moronao's blistering offensive in the winter of 1348.

The Southern Court was spared from annihilation because two factions of the Ashikaga *bakufu* attacked each other in 1350. Once again nearly all provinces became racked by war. A modicum of political stability was restored in the later 1350s as a result of the *hanzei* edict, promulgated by one faction of the Ashikaga, which allowed regional officers (*shugo*) to use "public" revenue of taxation for military supplies. *Shugo* became increasingly able to organize small, regionally based armies and to bring a preponderance of coercive force to bear in local disputes. A few prominent magnates, such as the Oyama in the east during the 1380s and 1390s, staged sporadic revolts, but generally only two regions of serious contention remained after 1355: Kyushu to the west and the Yamato heartland of the Southern Court.

If 1336 represents the peak of military activity during the contention between the two courts, 1370 represents the opposite, with fighting in Ise and Hizen Provinces and almost nowhere else.[5] Nevertheless, the logic of war continued to influence developments during even this seemingly peaceful year. As long as a contending political entity existed, the forces of its opponent continued to be directed toward its annihilation. Although the war was fought in an increasingly constricted terrain, the whole archipelago continued to be burdened by its systemic demands. Warriors still extracted revenue from the land for the sake of "military provisions." In some cases, these privileges were abrogated, but in other instances warriors fought battles (*kassen*) in order to retain their prerogatives.[6] Because such battles were perceived to be unrelated to political support for the Southern Court, they evoked hardly a shrug from Ashikaga authorities.[7]

The Ashikaga took advantage of the unprecedented peace of 1370 to dispatch an army, led by Imagawa Ryōshun and initially drawn from western warriors, on a campaign against the Southern Court stronghold of Kyushu.[8] This process of pacification did not, however, proceed smoothly. Regionally organized armies still had a propensity to disintegrate while engaged in distant campaigns. The Hatakeyama armies, drawn from the Kantō during the 1360s, collapsed in the mountains of Yoshino, while Imagawa Ryōshun

5. See NBIK 4830. Likewise, a warrior from Bungo Province lost his son in battle during this year. NBIK 4828. For the disturbance in Ise, see *Yokkaichi shishi* 7, *Shiryōhen kodai chūsei*, comp. Yokkaichi Shi (Yokkaichi Shi, 1988), document 182 (2.6.1370), p. 254.

6. See NBIC 3807, 3810.

7. NBIC 3809. For other examples of intransigence, see NBIC 3811, 3817–21.

8. The Akamatsu admitted as much, stating that Ryōshun's army was dispatched because all was quiet in the realm since the fall of 1369. See NBIK 4823. See also NBIK 4824–25, 4831, 4841–42, 4850–51.

quelled resistance in Kyushu only after surmounting considerable hardships and incorporating local warriors in his forces.

The consolidation of political power and the ability to prosecute the war were integrally related. These changes were propelled more by the organizational prowess of *shugo* than by any innovations in tactics or changes in the types of weapons used. The increased ability to extract surpluses, necessary for the waging of war, could best be expanded into a more comprehensive political authority—one that was inconceivable prior to the outbreak of war—after stability had been restored. The *shugo* and his officers could use their newly acquired *hanzei* rights to construct powerful networks of lordship once those capable of resisting by force were annihilated or quelled.

THE FOURTEENTH CENTURY'S LEGACY

War, once unleashed, carved new channels that endured long after the traces of battle and the lives of those who fought in them dissipated into obscurity. The political, social, economic, and intellectual landscape of Japan in 1392 was profoundly different from what it had been sixty years before when Aso Harutoki set off to quell an uprising at Chihaya castle. For, in contrast to 1332, when military service could be demanded, it could no longer be taken for granted. Whereas the outbreak of war had galvanized the country into action, its end did not entail a cessation of all violence. The sporadic revolts which accompanied the peace were conceived to be judicial, not political affairs, and became an integral aspect of daily life, evoking neither widespread fear, nor despair, nor insecurity.

Processes unleashed by the war continued to unfold relentlessly. The relationship between the Ashikaga shogun and regional magnates—*daimyō*, as they would increasingly be called—remained unstable. The Ōuchi, Yūki, and Akamatsu all "rebelled" against the Ashikaga during the next fifty years. Each was defeated in turn, but with the exception of the Akamatsu, who assassinated the sixth shogun Yoshinori in 1441, each was able to maintain his core holdings. The Ashikaga continued to respect these *daimyō*'s rights to the land and, indeed, recognized that each family had the hereditary right to certain positions within the *bakufu* itself.

Tensions between the Ashikaga and their *shugo* paled in comparison to the struggle between the *shugo* and the autonomous warriors of each province. The costs of war eroded *tozama* autonomy, and, increasingly, these men were no longer able to fight simply as they chose. Indeed, the need to secure adequate funds for the prosecution of war achieved such primacy that social status shifted from being a function of hereditary rights to one determined by control over wealth and resources. The burden caused by the waging of war meant that *tozama* autonomy was becoming increasingly difficult to sustain. Some warriors became retainers of the *shugo* and took advantage of their lord's newfound powers, while others tried to remain independent, although these men suffered accordingly. Tsuchiya Muneyoshi, for example, chose to fight for the Yamana and not the local *shugo* in 1391. His lands were declared "appropriable" (*kessho*) by the *shugo*'s retainers (*hikannin*). In 1398, Muneyoshi appealed to the *shugo*, boasted of his considerable military service, and asked that his lands be restored.[9] His wish was apparently granted, for five years later he passed his *jitō shiki* to his son, with the caveat that the *shugo* shall "exercise authority (*onsata*) over these lands in the matter of 'public' military affairs (*onkuji gun'yaku*)"[10] Muneyoshi managed to maintain his holdings only after sacrificing his military autonomy. His son Shinsaburō Kiyotō, bound to fight for the *shugo*, had even less freedom to choose his military allegiances. Nevertheless, although the parameters of *shugo* control had advanced markedly, the armies that they mobilized were inferior in size and organization to Harutoki's expeditionary force of 1332.

The 1398 petition of Tsuchiya Muneyoshi reveals that the powers of the *shugo*, well underway in the waning decades of the fourteenth century, were not confined to the person of the *shugo*. The *shugo*'s retainers were able to rely upon their authority and confiscate lands of those who committed "crimes" or "rebellions," and it is they who occupied Muneyoshi's lands.[11] This trend was already evident as early as 1366, when the deputy *shugo* used the pretext of military disorder to occupy estate lands,[12] and only became more prevalent as time passed. In 1377, for example, Urakami Tarō Saemon no jō Chikakage, a retainer of Akamatsu Mitsunori, attempted to arrest the *myōshu hyakushō* of Yano estate for their failure to pay taxes and, in addition, their temerity in launching a protest of his actions.[13] *Shugo* deputies such as the Urakami enforced *shugo* attempts to extract revenue, and their encroachments increased in number and magnitude once the wars of the fourteenth century came to a close. Again, in 1394, the Urakami entered an estate, confiscated cash, and took eleven as hostages, so as to procure unpaid taxes.[14] Other deputies possessed enough coercive force to enter estates repeatedly in Yamashiro province[15] under the pretext of levying provisional and *shugo* levies, even though their actions had been prohibited by the Ashikaga.[16]

9. *Hirakata shishi* 6, *shiryōhen* 1, Tsuchiyashi *monjo*, document 32, 4.1398 Tsuchiya Muneyoshi *meyasu an*, p. 230.

10. Ibid., Tsuchiyashi *monjo*, document 33, 6.15.1403 Tsuchiya Muneyoshi *yuzurijō*, p. 230.

11. Ibid., Tsuchiyashi *monjo*, document 32, 4.1398 Tsuchiya Muneyoshi *meyasu an*, p. 230.

12. *Okayama kenshi, Iewake shiryō*, document 185, 9.1366 Tōji zasshō Raiken *kasane moshijō*, p. 187.

13. *Aioi shishi*, vol. 7, Gakushūkata *hyōjō hikitsuke* no. 39, of 1378, pp. 238–43.

14. Ibid., Nijū ikko kata *hyōjō hikitsuke*, no. 55, of 1394.

15. *Mukō shishi, shiryōhen*, 11.1392 Kōmyōbuji zasshō *kasane moshijō an*, p. 233, and 10.1405 Tōji Chinju Hachimangū zasshō *moshijō an*, pp. 236–37.

16. Ibid., 4.19.1420 Ashikaga Shōgunke *migyōsho an*, p. 240, and 9.12.1431 Ashikaga Yoshinori *gohan migyōsho*, p. 242.

Because *shugo* deputies grasped the levers of bureaucratic control, they were ideally placed to control the administrative machinery of the provinces in the ensuing decades, and, ultimately, turn the mechanisms of local governance against the person of the *shugo* when circumstances allowed it. Although this process would not become common until the sixteenth century, the structure of regional power was established by the latter half of the fourteenth. Those not incorporated into the *shugo*'s structure of lordship or administration by 1392 had little chance of becoming regional magnates in the future.

Although the *hanzei* was designed to ensure that armies maintained adequate supplies, it also enabled *shugo* to direct these revenues toward their own immediate use. For example, already in 1352, the initial year of military crisis, levies were imposed by the Akamatsu, the *shugo* of Harima province, so that his messengers, horses, and guards could be fed. Furthermore, local estates were taxed so that his troops could purchase their own supply of saké, while the workers who fortified his Shirahata castle with lacquered walls were also provisioned with these *hanzei* levies of rice.[17] By 1359, funds were provided by laborers so that they could cut down lumber for the *shugo*, and transport military supplies.[18] Others were conscripted to perform guard duty, and to serve the shugo for periods ranging up to thirty days.[19] Yearly miscellaneous levies, ranging from two to ten *koku*, became normative, but this burden was compounded by levies of corvée labor and horse fodder.[20] At times these levies assumed extraordinary proportions, with Ōyama estate providing provisions for 755 laborers who performed service to their *shugo* in 1390.[21]

Shugo taxation became onerous precisely when the wars of the fourteenth century were drawing to a close. In spite of the decline in military activities, levies for horses, messengers, and workmen continued unabated. At times, some *shugo* assessed a supplemental tax of twenty percent, which was earmarked for "the shogun," but others attempted to translate their *hanzei* prerogatives into a landed lordship by confiscating half of each estate, thereby assuring their rights of income.[22] The *hanzei*, in other words, became the rationale for *shugo* and their deputies to confiscate lands.[23]

17. *Aioi shishi*, vol. 8, no. 1, document 1800, 4.27.1351 Nishikata Gakushū kata *nengu sanyōjō*, pp. 143–44.

18. Ibid., doc. 237, 4.1359 *Nengutō sanyōjō*, p. 212

19. Ibid., doc. 383, 2.1376 Gakushū kata *nengutō sanyōjō narabini mishin nengutō sanyōjō*, p. 386.

20. Ibid., doc. 471, 4.20.1390 Gakushū kata *nengutō sanyōjō*, pp. 504–6, and 2.24.1404 Gakushū kata *nengutō sanyōjō*, pp. 690–93.

21. *Hyōgo kenshi shiryōhen chūsei*, vol. 6, doc. 320, 1390 Ōyama no shō *shugo'yaku ninpu mokuroku*, pp. 237–38.

22. For an illuminating complaint dating from 1391, see NBIC 5386. For other records of lands divided, this time in 1393, see NBIC 5582 and 5587.

23. See NBIK, doc. 6231, of 9.17.1392. For another example, not necessarily claimed by the *shugo*, see NBIC 5608, of 6.1395.

Shugo confiscations thus continued to destabilize land rights even though the exigencies of war, the rationale for the *hanzei*, had passed. The *hanzei* allowed the *shugo* to reward their supporters generously, both warriors and shrines, and at the same time, further erode the autonomy of all warriors who maintained a wary distance.[24] Indeed, the notion that lands were subject to arbitrary appropriation seems to have become normative, and could only be overruled through special confirmations of an entire estate by the Ashikaga shogun,[25] or resisted through violence.

As *shugo* and their deputies reassembled the powers of the state on the provincial level, authorities in the capital emphasized their ritual prerogatives, which they continued to monopolize, as a way of interceding with the "otherworld." They concurrently continued to assert superiority over provincial magnates. This notion that the Ashikaga possessed transcendent political authority and were capable of influencing fate proved fleeting, and best characterize the reigns of only the first three Ashikaga shoguns (1336–1408). However, because the state had abandoned its monopoly over coercive force, violence gradually achieved transcendence while the authority of central control withered accordingly.

Conversely, the preponderance of economic and political power of the fifteenth-century *shugo* and their retainers ensured that *tozama* were increasingly unable to fight with autonomy, and submit their own petitions for rewards. The Ishikawa of Nagano continued submitting such documents, as did several eastern warriors intermittently during the first half of the fifteenth century, but these documents became increasingly rare.[26]

The performative nature of *tozama* status, coupled with the increasing difficulty in fighting with autonomy, led to a subtle shift in warrior identity. Gradually, it mattered less how one fought; instead, one's ties to shogunal or *shugo* authority became a crucial concern. Hence, over the ensuing centuries, the nature of the warrior became redefined as one who served as lord, rather than one who acted with autonomy.

---

24. For convenient references to the *hanzei* being used by *shugo* to reward their followers, see *Shiryō ni yoru Nihon no Ayumi, Kinseihen*, comp. Yasuda Motohisa et al. (Yoshikawa Kōbunkan, 1958), pp. 278, for a intercalary tenth month, fifth day of 1392, record from Tōji temple about *hanzei* lands being bestowed to *shugo* retainers, as well as an 11.28.1399 document from the Yamanaka document whereby Yamanaka Tachibana Roku is assigned *hanzei* lands. For another examples of *hanzei* lands being bestowed to a shrine, see NBIC 5500–3, 5523.

25. See for example, NBIC 5555–56. For other examples of the *bakufu* supporting local authority at Niimi estate, see NBIC 5571–72.

26. For some early fifteenth-century examples, see *Shinano shiryō*, vol. 7, p. 430, of 12.1404, for the Ishikawa fighting under a deputy *shugo*, and, for a later reference, see pp. 504–5, of 7.19.1415. For another example, dating from 1417, see *Ino Hachimangū monjo*, 4.26.1417 Ino Mitsutaka *gunchūjō*, p. 114. A perusal of the *Saitama kenshi* and *Gunma kenshi* reveals that slightly over a dozen petitions survive for the years 1414–23, while a few more survive for 1439–41. For one such example, see the 8.1423 Kamada Mikitane *chakutōgunchūjō utsushi*, in *Sekijō chōshi, Kodai chūsei shiryōhen*, document 58, pp. 408–9. For another, describing encounters of 1438, 1440–42, and 1454, see *Kanagawa kenshi shiryōhen, Kodai-chūsei*, vol. 3, no. 2, document 6187, 2.1455 Tsukuba Masutomo *gunchūjō an utsushi*, pp. 73–75.

Military documents dating from the mid–fifteenth century changed in both content and character. Instead of recording where one fought, it was sufficient to mention merely how warriors had been wounded, which suggests that armies were becoming more tightly organized, fighting in a discrete area under the command of one or several individuals.

A comparison between the documents of the latter fifteenth century with that of the fourteenth also reveals that pikes, the hallmark of tightly organized troops of infantry, became the preferred weapon of battle shortly after the 1467 outbreak of the Ōnin war. In contrast to the fourteenth century, where only fifteen out of approximately 720 wounds were caused by pikes, the fifteenth century witnessed a marked increase in the use of these weapons. During the autumn of 1467 twelve members of the Kikkawa family were stabbed by pikes in several encounters in Kyoto.[27] Of course, not all wounds stemmed from pikes—eight were injured by arrow, one by sword, and five by rocks—but the twelve pike wounds mentioned in these three documents nearly equals the fifteen recorded pike wounds of the fourteenth century. The increasing use of the pike reveals that battles had shifted from being ill-defined and haphazardly organized bloodlettings to well-organized affairs involving massed units of men.

Improvements in the ability to organize and sustain an army proved to be a far more significant development than changing patterns of weapons use, albeit one that is more difficult to trace. As we have seen in chapter two, semipermanent armies began to be organized on a regional basis in 1354. Further proof of this increasing sophistication can be found in a map created in 1493 which carefully delineates distinct semipermanent military encampments.[28] Military and coercive power now accrued to those most able to amass larger armies and to extract surplus provisions and revenue, rather than those most skilled at compensating warriors for their *chūsetsu*.

OF LAUGHTER AND FORGETTING:
THE FOURTEENTH-CENTURY TRANSFORMATION

So great were the changes that the fourteenth century engendered that the fifteenth century has been perceived as consisting of an entirely new era. Yamana Sōzen, the *shugo* of multiple provinces, is purported to have exclaimed during the mid–fifteenth century that "one cannot continue relying on precedents . . . but instead [must] replace this concept consistent with the spirit of our times."[29] Recent scholars would mirror Sōzen's statements

27. *Dai Nihon komonjo iewake* 9, *Kikkawa ke monjo*, comp. Tōkyō Teikoku Daigaku Shiryōhensanjo (Tōkyō Shiryōhensanjo, 1925), vol. 1, documents 320–24, pp. 272–77.
28. *Ōsaka fushi* 4, *Chūseihen* no. 2, plate four.
29. *Shiryō ni yoru Nihon no Ayumi, Kinseihen*, comp. Okubo Toshiaki et al. (Yoshikawa Kōbunkan, 1955), p. 1. This has also been translated in David Lu, *Japan: A Documentary History* (Armonk, N. Y.: M.E. Sharpe, 1997), p. 174.

by proclaiming that a rupture, or "systemic crisis in all relations of power" characterized the fifteenth century.[30] Nevertheless, as we have seen, this so-called "crisis" represents a linear outgrowth of the trends and fissures of fourteenth-century state and society, as *shugo* came to amass regional power through their control over land and erode the autonomy of *tozama*, who were increasingly forced to rely on violence to assert judicial ends.

Even though the wars of the fourteenth century caused profound change, they have nevertheless languished in obscurity because the warriors of that age fought with an idealized memory of the Genpei war (1180–85). Many were blind to the "newness" of their age and instead saw it as a rehash of the glories of past battles. By following too closely the script of the past, the epic of the twelfth century occurred, as it were, twice—the first time as tragedy, the second as farce.

The wars of the twelfth century were recounted and idealized in the literary classic, the *Tale of the Heike*. This tale reached its final form in 1371, nearly two hundred years after the events it purported to describe, and approximately forty years after the opening salvoes of the battles of the 1330s. This tale was immensely popular. Warriors wiled away their final hours before battle listening to blind lute priests reciting this yarn of brave warriors winning glory or stoically accepting their fate.[31] So persuasive and moving was this tale that warriors modeled their behavior on the semifictional heroes of this epic.

The warriors of the fourteenth century set themselves up for disappointment because they modeled their behavior on unattainable, idealized goals by following a script that was a hundred and fifty years old. Of course, there was nothing unusual about modeling one's behavior on the past, for nearly all legitimacy was based upon precedent. Ashikaga Takauji consciously mimicked the first of the Kamakura shoguns, Minamoto Yoritomo. Not only did he emphasize the fact that both he and Yoritomo achieved political prominence at the same age, but he also participated in ceremonies that consciously mirrored those Yoritomo had witnessed, and even used the same distinctive steel-blue ink to sign his documents.[32] Nevertheless, even Takauji abandoned these comparisons with Yoritomo after fifteen years of war, and instead chose to emphasize wholly unprecedented kingly prerogatives by adopting imperial rituals, and asserting links with the "otherworld." The wars of the fourteenth century undermined the notion of modeling one's behavior on the past. The

---

30. Berry, *The Culture of Civil War in Kyoto*, pp. 285–88.
31. *Taiheiki*, maki 21, "Enya Hangan zanshi no koto," p. 664 and *Gen'ishū*, p. 271.
32. For Uesugi Seishi's comparison between her son, Takauji, and Yoritomo, see Nakamura Naokatsu, "Ashikaga no Takauji," in Satō Kazuhiko, comp. *Ronshū Ashikaga Takauji* (Tōkyōdō Shuppan, 1991), p. 252. A similar comparison can be found in *Baishōron*, pp. 139–40. For Haga's assertion that the Tenryūji festival was based upon Yoritomo's visit to Tōdaiji, see Haga Norihiko, "Ashikaga Tadayoshi no tachiba 3, Ashikaga Tadayoshi shiron," in Haga Norihiko, *Chūsei seiji to shūkyō* (Yoshikawa Kōbunkan, 1994), pp. 130–31.

battlefield proved to be a particularly unforgiving arena for those who too closely attempted to relive the past.

This notion that the events of the twelfth century repeat themselves as farce pervades the *Taiheiki*, a fourteenth-century chronicle. One sees many examples of parody. For example, in one of the earlier *Tale of Heike*'s most famous episodes, a warrior named Nasu no Yōichi is commanded to shoot at a fan prominently displayed on enemy ships anchored far offshore. Nasu declines the honor three times, but fires in the end, and hits the target true.[33] The enemy yelled out "What a shot!" in admiration of his prowess. In the *Taiheiki*, one sees a mirror image of this scene. One warrior from a naval force is ordered to fire at an enemy target far ashore. The warrior, just like Nasu no Yoichi before him, states that he is not up to the task and refuses thrice, but he is commanded to fire. One of his comrades taunts him, "Behold the prowess of the warriors of the East." Thereupon the arrow sputters for twenty feet and plunges into the waves. The enemy yells out, "What a shot!" and doubles over with laughter.[34]

So ingrained were the ideals of the twelfth century that the warriors of the fourteenth century could not live up to them. By repeating the past, and laughing at it, they were gradually coming to grips with their idealized past and discarding it as well. And, once the next sequence of wars broke out, they were recognized by all as being new, although they owed more to the fourteenth century than has been acknowledged.[35]

War's great constant was its transformative power; it led to new associations, attitudes, and ideals. Fourteenth-century warfare transcended all contemporary boundaries and subverted political, intellectual and social norms. And from its bloodshed, and laughter, there arose a new order, a new way of thought, and a new sense that actions need no longer be linked to, and legitimated by, the deeds of an increasingly forgotten past.

Sixty years of civil war hastened the pace of political, social and even intellectual change. War also proved to be the catalyst for administrative development, although it was regional and not central government which reaped the greatest advantages. While allowing some magnates to assert greater control in regulating society and extracting revenue, the war also legitimated the recourse to violence, which served to hinder the exercise of all authority. The war between the two courts ended in 1392. And yet, in spite of the unification of courtly authority, and the ritual dominance achieved by the Ashikaga, *shugo* powers remained untrammeled, while judicial violence became systemic. The violent order of fourteenth-century Japan bequeathed a legacy of profoundly ordered violence.

---

33. *Heike monogatari*, vol. 2, pp. 318–19.
34. *Taiheiki*, maki 16, "Kairiku ni futasei Hyōgo no ura ni yoseru koto," pp. 483–85.
35. I intend to make the topic that I have alluded to in these last few pages the subject of my next monograph.

Bibliography

PRIMARY SOURCES AND REFERENCE MATERIALS IN JAPANESE

Aioi shishi 7, 8.1–2, *Shiryōhen*. Compiled by Aioi Shi. 3 vols. Aioi Shi, 1990–95.

Aro monogatari. Edited by Sawai Taizō. In *Muromachi monogatari shū* 1, *Shin nihon koten bungaku taikei*. Edited by Ichiko Teiji et al. Iwanami Shoten, 1989.

Azuma kagami. Edited by Kuroita Katsumi. In *Shintei zōho kokushi taikei*. 4 vols. Yoshikawa Kōbunkan, 1975–77.

Baishōron. Edited by Yashiro Kazuo and Kami Hiroshi. In *Shinsen Nihon koten bunko*. Gendai Shichōsha, 1975.

Buke myōmokushō. Compiled by Hanawa Hokinoichi. 8 vols. Meiji Tosho Shuppan, 1954.

Buki kōshō, maki 6, *Kaitei zōhō kojitsu sōsho* 19. Compiled by Kojitsu Sōsho Henshūbu. 1993.

Bungo no kuni Ōno no shō shiryō. Compiled by Watanabe Sumio. Yoshikawa Kōbunkan, 1979.

Chiba ken no rekishi, Shiryōhen chūsei 2. Compiled by Chiba Ken Shiryō Kenkyū Zaidan. Chiba, 1997.

Chūsei hōsei shiryō shū. Edited by Satō Shin'ichi and Ikeuchi Yoshisuke. 5 vols. Iwanami Shoten, 1955–65.

Chūsei Rusu ke monjo. Edited by Misawa Shiritsu Toshokan. Iwate: Misawa Kyōiku Iinkai, 1979.

Chūsei seiji shakai shisō, jō. Edited by Ishii Susumu, Ishimoda Shō, Kasamatsu Hiroshi, Katsumata Shizuo and Satō Shin'ichi. *Nihon shisō taikei* 21. Iwanami Shoten, 1972.

Chūsei seiji shakai shisō, ge. Edited by Kasamatsu Hiroshi, Satō Shin'ichi and Momose Kesao. In *Nihon shisō taikei* 22. Iwanami Shoten, 1981.

Dai Nihon komonjo iewake 5, *Sagara ke monjo*. Compiled by Tōkyō Teikoku Daigaku Shiryōhensanjo. 2 vols. 1927.

Dai Nihon komonjo iewake 6, *Kanshinji monjo*. Compiled by Tōkyō Teikoku Daigaku Shiryōhensanjo. 1917.

Dai Nihon komonjo iewake 9, *Kikkawa ke monjo*. Compiled by Tōkyō Teikoku Daigaku Shiryōhensanjo. 3 vols. 1925–32.

Dai Nihon komonjo iewake 10, *Tōji hyakugo monjo*. Compiled by Tōkyō Teikoku Daigaku Shiryōhensanjo. 8 vols. 1925–.

Dai Nihon komonjo iewake 11, *Kobayakawa ke monjo*. Compiled by Tōkyō Teikoku Daigaku Shiryōhensanjo. 2 vols. 1917–18.

Dai Nihon komonjo iewake 13, *Aso ke monjo*. Compiled by Tōkyō Teikoku Daigaku Shiryōhensanjo. 3 vols. 1932–34.

Dai Nihon komonjo iewake 14, *Kumagai ke monjo—Miura ke monjo—Hiraga ke monjo*. Compiled by Tōkyō Teikoku Daigaku Shiryōhensanjo. 1937.

Dai Nihon shiryō 6.1–43. Compiled by Tōkyō Teikoku Daigaku Shiryōhensanjo. 1901–.

Daigoji shinyōroku. Edited by Akamatsu Toshihide. 3 vols. Kyoto, 1951–53.

Emakimonoshū. Compiled by Habikinoshi Shiryōhensan Iinkai. Habikino, 1991.

Engi shiki. Compiled by Koten Kōkyūkai. Zenkoku Shinshokukai, 1992.

Entairyaku (Tōin Kinkata). Edited by Iwahashi Koyata and Saiki Kazuma. 7 vols. Zoku Gunsho Ruijū Kanseikai, 1973–86.

Entairyaku (Tōin Kinkata). Edited by Iwahashi Koyata. 4 vols. Taiyōsha, 1936–40.

Fūjinroku. Murata Masashi chosakushū 7. Compiled by Murata Masashi. Kyoto: Shibunkaku, 1986.

Fukui kenshi shiryōhen 3–9, *Chū-kinsei*. Compiled by Fukui Prefecture. 7 vols. Fukui Prefecture, 1982–92.

Fukushima kenshi 7, *Shiryōhen kodai chūsei*. Complied by Fukushima Prefecture. Fukushima Prefecture, 1966.

Gen'ishū. Edited by Kaji Hiroe. Heibonsha, 1996.

Genpei jōsuiki. Edited by Furutani Tomochika et al. Kokumin Bunko Kankōkai, 1911.

Genpei jōsuiki. Edited by Matsuo Ashie et al. Miyai Shoten, 1991–.

Gifu kenshi, Kodai-chūsei shiryō. Compiled by Gifu Prefecture. 4 vols. Gifu Prefecture, 1969–72.

Go-sannen ekotoba. In Nihon emaki taisei, vol. 15. Edited by Komatsu Shigemi. Chūōkōronsha, 1977.

Gukanki (Konoe Michitsugu). Edited by Tsuboi Kumezō, Kusaka Hiroshi, and Takeuchi Rizō. *Zōho shiryō taisei* 1–4. Kyoto: Rinsen Shoten, 1965.

Gukanshō (Jien). Edited by Okami Masao and Akamatsu Toshihide. *Nihon koten bungaku taikei* 86. Iwanami Shoten, 1967.

Gunma kenshi shiryōhen 6, *Chūsei* 2. Compiled by Gunma Prefecture. Gunma Prefecture, 1984.

Gunsho ruijū. Compiled by Hanawa Hokinoichi. Keizai Zasshisha, 1894.

Habikino shishi shiryōhen. Compiled by Habikino Shi. 3 vols. Habikino Shi. 1981–85.

Hakata nikki. In *Zoku zoku gunsho ruijū* 3 *Shidenbu*. Zoku Gunsho Ruijū Kanseikai, 1969–70.

Hanazono tennō shinki. In *Shiryō sanshū*. 3 vols. Zoku Gunsho Ruijū Kanseikai, 1982–86.

Heian ibun. Compiled by Takeuchi Rizō. 15 vols. Tōkyōdō Shuppan, 1963–80.

Heihō reizuisho. In *Shoryū heihō* 1 *Nihon heihō zenshū* 6. Edited by Ishioka Hisao. Jinbutsu Ōraisha, 1967.

Heiji monogatari emaki. In *Zen kyūnen kassen ekotoba, Heiji monogatari emaki, Yūki kassen e kotoba, Zoku Nihon emaki taisei* 17. Chūōkōronsha, 1983.

Heike monogatari. Edited by Takagi Ichinosuke et al. In *Nihon koten bungaku taikei*, vol. 32–33. Iwanami Shoten, 1964.

Heishō jinjun yōryaku shō. Zoku gunsho ruijū 25.1. Zoku Gunsho Ruijū Kanseikai, 1975.

Hekisan Nichiroku (Unsei Daigoku). In *Shintei Zōho Shiseki Shūran Shūkyōbu*, vol. 26. Kyoto: Rinsen Shoten, 1967.

Hennen Ōtomo shiryō. Compiled by Takita Manabu. 2 vols. Fuzanbō, 1942–46.

Hino shishi shiryoshū, Takahata Fudō tainai monjo hen. Compiled by Hino Shishi Hensan Iinkai. Tōkyō Inshokan, 1993.

Hino shishi tsushi hen 2, *jō.* Compiled by Hino Shi. Tōkyō Inshokan, 1994.

Hirakata shishi 6, *Shiryōhen* 1. Compiled by Hirakata Shishi Hensan Iinkai. Hirakata Shi, 1969.

Hiraoka shishi, Shiryōhen 1. Compiled by Hiraoka Shishi Iinkai. Hiraoka Shi, 1966.

Hizen Matsuratō Ariura ke monjo. Edited by Fukuda Ikuo and Murai Shōsuke. Osaka: Seibundō Shiryō Sōsho, 1982.

Hyōgo kenshi shiryōhen chūsei. Compiled by Hyōgo Kenshi Henshū Senmon Iinkai. 9 vols. Hyōgo Prefecture, 1983–1997.

Hyōshō jinkun yōryaku shō. In *Zoku gunsho ruijū* 25.1. Zoku Gunsho Ruijū Kanseikai, 1975.

Ibaragi kenshi chūseihen. Compiled by Ibaragi Prefecture. Mito, 1986.

Ibaragi ken shiryō chūseihen 1. Compiled by Ibaragi Prefecture. Mito, 1967.

Ibaragi no emaki. Compiled by Ibaragi Hakubutsukan. Mito: Ibaragi Kenritsu Rekishikan, 1989.

Ichinomiya shishi shiryōhen 6. Compiled by Iyanaga Teizō (Ichinomiya Shishi Hensanshitsu). Ichinomiya Shi, 1970.

Ino Hachimangū monjo. Edited by Tamayama Narimoto. Zoku Gunsho Ruijū Kanseikai, 1983.

Ippen hijiri e den (Shōkai). *Nihon emaki taisei* 27 *bekkan.* Chūōkōronsha, 1978.

Irie monjo. Edited by Ueda Jun'ichi. Zoku Gunsho Ruijū Kanseikai, 1986.

Iwate ken chūsei monjo 1. Compiled by Iwate Ken Kyōiku Iinkai. Morioka, 1960.

Izumi shishi 1, *Honpen shiryōhen.* Compiled by Izumi Shishi Hensan Iinkai. Osaka, 1960.

Jūnirui kassen emaki. In *Nihon emaki zenshū* 18. Kadokawa Shoten, 1968.

Kadokawa Nihon chimei daijiten. 49 vols. Kadokawa Shoten, 197890.

Kaei sandaiki. In *Gunsho ruijū* 12. Compiled by Hanawa Hokinoichi. Naigai Kabushiki Kaisha, 1929: 180–242.

Kagoshima ken shiryō, Kyūki zatsuroku jūi, Iewake 1–2. Kagoshima: Shunendō Bunkan, 1987.

Kamakura ibun. Compiled by Takeuchi Rizō. 51 vols. Tōkyōdō Shuppan, 1971–97.

Kamakura nendaiki uragaki, Buke nendai uragaki, Kamakura dai nikki. In *Zōho zoku shiryō taisei* 51. Kyoto: Rinsen Shoten, 1979.

Kamakura shishi 4–6, *Shiryōhen.* Compiled by Kamakura Shishi Hensan Iinkai. 3 vols. Kamakura, 1956–58.

Kanagawa kenshi shiryōhen, Kodai-chūsei 2, 3.1-2. Compiled by Kanagawa Kenshi Hensanshitsu. Yokohama: Kanagawa Kenshi Hensanshitsu, 1973–79.

Kanazawa bunko komonjo, Bushōhen. Compiled by Kanazawa Bunko. Yokohama, 1964.

Kannō ninen hinami ki. In *Zoku gunsho ruijū* 29.2. Zoku Gunsho Ruijū Kanseikai, 1975.

Kano shiryō, Nanbokuchō I. Compiled by Kano Shiryō Hensan Iinkai. Ishikawa Prefecture, 1992.

Kanringoroshū (Keijo Shūrin). Edited by Uemura Kankō. *Gozan bungaku zenshū* 4. Gozan Bungaku Zenshū Kankōkai, 1936.

Kassen emaki—Bushi no sekai. Edited by Torugashi Yuzuru. Mainichi Shinbunsha, 1990.

Kasuga gongen kenki e. In *Zoku Nihon no emaki* 13 *Kasuga gongen kenki e.* Compiled by Komatsu Shigemi. 2 vols. Chūōkōronsha, 1991.

Kasuga Shrine Art Masterpieces and Treasures, Kasuga taisha koshinhō takaramono zuroku. Compiled by Kasuga Taisha. Nara, 1987.

Kawano (Kōno) ke monjo. Compiled by Kageura Tsutomu (*Iyo shiryō shūsei* 3). Matsuyama, 1967.

Kinpu jinja monjo eshabon. Manuscript copy. Tōkyō Shiryōhen Sanjo.

Kinsō hitsuden. In *Zoku gunsho ruijū* 31.1, *Zatsubu.* Zoku Gunsho Ruijū Kanseikai, 1975.

Kitabatake Chikafusa monjo shūkō. Compiled by Yokoi Akio. Dai Nihon Hyakka Zensho Kankōkai, 1942.

Koga ke monjo. 5 vols. Compiled by Kokugakuin Daigaku Koga Ke Monjo Hensan Iinkai. Zoku Gunsho Ruijū Kanseikai, 1982–87.

Koji ruien. 60 vols. Koji Ruien Kankōkai, 1896–1912.

Kokinchōbunshū. In *Nihon koten bungaku taikei* 84. Iwanami Shoten, 1967.

Kokushi daijiten. 15 vols. Yoshikawa Kōbunkan, 1979–97.

Kongochōbunshū. Kokumin Kankōkai, 1910.

Kosaji monjo eshabon. Manuscript copy. Tōkyō Shiryōhensanjo.

Kōyasan monjo. Compiled by Kōyasanshi Hensanjo. 7 vols. Kyoto, 1935–41.

Kōyasan senhyakunenshi. Compiled by Kōyasan Kongōbuji Kinnen Daihō-e Jimukyoku. Kōyasan, 1914.

Kūge nichiyō kufū ryakushū (Gidō Shūshin). Edited by Tsuji Zennosuke. Kyoto: Taiyōsha, 1939.

Kugyō bunin. Edited by Kuroita Katsumi. 5 vols. In *Shintei zōho kokushi taikei* 53–57, 1964–66.

Kujō ke monjo. Compiled by Kunaichō Shoryōbu. 7 vols. Meiji Shoin, 1971–77.

Kumagai ke monjo. Compiled by Saitama Kenritsu Toshokan. Urawa, 1970.

Kuramaderashi. Edited by Hashikawa Shō. Kyoto, 1926.

Kusunoki kassen chūmon. In *Zoku zoku gunsho ruijū* 3, *Shidenbu.* Zoku Gunsho Ruijū Kanseikai, 1969–70.

Kutsuki monjo. Edited by Okuno Takahiro. 2 vols. Zoku Gunsho Ruijū Kanseikai, 1978.

Kyōto gekidō no chūsei. Compiled by Kyōto Bunka Hakubutsukan. November, 1996.

Masterpieces of Japanese Buddhist Art: Nara National Museum 100th Anniversary Commemorative Exhibition. Nara, April 22–June 4, 1995. Catalogue compiled by Nara National Museum. Nara, 1995.

Meitokuki. Edited by Tomikura Tokujirō. Iwanami Shoten, 1941.

Michiyukiburi (Imagawa Ryōshun). In *Chūsei nikki kigyō shū.* Shōgakkan, 1994.

Migita keizu. In *Zoku gunsho ruijū keizubu.* Zoku Gunsho Ruijū Kanseikai, 1975.

Minakuchi chōshi 2. Compiled by Minakuchi Chō. Minakuchi Chō, 1959.

Minoo shishi shiryōhen. Compiled by Minoo Shishi Hensan Iinkai. 2 vols. Minoo Shi, 1968–73.

Mōko shūrai ekotoba. Edited by Komatsu Shigemi. In *Nihon no emaki,* vol. 13. Chūōkōronsha, 1988.

Monyoki. In *Taishō shinshu daizōkyō* 78 *zoku shoshūbu* 9. Taishō Issaikyō Kankōkai, 1932.

Moromoriki (Nakahara Moromori). In *Shiryō sanshū.* Zoku Gunsho Ruijū Kanseikai, 1968.

Motegi chōshi. Compiled by Motegi Chōshi Hensan Iinkai. Motegi Chō, 1997.

Muchū mondō (Musō Kokushi). Edited by Satō Taishun. Iwanami Shoten, 1934.

Mukō shishi shiryōhen 1. Compiled by Mukō Shi. Mukō, 1988.

Mukō shishi jōkan. Compiled by Mukō Shi. Mukō Shi, 1983.

Nanbokuchō ibun, Chūgoku, Shikoku hen. Compiled by Matsuoka Hisatō. 6 vols. Tōkyōdō Shuppan, 1987–95.

Nanbokuchō ibun, Kyūshū hen. Compiled by Seno Sei'ichirō. 7 vols. Tōkyōdō Shuppan, 1980–92.

Nanbokuchō jidai no Tanba Kameoka. Compiled by *Kameokashi Bunka Shiryōkan.* Kameoka, 1993.

Nantaiheiki (Imagawa Ryōshun). In *Gunsho ruijū* 17 *kassen bu* 2 *buke bu* 1. Naigai Shoseki Kabushiki Kaishia, 1930.

Nanzan junjū roku tsuika 3. *Shinkō zōho shiseki shūran* 7. Kyoto, 1967.

Nihon no komonjo 2. Compiled by Aida Nirō. Iwanami Shoten, 1954.

Niigata kenshi, shiryōhen 3–5, *chūsei* 1–3. Compiled by Niigata Kenshi Hensan Iinkai. 3 vols. Niigata, 1981–83.

Obama shishi, shokemonjo hen. Compiled by Obama Shi. 4 vols. Obama, 1979–87.

Okayama kenshi, iewake shiryō. Compiled by Okayama Prefecture. Okayama, 1986.

Ōmi banba no shuku rengeji kakochō. In *Gunsho ruijū* 22, *zatsubu* 4. Compiled by Hanawa Hokinoichi. Naigai Shoseki Kabushiki Kaisha, 1931.

Ōninki. In *Gunsho ruijū* 20, *kassen bu* 1. Compiled by Hanawa Hokinoichi. Zoku Gunsho Ruijū Kanseikai, 1977.

Ōsaka fushi, chūsei 1. Compiled by Ōsaka Fu. Osaka, 1981.

Oyama ke monjo. In *Nihon chūsei shiryō no kadai,* ed. Amino Yoshihiko, pp. 283–319. Kōbundō, 1996.

Rai'in Daisōjōgyōjo ekotoba. In *Zoku gunsho ruijū* 9.1 *Denbu.* Zoku Gunsho Ruijū Kanseikai, 1975.

Reiranshū (Hosokawa Katsumoto). Unpublished manuscript, possession of the author.

Ruijū kokushi. Kokushi Taikei Kankōkai, 1965.

Rusu ke monjo. In *Sendai shishi shiryōhen, Kodai chūsei.* Compiled by Sendai Shi. 1995.

Ryōjin hisshō. Edited by Sasaki Nobutsuna. Iwanami Shoten, 1933.

Saga ken shiryō shūsei, Komonjo hen 2. Compiled by Saga Prefecture. Saga, 1956.

Sakaiki. Compiled by Kansai Daigaku Chūsei Bungaku Kenkyūkai. Sonkei Kakubunkozō, Izumi Shoin, 1990.

Sankō Taiheiki. Zoku Gunsho Ruijū Kanseikai, 1937.

Sano Izumi shishi shiryōhen. Compiled by Sano Izumi Shi. Osaka, 1958.

Santō chōshi shiryōhen. Compiled by Santō Chō. Shiga Prefecture, Santō, 1986.

Sata Mirensho. In *Zoku gunsho ruijū* 25. Zoku Gunsho Ruijū Kanseikai, 1975.

Sekijō chōshi, Kodai chūsei shiryōhen. Compiled by Sekikijō Chō. Sekikijō Chō, 1988.

Sendai shishi shiryōhen, Kodai chūsei. Compiled by Sendai Shi. Sendai, 1995.

Shibunkaku kosho shiryō mokuroku 150. Compiled by Shibunkakau. Kyoto, June, 1996.

Shinano shiryō 5–7. Compiled by Shinano Shiryō Kankōkai. Nagano Prefecture, 1954–56.

Shinpen Saitama kenshi shiryōhen 5, *Chūsei* 1. Compiled by Saitama-ken Shiryōhensan Iinkai. Saitama Prefecture, 1982.

Shiryō ni yoru Nihon no Ayumi, Kinseihen. Compiled by Okubo Toshiaki et al. Yoshikawa Kōbunkan, 1955.

Shizuoka kenshi shiryōhen, Chūsei. Compiled by Shizuoka Kenshi Iinkai Hensanshitsu. 4 vols. Shizuoka Prefecture, 1989–96.

Soga Monogatari. Shinsōban. Edited by Ōshima Tatehiko and Ichiko Teiji. Iwanami Shoten, 1992.

Sōma monjo. Edited by Toyoda Takeshi and Tashiro Osamu. Zoku Gunsho Ruijū Kanseikai, 1979.

Sonpi bunmyaku (Tōin Kinsada). 5 vols. In *Shintei zōho kokushi taikei.* Yoshikawa Kōbunkan, 1964.

Suwa daimyojin e-kotoba. In *Zoku gunsho ruijū, jingi bu* 3. Zoku Gunsho Ruijū Kanseikai, 1975.

Taiheiki (Jingū chōkōkan hon). Edited by Hasegawa Tadashi, Kami Hiroshi, Ōmori Kitayoshi, Nagasaka Shigeyuki. Osaka: Izumi Shoin, 1994.

Taiheiki (Keichō hon). Edited by Gotō Tanji and Kamada Kisaburō. 3 vols. *Nihon koten bungaku taikei.* Iwanami Shoten, 1961–62.

Taiheiki (Tenshō hon). Edited by Hasegawa Tadashi. 4 vols. In *Shinhen Nihon koten bungaku zenshū.* Shōgakkan, 1994–98.

Taiheiki. Edited by Okami Masao. 2 vols. Kadokawa Nihon Koten Bunko, 1975, 1982.

Takada ōyashiki iseki dai 8, Ji hakkutsu chōsa hōkokusho. Compiled by Kikugawa Shi, 1993.

Takaishi shishi 2, *Shiryōhen* 1. Compiled by Takaishi Hensan Iinkai. Takashi Shi, 1986.

Tannowa monjo. Original manuscript. Kyoto University Museum.

Teijō zakki (Ise Teijō/Sadatake). Edited by Shimada Isao. 4 vols. Heibonsha, 1985–86.

Tochigi kenshi shiryōhen chūsei. Compiled by Tochigi Kenshiryo Hensan Iinkai. Tochigi Prefecture, 1975–.

Toyama kenshi shiryōhen 2, *Chūsei*. Compiled by Toyama Prefecture. Toyama, 1975.

Wachi chōshi shiryōshū 1, *Chūsei kinsei* no. 1. Compiled by Wachi Chō. Wachi Chō, 1987.

Waseda daigaku shozō Ogino kenkyūshitsu monjo 2. Compiled by Waseda Daigaku Toshokan. Yoshikawa Kōbunkan, 1980.

Yamada Shōei Jikki (Yamada Shōei). In *Kagoshima kenshiryōshu* 7, pp. 39–107. Edited by Kagoshima Ken Kankō Iinkai. Kagoshima, 1967.

Yokkaichi shishi 7, *Shiryōhen kodai chūsei*. Compiled by Yokkaichi Shi. Yokkaichi Shi, 1988.

Yoshida ke hinami ki. Partially transcribed in *Dai Nihon shiryō* 7.5. Compiled by Tōkyō Teikoku Daigaku Shiryōhensanjo, 1933.

Yūrin Fukuden hō. Manuscript copy, Fujigawa Bunko, Kyoto University Fuzoku Library.

Yusoku kojitsu daijiten. Compiled by Suzuki Keizō. Yoshikawa Kōbunkan, 1995.

Zoku gunsho ruijū, Bukebu. Compiled by Hanawa Hokinoichi. Zoku Gunsho Ruijū Kanseikai, 1975.

Zoku gunsho ruijū, Keizubu. Zoku Gunsho Ruijū Kanseikai, 1975.

Zoku gunsho ruijū. Zoku Gunsho Ruijū Kanseikai, 1969–70.

Zōtei Kamakura bakufu saikyojō shū. 2nd ed. Compiled by Seno Sei'ichirō. 2 vols. Yoshikawa Kōbunkan, 1994.

Zōtei Kamakura bakufu shugo seido no kenkyū. Compiled by Satō Shin'ichi. 2 vols. Tōkyō Daigaku Shuppankai, 1971.

SECONDARY WORKS IN JAPANESE

Aida Nirō. *Mōkō shūrai no kenkyū*. Yoshikawa Kōbunkan, 1958.

Akamatsu Toshihide. *Kamakura bukkyō no kenkyū*. Kyoto: Heirakuji Shoten, 1957.

Amino Yoshihiko. *Nihon chūsei ni nani ga okita ka*. Nihon Editor's school, 1997.

———. *Nihon chūsei shiryō no kadai*. Kōbundō, 1996.

———. *Chūseishi o minaosu*. Yushisha, 1994.

———, ed. *Yomigaeru chūsei 3 Bushi no miyako Kamakura*. Heibonsha, 1989.

———. *Muen, kugai, raku*. 2nd ed. Heibonsha, 1987.

———. *Igyō no ōken*. Heibonsha, 1986.

———. Vol. 10 of *Mōko shūrai. Nihon no rekishi*. Shōgakkan, 1974.

Chūsei komonjo no sekai. Edited by Ogawa Makoto. Yoshikawa Kōbunkan, 1991.

Conlan, Thomas. "Nanbokuchōki kassen no ichikōsatsu." In Ōyama sensei taikan kinen ronshu kai, ed., *Nihon shakai no shiteki kōzō kodai chūsei*, pp. 417–39. Kyoto: Shibunkaku, 1997.

Fujigawa Yū. *Nihon igakushi*. Shōkabō, 1904.

Fujimoto Masayuki. "Eishō bunko shozō 'Aki no yo no nagamonogatari' ni mieru jōkaku ni tsuite." *Chūsei jōkaku kenkyū* 10 (1996): 330–33.

———. "Chūsei no eiga ni mieru chūsei jōkaku." *Chūsei jōkaku kenkyū* 8 (July 1994): 4–43.

Furusawa Naoto. *Kamakura bakufu to chūsei kokka*. Azekura Shobō, 1991.

Gomi Fumihiko. *Kamakura to Miyako*. Shōgakkan, 1992.

Gotō Shigeki, ed. *Nihon koji bijutsu zenshū*. Shūeisha, 1980.

Haga Norihiko, *Chūsei seiji to shūkyō*. Yoshikawa Kōbunkan, 1994.

———. "Kosen bōsen o megutte." In *Ronshū Chūsei no mado*, pp. 113–41. Yoshikawa Kōbunkan, 1977.

Hara Hidesaburō. "Denshi to tato to nomin." *Nihonshi kenkyū* 80 (November 1965).

Hattori Toshirō. "Tōdai ni okeru senshō byōsya no kyūgo to shūkyō katsudō." In *Muromachi Azuchi Momoyama jidai igakushi no kenkyū*. Yoshikawa Kōbunkan, 1971.

Hayami Tasuku. *Kannon Jizō Fudō*. Kōdansha, 1996.

———. *Shujutsu shūkyō no sekai*. Hanashinsho, 1987.

Hayashida Shigeyuki. *Nihon zairaba no keitō ni kansuru kenkyū*. Nihon Chūō Keibakai, 1978.

Honma Junji. *Nihontō*. Iwanami Shoten, 1939.

Hori Yutaka. "Gojisō to tennō." In Ōyama sensei taikan kinen ronshu kai, ed., *Nihon kokka no shikteki tokushitsu kodai chūsei*, 385–410. Kyoto: Shibunkaku Shuppan, 1997.

Hyōdō Hiromi. *Taiheiki 'yomi' no kanōsei*. Kōdansha, 1995.

Ichizawa Tetsu. "Nanbokuchō nairanki ni okeru Tennō to shoseiryoku." *Rekishigaku kenkyū* no. 688 (September 1996): 1–16.

Iimori Tomio. "Nobushi to sonraku." *Nairanshi kenkyū* 12 (May 1992): 34–41.

Ikushima Terumi. "Chūsei kōki ni okeru 'kirareta kubu' no tori atsukai." *Bunka shigaku* 50 (November 1994): 131–50.

Imaeda Aishin. *Chūsei zenshūshi no kenkyū*. Tōkyō daigaku shuppankai, 1970.

Imatani Akira. "Jū-yon go seiki no nihon," in *Iwanami kōza nihon tsūshi* 9, *Chūsei* 3. Iwanami Shoten, 1994.

Ishii Shirō. *Nihonjin no kokka seikatsu*. Tōkyōdō Shuppan, 1986.

Ishii Susumu. *Chūsei o yomitoku komonjo nyūmon*. Tōkyō Daigaku Shuppankai, 1990.

———. *Chūsei no bushidan, Nihon no rekishi* 12. Shōgakkan, 1974.

———. "Insei jidai." In *Hōken shakai no seiritsu, kōza nihonshi* 2. Tōkyō Daigaku Shuppankai, 1970.

Ishii Susumu and Hagihara Mitsuo, eds. *Chūsei no shiro to kōkogaku*. Shinjinbutsu Ōraisha, 1991.

Ishimoda Shō. *Chūseiteki sekai no keisei*. Tōkyō daigaku shuppankai, 1957.

Itō Masako. "Chūsei no mihata." *Rekishi hyōron* 497 (September 1991): 25–36.

Kasamatsu Hiroshi. *Chūseinin to no taiwa*. Tōkyō Daigaku Shuppankai, 1997.

———. *Hō to kotoba no chūseishi*. Heibonsha, 1993.

———. "Mimi o kiri, hana o sogu." In Amino Yoshihiko, ed., *Chūsei no tsumi to batsu*, 27–42. Tōkyōdō Shuppan, 1983.

Kasamatsu Hiroshi, Satō Shin'ichi, and Momose Kesao, eds. *Chūsei seiji shakai shisō*, vol. 2. In *Nihon shisō taihei* 22. Iwanami Shoten, 1981.

Katsumata Shizuo. "Jūgo-roku seiki no Nihon." In *Iwanami kōza Nihon tsūshi* 10, *Chūsei* 4. Iwanami Shoten, 1994.

Kawai Yasushi. *Genpei kassen no kyozō o hagu, Jishō Jūei nairanshi kenkyū*. Kōdansha, 1996.

Kawano Shinchirō. *Chūsei toshi Kamakura*. Kōdansha, 1995.

Kawazoe Shōji. "'Chinzei tandai' Ashikaga Tadafuyu: Kyūshū ni okeru Kannō seihen." In *Kyūshū chūsei kenkyū* 2: 187–242. Bunken Shuppan, 1980.

———. Imagawa Ryōshun. Yoshikawa Kōbunkan. 1964

Kimura Shigemitsu. *'Kokufū no bunka' no jidai*. Aoki Shoten, 1997.

Kondō Yoshikazu. *Chūseiteki bugu no seiritsu to bushi*. Yoshikawa Kōbunkan, 2000.

———. "Buki kara mita nairanki no sentō." *Nihonshi kenkyū* no. 373 (September 1993): 60–74.

Kōsaka Konomu. *Akamatsu Enshin, Michisuke*. Yoshikawa Kōbunkan, 1970.

Kume Kunitake. *Nanbokuchō jidaishi*. Waseda Daigaku Shuppan, 1907.

Kuroda Hideo. *Ō no shintai, ō no shōzō*. Heibonsha, 1993.

———. *Sugata to shigusa no chūseishi, Ezu to emaki no fukei kara*. Heibonsha, 1986.

Kuroda Toshio. *Jisha seiryoku*. Iwanami Shoten, 1980.

Matsui Teruaki. "Origami no chakutōjō ni tsuite." *Komonjo kenkyū* no. 34 (May 1991): 2–38.

Matsumoto Kazuo. "Nanbokuchō shoki Kamakura fu gunji taisei ni kansuru ichi kōsatsu." *Komonjo kenkyū* 41, 42 (December 1995): 63–80.

Matsumoto Shinpachirō. "Nanbokuchō nairan no shozentei." In *Chūsei shakai no kenkyū*. Tōkyō Daigaku, 1978.

Matsushita Shōji, ed. *Yomigaeru chūsei 8, Umoreta wanchō Kusado sengen*. Heibonsha, 1994.

Miya Tsugio. *Kassen no emaki*. Kadokawa Shoten, 1977.

Momose Kesao. "Gentoku gannen no 'chūgū onkainin.'" *Kanazawa bunko kenkyū* no. 274 (March 1985): 1–14.

Mori Shigeaki. *Go-Daigo tennō*. Chūkōshinsho, 2000.

———. *Yami no rekishi, Gonanchō*. Kadokawa Sensho, 1997.

———. "Ōtōnomiya Moriyoshi shinnō ryōji ni tsuite." In Ogawa Makoto, ed., *Chūsei komonjo no sekai*, pp. 192–218. Yoshikawa Kōbunkan, 1991.

———. *Taiheiki no gunzō*. Kadokawa Sensho, 1991.

———. *Ōjitachi no Nanbokuchō*. Chūkōshinsho, 1988.

Morimoto Masahiro. "Sensō to yōsei." *Chūsei nairanshi no kenkyū* 12 (May 1992): 43–50.

Murai Shōsuke. *Hōjō Tokimune to Mōko Shūrai: Jidai, sekai, kojin o yomu*. NHK Books, 2001.

Murata Masashi chosakushū. Compiled by Murata Masashi. Kyoto: Shibunkaku, 1986.

Nakamura Naokatsu. "Ashikaga no Takauji." In *Ronshū Ashikaga Takauji*, pp. 178–360, compiled by Satō Kazuhiko. Tōkyōdō Shuppan, 1991.

Nihon koji bitjutsu zenshū 10: *Enryakuji, Onjōji to Saikyōji.* Shūeisha, 1980.

Nihon no kokuhō 25, *Ehime.* Shūkan Asahi Hyakka, 8.10.1997.

Nihon no rekishi bekkan, Rekishi o yominaosu 15, *Shiro to kassen.* Shūkan Asahi Hyakka, 1993.

Nitta Ichirō. *Nihon chūsei no shakai to hō.* Tōkyō Daigaku Shuppankai, 1995.

Nuta Raiyū. *Nihon monshōgaku.* Shinjinbutsu Ōraisha, 1968.

Ogawa Makoto. *Yamana Sōzen to Hosokawa Katsumoto.* Shinjinbutsu Ōraisha, 1994.

———. *Ashikaga ichimon shugo hattenshi no kenkyū.* Yoshikawa Kōbunkan, 1980.

———. *Hosokawa Yoriyuki.* Yoshikawa Kōbunkan, 1972.

Ōhashi Toshio. *Jishū no seiritsu to tenkai.* Yoshikawa Kōbunkan, 1973.

Okubō Jinichi. *Mino no kuni Kasugadani no kassenshi.* Yahashi Insatsusho, 1982.

Ōmijima no Dōmaru. Compiled by Ōyamazumi Jinja. Ōyamazumi Shrine, Ehime, 1991.

Ōyama Kyōhei. "Shōensei." *Iwanami kōza Nihon tsūshi* 7 *chūsei* 1. Iwanami Shoten, 1993.

———. *Nihon chūsei nōsonshi no kenkyū.* Iwanami Shoten, 1978.

———. "Nihon chūsei shakai to nōmin." *Nihonshi kenkyū* no. 59 (March 1962).

Saitō, Shin'ichi. "Honkyo no tenkai; 14–15 seiki no kyokan to jōkaku yōgai." *Chūsei no shiro to kōkogaku,* pp. 243–64. Shinjinbutsu Ōraisha, 1991.

Satō Kazuhiko. *Zusetsu Taiheiki no jidai.* Kawadeshobō Shinsha, 1990.

———. *Nanbokuchō nairan shiron.* Tōkyōdō Shuppan, 1979.

Satō Kiyoshi. "Tokue Yorikazu chūjō ni mieru Nanbokuchōki Echizen no shiro to kassen ni tsuite." *Fukui kenshi kenkyū* no. 9 (March 1991): 29–52.

Satō Shin'ichi. *Nanbokuchō no dōran.* Chūōkōronsha, 1974.

Seki Yukihiko. "Busō," In Fukuda Toyohiko, ed., *Chūsei o kangaeru ikusa,* pp. 1–38. Yoshikawa Kōbunkan, 1993.

Seno Sei'ichirō. "Kankō shiryōshū seiri no hitsuyōsei." In *Kamakura jidai no seiji to keizai,* pp. 5–28. Compiled by Kamakura Ibun Kenkyūkai. Tōkyōdō Shuppan, 1999.

———, ed. *Bunretsu to dōran no seiki: Nihon rekishi tenbō* 5 *Nanbokuchō.* Ōbunsha, 1981.

———. *Chinzei gokenin no kenkyū.* Yoshikawa Kōbunkan, 1975.

Seya Yoshihiko. *Ibaragi ken no rekishi.* Yamakawa Shuppansha, 1975.

Shakadō Mitsuhiro. "Nanbokuchōki ni okeru senshō." *Nairanshi kenkyū* 13 (August 1992): 27–39

Shinjō Tsunezō. *Kamakura jidai no kōtsū.* 1967, Nihon Rekishi Soshō Shinsōban. Yoshikawa Kōbunkan, 1995.

Shūkan Asahi hyakka. Compiled by Fujiki Hisashi. *Shiro to kassen Nihon no rekishi bekkan Rekishi o yominaosu* no. 15. Asahi Shinbun, October 1993.

Sōson no jiritsu to seikatsu. Compiled by Shiga University, 1996.

Suzuki Hisashi. *Nihonjin no hone.* Iwanami Shoten, 1962.

———. *Kamakura zaimokuza hakken no chūsei iseki to sono jinkotsu.* Iwanami Shoten, 1956.

Suzuki Kenji. *Rekishi e no shōtai* 6. Nihon Hōsō Shuppankai, 1980.

Tachibana Shundō. "Taiheiki ni arawareta jishū no katsuyaku." *Jishūshi ronkō.* Kyoto: Hōzōkan, 1975.

Takahashi Masaaki. *Bushi no seiritsu bushizō no sōshutsu.* Tōkyō Daigaku Shuppan, 1999.

———. "Jōshikiteki kizokuzō, bushizō no sōshutsu katei." *Rekishi to hōhō* 1, *Nihonshi ni okeru kō to shi.* Aoki Shoten, 1996

Tanaka Minoru. "Samurai bonge kō." *Shirin* 59.4 (July 1976): 1–31.

Tanaka Yoshinari. *Nanbokuchō jidaishi.* Kōdansha gakujutsu bunko, 1979.

Tarashima Satoshi. "Nanbokuchō jidai no seisatsu to kinsei." *Komonjo kenkyū* 35 (December 1991): 1–10.

Tomita Masahiro. "Chūsei Tōji no kitō monjo ni tsuite." *Komonjo kenkyū* 11 (November 1977): 24–59.

Tsuda Sōkichi. *Bungaku ni arawaretaru kokumin shisō no kenkyū* 2. In *Tsuda Sōkichi zenshū* 5. Iwanami Shoten, 1964.

Tsuji Zennosuke. *Nihon Bukkyōshi* 4, *Chūsei* 3. Iwanami Shoten, 1949.

———. *Nihon Bukkyōshi no kenkyū.* Kinkōdō Shoseki Kabushiki Kaisha, 1919.

Uemura Seiji. *Kusunoki Masashige.* Shibundo, 1962.

Urushihara Tōru. *Chūsei gunchūjō to sono sekai.* Yoshikawa Kōbunkan, 1998.

———. "Nanbokuchō shoki ni okeru shugo hakkyū kanjō ni kansuru ichi kōsatsu." *Komonjo kenkyū* 38 (March 1994): 18–31.

———. "Nanbokuchō shoki ni okeru shugo kengen no ichi kōsatsu." *Komonjo kenkyū* 27 (July 1987): 57–72.

———. "Chakutōjō no kisoteki kōsatsu." *Shigaku* 54.2-3 (March 1985): 65–82.

———. "Gunchūjō ni kansuru jakkan no kōsatsu." *Komonjo kenkyū* 21 (June 1983): 33–52.

Usui Nobuyoshi. *Ashikaga Yoshimitsu.* Yoshikawa Kōbunkan, 1960.

Uwayokote Masataka. *Rekishi no kairaku.* Kōdansha, 1996.

———. *Kamakura jidai seijishi kenkyū.* Yoshikawa Kōbunkan, 1991.

Yamada Kuniaki. "Miura shi to Kamakura fu." In Ishii Susumu, ed., *Chūsei no hō to seiji,* pp. 22–51. Yoshikawa Kōbunkan, 1992.

Yamagishi Sumio. *Nihon kachū no kisoteki chishiki.* Yūzankaku, 1990.

Yamaguchi Takamasa. *Nanbokuchōki Kyūshū shugo no kenkyū.* Bunken Shuppan, 1989.

Yasui Hisayoshi. *Muneyoshi shinnō no kenkyū.* Kasama Shoin, 1993.

SOURCES IN WESTERN LANGUAGES

Adolphson, Mikael. *The Gates of Power: Monks, Courtiers and Warriors in Premodern Japan.* Honolulu: University of Hawai'i Press, 2000.

———. "Enryakuji—An Old Power in a New Era." In Jeffrey P. Mass, ed., *The Origins of Japan's Medieval World: Courtiers, Clerics, Warriors, and Peasants in the Fourteenth Century,* 237–60. Stanford: Stanford University Press, 1997.

Aoki, Michiko. *Records of Wind and Earth: A Translation of Fudoki with Introduction and Commentaries*. Association for Asian Studies Monographs and Occasional Papers Series, Number 53. Ann Arbor: Association for Asian Studies, 1997.

Arnesen, Peter Judd. "The Provincial Vassals of the Muromachi Shoguns." In Jeffrey P. Mass and William Hauser, eds., *The Bakufu in Japanese History*, pp. 99–128. Stanford: Stanford University Press, 1985.

———. "The Struggle for Lordship in Late Heian Japan: The Case of Aki." *Journal of Japanese Studies* 10.1 (Winter 1984): 101–41.

———. "Suō Province in the Age of Kamakura." In Jeffrey P. Mass, ed., *Court and Bakufu in Japan: Essays in Kamakura History*, pp. 92–120. New Haven: Yale University Press, 1982.

Asakawa, Kan'ichi. *The Documents of Iriki*. Japan Society for the Promotion of Science, 1955.

Aston, W. G., trans. *Nihongi: Chronicles of Japan from the Earliest Times to A.D. 697*. Rutland, VT: Charles E. Tuttle, 1972.

Berry, Mary Elizabeth. *The Culture of Civil War in Kyoto*. Berkeley: University of California Press, 1994.

Bourdieu, Pierre. *Language and Symbolic Power*. Cambridge: Harvard University Press, 1991.

———. *Outline of a Theory of Practice*. Cambridge: Cambridge University Press, 1977.

Braudel, Fernand. *The Mediterranean and the Mediterranean World in the Age of Philip II*. 2 vols. Berkeley: University of California Press, 1995.

Brown, Delmer, and Ishirō Ishida, trans. *The Future and the Past: A Translation and Study of the Gukanshō*. Berkeley: University of California Press, 1979.

Brunner, Otto. *Land and Lordship: Structures of Governance in Medieval Austria*. Philadelphia: University of Pennsylvania Press, 1992.

Clanchy, Michael. *From Memory to Written Record*. 2nd ed. Oxford: Basil Blackwell, 1993.

Collcutt, Martin. "Religion in the Formation of the Kamakura Bakufu: As seen through the *Azuma Kagami*." *Japan Review* 5 (1994): 55–86.

———. *Five Mountains*. Cambridge: Harvard University Press, 1981.

Conlan, Thomas D. *In Little Need of Divine Intervention: Takezaki Suenaga's Scrolls of the Monogl Invasion of Japan*. Cornell: Cornell East Asia Series, 2001.

———. "The Nature of Warfare in Fourteenth-Century Japan: The Record of Nomoto Tomoyuki." *The Journal of Japanese Studies* 25.2 (Summer 1999): 299–330.

———. "Largesse and the Limits of Loyalty in the Fourteenth Century." In Jeffrey P. Mass, ed., *The Origins of Japan's Medieval World: Courtiers, Clerics, Warriors, and Peasants in the Fourteenth Century*, pp. 39–64. Stanford: Stanford University Press, 1997.

Craig, Albert. *Choshu in the Meiji Restoration, 1853–1868*. Cambridge: Harvard University Press, 1961.

Duby, Georges. *The Legend of Bouvines*. Berkeley: University of California Press, 1990.

Elias, Norbert. *The History of Manners.* New York: Pantheon, 1978.

Erdmann, Carl. *The Origin of the Idea of Crusade.* Princeton: Princeton University Press, 1977.

Farris, William Wayne. *Heavenly Warriors: The Evolution of Japan's Military, 500 to 1300.* Cambridge: Harvard University Press, 1992.

Fichtenau, Heinrich. *The Carolingian Empire.* Toronto: University of Toronto Press, 1978.

Fisher, David Hackett. *Albion's Seed.* New York: Oxford University Press, 1989.

Friday, Karl. *Hired Swords: The Rise of Private Warrior Power in Early Japan.* Stanford: Stanford University Press, 1992.

Gay, Suzanne. "The Kawashima: Warrior-Peasants of Medieval Japan." *Harvard Journal of Asiatic Studies* 46 (1986): 81–119.

Geary, Patrick J. *Living with the Dead in the Middle Ages.* Ithaca: Cornell University Press, 1994.

Girard, René. *Violence and the Sacred.* Baltimore: Johns Hopkins University Press, 1977.

Gluckman, Max. "The Peace and the Feud," *Past and Present* 8 (1955): 1–14.

Goble, Andrew Edmund. "Visions of an Emperor." In Jeffrey P. Mass, ed., *The Origins of Japan's Medieval World: Courtiers, Clerics, Warriors, and Peasants in the Fourteenth Century*, pp. 113–37. Stanford: Stanford University Press, 1997.

———. *Kenmu: Go-Daigo's Revolution.* Cambridge: Harvard University Press, 1996

———. "Go-Daigo and the Kemmu Restoration." Ph. D. dissertation, Stanford University, 1987.

Goodwin, Janet. "Shadows of Transgression: Heian and Kamakura Constructions of Prostitution." *Monumenta Nipponica* vol. 55 no. 3 (2000): 327–68.

Grossberg, Kenneth A., and Kanamoto Nobuhisa, trans. *The Laws of the Muromachi Bakufu: Kemmu Shikimoku (1336) and Muromachi Bakufu Tsuikahō.* Monumenta Nipponica and Sophia University Press, 1981.

Hall, John Whitney. *Government and Local Power in Japan.* Princeton: Princeton University Press, 1966.

Hall, John W. and Jeffrey Mass, eds. *Medieval Japan: Essays in Institutional History.* Stanford: Stanford University Press, 1974.

Harrington, Lorraine F. "Social Control and the Significance of Akutō," In Jeffrey P. Mass, ed., *Court and Bakufu in Japan: Essays in Kamakura History*, pp. 221–50. New Haven: Yale University Press, 1982.

Huizinga, Johan. *The Autumn of the Middle Ages.* Chicago: University of Chicago Press, 1996.

Hurst, G. Cameron III. *Insei: Abdicated Sovereigns in the Politics of Late Heian Japan.* New York: Columbia University Press, 1976.

Ikegami, Eiko. *The Taming of the Samurai: Honorific Individualism and the Making of Modern Japan.* Cambridge: Harvard University Press, 1995.

Keegan, John. *The Face of Battle.* New York: The Viking Press, 1976.

Keeley, Lawrence H. *War Before Civilization: The Myth of the Peaceful Savage.* New York: Oxford University Press, 1996.

Keene, Donald. *Essays in Idleness: The Tsurezuregusa of Kenkō*. New York: Columbia University Press, 1967.

Keirstead, Thomas. *The Geography of Power in Medieval Japan*. Princeton: Princeton University Press, 1992.

Kiley, Cornelius J. "The Imperial Court as Legal Authority in the Kamakura Age." In Jeffrey P. Mass, ed., *Court and Bakufu in Japan: Essays in Kamakura History*, pp. 29–44. New Haven: Yale University Press, 1982.

———. "Estate and Property in the Late Heian Period." In John W. Hall and Jeffrey P. Mass, eds., *Medieval Japan: Essays in Institutional History*, pp. 109–24. Stanford: Stanford University Press, 1974.

Kondō, Shigekazu. "Leadership in the Medieval Japanese Warrior Family." In Ian Nearly, ed., *Leaders and Leadership in Japan*, pp. 14–25. London: Curzon Press, Japan Library, 1996.

Kraft, Kenneth, trans. "Musō Kokushi's *Dialogues in a Dream* Selections," *The Eastern Buddhist* n.s., 14. (Spring 1981): 75–93.

Leyser, Karl. *Rule and Conflict in an Early Medieval Society*. Oxford: Basil Blackwell, 1989.

———. "Early Medieval Canon Law and the Beginnings of Knighthood." In Lutz Fenske, Werner Rosener, and Thomas Zotz, eds., *Institutionen, Kulture and Gesellschaft im Mittelalter: Festschrift für Josef Fleckenstein zu seinem 65. Geburtstag*. pp. 549–66. Sigmaringen: Jan Thorbecke Verlag, 1984.

Little, Lester K. *Benedictine Maledictions: Liturgical Cursing in Romanesque France*. Ithaca: Cornell University Press, 1993.

Lu, David. *Japan: A Documentary History*. Armonk: M. E. Sharpe, 1997.

Mass, Jeffrey P. *Yoritomo and the Founding of the First Bakufu*. Stanford: Stanford University Press, 1999.

———. "Of Hierarchy and Authority at the End of Kamakura." In Jeffrey P. Mass, ed., *The Origins of Japan's Medieval World: Courtiers, Clerics, Warriors, and Peasants in the Fourteenth Century*, pp. 17–38. Stanford: Stanford University Press, 1997.

———. "The Missing Minamoto in the Twelfth-Century Kanto." *Journal of Japanese Studies* 19.1 (Winter 1993): 121–46.

———. *Antiquity and Anachronism in Japanese History*. Stanford: Stanford University Press, 1992.

———. "The Kamakura Bakufu." In Kozo Yamamura, ed., *The Cambridge History of Japan*, vol. 3, *Medieval Japan*, pp. 46–88. Cambridge: Cambridge University Press, 1990.

———. *Lordship and Inheritance in Early Medieval Japan: A Study of the Kamakura Soryō System*. Stanford: Stanford University Press, 1989.

———. "Patterns of Provincial Inheritance in Late Heian Japan." *Journal of Japanese Studies* 9.1 (Winter 1983): 67–95.

———. *The Development of Kamakura Rule, 1180–1250: A History with Documents*. Stanford: Stanford University Press, 1979.

———. *The Kamakura Bakufu: A Study in Documents*. Stanford: Stanford University Press, 1976.

————. "The Emergence of the Kamakura Bakufu." In John W. Hall and Jeffrey P. Mass, eds., *Medieval Japan: Essays in Institutional History*, pp. 127–56. Stanford: Stanford University Press, 1974.

————. *Warrior Government in Early Medieval Japan: A Study of Kamakura Bakufu, Shugo, and Jitō.* New Haven: Yale University Press, 1974.

Mauss, Marcel. *The Gift.* Translated by W. D. Hall. New York: W. W. Norton, 1990.

McCormick, Michael. *Eternal Victory.* New York: Cambridge University Press, 1986.

McCullough, Helen Craig, trans. *The Taiheiki: A Chronicle of Medieval Japan.* New York: Columbia University Press, 1959.

McMullin, Neil. "Historical and Historiographical Issues in the Study of Pre-Modern Japanese Religions." *Japanese Journal of Religious Studies* 16.1 (1989): 3–40.

Morris, Dana. "Land and Society." In *The Cambridge History of Japan*, vol. 2, *Heian Japan*, Donald Shively and William McCullough, eds., pp. 183–235. Cambridge: Cambridge University Press, 1999.

Murdoch, James. *A History of Japan*, vol. 1. Kobe: "The Chronicle," 1910.

Nagahara, Keiji. "Land Ownership Under the *Shōen Kokugaryō* System." *Journal of Japanese Studies* 1 (Spring 1975): 269–96.

Potter, David. *Prophets and Emperors.* Cambridge: Harvard University Press, 1994.

Ruppert, Brian D. *Jewel in the Ashes: Buddha Relics and Power in Early Medieval Japan.* Cambridge: Harvard University Press, 2000.

Sansom, George. *A History of Japan 1334-1615.* Stanford: Stanford University Press, 1961.

————. *A History of Japan to 1334.* Stanford: Stanford University Press, 1958.

————. *Japan: A Short Cultural History.* Stanford: Stanford University Press, 1931.

Schlesinger, Walter. "Lord and Follower in Germanic Institutional History." In Fredric L. Cheyette, ed., *Lordship and Community in Medieval Europe*, pp. 65–99. New York: Holt, Rinehart and Winston, 1968.

Shinoda, Minoru. *The Founding of the Kamakura Shogunate.* New York: Columbia University Press, 1960.

Smith, Bradley. *Japan: A History in Art.* New York: Doubleday, 1964.

Steenstrup, Carl. *A History of Law in Japan until 1868.* Leiden: E. J. Brill, 1991.

Steenstrup, Carl. "*Sata mirensho*: A Fourteenth-Century Law Primer." *Monumenta Nipponica* 35 (1980): 405–35.

Tambiah, Stanley. *Culture, Thought and Social Action.* Cambridge: Harvard University Press, 1985.

Tilly, Charles. *Coercion, Capital and European States, AD 990–1990.* London: Basil Blackwell, 1990.

Tonomura, Hitomi. *Community and Commerce in Late Medieval Japan: The Corporate Villages of Tokuchin-ho.* Stanford: Stanford University Press, 1992.

Varley, Paul. *Warriors of Japan as Portrayed in the War Tales.* Honolulu: University of Hawai'i Press, 1994.

Varley, Paul, trans. *A Chronicle of Gods and Sovereigns: Jinnō Shōtōki of Kitabatake Chikafusa.* New York: Columbia University Press, 1980.

Wallace-Hadrill, John Michael. *The Long-Haired Kings*. Toronto: University of Toronto Press, 1982.

Wilson, William R., trans. *Hōgen Monogatari: Tale of the Disorder in Hōgen*. Sophia University, 1971.

Yamaguchi, Hatirō, ed., *Japan's Ancient Armor*. Japan Tourist Library, 1940.

Glossary of Important Terms

akutō (悪党). "Evil bands" or brigands; a pejorative term describing those who resorted to violence, often in defense of their judicial claims. This term carries no social connotations, and can refer to provincial magnates, *tozama* warriors, or their more humble followers who engaged in violence. Most instances of *akutō* behavior arose with the upswing of judicial violence late in the thirteenth century, as the Kamakura *bakufu* began enforcing administrative law.

ando (安堵). Confirmation of lands, their transmission, or sale, by someone in higher authority. Unitary (*ichien*) confirmations were the most desired, and could be conveyed through edicts (see *kudashibumi*) or through merely notations scrawled on the reverse of documents (*uragaki ando*).

ashigaru (足軽). A term for foot soldiers, or literally "those with light feet." A synonym for minimal armor. This word initially appeared in fourteenth century chronicles (the *Taiheiki*) but most commonly describes formations of light-infantry during the Ōnin wars of 1467–77.

azukari dokoro (預所). Name for an estate manager, usually an official who attained the right to manage lands that had originally been commended to a central proprietor.

bakufu (幕府). Literally "tent government," this term describes three warrior governments of Japan: the Kamakura (1185–1333), Muromachi or Ashikaga (1338–1573) and Tokugawa (1603–1867) regimes. A shogun, or "barbarian-subduing generalissimo," headed each *bakufu*. Kamakura possessed judicial authority, appointed *shugo* and *jitō*, and mobilized *gokenin* for guard duty (*ōban'yaku*). The Ashikaga continued many Kamakura policies, but after 1351 they delegated considerable powers to the *shugo*.

bōhai (傍輩). Designated "comrades," or people of equal rank, capable of acting with autonomy on the battlefield (see *tozama*). This notion transcended gender, and the distinction between courtier and warrior, but excluded retainers (*miuchi*).

bonge (凡下). "Commoners," or "the base," who held almost no legal rights, and lacked surnames. Although *samurai* and other warrior retainers were immune from torture, the same did not hold true for *bonge*. See also *genin*.

bōrei (傍例). Notion of unwritten custom, frequently used to justify some type of proprietary or usufructuary right. Often used to legitimate resistance to new laws or appointments.

bōsen (防戦). Defensive warfare—the violent defense of rights—which achieved legitimation as an acceptable recourse during the fourteenth century.

buke (武家). Literally "warrior households," this term generally designated the Ashikaga or their supporters during the wars of the fourteenth century. See also *kangun*.

buppō (仏法). The laws of Buddhism; refers to the notion, existing since the eighth century, that secular or kingly laws, and buddhist laws together underpinned the state. See also *ōbō*.

chakutōjō (着到状). "Documents of arrival," submitted by warriors who arrived in camp. This format originated as a means of reporting for guard duty late in the thirteenth century. These documents merely proved a warrior's arrival, but did not necessarily indicate that he had performed military service. Some *chakutōjō* do, however, closely resemble petitions for reward in that they also describe military encounters. See *gunchūjō* and *kassen chūmon*.

chigyō (知行). A term of long lineage, but designating possession of lands in the fourteenth century.

chōbukohō (調伏法). Rituals of destruction, practiced by Shingon and Tendai priests, in order to destroy "those who cannot be saved," and by extension, enemies of the state. The Ninnōkyō sutra provided the scriptural authority for these prayers of destruction, designed to preserve and protect the state, that were offered to five potent Buddhist deities, the "wisdom kings" Fudō, Gozanze, Gundari, Dai-i-toku-ten, and Kongo. These prayers were performed by five ranking priests, from noble families, who individually burned offerings (*goma*) and chanted prayers to these deities, each of which was believed to destroy malevolence—be it hostile emotions, "evil spirits," or inhospitable aspects of the natural world. Although these rituals were primarily a prerogative of the court, they increasingly were patronized by the Ashikaga *shōguns*. See also *ōbō*, *buppō*, and *godanhō*.

chūgen (中間). Those obligated to serve a lord in battle, or perform various menial duties, but lacking a surname. Comprising men otherwise known as *bonge* or *genin*, *chūgen* could be granted surnames, and concomitant *samurai* rank, as a result of battle service.

chūsetsu (忠節). Service that required compensation. Only autonomous *tozama* warriors could submit petitions for reward (*gunchūjō*) and demand compensation. This term carries no connotation of "loyalty," and did not describe *miuchi* service for their lord.

daigūji (大宮司). The head, or chief administrative officer, of a large shrine. Could be a powerful warrior. See also *gūji*.

daikan (代官). A representative, acting on behalf of another. Such men were capable of serving as they saw fit, but their "lord" invariably received recognition for their actions.

dōmaru (胴丸). A type of armor fastened together on the right side. Although is more appropriate for combat on foot, this armor is of significantly higher quality than *haramaki*. The first reference to *dōmaru* appears in the 1270s. Several examples of this armor, fastened on the side, exist for the fourteenth century. Suits of *dōmaru* were embellished with accoutrements, including leggings, gloves, shin guards, and face guards (*hōate*).

dōri (道理). A sense of "justice" and propriety, which could transcend norms of codified law.

ebira (箙). A basketlike quiver, designed to be attached to a warrior's back.

fukunin (福人). A wealthy person.

gechijō (下知状). One of the three major forms of warrior documents, *gechijō* occupied a level of formality less than the edict (*kudashibumi*), but greater than that of the communique (*migyōsho*). *Gechijō* were increasingly used in the thirteenth century, and became the dominant vehicle for judicial decisions, which were signed during the Kamakura era by the *shikken* and co-signer, or officials of the Rokuhara or Chinzei *tandai*. Under early Ashikaga rule, the shōgun Takauji preferred issuing investitures in the *kudashibumi* format, while his brother Tadayoshi, continued the Kamakura tradition of adjudicating cases with *gechijō*. *Shitsuji* and *kanrei* in the Ashikaga *bakufu* also issued such documents, but they gradually fell out of favor during the fifteenth and sixteenth centuries.

gekokujō (下剋上). A term describing the lower conquering the higher. Although often used to describe the "Warring States" turmoil of the sixteenth century, early in the fourteenth century this term was used to criticize how members of the Kamakura *bakufu* had usurped prerogatives of the court.

genin (下人). A member of the "base" orders, lacking a surname. See *bonge*.

geshunin (下手人). A "double." This word designated those who were ordered by a higher authority to be handed over to another party, and subject to imprisonment, death, or release by their captors, in order to rectify a wrong that they, or their associates, had committed. An important mechanism for constraining feuds in an era when the state did not monopolize coercive violence. See also *migawari*.

gesu (下司). A local manager, appointed to an estate (*shōen*), who could be removed from his office by the proprietor. In such cases, the disgruntled *gesu* would frequently become an *akutō*. Kamakura replaced many of these offices with that of *jitō* during the late twelfth and early thirteenth centuries.

godanhō (五壇法). "Five altar rituals," were designed to harness the powers of the five wisdom kings, and protect the state (see *chōbukuhō*). First performed in the palace in the eleventh century, they maintained considerable importance. Go-Daigo apparently attributed his destruction of Kamakura to these rituals, which constituted an important prerogative of sovereignty. Takauji, the first Ashikaga shogun, and his brother Tadayoshi, had these rituals performed in their own residences, which marked a significant blurring of sovereign authority.

gojisō (御持僧). "Protector priests," a team of as many as eight esoteric specialists who were stationed in the palace from the eighth century onward. These priests prayed for the well-being of the emperor. Once the Ashikaga attained power in 1336, they had five *gojisō* pray for Ashikaga Takauji.

gokenin (御家人). "Honorable housemen," a social status drawn from the ranks of provincials who served Minamoto Yoritomo in the 1180s. *Gokenin* status became predicated upon the performance of guard duty and the possession of edicts (*kudashibumi*) from Kamakura. The advantages of this status were initially unclear, but as time passed, privileges, codified by Kamakura law, accrued to *gokenin*. By the mid–thirteenth century, the benefits associated with *gokenin* status outweighed the burdens of guard duty. Thereupon, the most ambitious men of the provinces aspired to become *gokenin.* No ironclad method existed of determining who was in fact a *gokenin.* This term continued to be used after the fall of the Kamakura *bakufu*, but it generally became replaced by the term *kokujin* or *tozama*.

goma (護摩). Sticks with prayers inscribed on them, to be offered to the "wisdom king" deities, such as Fudō or Aisen. Prayers would be burned in an altar in front of the deities. See also *godanhō* and *chōbukuhō*.

Goseibai Shikimoku (御成敗式目). Series of legal codes drawn up initially by Hōjō Yasutoki in 1232. Significant for it codified judicial norms of land ownership, and provided mechanisms for disputes to be adjudicated by the Kamakura *bakufu*. Administrative regulations, such as punishments for those who failed to report when summoned, were initially ignored, but their enforcement late in the thirteenth century led to an upswing in judicial violence (see *akutō*). Go Daigo attempted to nullify these laws, but they were largely upheld in the next sequence of legal codes, the *Kenmu Shikimoku*, which were promulgated by the Ashikaga in 1336.

gūji (宮司). The head of a shrine. Could also be a warrior in the fourteenth century. See also *kannushi*.

gunchūjō (軍忠状). Petition for rewards, documents submitted by warriors demanding compensation for their military service (*chūsetsu*) which described how and when they fought and which damages that they incurred. These documents were the hallmark of *tozama* warrior status, and arose out of military practices during the Mongol Invasions of 1274 and 1281. Most common in the fourteenth century, these documents became progressively rarer as armies became more systematically organized, and military service became more obligatory. See also *chakutōjō*, *kanjō*, *kassen chūmon*, and *tozama*.

hanzei (半済). Reference to a law passed in 1351, whereby half of a province's revenue was earmarked for the procurement of provisions and military supplies. This marks the first direct and sustained linkage of the ability to extract economic resources with the mobilization of military forces. This provisional tax became institutionalized, and served as the basis for *shugo* asserting rights to provincial revenue. With the *hanzei*, the post of *shugo* became coveted by aspiring magnates.

hara-ate (腹当). The simplest type of armor, which merely protects the chest and stomach. One is depicted in the *Rokudō-e,* but no examples survive. Reserved for the lowest ranking warriors.

haramaki (腹巻). A type of armor fastened in the back, this lightened, simplified armor first appeared early in the fourteenth century. As high-ranking warriors began wearing *dōmaru*, which was more suitable for fighting on foot than their larger suits of armor (*yoroi*), *haramaki* arose as a lighter alternative. In contrast to *dōmaru*, which were fastened on the side, with one plate attached to the top of the other, *haramaki* were merely fastened together at the back. This meant that they were far weaker than *dōmaru* and *yoroi*, and thus used almost exclusively by lower-ranking warriors. In most cases, *sode* and helmets were not worn with *haramaki*.

hihō (非法). A term for illegalities, but which refers more to unwritten judicial norms than to legality in the narrow sense of abiding by written laws. Often, *hihō* was associated with innovation (*shingi* 新儀) and used to castigate an opponent's actions.

hōate (頬当). "Face guards" designed to protect the neck and lower face from arrow wounds, which were adopted as a result of the endemic warfare of the fourteenth century. *Hōate* replaced the *hatsumuri* (半首), gear that remained widely used throughout the thirteenth century, which covered the forehead and the sides of the face, but not the jaw and neck.

hon'i (本意). One's fundamental desire or true belief which can or cannot be realized. Often used by warriors to justify temporary transfers of political and military allegiances.

honjo (本所). The proprietor or the primary owner of an estate. Generally referred to a centrally located courtier, be he a proprietor (*ryōke* 領家) or (from the twelfth century onward) a patron (*honke* 本家).

honryō (本領). Homelands. Generic term used to describe lands that were occupied by warriors and perceived as being their innate possession. Most claims were based the fact that the "owner," who often possessed the same surname as the lands in question, had either personally cleared or reclaimed the land, or was directly descended from one who had done so.

horo (母衣). A cape designed to physically and spiritually protect warriors. Billowing behind a mounted warrior, *horo* were thought to deflect arrows. Furthermore, warriors who wore bright crimson *horo* did so as an expression of their determination to fight to the death. A mandala would be placed in the *horo* so as to mitigate against the need for a funeral if one died in battle. The *horo* also served as a shroud for the head of those who had been decapitated.

hyakushō (百姓). Literally, "[members of] the hundred surnames," this term initially designated all members of society who held an obligation to pay taxes, had a surname, and who had not attained the fifth court rank or above. With social stratification in the ninth through thirteenth centuries, the term *hyakushō* came to designate provincials who possessed surnames and were entrusted with *shiki* office, or who were holders of local public office. Once Minamoto Yoritomo created the *gokenin* order late in the twelfth century, most ambitious provincials became associated with this term, while others preferred the designation *myōshu*. The first reference to *hyakushō* as designating cultivators appears in the late thirteenth century, but even as late as the mid–fifteenth century, one still sees powerful provincials with surnames referring to themselves as *hyakushō*. Although *hyakushō* of the thirteenth through fifteenth centuries could fight in battle, and even own horses, their allegiances were primarily lateral, to their compatriots, rather than directed toward a lord.

hyōrōmai (兵糧米). Military provisions, or a provisional levy of such provisions. The need to secure adequate *hyōrōmai* proved particularly problematic in the early fourteenth century, until the ability to extract revenue was linked with the ability to directly procure provisions as a result of the *hanzei* edict of 1351.

ichimon (一門). A lineage-based alliance formalized through oaths. Far more amorphous and broader than an *ichizoku*.

ichizoku (一族). "One family," or an autonomous house, capable of acting with autonomy. Headed by a chieftain, or *sōryō*, all the members of an *ichizoku* consisted of dependent relatives (*kenin*, or housemen). Both direct descendants, hereditary retainers, and relatives lacking autonomy could be subsumed into an *ichizoku*. By contrast, autonomous *tozama* relatives could only be incorporated into an *ichimon* grouping.

igoroshi (射殺). The act of being shot to death. Rare. Cases where those injured by arrows died at a later date are known as the more generic "killed" (*uchishi*).

ikki (一揆). A verb originally meaning "to be in accord," *ikki* came to be used as a noun to designate military units during the fourteenth century. *Ikki* were often cemented through oaths designed to show that all were in accord. Such groupings constituted corporate entities that possessed a status similar to that of a *tozama* warrior, but which remained dependant on a lord, and thus functioned like a *miuchi*. Warriors tended to form *ikki* as a means of resisting the increasing powers of regional magnates, or *shugo*, during the late fourteenth and early fifteenth centuries.

inzen (院宣). A retired emperor's edict, issued from his secretariat and having the force of law. In late thirteenth and early fourteenth century Japan, whether a retired emperor's edict, or a reigning emperor's edict (*rinji*) possessed the ultimate force of law remained in dispute. Supporters of the emperor Go-Daigo tended to view *rinji* as being supreme, while the Ashikaga relied more on *inzen* for legitimation.

ji (時) *priests.* Ippen (1239–89) founded a movement whose followers (*jishū* or congregation of itinerant priests) attempted to continually chant the *nenbutsu*, "Hail the Amida Bodhisattva." *Ji* priests danced while performing *nenbutsu* and traveled throughout Japan. They administered to the dying and also provided medical treatment.

jitō (地頭). A land steward, or one who was invested with the office of *jitō* in the aftermath of the Genpei wars (1180–85) by Yoritomo. Possessing powers of taxation and policing, this post proved most desirable for provincials, for they could only be dismissed by orders of the Kamakura *bakufu*. By contrast, local managers (*gesu*) could be terminated by the proprietor of an estate (see *akutō*). This office continued to be granted throughout the fourteenth and fifteenth centuries, but it became amalgamated with the social category of *gokenin* during the fourteenth century. After the destruction of Kamakura, this term lost its original meaning, but it still became associated with powers of local ownership and possession of land. *Jitō* were increasingly referred to as *tozama* or *kokujin* as the fourteenth century progressed.

kaburaya (鏑矢). A turnip-shaped arrow that emitted an eerie low hum. Fired during the onset of battle, this arrow both unnerved troops and demarcated the battlefield.

kaihatsu ryōshu (開発領主). Developer of the land, a crucial concern because with development was imparted a sense of innate rights to the land. This notion was integral to the fundamental rights of *chigyō*, or ownership. Often the "original cultivator" adopted the same surname as his lands, and would resist tenaciously if they were confiscated.

kan (貫). Three and three quarters kilograms of copper, the equivalent of one thousand *mon* of cash (Each mon constituted 3.75 grams). Fourteenth-century records reveal that horses could be purchased for a sum of three or four *kan*.

kangun (官軍). Term used to refer to the "imperial army," which designated supporters of Go Daigo, or his Southern Court successors, during the fourteenth century.

kanjō (感状). Written commendations, or documents of praise. These documents were first issued by generals fighting in 1333 to warriors who fought valiantly on their behalf, and were increasingly issued as the fourteenth and fifteenth centuries progressed. The recipients of these documents remained overwhelmingly *tozama*, although from the fifteenth century onward, some *miuchi* (or *hikan* 被官) of regional magnates (the *shugo*) received *kanjō* as well.

kannushi (神主). Head of a shrine, who could also be a warrior.

kanrei (管領). The chief of staff of the Muromachi *bakufu* from the time of Ashikaga Yoshimitsu's rule during the late fourteenth century. This post should be conceived as a deputy shogun, and became the preserve of three Ashikaga collateral lineages—the Hosokawa, Hatakeyama, and Shiba. Ultimately the Hosokawa proved most durable, achieving dominance within the *bakufu* and even launching a successful coup d' etat against an Ashikaga shogun in 1493.

kassen bugyō (合戦奉行). Battle administrators, literate warriors in the service of *shugo* or *taishō* who inspected battle reports (see *kassen chūmon*) and wounds in order to determine their veracity.

kassen chūmon (合戦注文). Battle reports, a detailed record of wounds submitted to battle administrators (*kassen bugyō*), who rigorously inspected the documents, sometimes adding notations making them more precise. These reports often later became summarized in petitions for reward (*gunchūjō*) and hence were less likely to be preserved than the later petitions. These reports had antecedents in late thirteenth-century petitions and complaints, which sometimes described violent acts in great detail. Although only a few fifteenth and sixteenth century *kassen chūmon* survive, this document remains unsurpassed as a means of reconstructing how warriors were wounded.

kenin (家人). Housemen; an ambiguous generic term for retainer. Any servant or follower in a particular house could use this term, thereby allowing some to obscure their origins, adopt their lord's surname, and achieve a more exalted status as *samurai*.

Kenmu Regime. A fleeting regime (1333–36) created by the emperor Go-Daigo after he destroyed the Kamakura *bakufu*. An uprising led by Ashikaga Takauji led to the demise of the Kenmu Regime early in 1336, and marked the onset of the *Nanbokuchō* era and sixty years of indeterminate civil war.

Kenmu Shikimoku (建武式目). Laws established by the Ashikaga *bakufu* after ousting Go-Daigo in 1336. Modeled after the *Goseibai Shikimoku*, these codes justified Ashikaga rule and provided mechanisms for the control over *shugo* and temples. During the mid–fourteenth century, these laws legitimated some recourse to judicial violence (see *bōsen* and *kosen*). Furthermore, the epochal *hanzei* edict was issued as an amendment to this code in 1351. Gradually, as Ashikaga power waned in the late fifteenth and early sixteenth centuries, these laws became directed toward economic regulations centered in the environs of the capital.

kessho (關所). Lands declared "appropriable" by those in authority as a result of "crimes" or "rebellions" by either their proprietor or manager.

koku (石). Ideally the amount of rice needed to feed one adult for a full year, *koku* represents a unit of measurement of rice for taxation purposes. For the sake of expedience, this term has been generally translated as a "bale of rice."

kokujin (国人). "Men of the provinces," or *tozama* warriors. A mid–fourteenth-century designation.

kokushi (国司). Originally a provincial governor during the Heian era, this institution was revived by Go-Daigo, who tended to appoint both *shugo* and *kokushi* to provinces during his short lived Kenmu Regime (1333–36). A few, such as the Kitabatake in Ise province, managed to retain local power for well over a century after the outbreak of civil war, but most became supplanted by *shugo*, particularly after the establishment of *hanzei* privileges.

kokyaku (沽却). The act of selling lands or goods.

kōsan (降参). The act of surrendering, or one who surrenders (*kōsannin*). An easy act for *tozama*, it entailed unstringing one's bow, and presenting it to an opposing warrior. Customarily, one would lose half of one's lands by surrendering, but this custom was observed more in the breach than in reality during most of the fourteenth century.

kosen (故戦). "Offensive warfare," which remained outlawed throughout the fourteenth through sixteenth centuries in name if not reality. Significantly, the characters for *kosen* mean "war with a reason," which suggests that violence was considered to be a predictable recourse for securing or maintaining judicial rights.

koshitate (楯). Shields, made from wood boards or doors, that were placed in front of foot soldiers to protect them from arrows. At times, they could be held by charging troops. Shields were often plundered from temples or other dwellings (*zaike*).

kubō (公方). "Mr. Public." A term originally used for the emperor or court. During the fourteenth century, this word was used designate members of the Ashikaga shogunate, or, on occasion, their plenipotentiaries as individual manifestations of a more public authority.

kudashibumi (下文). Edict having the force of law. One of three major types of documentary forms used by sovereigns, courtiers, and ranking warriors to convey grants of rank or lands. See also *gechijō* and *migyōsho*.

kugai (公界). The public realm, a term emphasized by Amino Yoshihiko as a counterpoint to his notion that the medieval state was littered with perceived immunities (*muen*).

kugyō (公卿). Otherwise known as *kandachime*, *kuge*, or courtiers, kugyō possessed the highest three court ranks. This position hinged upon appointment to the court, and so should best be conceived as an rank rather than a class. Of course, some imperial princes and members of notable families possessed an advantage in receiving appointments making themselves *kugyō*. The Ashikaga tended to be associated as *kugyō* from the late fourteenth century onward. Conversely, with the onset of civil war in the 1330s, many *kugyō* and imperial princes directed armies.

kumon shiki (公文職). Managerial rights to an estate. See *azukari dokoro*.

kyoshū no jiyū (去就の自由). A term coined by Satō Shin'ichi, meaning "freedom of movement." Satō initially explored how *tozama* warriors could fight for whomever they pleased.

kyūji sen (弓事銭). "Bow levies" issued with the outset of war in 1333. This marks one of the earlier attempts to rationalize a tax for military provisions. See also the *hanzei*.

kyūshu (給主). A resident of the *shōen*, often a priest, who was entrusted with collecting revenue, and who received a portion of this revenue as his salary. A 'tax-farmer.'

makai (魔界). Buddhist term, meaning a world of devils, or a hell on earth. Used by the courtier Tōin Kinkata to describe the violent order of mid–fourteenth-century Japan.

mandokoro (政所). Term possessing a variety of meanings, but here designating either the secretariat of a ranking official, or courtier, or a region in an estate where local administration was centered.

migawari (身代). Described a substitute or replacement—a person who would endure punishment, capture, or torture in order to atone for another related person's infraction. See also *geshunin*.

migyōsho (御教書). A communique, one of the three major types of *bakufu* documents, generally used in judicial decisions. The least formal of the three formats. See also *kudashibumi* and *gechijō*.

miuchi (御内). Term used to describe all dependent warriors. These men were not, however, confined to being followers of the Hōjō *shikken*, as was stipulated in the *Sata mirensho*. By contrast, see *tozama*.

muen (無縁). A state of immunity, or unattachedness, first hypothesized by Amino Yoshihiko. Although he characterizes the state as being fundamentally limited by these *muen* immunities, the fact that they proved paper-thin in times of war reveals that *muen* designated judicial rather than administrative or political boundaries.

musoku (無足). State of being landless, through either confiscation from above, or "illegal" occupation. Frequent complaint of warriors on the losing side of a land dispute.

myōshu (名主). Literally "lord of the *myō*." *Myō* represented a unit of taxation. During the eleventh and twelfth centuries, powerful *hyakushō* initially secured the right to assess taxes on particular lands. They became known as *myōshu* in order to create social space between themselves and their *hyakushō* brethren. With the creation of the *gokenin* order late in the twelfth century, tensions arose between members of these two categories. *Myōshu* sometimes refused to be called up by *gokenin* for guard duty in the thirteenth century, but both *myōshu* and *gokenin* became amalgamated into the *tozama* order once civil war broke out in the 1330s.

naginata (長刀). A weapon resembling a halberd, with a long curved blade attached to a wooden staff.

Nanbokuchō (南北朝). Term used to describe the period demarcated by supporters of two courts, the Northern, propped up the Ashikaga and residing for the most part in the capital of Kyoto, and the Southern, represented by Go-Daigo and his descendants and based in Yoshino, in Yamato Province. This term generally applies to the years 1336–92, although some date the period as beginning with the fall of the Kamakura *bakufu* in 1333.

nobushi (野伏). Also known as *nobuseri*, this word refers to skirmishers of all social rank, and not to a "class" of foot soldiers as been sometimes assumed. These skirmishers were generally archers, and were representative of the nature of fighting during the fourteenth century, when loosely scattered groups of soldiers predominated.

nuka (糠). "Rice chaff," or the husks of rice, after they had been hulled, frequently used as horse fodder.

ōban'yaku (大番役). Guard duty represented an obligation of all Kamakura-era *gokenin*, who were mobilized by the *shugo* of their province, and who served in the capital or Kamakura. Later on, warriors guarded northern Kyushu as well in the aftermath of the initial Mongol invasion of 1274. Guard duty continued throughout the *Nanbokuchō* era, and the need to provide records of one's service contributed to the creation of the documentary form of *chakutōjō*.

ōbō (王法). Kingly law. Kingly and Buddhist law represent two complementary and intertwined rationales for legitimating state authority. See also *buppō*.

ōbō (押妨). Interference with the land, usually denoting an "illegal" seizure and physical occupation.

ōdachi (大太刀). A long sword, otherwise known as a *nodachi*, or "field sword," over three feet in length, which appeared first in the thirteenth century and gained great popularity in the fourteenth. Increasing to seven feet in length, these swords were ideally suited for the scattered battles of the *Nanbokuchō* era, but were replaced by pikes in the fifteenth and sixteenth centuries as tactics shifted toward massed groups of infantrymen.

ongechi (御下知). An order with the force of law. See *gechijō*.

onryō (怨霊). An "evil spirit," generally arising where an individual had been wrongly or unfairly killed as the result of political machinations. *Onryō* haunted the perpetrators and wreaked general havoc.

onshōgata (恩賞方). (1) The administrative organ of the Kenmu Regime, responsible for granting rewards and established in 1333, whose authority extended throughout the land during its brief tenure. Ceased to function effectively by the end of 1335. (2) An organization of the Ashikaga regime responsible for rewards by the Muromachi bakufu, and dominated by Ashikaga Takauji and his chief of staff. See also *samurai dokoro*.

ōryō (押領). The "illegal" act of seizing, occupying, or plundering lands which one does not have a recognized right to.

ōyoroi (大鎧). Initially known only as *yoroi*, this term refers to the most expensive armor, which was worn with shoulder boards (*sode*), helmets, and all other accoutrements. By far the most expensive armor, *ōyoroi* was suited for generals or other ranking individuals. This boxlike armor was ideally suited for use on horseback and most effective in providing protection against arrows. Suits of *ōyoroi* open on the right side, but are supplemented with a special board to help fortify this vulnerable region. Gradually, as battles came to be fought on foot, *ōyoroi* came to resemble *dōmaru*.

ranbō (乱暴). Violent acts which do not necessarily represent an open defiance of authority. When these same acts continued in spite of orders from above to desist, then they become classified as *rōzeki*.

rinji (綸旨). Edict of a reigning emperor, with the force of law. Favorite of Go-Daigo and his heirs. Whether this document had precedence over a retired emperor's *inzen* remained disputed during the fourteenth century.

rōjū (郎従). Generalized term for retainer, but one who was not directly related to his "lord." One can find references to oath of service (*rōjū no reigi* [郎従之礼儀]), which implies that this subservient relationship was forged through some kind of oath. This term is synonymous with *miuchi*.

rōtō (郎等). Term for retainer, or follower, of more subservient status than a *wakatō*, and unrelated to his "lord." See also *miuchi, rōjū, kenin,* and *samurai*.

rōzeki (狼藉). An outrage. Open defiance of authority, frequently provoking military force after the promulgation of an order to cease and desist. From the viewpoint of authority, *rōzeki* represented a greater offence that did *ranbō*.

ryō (両). Unit of weight used to measure gold and silver which varied according to era and location in fourteenth and fifteenth century Japan; by extension, a synonym for cash. See also *kan*.

saisokujō (催促状). A mobilization order, or more functionally, an invitation for warriors to report to battle. These documents, dispatched by either princes, generals, or ranking *bakufu* officials, did not entail any obligation to fight. Mere receipt of such a document could allow warriors to assert *tozama* status, which is why they were commonly preserved.

samurai (侍). Arising originally from the ranks of "commoners" (*hyakushō*), *samurai* possessed surnames, and were obligated to a lord (*tozama*), rather than to their peers, and should be considered to be a retainer. They possessed considerably greater rights than did "the base" (i.e. immunity from torture. See *bonge, genin*). Best considered to be synonymous with *miuchi*, the term is inappropriate for *tozama* or *gokenin*.

samurai dokoro (侍所). Administrative organ of the Muromachi regime which was dominated by Ashikaga Takauji and his chief of staff (*shitsuji*), and was primarily responsible for overseeing affairs of the *shōgun*'s direct retainers. Most of this organ's powers were supplanted by the *kanrei*.

sata (沙汰). A generic term signifying administration, control, or judicial authority. Used in a variety of contexts.

Sata Mirensho (沙汰未練書). An early fourteenth-century law primer, useful for understanding judicial norms, but more misleading regarding social categories.

sekisho (関所). Barriers, or toll gates, where tariffs were assessed or supply routes blocked. Guarded by a small-to-medium number of troops, could be useful in blockades. In times of peace, their use as a means of controlling and taxing trade predominated. Go-Daigo attempted to abolish such barriers early in his reign, but the onset of civil war caused their numbers to increase.

shiki (職). Status-based rights of revenue. The distinction between these status-based rights withered in the fourteenth century as locals came to possess *shiki* that had previously been reserved for courtly proprietors. Gradually, rights to the land began to be conceived as more unitary. See *ando*, *shōen*, and *honryō*.

shikken (執権). The regent of the Kamakura *bakufu*, the chieftain of the Hōjō family. Wielded great power. When this *bakufu* was annihilated, the Ashikaga strove to make sure that their chief of staff (*shitsuji*, later *kanrei*) remained firmly under their control.

shinteki (身敵). Literally "enemies of the body," this word referred to mortal enemies or their associates.

shirabyōshi (白拍子). Itinerant female entertainers who sang popular songs, danced, and performed with handheld drums. Appearing late in the twelfth century, they initially wore court headgear (*eboshi*) and ceremonial swords, but this fell out of fashion by the fourteenth century. From the sixteenth century onward, this term became synonymous with prostitute.

shitaji (下地). Basic rights to the land. An important term, and a bridge from the notion of partible, status-based rights to the land, to a more fundamental and unitary sense of control and possession.

shitsuji (執事). The chief of staff of the Ashikaga regime, initially Kō no Moronao, who occupied an institutional position analogous to that of the *shikken*. The institutions of *onshōgata* and *samurai dokoro* were under the administrative control of the *shitsuji*. This post was replaced with that of *kanrei* during the reign of Ashikaga Yoshimitsu.

shōen (荘園). A commended estate, composed of partible *shiki* that expressed both status and function, appearing first in the eighth century, and continuing throughout the sixteenth. Most *shōen* had a far shorter life span. Although significant, they almost never constituted over half of a province's arable land. The "classic" estate of the twelfth and thirteenth century contained a hierarchy of *shiki* based on status and function, but this system of multiple ownership began to crumble in the fourteenth century as some local managers were granted *shiki* that had previously been the prerogative of central proprietors. Indeed, from the fourteenth century onward, the conception of singular or unitary (*ichien*) possession of lands strengthened. See *shiki* and *ando*.

shōgun (将軍). An eighth-century office, originally designed to quell barbarians, and hence known as *Sei-i-taishōgun* (征夷大将軍). This post became important as the highest authority within the *bakufu*, which contained delegated powers of military and judicial authority. Minamoto Yoritomo was appointed to this post in 1192, but he does not appear to have emphasized this office. After his death and the rise of the Hōjō regents, this position increased in importance as the symbolic head of the Kamakura *bakufu*, even though the shogun remained aloof from judicial matters and affairs of governance. During the late thirteenth and early fourteenth centuries, the post of shogun was reserved for court nobles or princes of imperial blood. With the downfall of the Kamakura *bakufu* in 1333, Ashikaga Takauji started laying claim to the post again, and was appointed shogun in 1338 (the Ashikaga or Muromachi *bakufu*). Nevertheless, he continued the princely tradition of remaining aloof from governance—save for enacting prayers and granting rewards—and delegated judicial and administrative powers to his brother Tadayoshi. Takauji's grandson Yoshimitsu resigned from the post of shogun at a young age, and relied on more courtly authority. The last Ashikaga shogun who attempted to rule directly was assassinated in 1441, and for the ensuing one-hundred and thirty years, shoguns of the Ashikaga *bakufu* came to wield little administrative power.

shu (主). Also known as *nushi*, refers to the lord of a *miuchi*. See *tozama*.

shugo (守護). In the Kamakura era, a "constable" responsible for investigating crimes, suppressing rebellion and organizing *gokenin* for guard duty. This position, originally held by warriors lacking particular local power, became the focus of ambitious warriors after the promulgation of the *hanzei* edicts. Prior to 1351, military powers accrued more to generals (*taishō*), but in later half of the fourteenth century *shugo* became incipient local magnates because they could directly extract economic surpluses for the waging of war.

sode (袖). Armor shoulder boards, covering the upper arms of warriors and used to protect the sides of warriors from arrows as they fought on horseback. *Sode*, best thought of as attachable shields, continued to be used only as long as warriors fought on horseback.

sōryō (総領). Family chieftain, one who has the ability to lead other dependent relatives of his family (*ichizoku*) in battle. A *tozama* warrior. As families increased in size and prosperity, the parameters of chieftain authority came to be contested, with some relatives attempting to assert autonomy.

tachi (太刀). A sword. During the fourteenth century, long-swords (see *ōdachi*) and, to a lesser extent, *naginata* were the preferred weapons for hand-to-hand combat. Nevertheless, the bow remained the dominant weapon throughout the fourteenth century.

taishō (大将). A general, appointed from the ranks of noted families on a provisional basis. With the fall of the Kamakura *bakufu*, most generals were either collaterals of the Ashikaga lineage, imperial princes, or court nobles. Their powers were formidable, but rarely institutionalized. Although *taishō* proved more capable of mobilizing troops than *shugo*, after the *hanzei* edicts of 1351, *shugo* could more effectively wield military force because they could systematically provision their armies.

tandai (探題). Two organs of the Kamakura *bakufu*, the Rokuhara *tandai* and the Chinzei *tandai*. The former was created in the aftermath of the 1221 Jōkyū war, and served to guard the capital and provide an arena for the preliminary adjudication of court cases, particularly those arising in western Japan. In the aftermath of the 1281 Mongol invasion, a similar office was established in Kyushu (the Chinzei). Both were annihilated with the fall of Kamakura in 1333.

tanji hatake (鍛治畠 sic). Fields reserved for the use of smiths, who were generally associated with the foundries of large Buddhist temples.

tenjō bito (殿上人). The rank of nobles capable of having an audience in the imperial palace. In addition to the highest three ranks of nobility (*kugyō*), members of the fourth and fifth rank were included as well. At times, members of the secretariat (*kurōdo* 蔵人) of the sixth rank could also be classified as *tenjō bito*.

tō (党). General term for a *miuchi* band of retainers. See also *ikki*.

tokusei (徳政). This term, "virtuous government," stemmed from the belief that possession of particular lands was innate, and that transfers due to economic exchange or commendations and confiscations were somehow wrong and needed to be rectified. Kamakura issued its first *tokusei* edict in 1297. This process seems integrally related to the increasing sense of transcendent rights to land that arose late in the thirteenth century, coupled with the tensions caused by Kamakura's enforcement of administrative law (see *Goseibai shikimoku* and *akutō*). *Tokusei* edicts would be repeatedly enacted by the court, Kamakura, and the subsequent Ashikaga *bakufu*. During the fifteenth century the *tokusei* became more of a devise for extracting income for the Ashikaga than as a means of restoring "innate" rights to the land.

tozama (外様). Literally an "outsider," this term refers to warriors who were capable of behaving with autonomy, receiving their own petitions for reward, and fighting for whomever they pleased. Designates warriors otherwise known as *myōshu* or *gokenin*. Ultimately, the expenses of fourteenth-century war eroded their autonomy, and they too either formed *ikki* or became the direct retainers (*hikan*) of regional magnates, the *daimyō* (大名). See also *miuchi*.

uchishi (打死). The generic term for being killed in battle. Can refer to death by either arrow, pike, or sword wounds.

wakatō (若党). Retainers possessing surname, but not autonomy. They were capable of riding horses, but not submitting their own petitions. The highest rank of *miuchi* retainers.

yoroi (鎧). See *ōyoroi*.

yōtō (用途). Also *yōto* or *yōdo*. Expenses or cash.

yumiya (弓箭). Literally "bow and arrow," but refers to the warrior social order. *Tozama* used such language to describe themselves in the fourteenth century. References exist for phrases such as the "house of the bow in arrow" (*yumiya no ie*); the "way of the bow and arrow" (*yumiya no michi*); and the "honor of the bow and arrow" (*yumiya no menboku*).

zaichō kanjin (在庁官人). Prominent local individuals, holding managerial office of some type in either *shōen* estates, or public lands. Prior to 1180, these individuals were also *hyakushō*, but in the aftermath of the Genpei war, they became the nucleus of the *gokenin* (*tozama*) order.

zaike (在家). Residence. One of perhaps several dwellings. Often burned, plundered, or sold in times of battle.

Index

About the Author

Thomas Donald Conlan is Assistant Professor of Japanese History at Bowdoin College. A Ph.D. from Stanford University, where his advisor was Professor Jeffrey Mass, and a graduate of The University of Michigan, his publications include *In Little Need of Divine Intervention: Takezaki Suenaga's Scrolls of the Mongol Invasions of Japan* (Cornell East Asia Series, 2001). He is currently engaged in a study of the Japanese court and the political role of Esoteric Buddhism.